T0192147

Communications
in Computer and Information Science   1701

More information about this series at https://link.springer.com/bookseries/7899

Shuo Yang · Huimin Lu (Eds.)

Artificial Intelligence and Robotics

7th International Symposium, ISAIR 2022
Shanghai, China, October 21–23, 2022
Proceedings, Part II

 Springer

Editors
Shuo Yang
Kyushu Institute of Technology
Kitakyushu, Japan

Huimin Lu
Kyushu Institute of Technology
Kitakyushu, Japan

ISSN 1865-0929   ISSN 1865-0937 (electronic)
Communications in Computer and Information Science
ISBN 978-981-19-7942-2   ISBN 978-981-19-7943-9 (eBook)
https://doi.org/10.1007/978-981-19-7943-9

This Springer imprint is published by the registered company Springer Nature Singapore Pte Ltd.
The registered company address is: 152 Beach Road, #21-01/04 Gateway East, Singapore 189721, Singapore

Preface

In recent years, artificial intelligence (AI) has attracted attention as a key for growth in developed countries and developing countries. The attention has been focused mainly on developing new deep learning-based information communication technology (ICT) and Internet of Things (IoT) applications. Although recently developed deep learning technology certainly excels in extracting certain patterns, there are many limitations. Most of recent models are overly dependent on big data, lack a self-idea function, and are complicated. In order to overcome these limitations and to solve the real-world industrial problems, cognitive computing (CC) and computational neuroscience (CN) are driving some of the best tools for future brain-inspired robots.

Rather than merely focusing on the development of next-generation AI models, the 7th International Symposium on Artificial Intelligence and Robotics (ISAIR 2022) aimed to provide a platform to share up-to-date scientific and industrial achievements of general-purpose intelligence cognition methods. These methods provide efficient tools to solve the issues of recent AI models, and capture remarkable human learning abilities, combining the strengths of CC/CN and deep generative neural networks.

This proceedings collects the state-of-the-art contributions on the cognitive intelligence, computer vision, multimedia, the Internet of Things, robotics, and related applications presented at ISAIR 2022, held during October 21–23 in Shanghai, China.

We received 285 submissions from authors in over 10 countries around the world. After the careful single-blind review process, 67 papers were selected based on their originality, significance, technical soundness, and clarity of exposition. Each submission was reviewed by at least 2 members of the Program Committee and the accepted papers underwent further rigorous rounds of review.

It is our sincere hope that this volume provides stimulation and inspiration, and that it will be used as a foundation for works to come.

October 2022

Shuo Yang
Huimin Lu
Shenglin Mu
Rushi Lan

Organization

Steering Committee

Manu Malek (Editor-in-Chief) Computers and Electrical Engineering, USA
Seiichi Serikawa Kyushu Institute of Technology, Japan
Huimin Lu Kyushu Institute of Technology, Japan

General Chairs

Tohru Kamiya Kyushu Institute of Technology, Japan
Zongyuan Ge Monash University, Australia
Jianru Li Tongji University, China

Program Chairs

Rushi Lan Guilin University of Electronic Technology, China
Shenglin Mu Ehime University, Japan
Shuo Yang Kyushu Institute of Technology, Japan

Publicity Chairs

Jože Guna University of Ljubljana, Slovenia
Guangwei Gao Nanjing University of Posts and Telecommunications, China
Shota Nakashima Yamaguchi University, Japan

Award Chairs

Quan Zhou Nanjing University of Posts and Telecommunications, China
Jihua Zhu Xi'an Jiaotong University, China
Zhibin Yu Ocean University of China, China
Dong Wang Dalian University of Technology, China

Area Chairs

Csaba Beleznai Austrian Institute of Technology, Austria
Hao Gao Nanjing University of Posts and Telecommunications, China

Ainul Akmar Mokhtar	Universiti Teknologi Petronas, Malaysia
Ting Wang	Nanjing University of Technology, China
Weihua Ou	Guizhou Normal University, China
Wenpeng Lu	Qilu University of Technology, China
Xing Xu	University of Electronic Science and Technology of China, China
Xin Jin	Beijing Electronic Science and Technology Institute, China
Amit Kumar Singh	National Institute of Technology Patna, India
Zhe Chen	Hohai University, China

Program Committee

Chiew-Foong Kwong	University of Nottingham, UK
Dario Lodi Rizzini	University of Parma, Italy
Danijel Skocaj	University of Ljubljana, Slovenia
Donald Dansereau	University of Sydney, Australia
Guangxu Li	Tianjin Polytechnic University, China
Giancarlo Fortino	Università della Calabria, Italy
Hossein Olya	University of Sheffield, UK
Iztok Humar	University of Ljubljana, Slovenia
Jianru Li	Tongji University, China
Jinjia Zhou	Hosei University, Japan
Keshav Seshadri	Carnegie Mellon University, USA
Levis Mei	Agilent, USA
Limei Peng	Kyungpook National University, South Korea
Liao Wu	University of New South Wales, Australia
Li He	Qualcomm Inc., USA
Mario G. C. A. Cimino	University of Pisa, Italy
M. Shamim Hossain	King Saud University, UAE
Matjaz Perc	University of Maribor, Slovenia
Oleg Sergiyenko	Baja California Autonomous University, Mexico
Sangeen Khan	COMSATS University, Pakistan
Shuai Chen	Chinese Academy of Sciences, China
Wendy Flores-Fuentes	Universidad Autonoma de Baja California, Mexico
Xin Li	Shanghai Jiao Tong University, China
Xinliang Liu	Beijing Technology and Business University, China
Yin Zhang	Zhongnan University of Economics and Law, China
Yichuan Wang	University of Sheffield, UK

Haitao Cheng	Nanjing University of Posts and Telecommunications, China
Fang Hu	Hubei University of Chinese Medicine, China
Xipeng Pan	Guilin University of Electronic Technology, China
Yun Liu	Southwest University, China
Huadeng Wang	Guilin University of Electronic Technology, China
Haigang Zhang	Shenzhen Polytechnic, China
Xianfeng Wu	Jianghan University, China
Zhihao Xu	Qingdao University, China
Junfei Wang	Jianghan University, China
Zhongyuan Lai	Jianghan University, China
Jianming Zhang	Changsha University of Science and Technology, China
Xiwang Xie	Dalian Maritime University, China
Heng Liu	Anhui University of Technology, China
Fenglian Li	Taiyuan University of Technology, China

Contents – Part II

Contents – Part I

Brain Modeling for Surgical Training
on the Basis of Unity 3D

Fengxin Zhang[1], Zhenxing Sun[2(✉)], and Ting Wang[2]

[1] Faculty of Mechanical and Power Engineering, Nanjing Tech University, Nanjing 211816, China
zhangfenfu@qq.com
[2] College of Electrical Engineering and Control Science, Nanjing Tech University, Nanjing 211816, China
sunzx@njtech.edu.cn

Abstract. Virtual surgical simulation trainings have advantages of repeatability, convinient operation, strong immersion, etc. It can greatly reduce the cost of surgical trainings and decrease the risk of surgery operations. In practice, virtual soft tissue models require real-time generation of deformations during the interaction, so as to provide force feedback. In this process, it requires that the rationality of the model deformation may be fully considered as building the model. Mass Spring Model is widely used in soft tissue modeling and deformation simulations due to its simple structure and high efficiency. In order to make the virtual surgical simulation more realistic and accurate, via the Unity3D software, a mass-spring physics model is established based on the biomechanical characteristics of soft tissue in this paper. Newtonian classical mechanics is used and the virtual brain modeling and collision are performed by numerical simulations. The platform is constructed using Unity 3D and C# software. Results show that our model may accurately reflects the deformations of soft brain issue.

Keywords: Virtual surgical simulation · Soft tissue modeling · Mass-Spring Model · Deformation

1 Introduction

With the rapid development of virtual reality technology and modern medicine, the cross-integration of various disciplines have gradually formed the medical virtual reality technology. A key difficulty in virtual surgery research is the simulation of soft tissue deformations, which provides users with virtual soft tissue force and deformations both in the visual and tactile real recovery of the surgical scene [1]. Soft tissue modelling techniques have been improved in the past decades, while there still exists many problems [2]. Currently, while real-time virtual surgery systems for soft tissues can meet the real-time requirements in computation, while the accuracy of the simulation still needs to be improved [3].

S. Yang and H. Lu (Eds.): ISAIR 2022, CCIS 1701, pp. 1–8, 2022.
https://doi.org/10.1007/978-981-19-7943-9_1

In exist researches, many methods have been proposed for modelling soft tissues, such as the Mass-Spring Model (MSM), the Finite Element Model (FEM) and the Boundary Element Method (BEM). Among them, the MSM and the FEM are the most commonly used. The central idea of the FEM is derived from engineering mechanics, which usually views a deformed object as a collection of elastic models. Thus, it is highly biomechanically realistic [4]. However, finite elements are relatively complex and inefficient to Ycompute. Courtecuisse H et al. proposed a non-linear FEM for modelling soft tissues [5]. The MSM is usually used for deformable surfaces and can simulate the force deformation of soft tissues more realistically [6]. Gao et al. proposed a mass-spring method that takes into account anisotropy to accurately model soft tissue deformations [7]. In recent years, most of the research has focused on improving the accuracy of the MSM.

Based on existing researches [8–12], this paper uses Unity3d software and MSM to model brain tissue according to the requirements of stability, accuracy and real time data for virtual surgery simulations. It not only enables the modelling of the required scenes, but also enables a better force feedback effect. Therefore, it may achieve a visual and haptical realistic reproduction of the surgical scenes. The rest of paper is organized as follows. The biomechanical properties of brain tissue and the MSM are presented in Sect. 2, in which a model with topological relationships is developed for brain tissues and the kinetic equations for the brain tissue model are accordingly given. The experimental platform and simulation results are described in Sect. 3. Section 4 draws some conclusions.

2 Tissue Deformation Modeling and Kinetic Equations

2.1 Biomechanical Properties of Brain Tissue

Soft tissues have major differences compared to traditional materials, and almost all soft tissues have both solid and liquid components. There are many types of soft tissues. Their mechanical properties vary with different tissues due to differences in structure and function [13, 14]. While the specific characteristics of soft tissues are different, they basically have the following three characteristics: (1) Anisotropy, the internal arrangement structure of soft tissues affects the tissue properties due to the different internal cellular and tissue composition. (2) Viscoplasticity, soft tissues are not only elastic, but also have frictional. (3) Nonlinearity, during the stress process of soft tissue, there is no linear relationship between the change of stress and the strain of biological tissue.

2.2 Mass-Spring Model

The MSM typically treats a deformed object as a collection of mass points connected to each other by springs. The deformation of soft tissues is caused by the motion of these discrete masses connected by springs. The types of springs can be classified according to their role: (1) Structural springs, maintain the structure of the soft tissue surface. (2) Bending springs, prevent excessive bending of the soft tissue, and (3) shear springs, simulate the shear properties of the soft tissue. The MSM is the first physical model proposed, and is also a classical deformation model, which is widely used in virtual surgical soft tissue simulation research due to its computational simplicity and fast modeling speed.

2.3 Physical Modeling of Brain Tissue

In this paper, we use MSM to model brain tissue. The classic MSM is a method of simulating the deformation of an object using Newton's laws of motion. Since the density of brain tissue is uniform, it can be approximated to the combinations of regularly arranged particles, and the mass of brain tissue is evenly distributed on each particle. This process is called discrete. Usually, the mass is connected to the particle with a spring of non-natural length of zero, which is used to simulate the force deformation of brain tissue.

The classic MSM topology model consists of structural springs, shear springs, and bending springs, as shown in Fig. 1. Among them, the structural spring is used to simulate the force along axis-X and axis-Y directions of brain tissue while the elastic coefficient is very large. It mainly prevents the brain tissue from being subjected to greater pulling force or pressure in the X and Y directions, avoid large deformation. Shear springs are used to simulate the force on the tilt direction within brain tissues, and the elastic coefficient is smaller relative to the structural spring. The purpose is to prevent unstable changes in brain tissue during stretching and torsions. A bend spring is a particle that connects two phased particles in the X and Y directions. It is used to simulate the brain tissue in the deformation process edge smooth, and its elastic coefficient is small in the simulation so that it can be ignored.

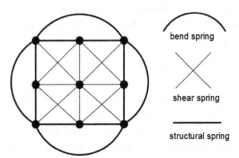

Fig. 1. Classic prime spring model topology

The MSM implemented in Unity3D is showed in Fig. 2 and Fig. 3. Figure 2 shows the original state of the model when it didn't hit by the ball, in which the ball in the figure simulates the particle. The green line simulates the real spring. Figure 3 shows the state of the MSM when it hits with a ball. If the ball hits with a large impact force, it turns yellow as the deformation occurs around the impacted ball.

Fig. 2. Original state

Fig. 3. Ball collision model

2.4 Kinetic Equations

In the MSM, the essence of the deformation of the model according to the external force is the motion of the mass. According to Newton's second law, the kinetic equation for the mass can be expressed as:

$$F = ma, \tag{1}$$

where F is the total force on a single mass. m is the current mass quality, and a is the acceleration obtained by the current mass. The total force on the mass includes the interaction force between the mass inside the model and the force exerted by the outside. Among mass points, the interaction force includes the spring force and the damping force during the movement of the mass point. The total force executed on the single mass point can be expressed as follow:

$$F = f_e + \sum_{n=1}^{n=m} (f_s^n + f_d^n), \tag{2}$$

where f_e is the external force. m means that there are m springs connected to the mass, and f_s^n, f_d^n indicate the spring force and damping force generated by the n-th spring.

From Hooke's law, the elastic force produced by a single spring f_s is defined as:

$$f_s = k(l - l^0), \tag{3}$$

where k is the spring elasticity coefficient. l indicates the real-time length of the spring and l_0 is the spring relaxation length.

Damping force f_d is defined as:

$$f_d = cv, \tag{4}$$

where c denotes the damping coefficient and v is the velocity of the mass at a given moment.

The kinetic equation for a single mass in the MSM can be derived from Eqs. 1, 2, 3, and 4 which is described as follows:

$$ma = f_e + \sum_{n=1}^{n=m} (k_n(l_n - l_n^0) + c_n v). \tag{5}$$

After obtaining the acceleration a at the current moment, the velocity and displacement of the mass can be expressed as follows:

$$v = at, \tag{6}$$

$$s = \frac{1}{2}at^2, \tag{7}$$

where t is the time interval, and the position of the mass at the next moment is the sum of the current position of the mass and the displacement of the mass. After obtaining the position of the mass at the next moment, the model can be updated and the spring length and force can be recalculated.

3 Experimental Environment and Experimental Results

3.1 Soft and Hardware Environment

The Brain tissue modeling is mainly based on the 3D drawing software 3DS MAX2020 and the Unity2020 game engine developed under the Windows operating system, with the modeling of virtual brain organization and the construction of virtual scenes.

The hardware part of the modeling of brain tissue is mainly composed of force feedback devices and computers. The experimental in this paper are based on computers and force feedback devices.

Force Feedback Device. The force feedback device is a high-performance force/haptic interaction device that accurately measures position in three-dimensional space (using x, y, and z axes) and the orientation of the handheld stylus (flip up and down, left and right shaking, and lateral movement).

Computer Configuration. The hardware configuration of the computer is 4.6GHz Intel Core i7-11800H processor, DDR4 3200MHz of memory, NVIDA GeForce RXT 3060 graphics card and Windows 11 operating system.

3.2 Experimental Platform

Based on the above-mentioned principles, structures, and software and hardware equipment, a virtual brain tissue modeling platform is built. The experimental platform is showed in Fig. 4. In it, the experiment is conducted a collision experiment with virtual brain tissues. The force feedback device in the figure is used as an interface device for human-computer interaction. As the human manipulates the force feedback device to move up and down in space, the small ball in the virtual environment also moves in the same way. When it touches the brain tissue in the virtual environment, the contact force is fed back in real time, so that the experimenter has an immersive feeling.

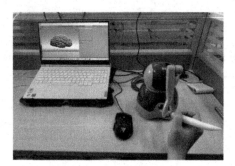

Fig. 4. Experimental platform

3.3 Experimental Simulation

First, the force feedback device is connected to the computer and debugged to realize the interaction between the force feedback device and the computer. Then take the following procedures: (1) export the brain model in 3DS MAX; (2) import the brain model in Unity3D, (3) adjust the program and required experimental parameters, and (4) run. Figure 5 reflects that at the beginning of the experiment, the virtual ball is located on the periphery of the brain and cannot collide with the brain. In this case, the force feedback at this time is 0. Figure 6 shows that the virtual ball is in contact with the surface tissue of the brain. When the human pushes the force feedback device with a small force, the surface tissue of the brain undergoes a small deformation. In this case, the force feedback is equal to the push force of the experimenter. Figure 7 displays that when the experimenter increased the thrust, in which the small ball in the virtual scene and the surface tissue of the brain are greatly deformed. Figure 8 illustrates that the virtual balls contact different parts of the surface tissue of the brain, which also deforms.

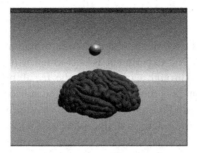

Fig. 5. Original state

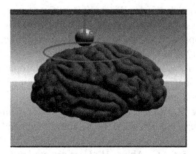

Fig. 6. Collide the brain with less force

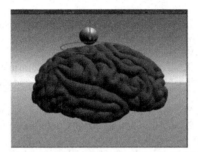

Fig. 7. Collide the brain with a larger force

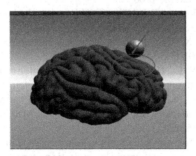

Fig. 8. Collide in different places

4   Conclusion

In this paper, the MSM is used to simulate brain deformation based on the biological properties of soft tissues. The experiment is performed using Unity3D software and a force feedback device. Through experiments, the feasibility of using the MSM to simulate brain deformation lays the foundation for the subsequent construction of the entire virtual surgical system. Future work will focus on improving the mesh size of the MSM, optimizing the collision detection algorithm, and improving the accuracy of the entire experiment.

References

1. Tan, Zhao, J., Shi, W., Li, X., Yang, H., Jiang, Z.: An improved soft tissue deformation simulation model based on mass spring. In: 2020 International Conference on Virtual Reality and Visualization(ICVRV), pp. 121–127 (2020)
2. Qiao, B., Chen, G., Ye, X.: The research of soft tissue deformation based on mass-spring model. In: 2009 International Conference on Mechatronics and Automation, pp. 4655–4660 (2009)
3. Bian, J., Chen, J., Sun, M.: Simulation of soft tissue deformation in virtual surgery based on physics engine. In: 2011 Third International Conference on Multimedia Information Networking and Security, pp. 60–64 (2011)
4. Liu, X., Yao, J.: Modelling and simulation of vascular tissue based on finite element method. In: 2018 5th International Conference on Information Science and Control Engineering (ICISCE), pp. 336–340 (2018)
5. Courtecuisse, H., Allard, J., Kerfriden, P., et al.: Real-time simulation of contact and cutting of heterogeneous soft-tissues[J]. Med. Image Anal. **18**(2), 394–410 (2013)
6. Tang, Y., et al.: An improved method for soft tissue modeling. Biomed. Signal Process. Control. **65**(6), 102367 (2021)
7. Gao, W., Chu, L., Fu, Y., Wang, S.: A non-linear, anisotropic mass spring model based simulation for soft tissue deformation. In: 2014 11th International Conference on Ubiquitous Robots and Ambient Intelligence (URAI), pp. 7–10 (2014)
8. Lu, H., Yang, R., Deng, Z., Zhang, Y., Gao, G., Lan, R.: Chinese image captioning via fuzzy attention-based DenseNet-BiLSTM. ACM Trans. Multimed. Comput. Commun. Appl. **17**(1s), 1–18 (2021)
9. Lu, H., Zhang, Y., Li, Y., Jiang, C., Abbas, H.: User-oriented virtual mobile network resource management for vehicle communications. IEEE Trans. Intell. Transp. Syst. (2020). https://doi.org/10.1109/TITS.2020.2991766
10. Lu, H., Qin, M, Zhang, F., et al. RSCNN: a CNN-based method to enhance low-light remote-sensing images. Remote Sens. **13**, 62 (2020)
11. Lu, H., Zhang, M., Xu, X.: Deep fuzzy hashing network for efficient image retrieval. IEEE Trans. Fuzzy Syst. (2020). https://doi.org/10.1109/TFUZZ.2020.2984991
12. Li, Y., Yang, S., Zheng, Y., Lu, H.: Improved point-voxel region convolutional neural network: 3D object detectors for autonomous driving. IEEE Trans. Intell. Trans. Syst. (2021)
13. Peng, Y., Wong, D.W.-C., et al.: Computational models of flatfoot with three-dimensional fascia and bulk soft tissue interaction for orthosis design. Med. Novel Technol. Devices. **9**, 100050, ISSN 2590-0935 (2021)
14. Castillo-Méndez, C., Ortiz, A.: Role of anisotropic invariants in numerically modeling soft biological tissues as transversely isotropic hyperelastic materials: a comparative study. Int. J. Non-Linear Mech. **138**, 103833, ISSN 0020-7462 (2022)

Motion Saliency Detection Based on Drosophila Vision-Inspired Model

Meng Zhou[1], Wencai Hu[2], Pingan Zhang[1], and Zhe Chen[2(✉)]

[1] School of Computer and Information, Hohai University, Nanjing 211100, China
[2] The Yi-Shu-Si River Basin Administration, Xuzhou 221018, China
chenzhe@hhu.edu.cn

Abstract. Drosophila vision is extremely sensitive to moving targets and color opponency, which provides rich biological enlightenment for the study of computer vision. Drosophila vision has been extensively studied in various aspects, but our understanding of the underlying neural computation remains poorly understood. We propose a Drosophila vision-inspired model that constructs a complete visual motion perception system and a color processing system by integrating continuous computing layers to gain insight into the neural mechanisms of Drosophila vision and make better use of its strengths in saliency detection. Drosophila vision-inspired model can also be used for saliency detection in dynamic scenes, especially in some scenes where the color distinction is significant, it can accurately identify the motion of interest (MOI) while suppressing background interference and self-motion because our model depends on the motion perception and color opponency based on the Drosophila vision. Experiments on two large-scale video saliency detection datasets demonstrate the superiority of our model in saliency detection compared with the state-of-the art methods.

Keywords: Drosophila vision · Motion perception · Color opponency · Saliency detection

1 Introduction

Biological vision research has always been a significant source of designing algorithms for computer vision. Biological vision is essential to maximize the efficiency of daily tasks such as feeding, avoiding predators, or finding mating partners. Although the natural scenes have high noise and chaos, the biological visual system shows extremely advanced perceptual ability. It is worth noting that in terms of information in the visual processing mechanism, some insects are similar to higher animals but their visual systems are relatively simple to construct [1]. For example, the medulla, the largest and most heavily populated optic neuropil, part of Drosophila vision, is organized into strata and columns in a manner reminiscent of the mammalian cortex [2]. Although the mechanisms behind the Drosophila vision have not been fully explained, however, the current modeling of Drosophila vision undoubtedly promote the further development of computer vision.

S. Yang and H. Lu (Eds.): ISAIR 2022, CCIS 1701, pp. 9–20, 2022.
https://doi.org/10.1007/978-981-19-7943-9_2

In Drosophila vision, motion vision is independent of color [3], however, the neural network behind the motion vision and color vision is a typical hierarchical structure [4]. First of all, the retina is the first layer of Drosophila vision, in retina, both motion vision and color vision depend on several photoreceptors (R1–R6, R7, R8), the R1–R6-based motion pathway is independent of R7/R8-based color pathway. Secondly, in lamina layer, the neurons specialize in the sensing spatial changes so that they are able to perceive the boundaries of MOI. Meanwhile, the R7 and R8 photoreceptors in the first layer penetrate the lamina and innervate the medulla directly. Medulla remind us of the color mechanism of mammalian cortex, which plays an important role in color boundary detection. Besides, the T cells in medulla can extract directional information. In the last layer, lobular, two motion-sensitive neurons called LPTC can integrate the direction information and reduce the background interference. At the high level of the Drosophila vision system, there is a central complex that has been found to play a role in multi-sensory integration [5], it connects the color vision and motion vision.

Generally speaking, most researches focus on a part of Drosophila vision or a single layer. There are few studies on their coordination ability in color processing and motion perception. We propose a model that integrate motion processing modules and color processing modules. It presents a novelty that can study the neural computation of color processing and motion perception in Drosophila.

This paper mainly consists of the following parts. Firstly, we introduce the related background about Drosophila vision and saliency detection. After this, we propose the model and detailed process. Then, an evaluation experiment is conducted to evaluate the accuracy of saliency detection. Finally, we give a conclusion.

2 Related Work

2.1 Drosophila Vision

Visual processing in Drosophila is divided into two parallel pathways in the first neuropiles: motion vision and color vision. In nature, lightweight and low-powered drosophila apply motion vision to detect a moving target in highly variable environments during flight, which are splendid paradigms to study motion detection strategies [26–30]. Color information is also important for survival as it conveys rich information about the external world and allows it to distinguish spectral stimuli and provides an extra dimension for computer vision. Some scholars have studied motion vision through the computation of local neural layers and neurons, however, there are few researches about applying color vision to motion detection.

Hassenstein and Reichardt tried to explain the mechanism of the insect vision and proposed an elaborated motion detector based on Hassenstein-Reichardt correlator model (HRC) [6]. Currently, behavioral and electrophysiological studies in the drosophila have demonstrated that the visual motion responses display the fundamental signatures predicted by the HRC. In Drosophila, there are four medulla neurons. The neurons Mi1 and Tm3 respond selectively to brightness increments, conversely, Tm1 and Tm2 respond selectively to brightness decrements [7]. The mechanism behind the four neurons corresponds with the HRC. The LPTCs in the adjacent layer will receive the result from medulla.

In Drosophila, photoreceptors R7–R8 in retina are required for color vision. Color vision cannot be executed by a single photoreceptor and requires complex comparisons. These comparisons have been shown to take place in the synaptic terminals of R7–R8 in medulla through mutual inhibition.

In the downstream of LPTCs, there is a central complex which can receive motion signals from LPTCs and color information. This finding suggests that the central complex plays a role in fusing motion information and color information.

Generally speaking, most researches focus on a part of Drosophila vision or a single layer. Besides, in current researches, motion vision and color vision have not work together to solve motion detection problems. This encourages us to propose a model fusing motion vision and color vision in Drosophila vision.

2.2 Saliency Detection

The study of visual saliency initially started with static information, i.e., a frame of an image, aimed at detecting attention-grabbing regions in a scene. Some models are inspired by biological vision mechanisms and aim to mimic the attentional mechanisms of biological vision and predict where an organism will focus its attention in an image. Itti et al. computed saliency by fusing multiple distinct feature channels and DoG (difference of Gaussian) filter responses at multiple scales [8]. Then, they simulated the features of "winner-take-all" and "inhibition of return" with a neural network, fully realizing the whole process of attentional selection. Later, discoveries in psychology and cognitive science sparked interest in salient object detection between consecutive frames. So far, we have witnessed the significant progress towards saliency detection. One of them is to mimic the mechanism of human visual sensitivity to motion, such as the motion features input into the Itti model. The starting point of other approaches is not to model the visual system, but to provide results similar to biological brains. Furthermore, there are many ways to design classifiers to identify motion saliency, such as graph theory-based models, regularized feature reconstruction, and compressed video saliency [9]. In recent years, the development of deep learning has facilitated motion saliency detection. Various deep models have been widely applied to the field of salient object detection, such as convolutional neural networks and recurrent neural networks [10].

While existing motion saliency methods have been successful in many applications, current research is increasingly deviating from the original saliency concept. Recall that salient object detection is implemented in the optic nervous system, where complex computations (like Fourier transform) or complex procedures (like deep learning) cannot be provided. Therefore, most of the existing motion detection models cannot simulate neural computation and cannot translate the advantages of biological vision into practice. It's time to go back to bionic models to detect salient objects.

2.3 Our Contributions

We propose a hybrid model fusing motion perception and color vision inspired by Drosophila vision in this paper, it is applied to saliency detection and is evaluated on benchmark datasets. The main contributions of our model are as follows:

i) The overall modeling of Drosophila motion vision and color vision. Unlike previous studies, our work established a hybrid model to simulate the process of perception from motion pathways and color pathways, revealing the intrinsic mechanisms of motion perception and color perception in Drosophila vision.

ii) Through functional simulation, we fill the gap between biological vision and computer vision. Current neural computational models only pay attention to explaining the motion characteristics of Drosophila, ignoring color information, which plays an important role in boundaries.

3   Methodology: Drosophila Vision-Inspired Model

Drosophila vision consists of motion pathways and color pathways, in which the motion pathway passes through the retinal, lamina, medulla, and lobula, and color pathway passes through the retina directly to the medulla. Neuro computing in these motion-sensitive organs is modeled and integrated sequentially, and finally the information from the two pathways is fused for further processing in the central complex, as shown in Fig. 1.

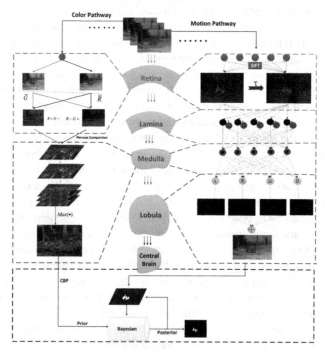

Fig. 1. Schematic illustration of the hybrid model fusing motion vision and color vision

3.1   Motion Pathway

Retina Layer. Retina mainly plays an important role in detecting illumination changes in motion pathways depending on a range of photoreceptors (R1–R6) [11]. Due to the scale-invariant feature of the retina, we combine scale-invariant feature transform [12] with the frame difference to obtain preliminary motion information through computation.

$$P_t = |H \otimes f_{t-1} - f_t| \tag{1}$$

where f_t is the frame in the time step t and H is the transform matrix based on SIFT features. The disturbance caused by self-motion can be largely removed in this way, as shown in Fig. 2(b).

Lamina Layer. Neurons in the lamina and medulla work together to enhance the spatial contrast of the MOI through lateral inhibition, where in the lamina, it is primarily used to generate inhibitory signals. Lateral inhibition strength is represented by a weighted sum of inhibitory signals from adjacent neural inputs.

$$I_t(x, y) = \sum_{i=-q}^{q} \sum_{-s}^{s} P_{t-1}(x + i, y + j) \times w(i + q, j + s) \tag{2}$$

where $q \times s$ represents the field of lateral inhibition, w is the lateral inhibition matrix with 0 and 1 elements.

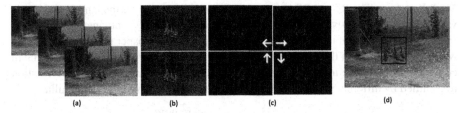

(a)   (b)   (c)   (d)

Fig. 2. MOI perception in Drosophila motion pathway. (a) Original scene, (b) Retina, (c) Lamina and Medulla (d) Lobula

Medulla Layer. T cells in the medulla play an important role in orientation. We consider motion information from four directions in a two-dimensional space, i.e., up, down, left, and right. The change of direction is achieved through changing the direction of lateral inhibition in T cells:

$$M_t^L(x, y) = [P_t(x, y) - I_t^L(x, y) \bullet W] \tag{3}$$

where L represents the direction "Left", other directions share the same steps, as shown in Fig. 2(c). W is a global inhibition weight. The direction selectivity is accomplished by adjusting the arrangement of the lateral inhibition matrix.

Lobula Layer. Giant LPTC cells existing in the lobula layer integrate all local motion signals along main directions [13], achieving a globally average perception for the MOI.

$$S_t(x, y) = \sum_{d=L,R,U,D} M_t^d(x, y) \tag{4}$$

So far, we finish the processing of motion pathways and get the orientation of targets, as shown in Fig. 2(d).

3.2 Color Pathway

Retina layer. In Retina, color vision depends on several photoreceptors(R7/R8), R7 and R8 photoreceptors inhibit each other within 'pale' and 'yellow' ommatidia, forming two channels of color opponency $R7_p - R8_p$ and $R7_y - R8_y$. Color vision cannot be performed alone by a single photoreceptor. It is encoded in color opponent neurons which are excited at one wavelength and suppressed at another [14].

Therefore, in retina, the input from the time step t is separated into four channels: red(R), green(G), blue(B), and yellow(Y), where Y = (R + G)/2. We simulate the receptive field in retina to preprocess the input by Gaussian filtering, the outputs are denoted $\overline{R}, \overline{G}, \overline{B}$ and $\overline{Y}$. The four outputs will inhibit each other.

$$Y(x, y) = \omega_1 \bullet \overline{R}(x, y; \delta) + \omega_2 \bullet \overline{G}(x, y; \delta)$$

$$\text{where,} \begin{cases} \omega_1 \bullet \omega_2 \leq 0 \\ |\omega_1|, |\omega_2| \in [0, 1] \end{cases} \tag{5}$$

where ω_1 and ω_2 are the inhibition weights. ω_1 and ω_2 always have the opposite sign. With $\omega_1 < 0$ and $\omega_2 > 0$, playing a role in mutual inhibition, δ is the standard deviate of the gaussian filter.

Medulla Layer. The R7 and R8 photoreceptors in retina penetrate the lamina and innervate the medulla directly. The medulla is the largest and densest optic nerve, and works in a way reminiscent of the vertebrate cortex, inspired by the paper [15], mimicking the working mechanism of the cortex, and most color-sensitive nerve cells are adversarial in color and space, so we mimic the processing mechanism of nerve cells for information transmitted by different photoreceptors in retina to get receptive field in medulla.

$$f(\overline{x}, \overline{y}) = \frac{1}{\sqrt{2\pi(k\delta)^2}} \exp(\frac{-(\overline{x}^2 + \gamma^2\overline{y}^2)}{2(k\delta)^2}) \tag{6}$$

$$\begin{bmatrix} \overline{x} \\ \overline{y} \end{bmatrix} = M \bullet \begin{bmatrix} x \\ y \end{bmatrix} M = \begin{bmatrix} \cos\theta \ \sin\theta \\ -\sin\theta \ \cos\theta \end{bmatrix} \tag{7}$$

$$F(x, y; \theta) = \left| \frac{\partial f(\overline{x}, \overline{y})}{\partial \overline{x}} \right| \tag{8}$$

where $f(\overline{x}, \overline{y})$ is a two-dimensional gaussian distribution in which γ can control the receptive field. M is a rotation matrix which controls the direction of the cells. We usually set k = 2, $\gamma = 0.5$ and δ to be the same as the scale of Gaussian filters used in the retina.

Thus, the output of medulla at each direction is given by

$$B(x, y, \theta_i) = \sum_{m,n \subseteq N_1} Y_1(x + m, y + n) \bullet F(m, n; \theta_i) + \sum_{m,n \subseteq N_2} Y_2(x + m, y + n) \bullet F(m, n; \theta_i) \tag{9}$$

where N_1 and N_2 represent the different region of color opponency, $\theta_i = \frac{2(i-1)}{N}, i = 1, 2...., N$, here we set N = 16. Then we take the maximum value in all directions as the response of the edge.

$$B(x, y) = \max\{B(x, y, \theta_i) | i = 1, 2, ..., N\} \tag{10}$$

So far, we finish the work of the color pathway.

3.3 Central Brain

In the high level of the Drosophila vision, there is a central brain involved in the multi-sensory integration. It can receive motion signals from LPTCs and color information. In motion pathway, we can obtain background information and approximate target area. In color pathway, we can get contour information. We simulate the interaction of top-down and bottom-up mechanism in Drosophila vision, based on rough salient area, we transform saliency detection problems into Bayesian inference [16].

With Bayesian inference, the likelihood of a point x belonging to saliency map can be computed as:

$$p(sal|x) = \frac{p(sal)p(x|sal)}{p(sal)p(x|sal) + p(bk)p(x|bk)} \tag{11}$$

where $p(sal)$ and $p(bk) = 1 - p(sal)$ are the prior probability. $p(x|sal)$ and $p(x|bk)$ are the likelihood based on saliency map and background. Here, we will further process the contour information to get the contour-based prior(CBP), we set CBP as the initial prior probability. The $p(x|sal)$ and $p(x|bk)$ will be set according to the target area and background information produced in the motion pathway. Finally, we further enhance the saliency map by iterating: we reset the prior according to the posterior calculated in the previous round.

4 Experiment Results

Our proposed model aims to explore and demonstrate the superior saliency detection capabilities of drosophila vision systems and attempt to apply them to classic computer vision tasks. To better highlight the performance of our model, we conducted a synthetic experiment on two challenging datasets: the FBMS [17] and DAVIS [18] datasets. There are various difficulties in these two datasets, such as huge self-movements and complex backgrounds. We conducted a thorough experimental comparison with the state-of-the-art saliency detection methods in recent years, such as the SGSP [19], SRP [20], SAGE [21], SG-FCN [22], SCGT [23], and PCSA [24]. Among the above-mentioned saliency detection methods, SGSP, SRP, SAGE, SCGT do not need pre-training and huge amounts of data, SG-FCN and PCSA depend on deep learning. The results of the above methods are achieved by running publicly available implementations provided by the original authors.

4.1 Evaluation Metrics

Different criteria, that is, Precision-Recall (PR) curves, F-Measure and MAE [25] are applied to evaluate the saliency detection results. PR curve, determined by precision and recall, is widely used to evaluate the performance of saliency detection. F-Measure is a comprehensive consideration of precision and recall, they are defined as:

$$Precision = \frac{\sum_x S_T(x) \bullet G_T(x)}{\sum_x S_T(x)}, Recall = \frac{\sum_x S_T(x) \bullet G_T(x)}{\sum_x G_T(x)}$$

$$F - measure = \frac{(1 + \beta^2) \bullet Precision \bullet Recall}{\beta^2 \bullet Precision + Recall} \tag{12}$$

$$MAE = \frac{1}{N}(S(x) - G_T(x))$$

where S_T represents the binary map of the saliency detection results, G_T is the ground truth, $\beta^2 = 0.3$ and N is the pixel number. MAE is the average per-pixel difference between saliency map S_T and ground truth map G_T.

4.2 Results on FBMS and DAVIS

A qualitative visual comparison of our Drosophila vision-inspired model and other prominent saliency detection methods are shown in Fig. 3. Among them, SGSP model improves the saliency detection performance on unconstrained videos through spatiotemporal propagation and superpixel-level graph, however, the result is not ideal. SRP model discovers the motion-related salient objects via sparsity-based reconstruction and propagation. SAGE depends on an unsupervised, geodesic distance-based saliency detection method. SCGT is model inspired by Gestalt theory, the saliency is influenced by high-level features from top-down knowledge. Both SAGE and SCGT can accurately detect the salient target areas, but still lack robustness in some video scenes. SG-FCN and PCSA are all deep learning methods, SG-FCN fully depends on CNNs, to efficiently detect salient regions. PCSA is a pyramid constrained self-attention model, which capture motion cues efficiently. However, more data may be needed for training.

Generally speaking, it can be clearly found that the saliency detection performance of the comparison method is not ideal.

Other methods may mistake some background regions as target area, and they cannot extract precise boundaries. Additionally, from Fig. 3, we also can find in severe dynamic scenes, the performance of some methods is degraded. In contrast, our method can extract precise MOI boundaries and a relatively complete target based on Drosophila vision. The below Fig. 4 will show the PR-curves, F-measure, and MAE results of our model and other comparison models. The Fig. 4 demonstrates that our model is the best. So it quantitatively shows that the detection performance of this method is better than other methods.

4.3 Performance Discussion

From the quantitative and qualitative results of different saliency detection methods above, our model has achieved better results in different scenes. In some scenes, although our model has not gotten the best result, there are some unique advantages: our method does not need additional training and a huge amount of data. Moreover, the time cost of our method is lower than others. Table 1 shows the cost for each saliency detection method.

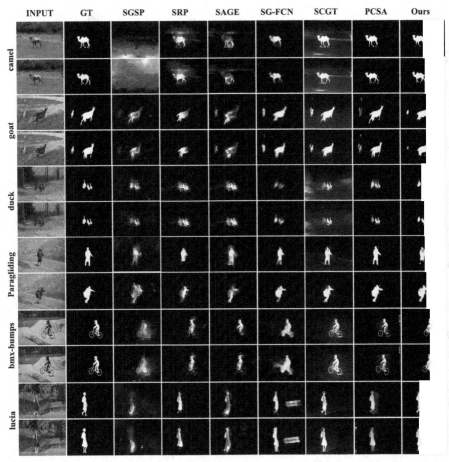

Fig. 3. Video saliency detection on the FBMS dataset (top three videos) and the DAVIS dataset (bottom three videos)

Generally speaking, deep learning methods with training tend to have a better performance than those who do not have pre-training process, such as PCSA. While our method shows better performance overall. It can contribute to the advantage of drosophila vision. The advantage of Drosophila vision has been fully reflected in our model.

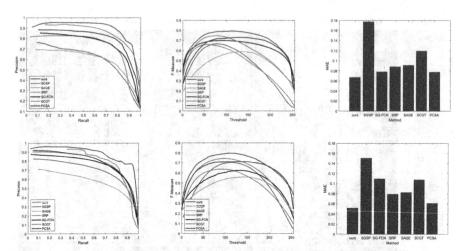

Fig. 4. Comparison of PR curves (left), F-Measure (middle) and MAE (right) on FBMS dataset (top row) and DAVIS dataset (bottom row)

Table 1. Time cost for saliency detection

Method	SGSP	SRP	SAGE	SG-FCN	SCGT	PCSA	Ours
Cost(s)	10.16	17.03	49.86	3.85	4.497	3.281	2.83

5 Conclusions

In this paper, a Drosophila vision-inspired model which integrates the motion pathway and color pathway is proposed. We establish a relatively complete model fusing motion cues and color features and it is applied to classic computer vision tasks. A bridge is built between computer vision and biological vision. Compared with other advanced methods, our method shows a better performance. As we all know, the deep neural networks came from biological inspiration in the very beginning, however, current neural networks have been separated from biological inspiration. Thus, in the future, we will continue to combine computer vision tasks with biological inspiration.

References

1. Medathati, N.V.K., Neumann, H., Masson, G.S., Kornprobst, P.: Bio-inspired computer vision: towards a synergistic approach of artificial and biological vision. Comput. Vis. Image Underst. **150**, 1–30 (2016)
2. Gao, S., et al.: The neural substrate of spectral preference in Drosophila (in eng). Neuron. **60**(2), 328–342 (2008)
3. Yamaguchi, S., Wolf, R., Desplan, C., Heisenberg, M.: Motion vision is independent of color in Drosophila (in eng). 1091–6490 (Electronic)
4. Longden, K.D.: Colour vision: a fresh view of lateral inhibition in drosophila. Curr. Biol. **28**(7), R308–R311 (2018)

5. de Andres-Bragado, L., Sprecher, S.G.: Mechanisms of vision in the fruit fly. Curr. Opin. Insect. Sci. **36**, 25–32 (2019)
6. Basch, M.-E., Cristea, D.-G., Tiponuţ, V., Slavici, T.: Elaborated motion detector based on Hassenstein-Reichardt correlator model (2010)
7. Behnia, R., Clark, D.A., Carter, A.G., Clandinin, T.R., Desplan, C.: Processing properties of ON and OFF pathways for Drosophila motion detection (in eng). Nature **512**(7515), 427–430 (2014)
8. Itti, L., Koch, C., Niebur, E.: A model of saliency-based visual attention for rapid scene analysis. IEEE Trans. Pattern Anal. Mach. Intell. **20**(11), 1254–1259 (1998)
9. Cong, R., Lei, J., Fu, H., Cheng, M.M., Lin, W., Huang, Q.: Review of visual saliency detection with comprehensive information. IEEE Trans. Circuits Syst. Video Technol. **29**(10), 2941–2959 (2019)
10. Kuen, J., Wang, Z., Wang, G.:Recurrent attentional networks for saliency detection. In: 2016 IEEE Conference on Computer Vision and Pattern Recognition (CVPR), pp. 3668–3677 (2016)
11. Paulk, A., Millard, S.S., van Swinderen, B.: Vision in Drosophila: seeing the world through a model's eyes (in eng). Annu. Rev. Entomol. **58**, 313–332 (2013)
12. Lowe, D.G.: Distinctive image features from scale-invariant keypoints. Int. J. Comput. Vision. **60**(2), 91–110 (2004)
13. Wienecke, C.F., Clandinin, T.R.: Drosophila vision: an eye for change (in eng). Curr. Biol. **30**(2), R66-r68 (2020)
14. Schnaitmann, C., Pagni, M., Reiff, D.F.: Color vision in insects: insights from Drosophila. J. Comp. Physiol. A. **206**(2), 183–198 (2020)
15. Yang, K., Gao, S., Li, C., Li, Y.:Efficient color boundary detection with color-opponent mechanisms. In: 2013 IEEE Conference on Computer Vision and Pattern Recognition, pp. 2810–2817 (2013)
16. Yang, K.F., Li, H., Li, C.-Y., Li, Y.-J.: A unified framework for salient structure detection by contour-guided visual search (in eng), 1941–0042 (Electronic)
17. Brox, T., Malik, J.: Object segmentation by long term analysis of point trajectories. In: Computer Vision – ECCV 2010, pp. 282–295. Springer, Berlin, Heidelberg (2010)
18. Perazzi, F., Pont-Tuset, J., McWilliams, B., Gool, L.V., Gross, M., Sorkine-Hornung, A.:A benchmark dataset and evaluation methodology for video object segmentation. In: 2016 IEEE Conference on Computer Vision and Pattern Recognition (CVPR), pp. 724–732 (2016)
19. Liu, Z., Li, J., Ye, L., Sun, G., Shen, L.: Saliency detection for unconstrained videos using superpixel-level graph and spatiotemporal propagation. IEEE Trans. Circuits Syst. Video Technol. **27**, 2527–2542 (2017)
20. Wenguan, W., Jianbing, S., Porikli, F.:Saliency-aware geodesic video object segmentation. In: 2015 IEEE Conference on Computer Vision and Pattern Recognition (CVPR), pp. 3395–3402 (2015)
21. Cong, R., Lei, J., Fu, H., Porikli, F., Huang, Q., Hou, C.: Video saliency detection via sparsity-based reconstruction and propagation. IEEE Trans. Image Process. **28**(10), 4819–4831 (2019)
22. Fang, Y., Zhang, X., Yuan, F., Imamoglu, N., Liu, H.: Video saliency detection by gestalt theory. Pattern Recognit. **96**, 106987 (2019)
23. Sun, M., Zhou, Z., Hu, Q., Wang, Z., Jiang, J.: SG-FCN: a motion and memory-based deep learning model for video saliency detection. IEEE Trans. Cybern. **49**(8), 2900–2911 (2019)
24. Gu, Y.-C., Wang, L., Wang, Z., Liu, Y., Cheng, M.-M., Lu, S.-P.: Pyramid constrained self-attention network for fast video salient object detection. In: AAAI (2020)
25. Guo, F., Wang, W., Shen, Z., Shen, J., Shao, L., Tao, D.: Motion-aware rapid video saliency detection. IEEE Trans. Circuits Syst. Video Technol. **30**(12), 4887–4898 (2020)

26. Lu, H., Yang, R., Deng, Z., Zhang, Y., Gao, G., Lan, R.: Chinese image captioning via fuzzy attention-based DenseNet-BiLSTM. ACM Trans. Multimed. Comput. Commun. Appl. **17**(1s), 1–18 (2021)

27. Lu, H., Zhang, Y., Li, Y., Jiang, C., Abbas, H.: User-oriented virtual mobile network resource management for vehicle communications. IEEE Trans. Intell. Transp. Syst. (2020). https://doi.org/10.1109/TITS.2020.2991766

28. Lu, H., Qin, M., Zhang, F., et al.: RSCNN: a CNN-based method to enhance low-light remote-sensing images. Remote Sens. **13**(1), 62 (2020)

29. Lu, H., Zhang, M., Xu, X.: Deep fuzzy hashing network for efficient image retrieval. IEEE Trans. Fuzzy Syst. (2020). https://doi.org/10.1109/TFUZZ.2020.2984991

30. Li, Y., Yang, S., Zheng, Y., Lu, H.: Improved Point-Voxel Region Convolutional Neural Network: 3D Object Detectors for Autonomous Driving. IEEE Trans. Intell. Trans. Syst. **23**(7), 9311–9317 (2022)

Research on Matching Mechanism and Route Planning of Intercity Carpool

Qunpeng Hu[1], Chao Li[2], Junwu Zhu[1(✉)], and Yu Xia[1]

[1] College of Information Engineering (College of Artificial Intelligence), Yangzhou University, Yangzhou, Jiangsu 225009, China
jwzhu@yzu.edu.cn
[2] China State Shipbuilding Corporation Limited, No.723 Research Institute, Yangzhou, Jiangsu 225127, China

Abstract. Under the influence of COVID-19, intercity ride-sharing has become more and more popular due to its relatively little contact and low price and has gradually become one of the important ways of intercity transportation. The ride-sharing platform provides functions of information interaction among passengers and drivers, allocating the transportation tasks and recommending the optimal route planning. Existing ride-sharing platforms fail to take user's personalized needs into account when assigning tasks, and users have low satisfaction with the planned routes. This paper designs an allocation algorithm (Allocation Algorithm 4 Inter-city Carpool) for intercity carpool and proposes a pricing function related to the detour distance and user's satisfaction, so as to ensure the optimal benefits for ride-sharing platforms and drivers, as well as the optimal passenger satisfaction. The AA4IC algorithm is proved to be incentive compatible and budget balanced theoretically, and the effectiveness of allocation scheme generation and path planning is verified by experiments. When the algorithm is iterated 1000 times, the time is less than 200 s, and the task assignment under the optimal user satisfaction can be achieved.

Keywords: Intercity carpool · Passenger satisfaction · Allocation mechanism · Path planning

1 Overview

1.1 Introduction

With the spread of COVID-19, the old intercity transport network is increasingly unsafe. Previously common modes of transportation, such as trains and buses, are highly intensive and have a high possibility of contact, which increases the possibility of infection with COVID-19. However, the cost of online car-sharing is high, which is difficult for ordinary people to afford, so online car-sharing becomes the optimal choice. However, the current online ride-hailing platform is still not very mature. As an intermediary for passengers and drivers, the online ride-hailing company's main function is to match and plan routes. But the existing ride-sharing companies can't perform these functions well.

© The Author(s), under exclusive license to Springer Nature Singapore Pte Ltd. 2022
S. Yang and H. Lu (Eds.): ISAIR 2022, CCIS 1701, pp. 21–39, 2022.
https://doi.org/10.1007/978-981-19-7943-9_3

Unreasonable matching leads to the waste of ride-sharing resources and the decrease of passenger satisfaction. Therefore, it is of great research value to further explore the distribution mechanism of online ride-sharing in different periods, on the one hand can improve the utilization of network about carpooling, and improve the net about carpooling company total income, on the other hand, can improve the passenger travel experience.

With the continuous expansion of the online ride-hailing market and the legalization of online ride-hailing platforms, the number of registered drivers and passengers on online ride-hailing platforms has increased sharply, and the problem of road congestion has gradually emerged. In order to solve the problems of high cost of ride-hailing, waste of resources and vehicle congestion, online ride-hailing arises. On the other hand, with the continuous urbanization, more and more working people choose to place their homes far away from the central urban area. Therefore, intercity network about carpooling matching mechanism is particularly important, however, at present, the mechanism of online ride-sharing platform is still not perfect, led to the advantage of network about carpooling can not well show, more detour, low passenger satisfaction problems emerging, therefore, it is of great importance to design a matching mechanism for ride-sharing.

1.2 Related Work

The matching mechanism of carpooling will affect the benefits of online ride-hailing platforms and the riding experience of passengers [25–29]. Document [1] demonstrates the feasibility of online ride-sharing. Considering the remarkable features of online ride-sharing in the document [2], we explore the formation mechanism of passengers' ride-sharing willingness from three different aspects of system, service and information. Document [3] analyzes the implementation of domestic net-contracting policies. Document [4] studied the price regulation strategy under the coexistence of online ride-hailing and online ride-sharing. Document [5] analyzed the existence value and development dilemma of ride-sharing patterns. Document [6] investigated the impact of socioeconomic attributes and pricing factors on user selection behavior. Document [7] studied the mechanism analysis of online carpooling behavior and its impact assessment. Document [8] uses three-party evolutionary game theory to describe the interaction mechanism between government regulators, online car platform safety regulators, and car-sharing owners during the operation of Internet car-hailing in China. Document [9] uses consumer behavior and bilateral market research theory to investigate the factors that influence pricing on online car platforms. Document [10] uses dynamic game theory and bilateral market theory to analyze pricing and cooperative revenue sharing problems between platforms and drivers. Document [11] analyzes the demand characteristics and service level influencing factors of intercity online ride-sharing, and understands the space-time characteristics of individual travel characteristics of intercity online ride-hailing. Through hybrid genetic algorithm and simulated annealing algorithm provides a minimum total mileage and minimum passenger variance optimization model, but minimum passenger variance does not guarantee high passenger total satisfaction, document [12] considered the waiting time of the net car. Document [13] designed a network car matching mechanism, but can not well assign passengers to each vehicle. In document [14], a coding and decoding rule is designed to realize the vehicle distribution and path planning problems, and the sequential matching relation of passenger vehicles and the route of vehicles can be given in a relatively short time. Document [15] builds a minimum travel cost model during peak hours, dynamically adjusts the route, and obtains the optimal route in real time. The static and dynamic optimal pricing and its sharing coefficient of online ride-hailing platforms is solved in document [16], which also reveals the impact of the average ride time and drivers and passengers' choice of online ride-hailing behavior on the platform pricing strategy. Document [17] uses improved particle swarm optimization algorithm to optimize the path. Document [18] uses game theory to set the optimal pricing and promotion strategy, which is inspiring for this paper. Document [19] considers the autonomous bargaining power of the passenger side and use a demand and supply function to describe the state of the passenger and the online taxi. In Document [20], an intermediary pricing model for transportation service markets is developed to assess the impact of spatial differentiation and network externalizations on the pricing mechanism of online taxi platforms. In Document [21], a genetic algorithm for mobile robot path planning is designed. Document [22] proposes dynamically adjustable route planning algorithms to avoid congestion through deep learning. A robot navigation test bed was designed and implemented in the Document [23] using a Markov decision process. Document [24] designed a platform pricing strategy based on maximizing the social welfare of the online taxi platform, drivers and passengers.

1.3 Study Content

This paper investigates the problem of detour distance and passenger satisfaction in online carpooling, and designs a matching mechanism for intercity online carpooling that increases passenger satisfaction while increasing the revenue of the online carpooling company, resulting in a win-win situation for the driver to stop detouring, the passenger to feel satisfied and the company to increase revenue.

1.4 Thesis Organization

The thesis is divided into six chapters, The main research content of each chapter is shown below:

Section 1: Overview. This chapter first introduces the research background and research significance of the online carpool matching and pricing mechanism. It then describes the current state of research and establishes the research content and research objectives of this paper.

Section 2: Problem definition and model. Formalizing the problem and a model is constructed to draw conclusions through mathematical derivation.

Section 3: Algorithm design. By analyzing the results of the model derivation, an algorithm is designed that can improve passenger satisfaction and the revenue of online carpooling.

Section 4: Theorem proof. Theoretical proofs are given for individual rationality, incentive compatibility and other aspects respectively to prove the rationality and effectiveness of the algorithm.

Section 5: Experiments. The effectiveness of the algorithm is verified by the simulation experiments, and ultimately constructing passenger satisfaction and the length of time consumed to arrive at a better number of cycles.

Section 6: Conclusion. This chapter summarizes and analyses the main research work and results, discusses some limitations of this paper, and provides an outlook on future research directions and work.

2 Problem Definition and Model

This section introduces a matching algorithm for carpooling that maximizes the total satisfaction of all passengers while making the carpooling company more profitable. Suppose there are n passengers who need to travel from several starting points in a city $((x_1, y_1), (x_2, y_2) \cdots (x_n, y_n))$ to several ending points in another city $((p_1, q_1), (p_2, q_2) \cdots (p_n, q_n))$. . The straight-line distance (effective transport distance) for each person d_i is easily obtained as $\sqrt{(x_i - p_i)^2 + (y_i - q_i)^2}$. The detour distance for each person is set as. $(l_1, l_2 \cdots l_n)$. Every four people ride in a ride-share, and we suppose that all the cars are filled with four people, that is

$$n\%4 = 0(0 \leq i \leq n) \tag{1}$$

Customer i's satisfaction equals to $\dfrac{l_i}{\sqrt{(x_i-p_i)^2+(y_i-q_i)^2}}$, and the total customer satisfaction is $\sum_{i=1}^{n} \dfrac{l_i}{\sqrt{(x_i-p_i)^2+(y_i-q_i)^2}}$.

The subsidy amount is

$$e_i = k * \frac{l_i}{\sqrt{(x_i - p_i)^2 + (y_i - q_i)^2}} + m \tag{2}$$

(where k, m are constants, determined by the carpooling platform based on actual conditions)

Assuming that carpooling drives at a uniform speed, there is the maximum charge as $\overline{f}$, for the customer i

$$\overline{f_i} = a * \sqrt{(x_i - p_i)^2 + (y_i - q_i)^2} \tag{3}$$

(where a is a constant, determined by the ride-sharing platform based on the reality)

Combined (2) and (3): The final cost for the customer i is f_i:

$$f_i = a * \sqrt{(x_i - p_i)^2 + (y_i - q_i)^2}$$
$$-k * \frac{l_i}{\sqrt{(x_i - p_i)^2 + (y_i - q_i)^2}} - m \tag{4}$$

Set the total revenue of the platform as r. Set advertising revenue as t. Income per driver is $0.8 * \overline{f_i}$. The total income of all drivers is $0.8 * \sum_{i=1}^{n} \overline{f_i}$. The final total profit of the platform is:

$$r = t + \sum_{i=1}^{n} f_i - 0.8 * \sum_{i=1}^{n} \overline{f_i} \tag{5}$$

Simplifying the formula 5:

$$r = t + 0.2 * \sum_{i=1}^{n} \overline{f_i} - \sum_{i=1}^{n} e_i \tag{6}$$

where:

$$e_i = k * \frac{l_i}{\sqrt{(x_i - p_i)^2 + (y_i - q_i)^2}} + m$$
$$\overline{f_i} = a * \sqrt{(x_i - p_i)^2 + (y_i - q_i)^2}$$

Because $\overline{f_i}$ is only related to coefficient a and distance, it is a fixed value. According to formula (6), the lower the $\sum_{i=1}^{n} e_i$, the higher the total gain. And because of the formula $e_i = k * \frac{l_i}{\sqrt{(x_i-p_i)^2+(y_i-q_i)^2}} + m$, it's easy to know the lower the $\sum_{i=1}^{n} \frac{l_i}{\sqrt{(x_i-p_i)^2+(y_i-q_i)^2}}$, the higher the total gain. And $\sum_{i=1}^{n} \frac{l_i}{\sqrt{(x_i-p_i)^2+(y_i-q_i)^2}}$ equals to overall satisfaction, so we can get the conclusion that when $\sum_{i=1}^{n} \frac{l_i}{\sqrt{(x_i-p_i)^2+(y_i-q_i)^2}}$'s minimum is taken, the overall satisfaction is the highest and the company has the highest earnings.

3 Algorithm Design

Based on the above formulas, we know that when the total passenger satisfaction are the highest, the path of each vehicle must also result in the highest passenger satisfaction. Based on the greedy algorithm, we first designed the optimal path for each car.

Algorithm 1 Shortest path value and best path

Input: Starting x_i;Destination y_i; $i \in [1,4]$

Output: Shortest path value for every four people

1. **for** i in range [1,4] **do**

2.   Calculate the linear distance from the beginning to the end;

3. **end**

4. $v \leftarrow 0, \text{minsize} \leftarrow 0$;

5. $c \leftarrow$ itertools.permulations$(x), d \leftarrow$ itertools.permulations(y);

6. **for** k in itertools.products(c,d) **do**

7.   Compute each of the starting indices a_m;

8.   Compute the subscripts of each endpoint b_m;

9.   **for** m in range [0,3] **do**

10.   **for** t in range $\left[a_m, b_m \right]$ **do**

11.   Calculate the distance from the start to the end of the detour;

12.   Calculate passenger satisfaction;

13.   **end**

14.   **end**

15. **end**

16. **while** $v < \text{minsize}$ **do**

17.   minsize=v ;

18.   Set the path to the shortest path;

19. **end**

The input to this algorithm is the starting and destination points of the 4 passengers, firstly by calculating the straight line path that each passenger needs to pass through, then by calculating the Cartesian product of the start and end point tuples to enumerate the optimal path for the passengers, the total satisfaction of the passengers calculated $\sum_{i=1}^{n} \frac{l_i}{\sqrt{(x_i-p_i)^2+(y_i-q_i)^2}}$, by continuously comparing the total satisfaction of each case with the previous optimal satisfaction, the final optimal path for the passengers and the optimal satisfaction is obtained.

In Algorithm 2, we devise a sampling algorithm that can only find sub-optimal solutions due to the high time complexity of the algorithm, so we need the sampling algorithm to make the results as accurate as possible without consuming too much time.

Algorithm 2 Sample

Input: Starting x_i ;Destination y_i ;total passengers number:n

Output: A randomly sorted list:c

1. $p \leftarrow TRUE$;

2. **while** $p = TRUE$ **do**

3.   b=random.sample(a,n) ;

4.   c.append(b);

5.   Removes selected elements from a;

6.   **if** there are elements in a **then**

7. $p \leftarrow TRUE$;

8.   **else**

9. $p \leftarrow FALSE$;

10.   **end**

11. **end**

What we input is the number of people in each group and the list of elements, and we can achieve the purpose of random sampling by constantly randomly extracting a fixed number of elements from the group until the elements are empty, so as to obtain a randomly sorted list.

In Algorithm 3, we obtain the suboptimal solution of the allocation algorithm by random sampling, and achieve the effect of obtaining the suboptimal solution in a certain time through the combination of Algorithm 1 and Algorithm 2.

Algorithm 3 Allocation Algorithm 4 Inter-city Carpool

Input: Starting x_i ;Destination y_i ;total passengers number:n

Output: Allocation plan and path

1. $r = list(range(0,n))$;

2. $\min \leftarrow 0, sum \leftarrow 0$;

3. **for** m in range $\left[1,t\right]$ (t is a preset value) **do**

4.   execute allocation algorithm shown in algorithm 2;

5.   execute allocation algorithm shown in algorithm 1;

6.   **while** sum of user satisfaction<minsize **do**

7. $\min \leftarrow$ sum of user satisfaction ;

8.   **end**

9. **end**

We can get n different grouping methods through n times random sampling, and then through the allocation method for each group can get the optimal path of each group and record, until there is a better allocation method to make passenger satisfaction higher, and replace the change scheme, in a certain number of times to get the best total satisfaction and path planning in these times.

4   Theorem Proof

Settings: There is a mechanism designer and an actor. They have to select an option a from some set A of the mutually exclusive option. If option a is selected and the actor pays the monetary transfer payment t, the utility of the actor is $u(a, \theta) - t$, θ is the type of the actor. The setting here includes the following scenario: A is a set of non-random options, and u is an expected utility function. Θ is the set of possible actor types, and is an abstract non-empty collection.

Definition 4.1: The direct mechanism (q, t) contains a mapping $q : \Theta \rightarrow A$ from each type of the actor to one option and a mapping $t : \Theta \rightarrow R$ from each type of the actor to the monetary transfer payment (positive t) or the monetary transfer payment (negative t), which we call q the "decision rule".

Definition 4.2: Incentive compatibility
If for all, we have all θ and $\theta' \in \Theta$

$$u(q(\theta), \theta) - t(\theta) \geq u(q(\theta'), \theta) - t(\theta')$$

A direct mechanism is "incentive-compatible".

Theorem 4.1: The carpool matching algorithm satisfies incentive compatibility

Proof: If the optimal algorithm of matching mechanism is l_i and the driver selected path distance is $l_i' > l_i$, it's easy to get:

$$\frac{l_i}{\sqrt{(x_i - p_i)^2 + (y_i - q_i)^2}} > \frac{l_i'}{\sqrt{(x_i - p_i)^2 + (y_i - q_i)^2}}$$

Since the total income is $t + 0.2 * \sum_{i=1}^{n} \overline{f_i} - \sum_{i=1}^{n} e_i$.

among:

$$e_i = k * \frac{l_i}{\sqrt{(x_i - p_i)^2 + (y_i - q_i)^2}} + m$$

$$\overline{f_i} = a * \sqrt{(x_i - p_i)^2 + (y_i - q_i)^2}$$

Then we know that since the driver chooses a path distance of l_i, the total revenue will increase and the total passenger satisfaction will increase, so we know that the driver will use the optimal path derived from the optimal algorithm of the matching mechanism.

Definition 4.3: Budget feasible

If, for all of those, there is $\theta \in \Theta$

$$\sum_{i=1}^{N} t_i(\theta) \geq 0$$

A direct mechanism is budget feasible.

Theorem 4.2: The online carpool matching algorithm is budget feasible

Proof: Since the platform takes a portion of the revenue, when a task worth f_i, is added to the grouping, the platform will not pay more than f_i for the driver in the grouping that matches the order, and because of the advertising fee revenue, the total expenses of the platform are $0.8 * \sum_{i=1}^{n} \overline{f_i}$ and the total revenue is $t + \sum_{i=1}^{n} f_i$, for which the following equations are available for expenses and revenue.

$$t + \sum_{i=1}^{n} f_i > \sum_{i=1}^{n} \overline{f_i}$$

Definition 4.4: Individual rationality

Let $a \in A$. If for all of the ones, $\theta \in \Theta$

$$u(q(\theta), \theta) - t(\theta) \geq u(a, \theta)$$

A direct mechanism is "individual rational".

Theorem 4.3: Online carpool matching algorithms are individually rational for both users and platforms

Proof: When the driver i matches the order j, the platform should pay the driver i more than the non-ride-sharing revenue and less than the sum of all passengers paying, that is, the total ride-sharing revenue. In the process of the algorithm, the passenger ride-sharing detour will reduce the charge, that is, the passenger carpooling expenditure will be less than the direct taxi expenditure, and the distribution scheme that pulls down the total passenger satisfaction arbitrarily will be replaced by the distribution scheme with a higher passenger total satisfaction. Therefore, there are all for any passenger i, $f_i > f_i'$.

Theorem 4.4: The total satisfaction is only the highest when the total satisfaction of passengers is the highest

Proof: Supposing that except for the car n, the total satisfaction of all cars is st, the highest satisfaction of the car n is st_n, and supposing that car n has the highest total satisfaction st_n' of the passengers, i. e:

$$st + st_n' > st + st_n$$

But since $st_n \geq st_n'$, we can easily obtain the highest overall satisfaction only and only when $st_n = st_n'$. The highest overall satisfaction can only be achieved when the total satisfaction of passengers on each carpool is the highest.

5   Experiments

This paper gives an example and conducts the simulation experiment with this example. Suppose 20 passengers need to travel from Yangzhou to Nanjing (with different starting and ending points) in five online carpooling vehicles. It is necessary to find an allocation such that the maximum user satisfaction can be minimized, so that the online carpooling platform has the highest revenue.

The experimental environment is:

Hardware: Lenovo y7000p, CPU: i7-10750H
Software: Pycharm.1.2 (Table 1)

The above starting and destination points correspond one to one, each passenger needs to start from a location in Yangzhou to a location in Nanjing, and we design an algorithm to enable every four passengers to ride an online taxi, making the highest total user satisfaction and the highest income of online ride-hailing companies.

After the code running, we can get the above experimental results, and through the analysis of the experimental results, we can get the following grouping results and paths.

By Fig. 1 and Fig. 2 we can get, and the paths are:

Route 1: He Yuan-> Zhu Ziqing's former residence-> The South Gate of Yangzhou University Slender West Lake Campus-> Yangzhou Hanjiang District Sansheng International Square-> Jiangsu Garden Expo Park-> Nanjing Institute of Physical Education-> The Presidential Palace-> Nanjing Yuhuatai Scenic Area

Table 1. Experimental data

Origin	The starting point coordinate	Terminal point	End point coordinates
The north gate of the Lotus Pond Campus of Yangzhou University	(119.423518,32.385394)	Nanjing University of Science & Technology	(118.855395,32.029061)
South gate of the Slender West Lake Campus of Yangzhou University	(119.424816,32.397457)	Nanjing Institute of Physical Education	(118.866682,32.044755)
East Gate of Yangzijin Campus, Yangzhou University	(119.405186,32.344317)	Xianlin Campus of Nanjing University of Posts and Telecommunications	(118.930841,32.113626)
North gate of Yangzhou University Road South Campus	(119.424445,32.376919)	Xianlin Campus of Nanjing University	(118.958109,32.119541)
Jiangsu North Jiangsu People's Hospital South 1	(119.431559,32.383945)	Jiulong University Campus of Southeast University	(118.820534,31.886956)
Yangzhou Hospital of Traditional Chinese Medicine	(119.419043,32.393011)	Nanjing Xuanwu Senior High School	(118.81387,32.056239)
Jiangsu Armed Police Corps Hospital	(119.461747,32.386705)	Silver city primary school	(118.732996,32.053013)
Yangzhou Museum	(119.371984,32.391699)	Jinling library	(118.717723,32.012447)

(*continued*)

Table 1. (*continued*)

Origin	The starting point coordinate	Terminal point	End point coordinates
Yangzhou railway station	(119.350827,32.389887)	Nanjing station	(118.797884,32.087039)
Yangzhou east station	(119.528684,32.404599)	Nanjing South Railway Station	(118.797636,31.968753)
Yangzhou Bus and Passenger Transport East Railway Station	(119.506024,32.386625)	Nanjing Lukou International Airport	(118.871253,31.731437)
Western Yangzhou traffic and passenger transport hub	(119.349108,32.38737)	Confucius Temple	(118.788941,32.020797)
Yangzhou municipal government	(119.412794,32.394328)	Nanjing Museum	(118.825269,32.040916)
The Grand Canal Museum of China	(119.428335,32.364615)	Zhongshan Mausoleum Scenic Spot	(118.848379,32.070414)
He yuan	(119.448591,32.385528)	office of the president	(118.797395,32.044481)
Zhu Ziqing's former residence	(119.44947,32.393682)	Nanjing Yuhuatai Scenic Area	(118.781774,31.998053)
Daming Temple	(119.412981,32.420044)	Nanjing Hospital of Traditional Chinese Medicine	(118.80791,31.995505)
Shi Kefa Memorial Hall	(119.440247,32.401725)	Nanjing People's Hospital	(118.766496,32.049166)
Yangzhou Hanjiang District Wanda Square	(119.399114,32.368887)	Jiangsu provincial government	(118.76375,32.061577)

(*continued*)

Table 1. (*continued*)

Origin	The starting point coordinate	Terminal point	End point coordinates
Yangzhou Hanjiang District Sansheng International Square	(119.397674,32.38106)	Jiangsu Garden Expo Park	(119.00974,32.076225)

8.7662899833005177
((119.448591, 32.385528), (119.44947, 32.393682), (119.424816, 32.397457), (119.397674, 32.38106), (119.00974, 32.076225), (118.866682, 32.044755), (118.797395, 32.044481), (118.781774, 31.998053))
((119.528684, 32.484599), (119.419043, 32.393811), (119.412794, 32.394328), (119.349108, 32.38737), (118.825269, 32.049916), (118.81387, 32.056239), (118.788941, 32.028797), (118.797636, 31.968753))
((119.596024, 32.386625), (119.431559, 32.383945), (119.423518, 32.385394), (119.405186, 32.344317), (118.938841, 32.113626), (118.855395, 32.829061), (118.820534, 31.886956), (118.871253, 31.731437))
((119.461747, 32.386795), (119.399114, 32.368887), (119.371984, 32.391699), (119.350827, 32.389887), (118.797884, 32.087039), (118.76375, 32.061577), (118.732996, 32.053013), (118.717723, 32.012447))
((119.412981, 32.420044), (119.448247, 32.401725), (119.424445, 32.376919), (119.428335, 32.364615), (118.958109, 32.119541), (118.848379, 32.078414), (118.80791, 31.995505), (118.766496, 32.049166))

Fig. 1. Experimental conclusion

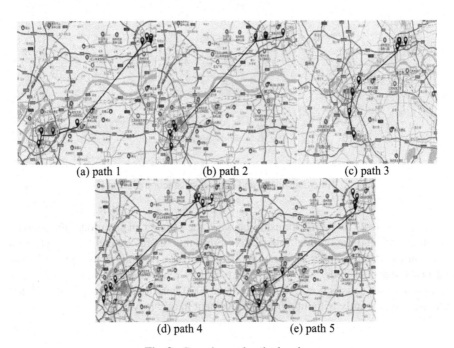

(a) path 1   (b) path 2   (c) path 3

(d) path 4   (e) path 5

Fig. 2. Grouping and path planning

Route 2: Yangzhou East Railway Station-> Yangzhou Hospital of Traditional Chinese Medicine-> Yangzhou Municipal Government-> Western Yangzhou Transportation and Passenger Transportation Hub-> Nanjing Museum-> Nanjing Xuanwu Senior High School-> Confucius Temple-> Nanjing South Railway Station
Route 3: Yangzhou Bus Passenger East Station-> South 1 of Jiangsu Subei People's Hospital-> North Gate of Yangzhou University Lianchi Campus-> East Gate of Yangzhou University Yangzijin Campus-> Nanjing University of Posts and Telecommunications Xianlin Campus-> Nanjing University of Technology-> Jiulong Lake Campus of Southeast University-> Nanjing Lukou International Airport
Route 4: Jiangsu Armed Police Corps Hospital-> Yangzhou Hanjiang District Wanda Plaza-> Yangzhou Museum-> Yangzhou Railway Station-> Nanjing Railway Station-> Jiangsu Provincial Government-> Yincheng Primary School-> Jinling Library
Route 5: Daming Temple-> Shikefa Memorial Hall-> The North Gate of Yangzhou University Road South Campus-> China Grand Canal Museum-> Nanjing University Xianlin Campus-> Sun Yat-sen Mausoleum Scenic Area-> Nanjing Hospital of Traditional Chinese Medicine-> Nanjing People's Hospital

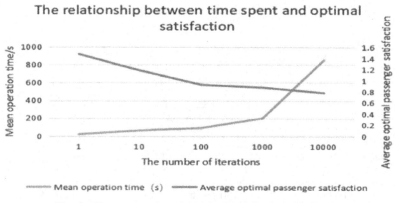

Fig. 3. Time-consuming and optimal satisfaction plots in Fig

Figure 3 shows us the relationship between the number of iterations, the average operation time and the optimal satisfaction. From this figure, we can know that when the accuracy of the number of iterations is about 1000, the time consumption is less and takes less than 200s, which can approximately reach the task assignment under the optimal user satisfaction. After more than 1000 iterations, the time consumption increased significantly without much improvement in accuracy.

6   Conclusion

In this paper, a matching algorithm is designed for intercity online ride-sharing. By changing the previous step pricing, online ride-sharing price is associated with the detour distance, so that online ride-sharing companies and drivers can get the highest benefits while ensuring the highest passenger satisfaction. A route planning algorithm was designed to significantly reduce the total number of detour routes for each passenger. Through experimental and theoretical analysis, the matching algorithm proposed in this paper can significantly improve the total satisfaction of passengers and the total revenue of online ride-sharing companies. This paper provides a novel method for online carpooling companies. However, due to the limitation of algorithm complexity and time, the proposed algorithm can only find the suboptimal solution, and cannot guarantee the optimal solution. In addition, in terms of improvement, if the API of the map is combined with the algorithm, it will make the algorithm more practical, as often the presence or absence of traffic jams on the map will also affect the optimized results of the algorithm.

Funding. This work was supported by National Natural Science Foundation of China (61872313); Jiangsu Province, China Education Informatization Research Key Project (20180012); Science and Technology Project of Emergency Management Department of Jiangsu Province, China (YJGL-YF-2021–3, YJGL-YF-2020–17); China Yangzhou Science and Technology Plan Project (YZ2019133, YZ2020174).

Vitae

Qunpeng Hu (2000-), undergraduate student of innovation class, has major research interests in algorithmic game theory and mechanism design; Chao Li (1982-), graduate student, has major research interests in electronic countermeasures and algorithmic game theory. Junwu Zhu (Corresponding author) (1972-), professor, PhD supervisor, PhD, CCF advanced member, has major research interests in knowledge engineering and algorithmic game theory in artificial intelligence; Yu Xia (1980-), Ph.D., has major research interests in game theory and e-commerce modeling.

Annex 1 Source Code (<u>code available for review only</u>)

```python
import itertools
import math
import os
import random
import datetime
os.environ["CUDA_VISIBLE_DEVICES"] = "0"

starting = [(119.423518, 32.385394),
(119.424816, 32.397457), (119.405186,
32.344317), (119.424445, 32.376919),
(119.431559, 32.383945), (119.419043,
32.393011), (119.461747, 32.386705),
(119.371984, 32.391699),
(119.350827, 32.389887), (119.528684,
32.404599), (119.506024, 32.386625),
(119.349108, 32.38737),
(119.412794, 32.394328), (119.428335,
32.364615), (119.448591, 32.385528),
(119.44947, 32.393682),
(119.412981, 32.420044), (119.440247,
32.401725), (119.399114, 32.368887),
(119.397674, 32.38106)]
destination = [(118.855395, 32.029061),
(118.866682, 32.044755), (118.930841,
32.113626), (118.958109, 32.119541),
(118.820534, 31.886956), (118.81387,
32.056239), (118.732996, 32.053013),
(118.717723, 32.012447),
(118.797884, 32.087039), (118.797636,
31.968753), (118.871253, 31.731437),
(118.788941, 32.020797),
(118.825269, 32.040916), (118.848379,
32.070414), (118.797395, 32.044481),
(118.781774, 31.998053),
(118.80791, 31.995505), (118.766496,
32.049166), (118.76375, 32.061577),
(119.00974, 32.076225)]

def pathvalue(x, y):
    s = 0
    m = 0
    n = 0
    p = 0
    q = 0
    w = 0
    e = 0
    r = 0

minsize = 10000
l = {}
for i in range(0, 4):
    l[i] = math.acos(math.sin(x[i][0]) *
math.sin(y[i][0]) + (math.cos(x[i][0]) *
math.cos(y[i][0])) * math.cos(
x[i][1] - y[i][1])) * 6371
c = itertools.permutations(x)
d = itertools.permutations(y)
for k in itertools.product(c, d):
    c = k[0] + k[1]
    a1 = c.index(x[0])
    b1 = c.index(y[0])
    a2 = c.index(x[1])
    b2 = c.index(y[1])
    a3 = c.index(x[2])
    b3 = c.index(y[2])
    a4 = c.index(x[3])
    b4 = c.index(y[3])
    for i in range(a1, b1):
        s += math.acos(
math.sin(c[i][0]) * math.sin(c[i + 1][0]) +
(math.cos(c[i][0]) * math.cos(c[i + 1][0]))
* math.cos(
c[i][1] - c[i + 1][1])) * 6371
    q = (s - l[0]) / l[0]
    for i in range(a2, b2):
        m += math.acos(
math.sin(c[i][0]) * math.sin(c[i + 1][0]) +
(math.cos(c[i][0]) * math.cos(c[i + 1][0]))
* math.cos(
c[i][1] - c[i + 1][1])) * 6371
    w = (m - l[1]) / l[1]
    for i in range(a3, b3):
        n += math.acos(
math.sin(c[i][0]) * math.sin(c[i + 1][0]) +
(math.cos(c[i][0]) * math.cos(c[i + 1][0]))
* math.cos(
c[i][1] - c[i + 1][1])) * 6371
    e = (n - l[2]) / l[2]
    for i in range(a4, b4):
        p += math.acos(
math.sin(c[i][0]) * math.sin(c[i + 1][0]) +
(math.cos(c[i][0]) * math.cos(c[i + 1][0]))
* math.cos(
c[i][1] - c[i + 1][1])) * 6371
    r = (p - l[3]) / l[3]
    v = e + r + q + w
```

```
if v < minsize:
minsize = v
s = 0
m = 0
n = 0
p = 0
return minsize


def minpath(x, y):
s1 = 0
m1 = 0
n1 = 0
p1 = 0
q1 = 0
w1 = 0
e1 = 0
r1 = 0
l1 = {}
for i in range(0, 4):
l1[i]  =  math.acos(math.sin(x[i][0])  *
math.sin(y[i][0])  +  (math.cos(x[i][0])  *
math.cos(y[i][0])) * math.cos(
x[i][1] - y[i][1])) * 6371
c = itertools.permutations(x)
d = itertools.permutations(y)
for k in itertools.product(c, d):
c1 = k[0] + k[1]
a1 = c1.index(x[0])
b1 = c1.index(y[0])
a2 = c1.index(x[1])
b2 = c1.index(y[1])
a3 = c1.index(x[2])
b3 = c1.index(y[2])
a4 = c1.index(x[3])
b4 = c1.index(y[3])
for i in range(a1, b1):
s1 += math.acos(
math.sin(c1[i][0]) * math.sin(c1[i + 1][0])
+ (math.cos(c1[i][0])  *  math.cos(c1[i +
1][0])) * math.cos(
c1[i][1] - c1[i + 1][1])) * 6371
q1 = (s1 - l1[0]) / l1[0]
for i in range(a2, b2):
m1 += math.acos(
math.sin(c1[i][0]) * math.sin(c1[i + 1][0])
+ (math.cos(c1[i][0])  *  math.cos(c1[i +
1][0])) * math.cos(
c1[i][1] - c1[i + 1][1])) * 6371

w1 = (m1 - l1[1]) / l1[1]
for i in range(a3, b3):
n1 += math.acos(
math.sin(c1[i][0]) * math.sin(c1[i + 1][0])
+ (math.cos(c1[i][0])  *  math.cos(c1[i +
1][0])) * math.cos(
c1[i][1] - c1[i + 1][1])) * 6371
e1 = (n1 - l1[2]) / l1[2]
for i in range(a4, b4):
p1 += math.acos(
math.sin(c1[i][0]) * math.sin(c1[i + 1][0])
+ (math.cos(c1[i][0])  *  math.cos(c1[i +
1][0])) * math.cos(
c1[i][1] - c1[i + 1][1])) * 6371
r1 = (p1 - l1[3]) / l1[3]
v1 = e1 + r1 + q1 + w1
while v1 == pathvalue(x, y):
return c1
s1 = 0
m1 = 0
n1 = 0
p1 = 0

def sample(a, n):
p = True
while p:
b = random.sample(a, n)
b.sort()
c.append(b)
a = list(set(a).difference(set(b)))
if len(a) > 0:
p = True
else:
p = False
start = datetime.datetime.now()
minpathall = ()
min1 = 1000000
for i in range(1,10001):
c = []
ran = list(range(0, 20))
n = 4
sample(ran, n)
x1 = []
x2 = []
x3 = []
x4 = []
x5 = []
y1 = []
y2 = []
```

```
y3 = []
y4 = []
y5 = []
for i in range(0, 4):
x1.append(starting[c[0][i]])
x2.append(starting[c[1][i]])
x3.append(starting[c[2][i]])
x4.append(starting[c[3][i]])
x5.append(starting[c[4][i]])
y1.append(destination[c[0][i]])
y2.append(destination[c[1][i]])
y3.append(destination[c[2][i]])
y4.append(destination[c[3][i]])
y5.append(destination[c[4][i]])
sum1 = pathvalue(x1, y1) + pathvalue(x2,
y2) + pathvalue(x3, y3) + pathvalue(x4,
y4) + pathvalue(x5, y5)
if sum1 < min1:
min1 = sum1
minpathall = minpath(x1, y1) + min-
path(x2, y2) + minpath(x3, y3) + min-
path(x4, y4) + minpath(x5, y5)
print(min1)
for i in range(0, 5):
print(minpathall[0 + 8 * i:8 + 8 * i])
end = datetime.datetime.now()
print ((end-start).seconds)
```

References

1. Peng, J., Lan, X.: Research on the feasibility of the promotion of carpool in Yi chang. Appl. Mech. Mater. **505–506**, 1179–1182 (2014)
2. Yu, W.: Research on the Formation Mechanism of Passengers' Willingness to Use Ride-Sharing Services. Hefei, University of Science and Technology of China (2021)
3. Meng, C., Li, T.: Analyzing the implementation of the policy of online car-hailing based on a structural equation model. In: 19th COTA International Conference of Transportation Professionals (2019)
4. Zhao, D.Z., Yang, J.: Price regulation strategy of online car-hailing service targeted at fairness. Control Decis. (2019)
5. Min, D.: Industry value, development dilemma and solutions of ride-sharing model. City. (10), 53–57 (2016)
6. Xing-Hua, L., Feiyu, F., Cheng, C., Wei, W., Peng-Cheng, T.: Selection preference analysis and modeling of ride-sharing service. J. Jilin Univ. (Engineering and Technology Edition). 1–7 (2021)
7. Xiaowei, C.: Analysis of Online Ride-Sharing System and Optimization of Platform Order Delivery. Zhejiang, Zhejiang University (2019)
8. Wang, W., Zhang, Y., Feng, L., et al. A system dynamics model for safety supervision of online car-hailing from an evolutionary game theory perspective. IEEE Access. **8**, 185045–185058 (2020)
9. Ying, X.: Research on pricing of online taxi platforms under competitive market structure. Value Eng. **39**(20), 168–170 (2020)
10. Yu, X.J.: On the Pricing Decision of Monopoly Online Car-Hailing Platform Considering Network Externality and Commission Rate (2021)
11. Shilong, W.: Research on End-Path Optimization of Intercity Ride-sharing Network. Chengdu, Southwest Jiaotong University (2019)
12. Daozhi, Z., Jie, Y., Zhibo, L.: A study on equilibrium pricing of online taxis and cabs considering waiting time. Syst. Eng. Theory Pract. **40**(5), 1229–1241 (2020). https://doi.org/10.12011/1000-6788-2018-2092-13
13. Yu, X.: Research on Matching Mechanism and Pricing Strategy Related to Ride-Hailing Capacity. Yangzhou, Yangzhou University (2021)
14. Ling-juan, C., Si-jia, K., Zu-peng, L.: Passenger-vehicle matching and route optimization of network carpooling. Comput. Modern. **0**(07), 6–11 (2021)

15. Yang, R., Yao, J., Lin, Q.: Research on optimization of car-hailing driving route based on short-term traffic speed. In: 2021 6th International Conference on Inventive Computation Technologies (ICICT) (2021)
16. Xiang, P., Tianyu, H., Junfang, S., Yong, Z.: Research on pricing model of ride-hailing platform based on social welfare maximization. Syst. Eng. Theory Pract. **41**(07), 1806–1818 (201)
17. Jianhu, F., Tingyu, Z., Shuo, F., Baojuan, Z.: Improved particle swarm optimization algorithm for robot path planning. Mach. Design Manuf. (09), 291–294+298 (2021)
18. Jin, L., Hao, G.S.: Research on pricing and promotion strategies of online retail supply chain considering socially responsible. Soft Sci. (2018)
19. Wang, J., Wang, H., Hu, X.W., et al.: Optimization of online taxi pricing with platform revenue and social welfare considering passenger bargaining during peak periods. Trans. Syst. Eng. Inform. **22**(2), 54–63 (2022). https://doi.org/10.16097/j.cnki.1009-6744.2022.02.006
20. Wu, T., Zhang, M., Tian, X., et al.: Spatial differentiation and network externality in pricing mechanism of online car hailing platform. Int. J. Prod. Econ. **219** (2020)
21. Xing, X., Xuyang, Y., Yun, Z., Chengxing, L., Xiang, W.: Global path planning for mobile Robots Based on Improved Genetic Algorithm. Comput. Integr. Manuf. Syst. 1–20 (2021)
22. Geng, Y., Liu, E., Wang, R., et al.: Deep reinforcement learning based dynamic route planning for minimizing travel time. In: 2021 IEEE International Conference on Communications Workshops (ICC Workshops). IEEE (2021)
23. Penmetcha, M., Min, B.C.: A deep reinforcement learning-based dynamic computa tional offloading method for cloud robotics. IEEE Access. PP(99), 1–1 (2021)
24. Hu, T., Zhang, Y., Cheng, M.: Pricing strategy of car-hailing platform with maximizing social welfare. In: 2019 6th International Conference on Frontiers of Industrial Engineering (ICFIE), pp. 33–39 (2019). https://doi.org/10.1109/ICFIE.2019.8907775
25. Lu, H., Liu, G., Li, Y., Kim, H., Serikawa, S.: The cognitive internet of vehicles for automatic driving. IEEE Net. **33**(3), 65–73 (2019)
26. Lu, H., et al.: CONet: a cognitive ocean network. IEEE Wirel. Commun. **26**(3), 90–96 (2019)
27. Lu, H., Zhang, Y., Li, Y., Jiang, C., Abbas, H.: User-oriented virtual mobile network resource management for vehicle communications. IEEE Trans. Intell. Transp. Syst. (2020). https://doi.org/10.1109/TITS.2020.2991766
28. Lu, H., Yu, T., Sun, Y.: DRRS-BC: decentralized routing registration system based on blockchain. IEEE/CAA J. Autom. Sin. 8(12), 1868–1876 (2021)
29. Lu, H., Wang, T., Xu, X., Wang, T.: Cognitive memory-guided AutoEncoder for effective intrusion detection in IoT. IEEE Trans. Ind. Inform. **18**(5), 3358–3366 (2022)

Image Undistortion and Stereo Rectification Based on Central Ray-Pixel Models

Zhao Zheng, Xiaohua Xie[✉], and Yang Yu

Sun Yat-sen University, Guangzhou, China
zhengzh28@mail2.sysu.edu.cn, xiexiaoh6@mail.sysu.edu.cn

Abstract. Recently ray-pixel imaging models which work on pixels and their related incoming rays have attracted much attention in the computer vision community. Having many more parameters than traditional models, ray-pixel models are capable of describing cameras more accurately. Despite this, ray-pixel models are still rarely used in practice due to the lack of mature modules for image undistortion and stereo rectification. Perceived that optical centers can be used as the bridge between pinhole and central ray-pixel models, we thus propose algorithms for image undistortion and stereo rectification based on central ray-pixel models. Besides, we propose sector grids in the B-spline interpolation procedure, which significantly reduces the calibration time. With a focus on accuracy, we show that ray-pixel models outperform traditional models in terms of image undistortion, stereo rectification and 3D reconstruction. Our calibration pipeline has been released at https://github.com/painterdrown/raxel.

Keywords: Camera calibration · Ray-pixel · Image undistortion · Stereo rectification

1 Introduction

Camera calibration is part of the infrastructure of computer vision. The nature of camera calibration is to compute specific parameters of some geometric imaging model, which describes how a beam of light in the world coordinate system passes through lenses and finally arrives at some pixel on camera sensors. It enables applications such as image undistortion [1–3], 3D reconstruction [4, 5], SLAM [6, 7], autonomous driving [8] and so on. In many scenarios, dual or multiple cameras are used to generate stereo visual information. Extrinsics of calibration describe the relative rotation and translation from one camera to another. These cameras should be well calibrated before being applied in various fields.

Zhang [9] proposed the most widely used calibration method in the camera industry. It adopts pinhole models, which perform linear perspective transformations on 3D objects to project a 2D image through a single optical center. Pinhole models only have around 20 parameters even though distortion coefficients are considered. They can handle lenses with slight distortion. However, for some cameras with severe image distortion, or having complex optics inside, such models should have poor performance because they are too simple to describe the whole imaging system. More specifically, they may calibrate central image regions well, but fail when it comes to border regions.

© The Author(s), under exclusive license to Springer Nature Singapore Pte Ltd. 2022
S. Yang and H. Lu (Eds.): ISAIR 2022, CCIS 1701, pp. 40–55, 2022.
https://doi.org/10.1007/978-981-19-7943-9_4

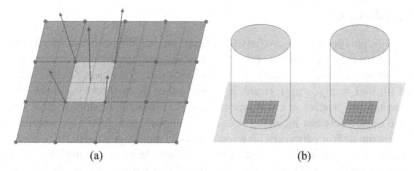

Fig. 1. A ray-pixel model (a) containing 8 × 6 pixels is divided into 4 × 3 cells. The original calibration method requires ray directions of each pixel, while using B-spline curves, we can just calibrate rays of cell corners (darker gray). A ray (orange) is interpolated using four corner rays (blue) from its cell. (b) is a dual-camera system which we mainly use in our experiments.

Ray-pixel models [10], also known as generic models, relate each pixel to its corresponding incoming ray outside cameras. Each ray consists of two 3D vectors, of which one represents the endpoint and the other one represents the direction. Ray-pixel models are more intuitive because they care neither how rays are redirected when passing lenses, nor how images are distorted. They have enough parameters to calibrate every region in the image. Some comparisons [11] showed that ray-pixel models outperform pinhole models for lenses with large distortion. However, methodologies about image undistortion and stereo rectification based on ray-pixel models are lacking, which hinders practical applications of ray-pixel models.

In order to break through the above dilemma, we provide theories and implementations for image undistortion and stereo rectification algorithms based on ray-pixel models. We also release an extended pipeline from calibration to application for multi-camera systems. Finally, we show the experimental results of our algorithms and how they defeat traditional models in terms of accuracy.

2   Related Work

2.1   Corner Detection

In camera calibration, both 3D object points and 2D image points are required during Bundle Adjustment [12]. We need an accurate detection method to extract corner coordinates in sub-pixel precision from original images. Bradski's toolbox [13] and OpenCV [14] both provide simple and useful methods, but they are likely to have poor performance on rather distorted images. Geiger *et al.* [15] and Schonbein *et al.* [16] developed a growing-based method, which is able to detect multiple patterns (normally chessboards) in a single image without prior knowledge about pattern sizes. To have more robustness against motion blur and defocus [17], Ha *et al.* [18] used triangular patterns to detect ridge lines, which can also provide more gradient information for corner refinement.

2.2 Pinhole Models

In the 1970s, photography researchers found that camera calibration was needed to get lines straight in their captured images [19]. They've germinated basic concepts of camera calibration and discovered that lens distortion varies with object distance. Zhang's method [9] took a huge step forward. It's quite a flexible method to calibrate in both experimental and productive environments. Based on pinhole models, fisheye models [20] used angles between incoming rays and the optical axis for image undistortion, which are mapped from distances between pixels and the image center. There're several fisheye mapping functions such as rectilinear mapping, stereographic mapping, equidistant mapping and so on. Geyer *et al.* [21] provided a unifying theory for all central catadioptric systems, enabling panoramic calibration. CNNs [22–24] attempted to apply the features of neural networks to imaging models, but there is still a lot of room for progress.

2.3 Ray-Pixel Models

Grossberg *et al.* [10] first proposed the concept of ray-pixel models. They argued that we should apply this kind of "blackbox" calibration to arbitrary camera systems.

Central Ray-Pixel Models. Central ray-pixel models [8, 25–27] are simplified versions which assume that all rays will intersect at a single optical center, making it easier to calibrate. This is also why optical centers can be regarded as the bridge between pinhole models and ray-pixel models (Sect. 3.3). While in non-central models, endpoints and directions of rays are arbitrary.

Unknown Camera Motion. The original ray-pixel calibration method requires prior motion information of the camera when capturing images, which means that some kind of sophisticated and expense instruments should be set up to carry cameras. Sturm *et al.* [28–30] proposed a unifying theory for central, non-central and axial cameras. During calibration, camera motions can be automatically calculated.

B-Spline Interpolation. Ray-pixel models are dense, where each pixel has to store a ray. For example, a 12MP camera has around 72 million parameters when using non-central models. Time and computation costs to refine such massive parameters are beyond tolerance. B-spline interpolation [8, 13] thus is necessary in practice, where an image will be divided into cells. As shown in Fig. 1(a), the four rays of corners in some cell define a cubic B-spline curve to interpolate every other ray in the cell. Schops *et al.* [32] have combined and implemented these new features together in their calibration pipeline.

2.4 Image Undistortion and Stereo Rectification

Image undistortion is important especially for wide-angle lenses. Although solutions for radial distortion, tangential distortion and thin prism distortion [2] are mature in OpenCV and many other implementations, they cannot meet increasing demands on high accuracy. Hartley *et al.* [3] managed to calibrate radial distortion and intrinsics simultaneously in a parameter-free manner. Tang *et al.* [33] used high-degree polynomial coefficients and claimed that they can reach a high precision of 0.01 pixels. However, none of them has satisfying performance on lenses with severe distortion. Besides, in recent years, deep learning methods have also been proposed to solve problems of image undistortion. Sunet [34] trained a symmetric convolutional neural network to reduce blur and distortion when the camera is moving fast.

We realized that optical centers could be the connection between central ray-pixel models and pinhole models. An optical center is the intersection of all rays in ray-pixel models and is used to project in pinhole models. We thus come up with a procedure that firstly unproject using pinhole and then project using ray-pixel to achieve image undistortion. Thanks to such a bridge, we can also achieve stereo rectification.

3 Algorithms and Pipeline

In Sect. 3.1 we propose theories of projection and unprojection for central ray-pixel models; In Sect. 3.2 we detail about how Bundle Adjustment refines ray-pixel models; In Sect. 3.3 and Sect. 3.4 we respectively describe image undistortion and stereo rectification algorithms for ray-pixel models, which are integrated into our pipeline in Sect. 3.5.

3.1 Projection and Unprojection

In computational photography, projection means to project an object point P or its direction d in 3D space into a 2D image point p, while unprojection means to obtain the incoming ray direction d from a pixel. Unprojection of a single camera just gets directions with unknown depth. In pinhole models, both projection and unprojection without distortion are linear transformations:

$$p = \mathbf{K}P$$

$$sd = \mathbf{K}^{-1}p$$

Here, $\mathbf{K}$ is the camera matrix consisting of the focal length and the principle point (the intersection of the optical axis and the image plane); s is an arbitrary scaling factor.

To achieve projection for ray-pixel models, we will need a non-linear iteration procedure. More specifically, once given an incoming ray direction d_0, we pick up the center of the image as the initialization. Surely any other pixel is an acceptable candidate. Then, Levenberg–Marquardt algorithm [35, 36] is applied to refine the objective position, taking the Euclidean distance between the current unprojected direction d and the input direction d_0 as the cost function. Finally, in general, when the cost function is minimized enough, or when the direction change from previous iteration is below some threshold (10^{-6}), the iteration should end.

$$\min_{x,y}(S(x, y) - d_0)$$

In the above cost function, $S(x, y)$ denotes the interpolated ray direction at pixel (x, y) using B-spline.

3.2 Bundle Adjustment

Given original images with extracted corners C and the physical sizes of the pattern α, we can feed them into Bundle Adjustment, where ray directions of pixels and camera poses (rotation and translation from the pattern to the camera per image) will be jointly refined. Our goal is to minimize the reprojection error, described as the following objective function:

$$\min_{\mathcal{D},\mathcal{M}} \sum_{i \in \mathcal{I}} \sum_{j \in \mathcal{C}} \Delta(\Psi(\mathcal{D}, \mathbf{M}_i, \mathbf{P}_j), \mathbf{p}_j)$$

Here, $\mathcal{D}$ denotes the set of cell directions to be calibrated. We don't have a corresponding ray for each pixel, instead we divide the whole image into cells and use B-spline interpolation as described in Sect. 2.3. $\mathcal{M}$ denotes the set of camera poses per image to be calibrated, in which $\mathbf{M}_i$ denotes the transformation from the pattern coordinate system to the camera coordinate system of the i-th image. $\mathbf{P}_j$ denotes the j-th generated corner location using α while $\mathbf{p}_j$ is the corresponding detected corner location. Ψ denotes the function that projects $\mathbf{P}_j$ into the image. Δ denotes the Euclidean distance between the projection result and $\mathbf{p}_j$. Similar to projection in Sect. 3.1, Bundle Adjustment also adopts Levenberg-Marquardt algorithm for non-linear iteration.

3.3 Image Undistortion

Image undistortion is done mainly via two steps: we firstly compute a pinhole model and then apply the unprojection - projection procedure.

Pinhole Model Computation. Intrinsics parameters of pinhole models are required for image undistortion here. We will compute a camera matrix $\mathbf{K}$ which should be as close to the real one $\widehat{\mathbf{K}}$ as possible. The closer to the real one, the FOV (field-of-view) will also be closer to the original FOV. If we already know the specifications of the camera: 1) the focal length of the lens; 2) the physical size of the pixel on the sensor, we can just easily create a camera matrix based on them. Otherwise we also find an effective way to calculate $\mathbf{K}$ using the corners C in Sect. 3.2 via:

a. **Homography Calculation:** We pick up m image combinations, of which each image contains n points, to compute m homography matrices $\mathbf{H}$ using maximum likelihood criterion. Levenberg-Marquardt algorithm is applied to optimize each homography $\mathbf{H}$. The initialization can be obtained by solving a linear system $\mathbf{LH} = 0$. Here, $\mathbf{L}$ is a normalized $2n \times 9$ matrix consisting of constant 1 and corner coordinates.
b. **Intrinsics Extraction:** Homography is a combination of intrinsics and extrinsics. Referring to Zhang's method [9], once $\mathbf{H}$ is obtained, we can construct a symmetric matrix $\mathbf{B}$. Without difficulty, the intrinsic parameters of each image combination can be extracted via:

$$c_y = (B_{12}B_{13} - B_{11}B_{23})/(B_{11}B_{22} - B_{12}^2)$$

$$\lambda = B_{33} - [B_{13}^2 + c_y(B_{12}B_{13} - B_{11}B_{23})]/B_{11}$$

$$f_x = \sqrt{\lambda/B_{11}}$$

$$f_y = \sqrt{\lambda B_{11}/(B_{11}B_{22} - B_{12}^2)}$$

$$c_x = \gamma c_y/f_y - B_{13}f_x^2/\lambda$$

iii. Averaging: We can simply get the wanted camera matrix by averaging the resulting camera matrices from the previous step: $\mathbf{K} = \frac{1}{m}\sum_{i=1}^m \mathbf{K}_i$

Unprojection - Projection Procedure. We achieve image undistortion in a reverse way. Starting from an image plane without distortion, and for each pixel on it, we find the location in the original image. In such a way we can make sure the undistorted image is blank-free. It includes three steps: Firstly, unproject a pixel $\boldsymbol{p}(p_x, p_y)$ to a direction $\boldsymbol{d}$ using pinhole models; Secondly, project the direction $\boldsymbol{d}$ to a sub-pixel $\boldsymbol{p}'$ in the original image using ray-pixel models; Thirdly, apply bilinear interpolation to get the color of $\boldsymbol{p}$ from $\boldsymbol{p}'$. The pseudocode is shown in Algorithm 1.

Algorithm 1. Unprojection – Projection Procedure.

Require: $\mathcal{J}, \mathbf{K}$
for $p \in \mathcal{P}$ **do**
  $\boldsymbol{d} \leftarrow ((p_x - c_x),,1)$ ▷ Unproject
  $\boldsymbol{p}' \leftarrow \Psi(\mathcal{D}, \mathbf{I}, \boldsymbol{d})$ ▷ Project
  $\Gamma(\boldsymbol{p}) \leftarrow \Pi(\mathcal{J}, \boldsymbol{p}')$
end for

Input $\mathcal{I}$ is the original image; Input $\mathbf{K}$ is the computed camera matrix of pinhole models in Sect. 3.3; $\mathcal{P}$ refers to the collection of all pixels in the image; The transformation between original and undistorted images is an identity matrix $\mathbf{I}$ because it has neither rotation nor translation; Ψ denotes the function that projects direction $\boldsymbol{d}$ into the image at pixel $\boldsymbol{p}'$; Π denotes the bilinear interpolation while $\Gamma(\boldsymbol{p})$ refers to the color of $\boldsymbol{p}$.

3.4 Stereo Rectification

Stereo rectification is a general demand for dual-camera or multi-camera systems, which aligns all the cameras in some unified camera coordinate system after undistorting every single camera. In this section, we take dual-camera systems as shown in Fig. 1(b) for example. The algorithm can be easily extended to multi-camera systems.

During Bundle Adjustment in Sect. 3.2, we optimize the camera poses $\mathcal{M}$ for all images. For dual-camera systems, we have 2 camera pose sets $\mathcal{M}_1$ and $\mathcal{M}_2$ of the left camera and the right camera. Each camera pose consists of a rotation matrix and a translation vector so we have $\mathbf{M}_1 = [\mathbf{R}_1 \mathbf{T}_1]$ and $\mathbf{M}_2 = [\mathbf{R}_2 \mathbf{T}_2]$. Note that the left camera and the right camera share the same pattern coordinate system when capturing an image. Thus:

$$\overleftarrow{\mathbf{R}} = \mathbf{R}_2 \mathbf{R}_1^{-1}$$

$$\overleftarrow{\mathbf{T}} = -\overleftarrow{\mathbf{R}} \mathbf{T}_1 + \mathbf{T}_2$$

$\overleftarrow{\mathbf{R}}$ and $\overleftarrow{\mathbf{T}}$ denotes the relative rotation and translation from the right camera coordinate system to the left. We half rotate both of them to obtain the largest common FOV. To this point, the orientations of these 2 coordinate systems settle down.

$$\mathbf{R}' = \overleftarrow{\mathbf{R}}^{-\frac{1}{2}}$$

$$\mathbf{T}' = \mathbf{R}' \overleftarrow{\mathbf{T}}$$

$\mathbf{R}'$ and $\mathbf{T}'$ are the intermediate results used to generate the final rotation $\mathbf{R}''$. Stereo rectification can be summarized by applying the following $\overline{\mathbf{R}_1}$ and $\overline{\mathbf{R}_2}$ to the original left and right camera coordinate systems respectively:

$$\overline{\mathbf{R}_1} = \mathbf{R}'' \mathbf{R}'$$

$$\overline{\mathbf{R}_2} = \mathbf{R}'' \mathbf{R}'^T$$

3.5   Calibration Pipeline

Although Schops's calibration pipeline [32] provides corner detection and camera calibration based on ray-pixel models, it's difficult for people to apply ray-pixel models in practice. There are two main reasons: 1) it still costs much time to complete the calibration procedure even when using B-spline interpolation, especially for non-central models. 2) the pipeline does not support image undistortion and stereo rectification, which are essential for wide-angle lenses and stereo cameras. We extend the pipeline in the following two ways.

Sector Grids. Original B-spline interpolation is based on rectangular grids, where the number of parameters would grow fast as we use high resolution images.

For example, using 15 pixels as the cell size, there are 128×72 rectangular cells for 1920×1080 images. In our pipeline, we use sector grids instead, as shown in Fig. 2(b). Firstly, we divide the image by 16 identical angles. Secondly, considering that distortion is not distributed evenly in images and central regions are much less distorted, we use dynamic sector widths - sector cells are sparse in central regions while they are dense in border regions. The number of sector cells only depends on the diagonal length of the image. As a result, we reduce the number of parameters (for 1920×1080 images, it's around 16×100 cells) and have most of them focus on border regions in the images.

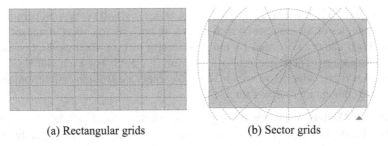

(a) Rectangular grids   (b) Sector grids

Fig. 2. Ray-pixel models using different grids for B-spline interpolation.

In Sect. 4.3 we show the performance of ray-pixel models using sector grids.

Image Undistortion and Stereo Rectification. Our pipeline implements the proposed image undistortion and stereo rectification algorithms. Using corner coordinates and calibrated camera parameters, we generate a mapping from the undistorted image to the original image. For stereo cameras, our pipeline will save the camera poses during Bundle Adjustment to compute relative rotation and translation matrices, which are then used in the stereo rectification to align cameras. We also provide APIs to combine these two procedures as a generic geometrical transformation:

$$dst(x, y) = src(map_x(x, y), map_y(x, y))$$

We calculate the final mapping from undistorted and aligned images to original images, so that we can just input original images $src(x, y)$ and the combined mapping $map_x(x, y)$, $map_y(x, y)$ into OpenCV's remap function to get resulting images $dst(x, y)$.

Overall, our pipeline contains the following functionalities. We have released it as an open source software to make ray-pixel models easier to use in practice.

- Adopt the growing-based method to detect corners in original images.
- Use Bundle Adjustment to calibrate ray-pixel models (using sector grids).
- Apply image undistortion to original images.
- Apply stereo rectification to multiple cameras.
- Integrate a stereo matching method to get disparity maps from stereo rectified image pairs.
- Reconstruct 3D scenes as point clouds from disparity maps.

4 Evaluation

In this section, we design and carry out three experiments to evaluate performances on our proposed algorithms and pipeline. Note that we mainly care about performances on cameras with severe distortion. Experiments are carried out on a MacBook Pro (16-inch 2019) laptop, with 2.3 GHz 8-Core Intel Core i9, AMD Radeon Pro 5500M 4 GB and Intel UHD Graphics 630 1536 MB.

Data Collection. In order to obtain consistent calibration data for each camera, a robotic arm is programmed to steadily carry cameras. We plan a motion trajectory around the calibration pattern in the world coordinate. The trajectory will cover the operating distances and angles of the cameras, which ensure we are able to collect abundant corner features. Each camera is carried by the robotic arm to take 4000 calibration images along the trajectory. The frame rate of capturing is 2 FPS. For each camera, around 400,000 corners are detected, of which 300,000 corners are fed into calibration, and the left 100,000 corners are reserved for testing.

Camera and Models. We use wide-angle lenses of three focal lengths - 1.9 mm, 2.2 mm and 2.6 mm. We also prepare 10 dual-camera rigs for each focus to get the results more generalized. All cameras use the same type of sensor - SONY IMX327, which has at most 1920×1080 2.9 μm pixels. For comparison, these cameras are calibrated using the following models:

- Pinhole with radial and tangential distortion (OpenCV)
- Fisheye with radial distortion (OpenCV)
- Central ray-pixel using rectangular grids (Schops's implementation [32])
- Central ray-pixel using sector grids (ours)

In terms of image undistortion, stereo rectification and 3D reconstruction, their performances are shown in Table 1.

4.1   Image Undistortion Results

An outcome image using our proposed undistortion algorithm is shown in Fig. 3(b). For more quantitative analysis, we design an experiment including the following steps:

a. Use calibrated cameras to take images of the chessboard pattern from different distances and orientations.
b. Undistort these images to get distortion-free chessboard image regions.
c. Apply a corner detection method to these regions to get sub-pixel corner coordinates.
d. Connect adjacent corners on each row and column, and calculate the slope of each connection.

For example in Fig. 3(b), we believe that corners on the same row or same column in the original image, should lie on a straight line instead of a curve after being well undistorted. Their connection slopes should be identical. Hence, smaller standard deviation of connection slopes in the whole image means better image undistortion performance. We test at four distances: 25 cm, 50 cm, 75 cm and 100 cm, denoted as σ_1, σ_2, σ_3 and σ_4.

Table 1 shows that the largest standard deviation goes to pinhole models. Fisheye models slightly outperform pinhole models but also have large standard deviation. The standard deviation of rectangular or sector ray-pixel model reduces by 59.4%, 50.8% and 46.6% respectively in terms of different focal lengths. In addition, we notice that as the focal length becomes shorter (the camera has severer distortion), ray-pixel models represent more advantages. Note that our proposed sector ray-pixel models keep almost the same performance as rectangular models.

Table 1. Performances of camera models.

Camera	Calibration		Image undistortion				Stereo rectification				3D reconstruction			
	Model	ε	σ_1	σ_2	σ_3	σ_4	δ_1	δ_2	δ_3	δ_4	η_1	η_2	η_3	η_4
1.9 mm + 1920 × 1080	Pinhole	0.35	1.69	1.61	1.53	1.42	0.42	0.40	0.39	0.37	2.83	5.80	10.80	16.20
1.9 mm + 1920 × 1080	Fisheye	0.32	1.65	1.56	1.44	1.36	0.38	0.35	0.36	0.33	2.52	5.59	9.56	15.44
1.9 mm + 1920 × 1080	Ray-pixel (rect)	0.10	0.67	0.62	0.57	0.55	0.23	0.22	0.22	0.21	1.12	2.39	4.86	6.49
1.9 mm + 1920 × 1080	Ray-pixel (sect)	0.11	0.68	0.64	0.59	0.55	0.24	0.22	0.23	0.21	1.11	2.42	4.80	6.45
2.2 mm + 1920 × 1080	Pinhole	0.34	1.24	1.23	1.20	1.17	0.39	0.38	0.36	0.34	2.64	5.77	9.72	15.24
2.2 mm + 1920 × 1080	Fisheye	0.32	1.20	1.18	1.14	1.07	0.38	0.34	0.33	0.31	2.45	5.43	9.31	14.28
2.2 mm + 1920 × 1080	Ray-pixel (rect)	0.09	0.59	0.58	0.56	0.53	0.22	0.20	0.19	0.18	1.08	2.27	4.21	6.02
2.2 mm + 1920 × 1080	Ray-pixel (sect)	0.09	0.59	0.59	0.57	0.54	0.23	0.22	0.19	0.19	1.09	2.32	4.25	6.03
2.6 mm + 1920 × 1080	Pinhole	0.33	1.11	1.05	0.99	0.98	0.40	0.38	0.35	0.34	2.55	5.43	9.48	13.88
2.6 mm + 1920 × 1080	Fisheye	0.30	1.03	0.99	0.96	0.93	0.37	0.35	0.33	0.30	2.38	5.09	9.33	13.05
2.6 mm + 1920 × 1080	Ray-pixel (rect)	0.08	0.55	0.54	0.52	0.50	0.20	0.19	0.17	0.17	0.95	2.11	3.94	5.77
2.6 mm + 1920 × 1080	Ray-pixel (sect)	0.09	0.56	0.56	0.53	0.50	0.22	0.19	0.17	0.18	0.97	2.15	4.07	5.59

Note that in calibration, ε denotes reprojection errors (in pixels); In image undistortion, σ_1, σ_2, σ_3, σ_4 denote standard deviations of corner connection slopes; In stereo rectification, δ_1, δ_2, δ_3, δ_4 denote y-coordinate differences (in pixels) of detected corners in the left and right cameras; In 3D reconstruction, η_1, η_2, η_3, η_4 denote reconstruction errors (in centimeters)

4.2 Stereo Rectification Results

Figure 4 shows the outcome of our stereo rectification algorithm. It's difficult to distinguish whether rectification results are good or bad with our naked eyes because row alignment differences are normally less than a pixel. After stereo rectification, we calculate y-coordinate differences of detected corners between the left images and the right

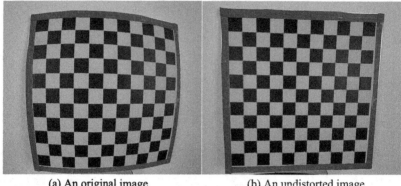

(a) An original image   (b) An undistorted image

Fig. 3. Image undistortion of ray-pixel models. After image undistortion, we detect corner positions (red circle) and connect corners on the same row (green arrow) or column (blue arrow). Only one row and one column are demonstrated here.

images, which should be 0 under ideal circumstances. We use the detected chessboard corners in Sect. 4.1. Note that the corner detection not only gives the accurate corner positions, but also gives the ordered number of each corner. We make 2 corners a pair if they have the same ordered number in the left and right images. Then we can directly get the y-coordinate differences of each corner pair. We also test image corners at four distances: 25 cm, 50 cm, 75 cm and 100 cm, denoted as δ_1, δ_2, δ_3 and δ_4.

From the results in Table 1, the conclusion is similar to Sect. 4.1. The averaged y-coordinate differences of pinhole and fisheye models are below 0.5 pixel and fisheye models outperform slightly than pinhole models. Our proposed stereo rectification algorithm reduces the differences by over 40% with comparison to fisheye models, no matter using rectangular girds or sector grids. We think such an improvement benefits from the better undistortion of ray-pixel models. We are confident that with higher accuracy (around 0.2 pixel) on stereo rectification, we can achieve better performance on stereo matching and 3D reconstruction.

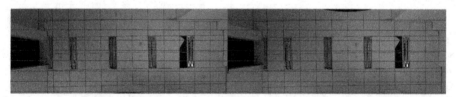

Fig. 4. An image pair after stereo rectification. Auxiliary lines (blue) can help distinguish whether positions of objects in the left and right image are row-aligned.

4.3 Sector Grid Results

This section we focus on the performance of ray-pixel models using rectangular grids versus sector grids. We test on cameras with 1.9mm focal length under 3 different image resolutions: $1920 \times 1080, 960 \times 540$ and 480×270. We don't directly resize the corner coordinates because it will lose accuracy to a certain degree. For each camera, the 1920×1080 original corner images are resized to 960×540 and 480×270, respectively. Then we apply corner detection on resized images to get resized corner coordinates. We use central ray-pixel models to calibrate each camera using 2 types of grids: rectangular and sector. In 1920×1080 images, there are 9,216 rectangular grids and 1600 sector grids; In 960×540 images, there are 2304 rectangular grids and 800 sector grids; In 480×270 images, there are 576 rectangular grids and 400 sector grids. As a controlled experiment, we also prepare sparse rectangular grids by increasing the cell size so that they have the same number of grids as sector grids.

The calibration time and reprojection error are shown in Fig. 5. For images of high resolution, our proposed sector ray-pixel models reduce 83% of calibration time, while maintaining almost the same calibration accuracy - reprojection error is less than 0.12 pixel. For images of low resolution like 480×270, sector grids are also faster in terms of calibration time, but we don't recommend using low resolution for calibration because many details on image will not be reserved. Although it takes almost the same time to calibrate sector grids and the sparse rectangular grids, the latter has 2 more times reprojection error.

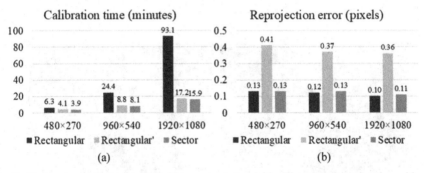

Fig. 5. Comparison of rectangular grids versus sector grids. The sparse rectangular grids are marked as Rectangular' (orange)

4.4   3D Reconstruction Results

In this experiment, we evaluate the performance on 3D reconstruction. Firstly, we apply both image undistortion and stereo rectification algorithms to get row-aligned image pairs. At certain distances, we then take photos (Fig. 6(a)) of a plain full of random and colorful texture, which helps the stereo matching algorithm to find more details in the image. We then feed image pairs into SGBM method [37] to get disparity maps and then reconstruct 3D point clouds. The idea is to see the reconstruction errors (in terms of z-coordinate) at three distances: 50 cm, 100 cm, 150 cm and 200 cm, denoted as η_1, η_2, η_3 and η_4. Some of the SGBM parameters are: image channel is set to 1, the number of disparities is set to 128, the SAD window size is set to 15, the dynamic programming is set to full-scale and two-pass mode.

There is a concern that we shall introduce the error of stereo matching, which will affect the reconstruction results. We design another experiment to use OpenCV's CharUco patterns (Fig. 6(b)) and relative detection methods, which can provide accurate corner coordinates. In the same way, we take photos of CharUco patterns at certain distances, then we detect CharUco corners and get sub-pixel coordinates. The disparity is obtained from the x-coordinate difference of CharUco corners in the left and right images.

In Table 1, it's obvious that ray-pixel models have higher 3D reconstruction accuracy. At the distance of 50 cm, the reconstruction error of ray-pixel models is 60.4% smaller than pinhole models, and 55.6% smaller than fisheye models. At the distance of 200 cm, the advantages of ray-pixel models are also obvious. The visualization results of dense 3D reconstruction using stereo matching are shown in Fig. 7. We can see that in the central regions, both models have good performances. The main difference between ray-pixel models and fisheye models is: ray-pixel models are able to maintain small reconstruction error in the border image regions, where pinhole and fisheye models have poor reconstruction ability. The above reconstruction errors (η_1, η_2, η_3, η_4) are the average from the whole image field, so we then focus on the border regions (the first and last 25% rows and columns of the image). The results are as expected: at the distances of 50 cm and 200 cm, ray-pixel models have 71.6% and 63.3% smaller reconstruction error, respectively.

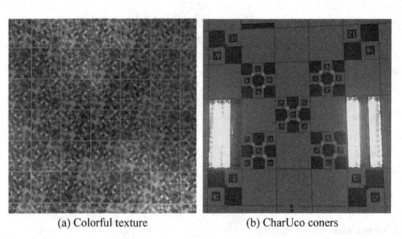

(a) Colorful texture   (b) CharUco coners

Fig. 6. Images for 3D reconstruction

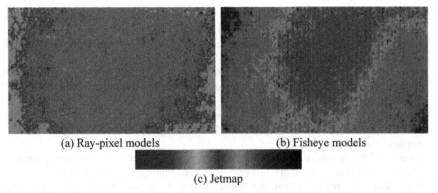

(a) Ray-pixel models   (b) Fisheye models

(c) Jetmap

Fig. 7. Visualization of dense reconstruction error (150 cm). OpenCV's Jetmap is used to represent the reconstruction error. Error near ground truth is marked as green (middle). Error less than ground truth is marked as red (right). Error greater than ground truth is marked as blue (left).

5 Evaluation

In this paper, we propose algorithms and implementations of image undistortion and stereo rectification based on central ray-pixel models. We also provide an extended pipeline from calibration to application. The evaluation consisting of several experiments shows that our algorithms work better in terms of various aspects: calibration time, image undistortion, stereo rectification and 3D reconstruction. We believe that our work should make ray-pixel models much easier and more attractive in practice.

In the future, we would like to complete ray-pixel models, such as supporting non-central models.

References

1. Fryer, J.G., Brown, D.C.: Lens distortion for close-range photogrammetry. Photogramm. Eng. Remote. Sens. **52**, 51–58 (1986)
2. Weng, J., Cohen, P., Herniou, M., et al.: Camera calibration with distortion models and accuracy evaluation. IEEE Trans. Pattern Anal. Mach. Intell. **14**(10), 965–980 (1992)
3. Hartley, R., Kang, S.B.: Parameter-free radial distortion correction with center of distortion estimation. IEEE Trans. Pattern Anal. Mach. Intell. **29**(8), 1309–1321 (2007)
4. Pons, J.-P., Keriven, R., Faugeras, O.: Modelling dynamic scenes by registering multi-view image sequences. In: 2005 IEEE Computer Society Conference on Computer Vision and Pattern Recognition (CVPR'05), vol. 2, pp. 822–827. IEEE (2005)
5. Woodford, O., Torr, P., Reid, I., Fitzgibbon, A.: Global stereo reconstruction under second-order smoothness priors. IEEE Trans. Pattern Anal. Mach. Intell. **31**(12), 2115–2128 (2009)
6. Mur-Artal, R., Montiel, J.M.M., Tardos, J.D.: Orb-slam: a versatile and accurate monocular slam system. IEEE Trans. Rob. **31**(5), 1147–1163 (2015)
7. Schops, T., Schonberger, J.L., Galliani, S., Sattler, T., Schindler, K., Pollefeys, M., Geiger, A.: A multi-view stereo benchmark with high-resolution images and multi-camera videos. In: Proceedings of the IEEE Conference on Computer Vision and Pattern Recognition, pp. 3260–3269 (2017)

8. Beck, J., Stiller, C.: Generalized b-spline camera model. In: 2018 IEEE Intelligent Vehicles Symposium (IV), pp. 2137–2142. IEEE (2018)
9. Zhang, Z.: A flexible new technique for camera calibration. IEEE Trans. Pattern Anal. Mach. Intell. **22**(11), 1330–1334 (2000)
10. Grossberg, M.D., Nayar, S.K.: A general imaging model and a method for finding its parameters. In: Proceedings Eighth IEEE International Conference on Computer Vision. ICCV 2001, vol. 2, pp. 108–115. IEEE (2001)
11. Dunne, A.K., Mallon, J., Whelan, P.F.: A comparison of new generic camera calibration with the standard parametric approach. In: MVA2007 IAPR Conference on Machine Vision Applications (2007)
12. Triggs, B., McLauchlan, P.F., Hartley, R.I., Fitzgibbon, A.W.: Bundle adjustment—a modern synthesis. In: International Workshop on Vision Algorithms, pp. 298–372. Springer (1999)
13. Bouguet, J.-Y.: Camera calibration toolbox for matlab. http://www.vision.caltech.edu/bouguetj/calib/doc/index.html (2004)
14. Bradski, G.: The openCV library. Dr. Dobb's J. Soft. Tools Prof. Prog. **25**(11), 120–123 (2000)
15. Geiger, A., Moosmann, F., Car, O., Schuster, B.: Automatic camera and range sensor calibration using a single shot. In: 2012 IEEE International Conference on Robotics and Automation, pp. 3936–3943. IEEE (2012)
16. Schonbein, M., Strauß, T., Geiger, A.: Calibrating and centering quasi-central catadioptric cameras. In: 2014 IEEE International Conference on Robotics and Automation (ICRA), pp. 4443–4450. IEEE (2014)
17. Ding, W., Liu, X., Xu, D., Zhang, D., Zhang, Z.: A robust detection method of control points for calibration and measurement with defocused images. IEEE Trans. Instrum. Meas. **66**(10), 2725–2735 (2017)
18. Ha, H., Perdoch, M., Alismail, H., So Kweon, I., Sheikh, Y.: Deltille grids for geometric camera calibration. In: Proceedings of the IEEE International Conference on Computer Vision, pp. 5344–5352 (2017)
19. Duane, C.B.: Close-range camera calibration. Photogramm. Eng **37**(8), 855–866 (1971)
20. Kannala, J., Brandt, S.S.: A generic camera model and calibration method for conventional, wide-angle, and fish-eye lenses. IEEE Trans. Pattern Anal. Mach. Intell. **28**(8), 1335–1340 (2006)
21. Geyer, C., Daniilidis, K.: A unifying theory for central panoramic systems and practical implications. In: European Conference on Computer Vision, pp. 445–461. Springer (2000)
22. Bogdan, O., Eckstein, V., Rameau, F., Bazin, J.-C.: Deepcalib: a deep learning approach for automatic intrinsic calibration of wide field-of-view cameras. In: Proceedings of the 15th ACM SIGGRAPH European Conference on Visual Media Production, pp. 1–10 (2018)
23. Iyer, G., Ram, R.K., Murthy, J.K., Krishna, K.M.: Calibnet: Geometrically supervised extrinsic calibration using 3d spatial transformer networks. In: 2018 IEEE/RSJ International Conference on Intelligent Robots and Systems (IROS), pp. 1110–1117. IEEE (2018)
24. Shi, J., Zhu, Z., Zhang, J., Liu, R., Wang, Z., Chen, S., Liu, H.: Calibrcnn: calibrating camera and lidar by recurrent convolutional neural network and geometric constraints. In: 2020 IEEE/RSJ International Conference on Intelligent Robots and Systems (IROS), pp. 10197–10202. IEEE (2020)
25. Bergamasco, F., Cosmo, L., Gasparetto, A., Albarelli, A., Torsello, A.: Parameter-free lens distortion calibration of central cameras. In: Proceedings of the IEEE International Conference on Computer Vision, pp. 3847–3855 (2017)
26. Dunne, A.K., Mallon, J., Whelan, P.F.: Efficient generic calibration method for general cameras with single centre of projection. Comput. Vis. Image Underst. **114**(2), 220–233 (2010)
27. Nister, D., Stewenius, H., Grossmann, E.: Non-parametric self-calibration. In: Tenth IEEE International Conference on Computer Vision (ICCV'05), vol. 1, pp. 120–127. IEEE (2005)

28. Sturm, P., Ramalingam, S.: A generic concept for camera calibration. In: European Conference on Computer Vision, pp. 1–13. Springer (2004)
29. Ramalingam, S., Sturm, P.: Minimal solutions for generic imaging models. In: 2008 IEEE Conference on Computer Vision and Pattern Recognition, pp. 1–8. IEEE (2008)
30. Ramalingam, S., Sturm, P.: A unifying model for camera calibration. IEEE Trans. Pattern Anal. Mach. Intell. **39**(7), 1309–1319 (2016)
31. Rosebrock, D., Wahl, F.M.: Generic camera calibration and modeling using spline surfaces. In: 2012 IEEE Intelligent Vehicles Symposium, pp. 51–56. IEEE (2012)
32. Schops, T., Larsson, V., Pollefeys, M., Sattler, T.: Why having 10,000 parameters in your camera model is better than twelve. In: Proceedings of the IEEE/CVF Conference on Computer Vision and Pattern Recognition, pp. 2535–2544 (2020)
33. Tang, Z., von Gioi, R.G., Monasse, P., Morel, J.-M.: A precision analysis of camera distortion models. IEEE Trans. Image Process. **26**(6), 2694–2704 (2017)
34. Fan, B., Dai, Y., He, M.: Sunet: symmetric undistortion network for rolling shutter correction. In: Proceedings of the IEEE/CVF International Conference on Computer Vision, pp. 4541–4550 (2021)
35. Levenberg, K.: A method for the solution of certain non-linear problems in least squares. Q. Appl. Math. **2**(2), 164–168 (1944)
36. Marquardt, D.W.: An algorithm for least-squares estimation of nonlinear parameters. J. Soc. Ind. Appl. Math. **11**(2), 431–441 (1963)
37. Hirschmuller, H.: Stereo processing by semiglobal matching and mutual information. IEEE Trans. Pattern Anal. Mach. Intell. **30**(2), 328–341 (2007)
38. Lu, H., Yang, R., Deng, Z., Zhang, Y., Gao, G., Lan, R.: Chinese image captioning via fuzzy attention-based DenseNet-BiLSTM. ACM Trans. Multimed. Comput. Commun. Appl. **17**(1s), 1–18 (2021)
39. Lu, H., Zhang, Y., Li, Y., Jiang, C., Abbas, H.: User-oriented virtual mobile network resource management for vehicle communications. IEEE Trans. Intell. Transp. Syst. (2020). https://doi.org/10.1109/TITS.2020.2991766
40. Lu, H., Qin, M., Zhang, F., et al.: RSCNN: a CNN-based method to enhance low-light remote-sensing images. Remote Sens. **13**(1), 62 (2020)
41. Lu, H., Zhang, M., Xu, X.: Deep fuzzy hashing network for efficient image retrieval. IEEE Trans. Fuzzy Syst. (2020). https://doi.org/10.1109/TFUZZ.2020.2984991
42. Li, Y., Yang, S., Zheng, Y., Lu, H.: Improved point-voxel region convolutional neural network: 3D object detectors for autonomous driving. IEEE Trans. Intell. Trans. Syst. **23**(7), 9311–9317 (2022)

GGM-Net: Gradient Constraint on Multi-category Brain MRI Segmentation

Yuanyuan Wang[1] and Xiangzhi Bai[1,2,3(✉)]

[1] Image Processing Center, Beihang University, Beijing 102206, China
{wangyuanyuan,jackybxz}@buaa.edu.cn
[2] The State Key Laboratory of Virtual Reality Technology and Systems, Beihang University, Beijing 100191, China
[3] Beijing Advanced Innovation Center for Biomedical Engineering, Beihang University, Beijing 100083, China

Abstract. In the diagnosis and treatment of brain tumor, the position, shape, and size of tumor are the key factors to be taken into account. However, for the multi-category brain tumor segmentation task, complexity of tumor growth lead to poor segmentation performance near intersection area. Most medical image segmentation methods extract the region of interest based on the gray information of the image, rather than introducing gradient information. In addition, the complexity of multi-modality medical images and the huge differences between brain tumor areas make it difficult to segment brain tumors. To solve the above problems, we propose an gradient-guided multi-category brain tumor segmentation method. Proposed algorithm includes three branches: Dual-ConvD encoding branch, gradient detecting branch, and multi-category segmentation branch. We used 295 patients as training set and 74 as validation set to validate the performance of the algorithm. The proposed method has 1.25% improved to the latest method on averaged Dice Score.

Keywords: Deep learning · Multi-modality MRI · Brain tumor segmentation · Gradient-guided

1 Introduction

Magnetic Resonance Imaging (MRI) technology obtains information on human tissue structure through non-invasive imaging [1]. MRI has an excellent performance in reflecting the brain tissue. It is used for the diagnosis and treatment of brain tumors commonly. Tumor segmentation of tumor areas can help doctors better judge current situation of patients to formulate diagnosis and treatment strategies [2]. Glioma is the most common malignant tumor in the brain, which is very aggressive and poses a severe threat to the lives of people all over the world [3–5]. The median survival time of glioma patients is about 15 months, and the 5-year survival rate is less than 10% [6]. It is almost incurable. Gliomas grow in the brain parenchyma and mix with normal brain tissues [7]. In the same tumor area, tumor cells and tissue have complex and changeable tumor characteristics.

Because of the complexity of the same tumor, different regions have their own relatively specific characteristics and clinical manifestations. These all lead to the high complexity of glioma segmentation. According to the malignant degree, tumor cells can be divided into low-grade glioma (LGG) and high-grade glioma (HGG) [8]. The volume, shape, and location of the tumor site are essential factors in evaluating brain tumors. Therefore, the segmentation of brain tumor regions is significant for diagnosing and treating brain tumors.

Generally, MRI images of a patient include the following: native (T1), post-contrast T1-weighted (T1ce), T2-weighted (T2), and T2-weighted fluid attenuated inversion recovery (T2-Flair) [9]. These four kinds of images have different sensitivity to different areas in tumor tissue. Glioma segmentation needs to be abtained at the pixel level, and the following four regions need to be generated: Enhanced Tumor (ET), Tumor Core (TC), Whole Tumor (WT), and normal tissue.

In order to use the generated MRI images to evaluate the condition of patient and help doctors make diagnoses and treatment plans, professional radiologists need to use professional physiological anatomy knowledge to sketch pixel-level spatial information. Manual drawing of the target area takes time and effort, leading to unstable effects and error-prone [10, 11]. It usually takes a radiologist 3–5 hours to sketch the image of a patient [12, 13]. Therefore, scholars are studying powerful automatic methods, hoping to reduce the tedious workload of radiologists. Radiologists can save time for other meaningful work. At the same time, the automatic segmentation algorithms can also ensure the accuracy and stability of segmentation results, thus helping clinicians in diagnosis and treatment [14]. Deep learning has made remarkable achievements in the field of segmentation [15], and has also made some progress in multi-modality [16, 17]. For medical images, due to the complexity and diversity of its imaging principles and the limitation of small amount of data, accurate image segmentation is being explored.

In MRI brain tumor analysis, segmentation techniques are mainly divided into traditional segmentation and deep learning algorithms [18]. Traditional algorithms are usually based on hand-designed features to perform pixel-level segmentation [19–21]. Kaihu et al. [19]. Designed the patch's 3-D texture features using the gray co-occurrence matrix (GLCM) statistics, thus constructing the random field of texture features. Recently, the methods based on deep learning have made the cutting-edge achievements in the field of medical image analysis [22–24], especially the UNet [25] structure and its derivative networks [24–26] networks are vital in medical images. There are two difficulties that limit the improvement of algorithm performance. The one is that the medical image data is in the form of three-dimensional voxels. The other is imbalanced data. For brain tumor segmentation, the situation is more complicated. We need to get multiple regions of the tumor from multi-modality MRI. The existing multi-modality image data are usually input to the neural network, which does not effectively utilize the multi-modality characteristics of data. Therefore, this paper proposes a brain tumor segmentation algorithm consisting of one encoding branch and two decoding branches. The main contributions are as follows: 1) A encoding structure is designed to extract the features of multi-modality image data; 2) An gradient extraction decoding structure is designed to guide region segmentation; 3) Segmentation network branch is designed to utilize gradient features and abstract features generated by the encoder effectively. The proposed algorithm achieves the Dice score of WT, ET, and TC of 0.9010, 0.8289, and 0.7543 on Brats2020 dataset. The effectiveness of proposed algorithm has been verified.

In the following sections, we first introduces the proposed method in detail from three aspects, and then introduces the training related settings based on the proposed method, including loss function and parameter settings. Finally, relevant experiments are carried out on the dataset, including ablation experiment and advanced contrast experiment.

2 Methods

2.1 Image Acquisition and Preprocessing

The algorithm proposed in this paper is verified on the multi-modality Brain Tumor Segmentation Dataset. The classical 3D segmentation algorithms are evaluated on the same dataset. This dataset published four modality MRI image data of 369 patients, namely T2-flair, T1, T1-CE and T2. These patients are divided into two different disease development processes: HGG and LGG. The images needs to be divided into three parts: whole tumor (WT), enhanced tumor (ET), and tumor core (TC). In the published official tumor labeling data, there are four kinds of numerical values: 0, 1, 2, and 4. Integer 0 represents the background area. The true value of WT, TC, ET area are $1 \cup 2 \cup 4$, $1 \cup 4$, and 4, respectively. The original volume data size of each 3D image is $240 \times 240 \times 155$. In data preprocessing, we mainly adopt three operations: Z-value normalization, random (center) cropping, and random flipping.

As for Z-score normalization [27], we use the linear change between the gray levels of the original image to obtain the mean and variance of the whole image. The specific mathematical transformation is shown in Eq. 1.

$$X = \frac{Z - \mu}{\sigma} \tag{1}$$

where Z represents the initial input image and X represents the normalized image. μ and σ represent the mean and variance of the image respectively.

As for random (center) cropping, based on the original data size of $240 \times 240 \times 155$, we crop the training data and test data to $160 \times 192 \times 128$. In the training process, the random cutting operation can expand the amount of original data. During the testing process, the central cropping operation can ensure the same size as the training data and remove the redundant background. In addition, four times of down-sampling are carried out in this paper, and the input data are collected to 1/16 of the original data in each dimension.

As for random flipping, if the random value is set every time data is read less than 0.5, the data will be flipped around the X-axis. Every flip data enhancement includes three random flips on the X, Y, and Z axes.

2.2 Gradient-Guided Multi-category Segmentation Network

The overall network structure flow proposed in this paper is shown in Fig. 1. The proposed algorithm comprises three modules: dual feature extraction network module (D-Conv

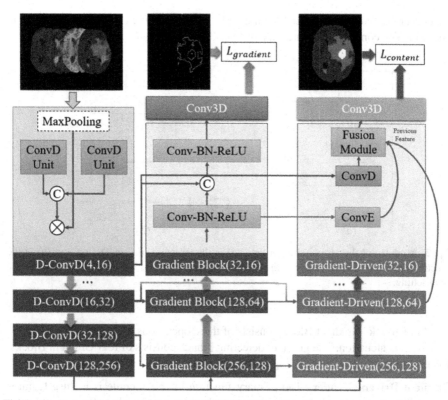

Fig. 1. Pipeline of the proposed method GGM-Net. The algorithm is composed of four part: D-ConvD Block, Gradient Block, Gradient Driven Block

Block), gradient extraction module (Gradient Block), and gradient driven decoder module (GDD Block). The dual convolution feature extraction network module can skillfully deal with the problem that multi-modality images are uniformly input into the network model and effectively extract multi-modality features. The gradient extraction module can effectively use the features output by the Encoder to obtain gradient information to guide the network to generate pixel-level segmentation results. The gradient driven decoder module is driven to receive the corresponding features output by the dual feature extraction encoder and the gradient extraction module simultaneously and fuse the information to generate accurate multi-category segmentation results.

D-ConvD Block: This module consists of four operations: MaxPooling, ConvD Unit, concatenation, and adding. There are five D-ConvD Blocks in the proposed algorithm. If the module is located at the first position, the Maxpooling indicated by the dotted line in Fig. 1 will be omitted, and next operations will be carried out directly. If the D-ConvD Block are not at the first position, MaxPooling is the first operations to be performed. In this paper, all Maxpooling kernel size and stride of MaxPooling are set to be 2. After the Maxpooling operation, two ConvD Units are used to extract features separately. Then the two streamline features are concatenated. Finally the concatenated features are added with the initial features. The structure of the ConvD Unit is shown in Fig. 2(a). The convolution kernel size of Conv3d is $3 \times 3 \times 3$.

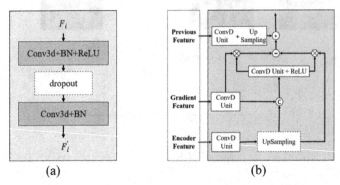

(a)   (b)

Fig. 2. Modules of the proposed algorithm. (a) is the structure of ConvD Unit and (b) is the structure of GDD. The dotted box indicates that the operation can be omitted according to the input setting.

Gradient Block: Gradient Block consists of three operations, two convolution blocks, and one concatenation. The gradient detecting branch consists of four Gradient Blocks. The convolution kernel sizes in Fig. 1 are $3 \times 3 \times 3$.

Gradient-Driven-Decoder: The primary function of this module is to fuse features from different network branches to decode and get accurate multi-category segmentation results. Segmentation network branch consists of four GDD Blocks. As shown in Fig. 2(b), the input of GDD block has no previous feature for the first fusion block, the top branch is cut off. We indicate the corresponding branch as a dotted line. For the fusion modules at other positions, the features output by encoder are up-sampled and then concatenated with the gradient features. After that, ConvD Unit is multiplied by the processed gradient feature and encoder feature, respectively. Finally, the obtained two features are subtracted and added with the previous feature.

2.3 Training

2.3.1 Loss Function

The brain tumor segmentation task has three significant characteristics: 1) a large proportion of HGG and LGG, 2) large differences in tumor morphology, sometimes discrete, and 3) small tumor area, especially non-enhancing tumor. Therefore, we use soft Dice loss [28] as the objective function of the task, consider each category separately, and then average the final result. Dice loss is expressed as follows:

$$L_{content} = 1 - \frac{1}{M} \sum_{c=1}^{M} \frac{2 \times \sum_{i=1}^{W}\sum_{j=1}^{H}\sum_{k=1}^{D} Y_{cijk}\Theta(X) + \varepsilon}{\sum_{i=1}^{W}\sum_{j=1}^{H}\sum_{k=1}^{D} Y_{cijk} + \sum_{i=1}^{W}\sum_{j=1}^{H}\sum_{k=1}^{D}\Theta(X) + \varepsilon}. \qquad (2)$$

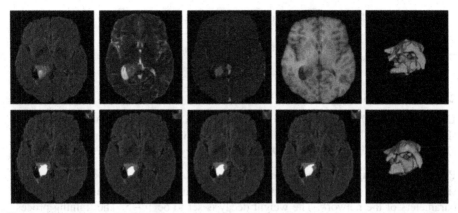

Fig. 3. Visualization of HGG segmentation results. The first line is the four modes of input image and the visualization of the manual label. The second line is annotation, UNet, ResUnet, and proposed methods.

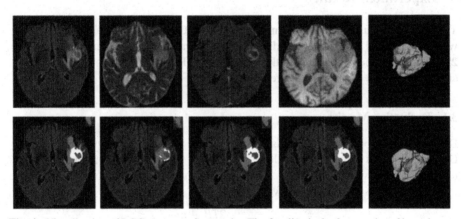

Fig. 4. Visualization of LGG segmentation results. The first line is the four modes of input image and the visualization of the manual label. The second line is annotation, UNet, ResUnet, and proposed methods.

where X and Y_{cijk} represents the original input and predicted segmentation respectively. M is the total number of segmentation categories. Θ is the set of MCCNet parameters. W, H and D are the size of the input image in three dimensions. Our input patches are cropped to the size of $160 \times 192 \times 128$. ε is to prevent the denominator from being 0. It is set to 1.

In addition, in order to strengthen the guidance of gradient information to segmentation tasks, we introduce gradient supervision information in the training process, and its loss function is shown as follows:

$$L_{gradient} = -\frac{1}{M}\sum_{c=1}^{M}\sum_{i=1}^{W}\sum_{j=1}^{H}\sum_{k=1}^{D} G_{cijk} log\left(\Theta(X) + \left(1 - G_{cijk}\right) log(1 - \Theta(X))\right). \quad (3)$$

where X and G_{cijk} represents the original input and gradient information respectively.

The final loss function is as follows, α is set to be 0.1:

$$L_{final} = L_{content} + \alpha \times L_{gradient}. \tag{4}$$

2.3.2 Training Setting

Configuration: Our experiment is performed on a workstation equipped with Intel (R)Intel(R) Core(TM) i9-10980XE CPU at 3.00 GHz, 24 GB memory. The model of GPU is NVIDIA GeForce RTX 3090, 24 GB memory.

Parameter Setting: The patch size of the input data is $160 \times 192 \times 128$. The batch size is set to be 1. Adam optimizer with initial learning rate 1e−4 is adopted to update parameters of the network. The weight decay is set to be 1e−5. The training process epoch of iteration is 100. And the initial channels is 16.

3 Experiment Result

The training data used in this experiment is the Brats2020 dataset, a total of 369 patients, which are divided into train set and test set. The number of patients in the train set is 295 and the number of patients in the test set is 74. The training images are randomly cropped while the testing images are center cropped.

3.1 Evaluation Metric

Dice similarity coefficient (DSC) is the main rating standard for segmentation tasks. Dice coefficient is a measure of collective similarity, which is usually used to calculate the similarity between two samples. The optimal value of segmentation result is 1 and the worst is 0. It is defined as follows:

$$DSC = \frac{2TP}{FP + 2TP + FN} \tag{5}$$

where FP, FN and TP are false positive, false negative and true positive respectively.

3.2 Analysis and Presentation of Results

To verify the effectiveness of the proposed algorithm, we analyzed the output results qualitatively and quantitatively and compared our algorithm with 3D-Unet, 3D-ResUnet, and Vnet. The output results of various algorithms are shown in Fig. 3 and Fig. 4. The first line is the original image data of the patient, and the last column of the first line is the three-dimensional visualization effect of the true value of the tumor sketched by hand. It can be seen that the tumor in Fig. 3 has a complex shape and a star-shaped emission. The first four pictures in the second row are the manually sketched truth values, the output of 3D-Unet algorithm, the output of 3D-ResUnet, and the output results of the proposed algorithm. The last column in the second row is the 3D visualization effect of the output result of the proposed algorithm. It can be seen from the resulting diagram that all three algorithms can determine the general location of the tumor, but there are some differences in performance in detail. The proposed algorithm can capture the detailed features better.

Table 1 shows the performance of the algorithm in indicators. All the comparative experiments performed are based on the framework given by the official literature. We set the number of initial channels to 16, which is consistent with the number of channels in the proposed algorithm. It can be found from the table that the DSC obtained by our proposed method is 0.9010, 0.8289, and 0.7543 respectively. The average DSC index reached 0.8278, 1.5% higher than that of 3D-ResUnet. The correlation results of three tumor regions prove the effectiveness of the proposed method.

Table 1. Quantitative comparisons of segmentation results

Methods	DSC				HD95			
	WT	TC	ET	Average	WT	TC	ET	Average
Unet [25]	0.6858	0.5280	0.5509	0.5882	16.8238	14.6242	11.2896	14.2459
VNet [28]	0.6578	0.6145	0.6330	0.6351	25.1337	15.0412	11.8130	17.3293
Res-Unet	0.8927	0.8331	0.7200	0.8152	5.7462	6.3212	6.5573	6.2082
RAL [29]	0.8873	0.8426	0.7432	0.8244	7.7767	7.7917	4.5934	6.7206
Proposed	0.9010	0.8289	0.7543	**0.8278**	6.4465	5.5104	5.6123	**5.8564**

4 Conclusion

In this work, we propose an gradient-guided multi-category segmentation algorithm (GGM-Net) to segment three sub-regions of multi-modality glioma. GGM-Net comprises a three-branch coding structure, gradient extraction branch, and decoding branch, effectively using various features with different modes. The gradient extraction branch generates gradient features, thus guiding the decoding branch to generate more accurate multi-category segmentation results. The fusion module applied in the decoding structure can fuse the details extracted by the Encoder and the contour information extracted by the gradient structure. We put forward a supervision training method combining gradient information with content information in the objective function, making the training process more effective. The proposed algorithm is superior to the widely used coding and decoding structure in brain tumor segmentation. Our algorithm has substantial advantages in WT region segmentation and competitiveness in ET region segmentation through qualitative and quantitative analysis and comparison. Overall, the proposed algorithm is an effective brain tumor segmentation method and an essential tool for studying three-dimensional medical images.

Acknowledgments. This work was supported in part by the National Key R&D Program of China (2019YFB1311301), and Beijing Natural Science Foundation (4222007).

References

1. Gandon, Y., Olivié, D., Guyader, D., Aubé, C., Oberti, F., Sebille, V., Deugnier, Y.: Non-invasive assessment of hepatic iron stores by MRI. Lancet. **363**(9406), 357–362 (2004)
2. Ae, A., Aiab, C., Aamk, D., Hfah, D.: A review on brain tumor diagnosis from MRI images: practical implications, key achievements, and lessons learned. Magn. Reson. Imaging **61**, 300–318 (2019)
3. Menze, B.H., et al.: The multimodal brain tumor image segmentation benchmark (brats). IEEE Trans. Med. Imaging **34**(10), 1993–2024 (2014)
4. Işın, A., Direkoğlu, C., Şah, M.: Review of MRI-based brain tumor image segmentation using deep learning methods. Procedia Comput. Sci. **102**, 317–324 (2016)
5. Pereira, S., Pinto, A., Alves, V., Silva, C.A.: Brain tumor segmentation using convolutional neural networks in MRI images. IEEE Trans. Med. Imaging **35**(5), 1240–1251 (2016)
6. Perry, J.R., Laperriere, N., Mason, W.P.: Radiation plus temozolomide in patients with glioblastoma. N. Engl. J. Med. **376**(22), 2197 (2017)
7. Selbekk, T., Brekken, R., Solheim, O., Lydersen, S., Unsgaard, G.: Tissue motion and strain in the human brain assessed by intraoperative ultrasound in glioma patients. Ultrasound Med. Biol. **36**(1), 2–10 (2010)
8. Magadza, T., Viriri, S.: Deep learning for brain tumor segmentation: a survey of state-of-the-art. Multidiscip. Digital Pub. Inst. **7**(2), 19 (2021)
9. Luo, Z., Jia, Z., Yuan, Z., Peng, J.: HDC-net: hierarchical decoupled convolution network for brain tumor segmentation. IEEE J. Biomed. Health Inform. PP(99), 1–1 (2020)
10. Akkus, Z., Galimzianova, A., Hoogi, A., Rubin, D.L., Erickson, B.J.: Deep learning for brain MRI segmentation: state of the art and future directions. J. Digit. Imaging **30**(4), 449–459 (2017)
11. Yue, W., Wang, Z., Tian, B., Pook, M., Liu, X.: A hybrid model-and memory-based collaborative filtering algorithm for baseline data prediction of friedreich's ataxia patients. IEEE Trans. Industr. Inf. **17**(2), 1428–1437 (2020)
12. Kaus, M.R., Warfield, S.K., Nabavi, A., Black, P.M., Jolesz, F.A., Kikinis, R.: Automated segmentation of MR images of brain tumors. Radiology **218**(2), 586–591 (2001)
13. Liu, W., Wang, Z., Liu, X., Zeng, N., Bell, D.: A novel particle swarm optimization approach for patient clustering from emergency departments. IEEE Trans. Evol. Comput. **23**(4), 632–644 (2018)
14. Li, Y., Jia, F., Qin, J.: Brain tumor segmentation from multimodal magnetic resonance images via sparse representation. Artif. Intell. Med. **73**, 1–13 (2016)
15. Nakayama, Y., Lu, H., Li, Y., Kamiya, T.: Widesegnext: semantic image segmentation using wide residual network and next dilated unit. IEEE Sens. J. PP(99), 1–1 (2020)
16. Xu, X., Lin, K., Gao, L., Lu, H., Shen, H.T., Li, X.: Learning cross-modal common representations by private–shared subspaces separation. IEEE Trans. Cyber. **52**(5), 3261–3275 (2022)
17. Xu, X., Wang, T., Yang, Y., Zuo, L., Shen, F., Shen, H.T.: Cross-modal attention with semantic consistence for image-text matching. IEEE Trans. Neural Net. Learn. Syst. **31**(12), 5412–5425 (2020)
18. Saman, S., Jamjala Narayanan, S.: Survey on brain tumor segmentation and feature extraction of MR images. Int. J. Multimedia Inform. Retr. **8**(2), 79–99 (2019)
19. Hu, K., Gao, X., Zhang, Y.: Markov multiple feature random fields model for the segmentation of brain MR images. Expert Syst. Appl. **134**, 79–92 (2019)
20. Ahmadvand, A., Yousefi, S., Manzuri Shalmani, M.: A novel markov random field model based on region adjacency graph for T1 magnetic resonance imaging brain segmentation. Int. J. Imaging Syst. Technol. **27**(1), 78–88 (2017)

21. Ahmadvand, A., Daliri, M.R.: Improving the runtime of MRF based method for MRI brain segmentation. Appl. Math. Comput. **256**, 808–818 (2015)
22. Lopes, R., Dubois, P., Bhouri, I., Bedoui, M.H., Maouche, S., Betrouni, N.: Local fractal and multifractal features for volumic texture characterization. Pattern Recogn. **44**(8), 1690–1697 (2011)
23. Wels, M., Carneiro, G., Aplas, A., Huber, M., Hornegger, J., Comaniciu, D.: A discriminative model-constrained graph cuts approach to fully automated pediatric brain tumor segmentation in 3-D MRI. In: International Conference on Medical Image Computing and Computer-Assisted Intervention, pp. 67–75. Springer (2008)
24. Liu, Z., et al.: Liver CT sequence segmentation based with improved U-Net and graph cut. Expert Syst. Appl. **126**, 54–63 (2019)
25. Çiçek, O., Abdulkadir, A., Lienkamp, S.S., Brox, T., Ronneberger, O.: 3D U-Net: learning dense volumetric segmentation from sparse annotation. In: International conference on medical image computing and computer-assisted intervention, pp. 424–432. Springer (2016)
26. Zhou, X., Li, X., Hu, K., Zhang, Y., Chen, Z., Gao, X.: ERV-Net: an efficient 3D residual neural network for brain tumor segmentation. Expert Syst. Appl. **170**, 114566 (2021)
27. Jain, A., Nandakumar, K., Ross, A.: Score normalization in multimodal biometric systems. Pattern Recogn. **38**(12), 2270–2285 (2005)
28. Milletari, F., Navab, N., Ahmadi, S.-A.: V-Net: fully convolutional neural networks for volumetric medical image segmentation. In: 2016 Fourth International Conference on 3D Vision (3DV), pp. 565–571. IEEE (2016)
29. Peiris, H., Chen, Z., Egan, G., Harandi, M.: Reciprocal adversarial learning for brain tumor segmentation: a solution to brats challenge 2021 segmentation task. In: Crimi, A., Bakas, S. (eds.) Brainlesion: Glioma, Multiple Sclerosis, Stroke and Traumatic Brain Injuries: 7th International Workshop, BrainLes 2021, Held in Conjunction with MICCAI 2021, Virtual Event, September 27, 2021, Revised Selected Papers, Part I, pp. 171–181. Springer International Publishing, Cham (2022)
30. Lu, H., Yang, R., Deng, Z., Zhang, Y., Gao, G., Lan, R.: Chinese image captioning via fuzzy attention-based DenseNet-BiLSTM. ACM Trans. Multimed. Comput. Commun. Appl. **17**(1s), 1–18 (2021)
31. Lu, H., Zhang, Y., Li, Y., Jiang, C., Abbas, H.: User-oriented virtual mobile network resource management for vehicle communications. IEEE Trans. Intell. Transp. Syst. (2020). https://doi.org/10.1109/TITS.2020.2991766
32. Lu, H., Qin, M., Zhang, F., et al.: RSCNN: a CNN-based method to enhance low-light remote-sensing images. Remote Sens. **13**(1), 62 (2020)
33. Lu, H., Zhang, M., Xu, X.: Deep fuzzy hashing network for efficient image retrieval. IEEE Trans. Fuzzy Syst. (2020). https://doi.org/10.1109/TFUZZ.2020.2984991
34. Li, Y., Yang, S., Zheng, Y., Lu, H.: Improved point-voxel region convolutional neural network: 3D object detectors for autonomous driving. IEEE Trans. Intell. Trans. Syst. **23**(7), 9377–9317 (2021)

Linear Split Attention for Pavement Crack Detection

Guoliang Yan[✉] and Chenyin Ni

Nanjing University of Science and Technology, Nanjing, Jiangsu 210094, China
y731784849@163.com

Abstract. The number of vehicles is increasing rapidly, the road is aging faster than ever, cracks are an early manifestation of road aging. To avoid high maintenance costs, this method was designed for realizing early detection of various cracks on the surface of pavement, which are mostly made of concrete, asphalt and other materials. To improve the accuracy of crack detection, this paper slightly modifies the backbone network vgg16 to retain the crack features in the depth information. We designed Linear Split Attention Module (LSAM) to extract more location information and linear features from deep feature map. Multi-scale Feature Fusion module (MFFM) was designed for last layer to capture higher information features and make connections with low level features. Then different upsample methods are used in high-level and low-level convolutional layer to improve the position ability for crack pixels. Finally, compared with the other 5 methods in two datasets, prediction results of this method on DeepCrack dataset have an overall improvement of 1%–2.5%. Recall of this method on CrackForest dataset is 2.2% higher than traditional method.

Keywords: Crack detection · Deep learning · Linear split attention · Multi-scale feature fusion

1 Introduction

Cracks are one early sign of a variety of road damage types that can shorten the road's useful life and render it incapable of supporting large loads. It is crucial to promptly identify and fix road cracks since they can endanger pedestrians and traffic safety. Traditional manual survey techniques typically need labor at the target site, which can be slowed down by keeping the road closed to traffic. In addition, since manual detection is common, human error may have a detrimental effect on evaluation outcomes. Because of its quick speed, practical detection method, and low cost, digital image processing-based fracture detection technology has replaced human survey. The detection accuracy is currently not very high because the standard digital image processing algorithm design depends on the designer's experience. Accurate crack identification is quite challenging due to the complicated environment, as well as the difficulty of gathering fracture texture data.

Deep learning is widely utilized in the area of autonomous image processing, fortunately, and is much more accurate than conventional image processing techniques in

© The Author(s), under exclusive license to Springer Nature Singapore Pte Ltd. 2022
S. Yang and H. Lu (Eds.): ISAIR 2022, CCIS 1701, pp. 66–80, 2022.
https://doi.org/10.1007/978-981-19-7943-9_6

areas like shadow detection and face detection. This is thanks to the rapid growth of machine learning. The vast majority of crack identification jobs use supervised learning. Convoluted Neural Networks (CNN) are used in supervised learning to execute a crack detection job, matching each training input with a labeled output. The neural network model is optimized so that the input can be predicted later by changing the parameters of each node. In the task of monitoring and learning to detect cracks, there are two methods: mesh recognition and pixel segmentation. They split the picture lattice into numerous blocks and categorise each one in order to find fractures at the beginning of the detection development process, like in the 1993 article [1]. However, this approach is too crude to identify cracks; it can only precisely identify the position of cracks, not their exact profile. As a result of its high accuracy prediction capability, pixelated segmentation crack has emerged as the most active detection technique in this area. U-Net was applied by Cheng et al. [2] on complete Crack pictures to successfully forecast fractures. However, the network struggles when faced with multi-target identification and pays little attention to deep information. SegNet design has been used by Zou et al. to construct a novel encoder-decoder [3]. Its drawbacks include poor crack edge prediction accuracy and inadequate predictive placement capabilities. A deep-supervised encoderdecoder architecture [4] is created for the deep feature extraction issue that can handle the training of various feature levels and multi-scale feature fusion. May enhance fracture detection skills in addition to attention methods and residual modules [5]. However, the operational memory is increased by the blind addition of the attention mechanism, which makes the deep supervision network ineffective. Supersamples and structure employing encoders were proven to be quicker and more efficient by Liu et al. [6]. However, this structure missed a lot of deep information, overlooked the specifics of high-level and low-level information, and the inaccurate localization of crack from the whole network.

In summary, our proposed a linear split attention for pavement crack detection has the following contributions:

we take vgg16 [7] as the backbone network, eliminates the pool operation after the last convolution layer and the full connection layer operation, which can improve the efficiency and recoverthe loss of deep information.

we desigin Linear Split Attention Module (LSAM) to focusing on the crack pixels along the two dimensions of channel and space, which can improve the localization of crack and reduce noise interference. Then we desigin Multiscale Feature Fusion module (MFFM) to enhance the ability of deep information feature extraction, strengthening the connection between high level features and low level features. Because the low level feature information is missing less, the two modules are only used to extract the deep feature information, which can improve the efficiency of the whole network and avoid taking up too much operating memory.

According to the particularity of high level feature information and low level feature information, we optimize the upsample module, and different upper adoption methods are used in high-level and low-level convolutional layer. Prediction accuracy of whole network can be improved by combining with deep supervision.

The rest of this paper is organized as follows. Section 2 introduces the related work. In Sect. 3, we introduce the proposed deep convolutional neural network architecture.

Section 4 gives the experimental results and discusses the performance of the results. Section 5 draws the conclusion for this paper.

2 Related Work

2.1 Traditional Methods

Image processing and conventional machine vision are examples of classic detection techniques. For image processing to achieve crack detection, the crack image must first be captured by a camera. The data must then be uploaded to a computer for prepro-cessing. The crack image's features must then be manually extracted and the crack's recognition achieved using techniques like histogram estimation [8, 28, 29], trapezoidal histogram [9], local binary mode [10], Gabor filter [11], and multi-feature fusion [12]. Although under ideal circumstances these approaches can effectively identify cracks, the actual operation will be impacted by the fissures' surrounding environment, such as uneven illumination and noise interference. The latter makes use of machine vision technologies, including basic video capture and image inspection [13], a lidar scanner [14], and ultrasonic detection [15], to collect crack data. While employing 3D data in the form of 2D photos, video, or point clouds makes the detection process more chal-lenging, these systems can nonetheless automatically detect fissures in road surfaces. The development of more potent hardware and software tools has accelerated research into machine learning algorithms in the field of computer vision, and more researchers are now studying the semantic segmentation crack detection based on Deep Learning [30–32].

2.2 Deep Learning Based Methods

Based on deep learning semantic segmentation, there are two different types of frac-ture detection techniques. One method is to identify the pixel by taking into account how it relates to the pixels around it. For pixels, this is a two-category issue [16]. This approach requires an excessive amount of operational memory and is difficult to train because to the enormous number of pixels in the image. Another strategy is to begin with the entire image. As coders, network models like FCN [17] and SegNet [18] are frequently employed. To decrypt the deep feature information, Zou et al. [3] constructed a SegNet encoder decoder framework and had success on the dataset. CrackSeg is a deep-convolution neural network that Song et al. [19] devised. It is more effective at automatically detecting advanced characteristics in pictures. To solve the imbalance of contextual information during detection [26, 27, 33, 34], Yang et al. [20] suggested the topology of the Feature Pyramid Hierarchical Boost Network (FPHBN), which lever-ages edge detection HED [21] as its backbone network to enable automatic end-to-end crack detection. In order to improve the ability to detect cracks and strengthen the con-nection between the high level layer and low level layer, this paper summarises the prior experience by using Vgg16 as the network's backbone and adding LSAM atten-tional mechanism and MFFM linear multi-scale sensing field modules in the deep layer. Last but not least, the network's upsample module is tuned to record and restore the information typically lost during bilinear interpolation.

3 Proposed Method

3.1 Model Architecture

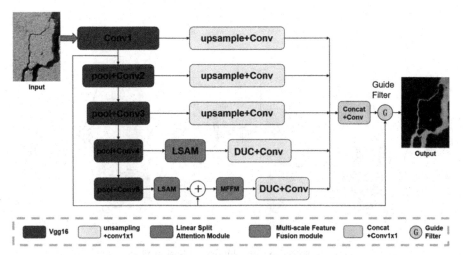

Fig. 1. The suggested network's basic architecture is made up of the following components: LSAM, MFFM, an upsample module, and guided filtering. To get additional linear characteristics and localization data, LSAM is suggested. To improve the contextual relationship and acquire deeper characteristics, MFFM is offered. Only bilinear interpolation is utilised as an upsample at low values. Here, the DUC is employed as an upsample due to the high level. Each measured output is then combined, and guided filtering is employed to improve the forecast.

Vgg16 is utilised as the primary component of the network structure in this study. Only the pool operation following the last convolution layer and the whole connection layer are removed from the structure, as seen in Fig. 1. The feature map is recovered to its original size using sample operation on bilinear interpolation after the first, second, and third layers have been convolutioned. We employ LSAM and MFFM to extract the linear features, position information, and channel information of fractures in the fourth and fifth layers after the fourth and fifth layers have been convolutioned. Then, we sample the deep layer's features using DUC [22] and restore them to their original size. After the final sampling operation, each layer is exposed to a loss function to modify its model parameters using the knowledge gained by the deep supervision network DSN [23]. A guidance filter is then applied here [24]. Each layer's output is combined, and the first convolution layer's output serves as the guide image for the guide filter. Finally, we may obtain the prediction result for each pixel in the picture by adjusting the weight of each layer and other network parameters.

Utilizing LSAM in the final two layers will enable us to concentrate on the crack pixels along the channel and spatial dimensions, improving crack localization and lowering noise interference. In order to improve the ability of deep information feature extraction and strengthen the connection between high level and low level features, MFFM must be added as the final layer after LSAM. After employing LSAM and MFFM, we should switch to using DUC and a different upsample approach.

3.2 Linear Split Attention Module

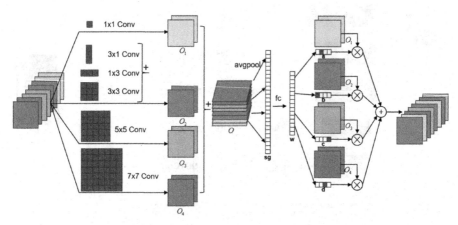

Fig. 2. Selective Convolution and Fusion Model

The attentional process that has been investigated only applies to the network as a whole; adding without considering the consequences would increase operational memory and reduce the network's ability to forecast outcomes accurately. Therefore, there haven't been many research to enhance deep feature extraction's capabilities. Therefore, starting with the Selective Convolution and Fusion Model (SFM), with the module specifics provided in Fig. 2, this research has built an attention mechanism LSAM that focuses on deep spatial and channel information.

The mission of the SFM module is to focus on channel characteristics in deep feature maps. First, the input feature map is passed through convolution layers of different scales. The length of the feature map is H, the width is W and the number of channels is C. where, Conv1 uses the convolution layer of 1×1 with an output of O_1; Conv2 is to pass through the convolution layers of $1 \times 3, 3 \times 1$, and 3×3 respectively and fuse them into output O_2, and pass through the convolution of 1×3 and 3×1 respectively to become more sensitive to the linear features of the convolution. Conv3 uses 5×5 convolution layers with output of O_3; Conv4 uses the convolution layer of 7×7. A dense sampling layer of feature map information can be implemented with output of O_4. Finally, the characteristic mosaic of four convolution layers with different scales is output as O. The feature map O of the mosaic output is Golbal Average Pooling and the information is embedded in the vector sg, which has a length of C and a formula such as o below:

$$sg = \frac{1}{H \times W} \sum_{i=1}^{H} \sum_{j=1}^{W} O(i,j) \tag{1}$$

Vector sg is then reduced in size and refined through the full connection layer to improve efficiency, and the output is defined as w:

$$w = fc(sg) = \text{relu}\big(B\big(W_{sg}\big)\big) \tag{2}$$

where fc is the full connection layer formula. *Relu* is the activation function. B is the normalized BN layer in the algorithm. W is the matrix, whose dimension is $d \times C$ and due to the full connection operation, the dimension of w of the output fc is $d \times 1$, which is defined as follows:

$$d = \max\left(\frac{C}{r}, 32\right) \tag{3}$$

where C is for the number of channels in the feature map, r is for the re- duction dimension ratio, and d is restricted to 32 when the channel after the reduction dimension is less than 32.

After the above operations, four smooth attention vectors a, b, c and d can be obtained to determine the results of convolution layers of different scales. Assume that channel k of the feature map corresponds to the a_k, b_k, c_k, d_k elements of the four attention vectors, and that the weighted combination of the channel is Y_k. The final output Y can be obtained by combining the weighted combinations of each channel as follows:

$$1 = a + b + c + d \tag{4}$$

$$Y_k = a_k O_{1,k} + b_k O_{2,k} + c_k O_{3,k} + d_k O_{4,k} \tag{5}$$

$$Y = [Y_1, Y_2, \cdots, Y_C] \tag{6}$$

where $O_{1,k}$ is the output of the first convolution layer of the module when the channel is k. The dimension of Y_k is $H \times W$. The dimension of Y is $H \times W \times C$.

As shown in Fig. 3, the input characteristic map X is weighted after passing through the SFM module and the output is $Z = X \times Y$. The subsequent oper- ation is similar to that of the SFM module, in which the feature Z is averaged and maximized, respectively, and then each pixel is summed up and fed into a convoluted layer with a core of 7×7. This operation reduces the feature to a single 1-channel number and generates spatial features Y_s through the sigmoid activation function. The overall formula is as follows:

$$Y_s = \text{sigmoid}\big(\text{Conv}_{7 \times 7}\big([\text{avgpool}(Z) + \text{maxpool}(Z)]\big)\big) \tag{7}$$

Finally, the input Z is weighted with the generated spatial features Y_s to obtain the final generated features.

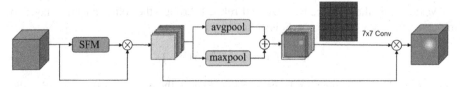

Fig. 3. Linear split attention module

3.3 Multi-scale Feature Fusion Module

With the deepening of the network, the positioning performance in areas with weak recognition, the resolution of feature images will decrease continuously as the network deepens, and the location performance will gradually decline. Based on dilated convolution, we can set different dilated rates to obtain multi-scale semantic feature information by, and improve the ability of network to locate and identify target areas. It can increase the effective information around the target by expanding the receptive domain of convolution kernel, and improves the target areas with weak recognition ability. By operating the convolutions in a cascade way, not only can obtain the position mapping of the target, but also the target area with weak recognition ability can be accurately located.

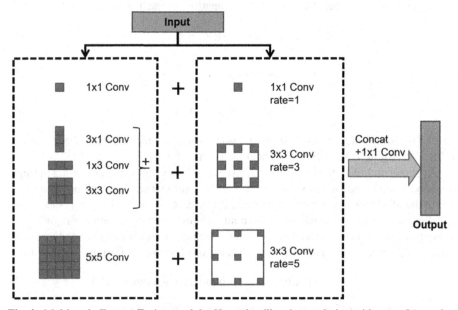

Fig. 4. Multi-scale Feature Fusion module. Here, the dilated convolution with rate of 1 can be regarded as a the 1 × 1 convolution.

We add MFFM to the backbone after the final layer of the network passes through the attentional mechanism LSAM to increase the network's sensory field, allowing for more high level feature and low level feature connections because the backbone network Vgg16 has a shallower receptive field than theoretical val- ues. The MFFM structure, as shown in Fig. 4, is a parallel mosaic of multi-scale sensory field modules. First, the input is divided into three convolution cores with different convolution rates. The process of operation is that the input char- acteristic map is passed through the 1×1 convolution and the dilated convolution with rate of 1, respectively, and the result is spliced into D_1. At the same time, the input feature passed through 1×3 convolution, 3×1 convolution and 3×3convolution and the 3×3 dilated convolution with rate of 3, respectively, and the result was patched out as D_2. At the same time, the input feature map was divided into 5×5 convolution and the 3×3 dilated convolution with rate of 5, and the output was spliced into D_3. Finally, the output of three different paths was combined into a convolution with a kernel of 1×1.

As the comparison before and after adding MFFM in the fifth layer shown in Fig. 5. After adding MFFM, we can see the ability of locating crack pixels is obviously improved, the detailed information is richer and the edge of crack is clearer.

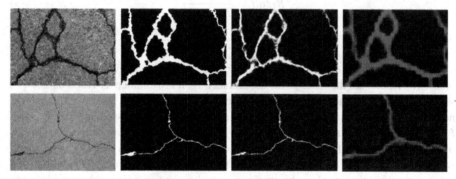

Fig. 5. The effect comparison before and after adding MFFM. (a) input (b) GT (c) sideoutput5 after using MFFM (d) sideoutput5 before using MFFM.

4 Experimental Result and Analysis

4.1 Experimental Setting

This chapter conducted network training and experiments on a computer with an NVIDIA GeForce 2080Ti GPU with I9900K performance and 32 gigabytes of RAM. The version of Python is 3.6, with Pytorch, and others using default settings. The parameters of network tuning are an initial learning rate of 1e−4, an adaptive learning rate of 1/5, the loss weight for each side output layer and final fusion layer is 1.0, and a weight attenuation of 2e−4. The momentum is 0.9.

5 Dataset Introduction

Two crack datasets are used. Deepcrack [6] and CrackForest [25] datasets. Deep- crack is a manually annotated multi-scale and multi-scenario public infrastruc- ture dataset.

The dataset consisted of 537 RGB color images, of which 300 were selected for training and the rest for testing with CrackForest. CrackForest is a collection of 118 480 320 images, each with a hand-drawn realistic outline. Data augmentation is a key technique in deep learning networks. Rotation parameters are set to 0, 45, 90, etc., up to 360°, with each rotation separated by 45° and the largest rectangle cut out; Horizontal flip of the above rotated image. In all, the dataset were augmented by 16 times.

6　Evaluation Metrics

To assess network performance, six metrics were used: *Precision, recall, F 1Score, ttlobalaccessibility, Classaverageaccessibility*, and *MeanIU*.

$$Precision = \frac{TP}{TP + FP} \tag{8}$$

$$Recall = \frac{TP}{TP + FN} \tag{9}$$

$$F1score = \frac{2 * (Precision * Recall)}{(Precision + Recall)} \tag{10}$$

When the prediction is positive and the true value is positive, that is, when the prediction results are the same as the actual labeling, it is evaluated as True Positive *TP*; When the predicted value is positive and the true value results in negative, that is, it is not actually a crack but is mistakenly predicted as a crack, assessed as False Positive *FP*; When the predictive value is negative and the true value is positive, the broken pixel cannot be identified and the system mistakenly treats it as a background pixel, which is assessed as False Negative *FN*; When the prediction is negative and the true value is negative, that is, when the prediction matches the true value without a crack, the assessment is True Negative *TN*.

$$\text{Global accuracy (G)} = \frac{\sum_i n_{ii}}{\sum_i t_i} \tag{11}$$

$$\text{Global average accuracy (C)} = \frac{(1/n_{cls}) \sum_i n_{ii}}{t_i} \tag{12}$$

$$\text{MeanIU (MIU)} = \frac{(1/n_{cls}) \sum_i n_{ii}}{\left(t_i + \sum_j n_{ji} - n_{ii}\right)} \tag{13}$$

where N_{ij} is the number of pixels predicted as j for the i class, which has $n_c ls$ in different classes, and $t_i = \Sigma_j n_{ii}$ is the total number of pixels for the i class (true positive and includes misinformation).

$$TPR(TruePositiveRate) = \frac{TP}{TP + FN} \tag{14}$$

$$FPR(FalsePositiveRate) = \frac{FP}{TN + FP} \tag{15}$$

At last, we use a classical metric Receiver Operating Characteristic (ROC) curve. For the ROC curve, we calculate three metrics TPR, FPR and AUC is the area under the ROC Curve.

7 Evaluation on Image Datasets

The network in this chapter compared five of the best experimental methods in the DeepCrack and CrackForest datasets with crack detection, DeepCrack [6], SegNet [18], CrackSeg [19], FPHBN [20], and HED [21]. Table 1 predicted the results of the DeepCrack experiment and Table 2 predicted the results of the CrackForest experiment.

In the above two tables, the optimal data of crack detection method compared with other methods are put forward. You can see an overall improvement in the assessment on the DeepCrack dataset. These metrics results are shown in Table 1. On DeepCrack dataset Precision of Our method reaches 87.5%, Recall reaches 86.3%, F-score reaches 86.9%, and MIOU reaches 87.8%, it outperforms DeepCrack, the second best.

Then we verify the crack detection ability of our methods in another environments, we test the network model on CrackForest dataset. The results are shown in Table 2. Comparing with the second highest result, the Recall, GAccuracy, CAccuracy of our method are improved by 2.2%, 0.1% and 1.5% respectively. The results show that our proposed network model has good generalization ability.

Fracture prediction maps of various fracture detection methods are shown in Fig. 6. By comparing the results of different prediction methods, it can beclearly observed that the fracture detection methods in this paper can accurately predict the fracture maps in different complex environments. It can be seen that CrackSeg is seriously disturbed by noise, and the anti-noise performance of this paper is good, not only can correctly point out the location of the crack area, but also can accurately generate the crack boundary.

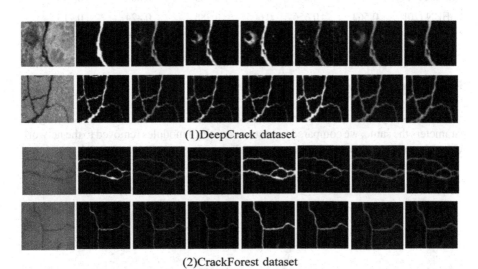

(1)DeepCrack dataset

(2)CrackForest dataset

Fig. 6. The visualization results of different crack detection methods are obtained in two datasets.

Table 1. The evaluation metrics of competing methods on Deepcrack dataset.

DeepCrack

Methods	Precision	Recall	F-score	GAccuracy	CAccuracy	Mean IOU
DeepCrack [6]	0.850	0.850	0.850	0.987	0.922	0.863
HED [21]	0.825	0.838	0.746	0.986	0.922	0.853
SegNet [18]	0.733	0.693	0.712	0.980	0.877	0.800
CrackSeg [19]	0.789	0.813	0.801	0.983	0.900	0.825
FPHBN [20]	0.827	0.766	0.796	0.988	0.884	0.824
Ours	0.875	0.863	0.869	0.989	0.931	0.878

Table 2. The evaluation metrics of competing methods on Crackforest dataset.

Crackforest

Methods	Precision	Recall	F-score	GAccuracy	CAccuracy	Mean IOU
DeepCrack [6]	0.558	0.664	0.601	0.988	0.822	0.712
HED [21]	0.520	0.635	0.572	0.985	0.813	0.692
SegNet [18]	0.710	0.658	0.683	0.979	0.820	0.749
CrackSeg [19]	0.506	0.648	0.568	0.985	0.800	0.690
FPHBN [20]	0.562	0.656	0.605	0.986	0.824	0.710
Ours	0.622	0.686	0.652	0.989	0.839	0.736

8 Ablation Studies

In order to study the effectiveness of LSAM and MFFM in this network. Keeping all parameters the same, we compared the network with all modules removed to the network with only some modules added, and the results are shown in Tables 3 and 4.

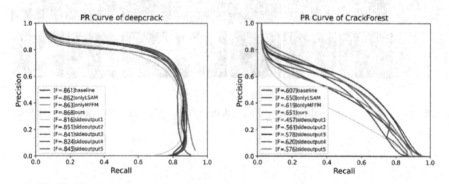

Fig. 7. The Precision-Recall (PR) curve for crack segmentation on two database

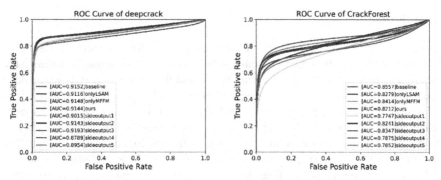

Fig. 8. The ROC curve for crack segmentation on two database.

It performed better than either LSAM or MFFM alone to combine the two. It is clear that the two modules do not limit one another but rather improve the network's crack detection ability, enabling the network to identify more varieties of fractures in situations with more complexity. The MFFM module additionally gives deep location information, linear edge characteristics, and contextual connections, whereas the LSAM attentional mechanism just provides rough position and edge information. The ROC metrics and PR metrics are shown in Figs. 7 and 8. Though there are only small differences in the curve, our strategy achieves the better performances than baseline.

Table 3. Ablation analyze for the proposed architecture on DeepCrack dataset.

DeepCrack						
Methods	Precision	Recall	F-score	GAccuracy	CAccuracy	Mean IOU
baseline	0.8637	0.8593	0.8615	0.9880	0.9266	0.8721
onlyLSAM	0.8634	0.8619	0.8627	0.9881	0.9279	0.8731
onlyMFFM	0.8739	0.8529	0.8633	0.9883	0.9237	0.8737
LSAM + MFFM	0.8747	0.8622	0.8684	0.9886	0.9307	0.8778

Table 4. Ablation analyze for the proposed architecture on CrackForest dataset.

CrackForest						
Methods	Precision	Recall	F-score	GAccuracy	CAccuracy	Mean IOU
baseline	0.5588	0.6666	0.6079	0.9861	0.8290	0.7113
onlyLSAM	0.6187	0.6855	0.6504	0.9881	0.8393	0.7350
onlyMFFM	0.5816	0.6628	0.6196	0.9868	0.8275	0.7178
LSAM + MFFM	0.6216	0.6855	0.6519	0.9882	0.8393	0.7358

9   Conclusions

Our work contributes to the idea of a linear split attention for pavement fracture identification that can partition the fine-grained crack areas in pixel terms. To enhance the extraction of position and edge information, we add the attention module to the deep feature map. Then, to enhance the deep orientation and edge linearity characteristic and increase the relationship between high-level and lowlevel, we create a linear multiscale sensing field module. In order to increase the network's detection precision and operational effectiveness, we additionally optimise the upsampling module and employ several upsampling techniques in both the high-level and low-level convolutional layers. Finally, the experimental findings demonstrate that our technique outperforms other cutting-edge fracture identification methods in dataset. The LSAM and MFFM modules can both boost the underlying network's predictive ability, according to ablation studies. The usefulness of the suggested strategy is demonstrated by experiments on two datasets, which also show that it outperforms other methods in terms of detection accuracy. We intend to develop a more effective approach in the future to improve network performance and achieve accurate automatic crack detection. We also need to develop a Data Augmentation plan due to the dearth and unreliability of datasets. To satisfy the demands of real-time detection, the network must, meanwhile, speed up crack detection. Therefore, our future equipment needs higher memory than 2080ti, and also need hardware knowledge.

References

1. Kaseko, M.S., Ritchie, S.G.: A neural network-based methodology for pavement crack detection and classification. Transp. Res. C Emerg. Technol. 1(4), 275–291 (1993)
2. Jenkins, M.D., Carr, T.A., Iglesias, M.I., Buggy, T., Morison, G.: A deep convolutional neural network for semantic pixel-wise segmentation of road and pavement surface cracks. In: European Signal Processing Conference, pp. 2120–2124. IEEE, New York (2018)
3. Zou, Q., Zhang, Z., Li, Q., Qi, X., Wang, Q., Wang, S.: DeepCrack: Learning hierarchical convolutional features for crack detection. IEEE Trans. Image Process. 28, 1498–1512 (2018)
4. Qu, Z., Cao, C., Liu, L., Zhou, D.Y.: A deeply supervised convolutional neural net-work for pavement crack detection with multiscale feature fusion. In: IEEE Transactions on Neural Networks and Learning Systems (2021)
5. Qu, Z., Chen, W., Wang, S. Y., Yi, T. M., Liu, L.: A crack detection algorithm for concrete pavement based on attention mechanism and multi-features fusion. In: IEEE Transactions on Intelligent Transportation Systems (2021)
6. Liu, Y., Yao, J., Lu, X., Xie, R., Li, L.: DeepCrack: A deep hierarchical feature learning architecture for crack segmentation. Neurocomputing 338, 139–153 (2019)
7. Simonyan, K., Zisserman, A.: Very deep convolutional networks for largescale image recognition. In: International Conference on Learning Representations (ICLR) (2015)
8. Zhigang, X., Xiangmo, Z., Huansheng, S., et al.: Asphalt pavement crack recognition algorithm based on histogram estimation and shape analysis. Chin. J. Sci. Instrum. 31(10), 2260–2266 (2010)
9. Huazhong, J., Fang, W., Zhiwei, Y.: Pavement crack detection fused HOG and watershed algorithm of range image. J. Cent. China Norm. Univ. Nat. Sci. 51(5) 715–722 (2017)
10. Quintana, M., Torres, J., Menendez, J.M.: A simplified computer vision system for road surface inspection and maintenance. IEEE Trans. Intell. Transp. Syst. 17(3), 608–619 (2016)

11. Medina, R., Llamas, J., Zalama, E. et al.: Enhanced automatic detection of road surface cracks by combining 2D/3D image processing techniques. In: Proceedings of the IEEE International Conference on Image Processing, pp. 778–782. IEEE Computer Society Press, Los Alamitos (2014)

12. Wei, X., Zhenmin, T., Dan, X., et al.: Integrating multi-features fusion and gestalt principles for pavement crack detection. J. Comput.-Aid Des. Comput. Graph. **27**(1), 147–156(2015)

13. Sony, S., Laventure, S., Sadhu, A.: A literature review of nextgeneration smart sensing technology in structural health monitoring. Struct. Control Health Monitor. **26**(3), e2321(2019)

14. Riveiro, B., DeJong, M., Conde, B.: Automated processing of large point clouds for structural health monitoring of masonry arch bridges. Autom. Constr. **72**, 258–268 (2016)

15. Mutlib, N.K., Baharom, S.B., El-Shafie, A., Nuawi, M.Z.: Ultrasonic health monitoring in structural engineering: buildings and bridges. Struct. Control Health Monitor. **23**(3), 409–422 (2016)

16. Fan, Z, Wu, Y.M., Lu, J.W., et al.: Automatic pavement crack detection based on structured prediction with the convolutional neural network (2019). org/abs/1802. 02208

17. Shelhamer, E., Long, J., Darrell, T.: Fully convolutional networks for semantic segmentation. IEEE Trans. Pattern Anal. Mach. Intell. **39**(4), 640–651 (2017)

18. Badrinarayanan, V., Kendall, A., Cipolla, R.: SegNet: A deep convolutional encoder-decoder architecture for image segmentation. IEEE Trans. Pattern Anal. Mach. **39**(12), 2481–2495 (2017)

19. Song, W., Jia, G., Zhu, H., Jia, D., Gao, L.: Automated pavement crack damage detection using deep multi-scale convolutional features. Hindawi J. Adv. Transport. Jan. **2020**, 11 (2020)

20. Yang, F., Zhang, L., Yu, S., Prokhorov, D., Mei, X., Ling, H.: Feature pyramid and hierarchical boosting network for pavement crack detection. IEEE Trans. Intell. Transp. Syst. **21**(4), 1525–1535 (2020)

21. Xie, S., Tu, Z.: Holistically-nested edge detection. In: Proceedings of IEEE International Conference Computer Vision (ICCV), Santiago, pp. 1395–1403 (2015)

22. Panqu, W., Pengfei Chen, Y.Y., et al.: Understanding convolution for semantic segmentation. In: IEEE Winter Conference on Applications of Computer Vision (WACV), pp. 13–21 (2018)

23. Lee, C. Y., Xie, S., Gallagher, P., Zhang, Z., Tu, Z.: Deeply-supervised nets. In: Proceedings of the AISTATS, p. 6 (2015)

24. He, K., Sun, J., Tang, X.: Guided image filtering. In: IEEE Trans. Pattern Anal. Intell. Mach. **35**(6) 1397–1409 (2013)

25. Dollar, P., Zitnick, L.C.: Structured forests for fast edge detection. In: Proceedings of IEEE International Conference Computer Vision (ICCV), Sydney, pp. 1841–1848 (2013)

26. Deep Fuzzy Hashing Network for Efficient Image Retrieval: IEEE Trans. Fuzzy Syst. (2020). https://doi.org/10.1109/TFUZZ.2020.2984991

27. Visual information processing for deep-sea visual monitoring system: Cogn. Robot. **1**, 3–11 (2021)

28. Brain Intelligence: Go beyond artificial intelligence. Mob. Netw. Appl. **23**(2), 368–375 (2018)

29. WideSegNeXt: Semantic image segmentation using wide residual network and NeXt dilated unit. IEEE Sens. J. (2021)

30. Global-PBNet: A novel point cloud registration for autonomous driving. In: IEEE Transactions on Intelligent Transportation Systems (2022)

31. Multifeature fusion-based object detection for intelligent transportation systems. In: IEEE Transactions on Intelligent Transportation Systems (2022)

32. Cross-Modal Common Representations by Private-Shared Subspaces Separation. In: IEEE Transactions on Cybernetics (2020)

33. DRRS-BC: Decentralized Routing Registration System Based on Blockchain. IEEE/CAA J. Automat. Sin. (2020)

34. Cross-Modal Attention with Semantic Consistence for Image-Text Matching. In: IEEE Transactions on Neural Networks and Learning Systems (2020)
35. Lu, H., Yang, R., Deng, Z., Zhang, Y., Gao, G., Lan, R.: Chinese image captioning via fuzzy attention-based DenseNet-BiLSTM. ACM Trans. Multim. Comput. Commun. Appl. **17**(1s), 1–18 (2021)
36. Lu, H., Zhang, Y., Li, Y., Jiang, C., Abbas, H.: User-oriented virtual mobile network resource management for vehicle communications. IEEE Trans. Intell. Transp. Syst. **10**, 2991766 (2020)
37. Lu, H., Qin, M., Zhang, F., et al.: RSCNN: A CNN-based method to enhance low-light remote-sensing images. In: Remote Sensing, p. 62 (2020)
38. Lu, H., Zhang, M., Xu, X.: Deep fuzzy hashing network for efficient image retrieval. In: IEEE Transactions on Fuzzy Systems (2020)
39. Li, Y., Yang, S., Zheng, Y., Lu, H.: Improved point-voxel region convolutional neural network: 3D object detectors for autonomous driving. In: IEEE Transactions on Intelligent Transportation Systems (2021)

Information Acquisition and Feature Extraction
of Motor Imagery EEG

Chen Ma and Mei Wang[✉]

Xi'an University of Science and Technology, Xi'an 710054, China
wangm@xust.edu.cn

Abstract. Brain-computer interface (BCI) is a new interaction model that directly connects the human brain or animal brain with external devices, which has a wide range of application scenarios. Through the BCI technology based on electroencephalography (EEG) signal, the communication and control of external devices can be realized independently of the peripheral nervous system and muscle tissue. Motor imagery (MI) is a process in which people imagine their limbs or muscles moving, to control some external auxiliary devices (wheelchairs, robotic arms, robots etc.) so that people without motor ability can restore their communication and motor ability to a certain extent. In this paper, the basic situation of EEG and EEG signal acquisition is introduced first. Then, the analysis methods and research contents of EEG signal preprocessing, feature extraction, and feature classification based on motor imagery are introduced in detail. Finally, the brain-computer interface technology based on motor imagery is summarized and prospected.

Keywords: Brain-computer Interface (BCI) · Motor Imagery (MI) · EEG signals · Feature extraction

1 Introduction

Brain-computer interface (BCI), also known as brain-computer fusion sense, is a means of communication between a human or animal brain and an external auxiliary device. Using this communication technology, the control and interaction of external auxiliary devices can be realized without the help of the brain nervous system and muscle tissue [1], Nicolas [2] define this as a hardware and software communication strategy.

There are many classification methods for BCI. Figure 1 illustrates four classification schemes, which are classified according to the direction of control, dependability, recording method, and operation method respectively. According to the direction of control, it can be divided into unidirectional BCI and bidirectional BCI. In a unidirectional BCI, only one end can send instructions to the other end at the same time. For example, the brain sends instructions to an external auxiliary device, or an external device sends instructions to the brain. Bidirectional BCI allows two-way information exchange between the brain and external devices. At present, the research on BCI is mainly on unidirectional BCI, and can only realize the brain sends instructions to external auxiliary devices.

S. Yang and H. Lu (Eds.): ISAIR 2022, CCIS 1701, pp. 81–94, 2022.
https://doi.org/10.1007/978-981-19-7943-9_7

According to dependability, it can be classified into dependent BCI and independent BCI. Dependent BCI requires subjects to carry out some form of motor control, such as visual evoked control and motor imagery control, which has been widely used. Independent BCI, which does not require subject control, is ideal for patients with eye movement disorders or severe physical paralysis. Tello [3] proposed a novel independent BCI based on conventional steady-state visual evoked potentials, they use figure-ground perception to identify two different targets, send commands in limited visual space without shifting eyes, and proved to be effective.

According to the recording method, it can be divided into non-invasive BCI and invasive BCI. Non-invasive BCI involves placing physical electrodes to collect electrical signals on the scalp, and invasive BCI involves placing physical electrodes into the skull. Invasive BCI requires physical electrodes to be surgically implanted in different parts of the brain and has the characteristics of strong signal acquisition, stable signal, and long duration. But with time, scar tissue is easy to produce, resulting in signal interference and loss. Although the signal of non-invasive BCI is not as strong and stable as that of invasive BCI, it does not harm the human body, there is no need to worry about immune effects on the human body. Common non-invasive methods include EEG, MEG, PET, functional magnetic resonance imaging, and functional near-infrared spectroscopy etc. Due to the advantages of non-invasive, easy to use, safe, easy to collect, and cost-effective, EEG is widely used and can induce SCP, SSVEP, MI, ERRP, P300, and other control signals [4].

Finally, according to whether the user depends on the time when operating the system, the BCI can be divided into synchronous BCI and asynchronous BCI. If the interaction is based on a prompt imposed by the system at some point in time, it is called asynchronous BCI. At this point, the brain activity is generated by the user. Based on this cue, it can be distinguished whether the neural activity generated by the user is intentional or unintentional [5]. Asynchronous BCI means that the user can generate a mental task to interact with the application at any time, regardless of time and system prompt. But asynchronous BCI needs to actively distinguish between intentional and unintentional neural activity generated by the user. The synchronous BCI system is simple in design but has many limitations. By comparison, synchronous BCI is not user-friendly.

Motor imagery (MI), one of the four main paradigms of BCI, focuses on controlling the movement of objects (such as the movement of hands, arms, or feet) through visual-motor imagery visualization. Unlike other paradigms, it primarily characterizes an intention to move, controls limb movement through neural activity and has no actual movement output, and does not require external stimulation [6]. When subjects imagine different limb movements, they generate EEG signals in the sensorimotor cortex of the brain that is similar to the actual signals, allowing researchers to determine the user's intention to achieve control of the limb by identifying the activation effects in different brain areas. 28-year-old paraplegic Giuliano Pinto successfully kicked off the World Cup in Brazil through MI-BCI.

The MI-BCI is important for the therapeutic recovery of stroke patients, people with motor disorders, severe muscle disorders, and paralysis etc., and this active motor rehabilitation training approach has been studied to effectively restore the function of impaired brain motor perceptual areas [7]. It also allows people with motor disabilities, cerebral palsy, and other mobility impairments to control some external assistive devices (such as wheelchairs, nursing beds, and robotic arms) through the MI paradigm to restore their ability to communicate and move to some extent.

The structure of this paper is as follows: Sect. 2 introduces the basic information about EEG signal and EEG signal acquisition; Sect. 3 introduces the pre-processing method of MI-EEG signal; Sect. 4 introduces the feature extraction method of MI-EEG signal; Sect. 5 introduces the feature classification method of MI-EEG signal; Sect. 6 makes a conclusion and outlook on the MI-BCI.

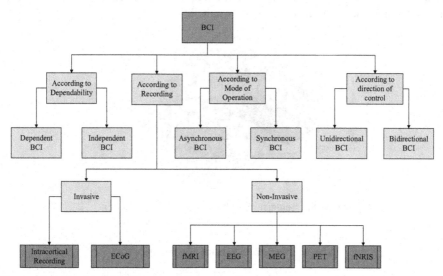

Fig. 1. Classification of BCI systems in terms of control direction, dependability, recording method, and mode of operation.

2 EEG Signals and Signals Acquisition

The EEG signals are the sum of the changes in extracellular field potentials caused by the electrophysiological activity of a large number of nerve cells in the brain in the cerebral cortex or on the surface of the scalp, and data on brain activity can be recorded using EEG acquisition equipment. EEG signal is generally classified as spontaneous EEG and evoked EEG [8], with spontaneous EEG being the spontaneous changes in extracellular field potentials induced by the brain's nervous system without any external stimuli applied, such as slow cortical potentials and sensorimotor rhythms. Evoked EEG is an external stimulus (such as sound, light, picture, video etc.) applied to a person's sensory organs that cause fluctuations in the nervous system of the brain which in turn causes potential changes in the corresponding parts of the brain, such as steady-state visual evoked potentials, visual evoked potentials, and P300.

The human brain is generally divided into the cerebral cortex and the subcortex, of which the cerebral cortex is generally the focus of scientists' research. It is the most central and complex region of the brain, controlling human emotions, memory, thinking, behavior, language, and other functions. The cerebral cortex is divided into two hemispheres, as shown in Fig. 2, each of which contains five parts: frontal, parietal, occipital, temporal lobes, and cerebellum [9]. With the advancement of science and technology, scientists have found that subjects in different mental states show different EEG signal characteristics, and EEG activity is closely related to the subject's emotion and thinking. Since the frequency domain signal of the EEG signal fluctuates more obviously, the fluctuation range is 0.5–0 Hz, so the EEG signal is divided into 5 bands δ wave, θ wave, α wave, β wave, and γ wave according to the frequency, and each band can reflect the different activity states of the brain, as shown in Table 1.

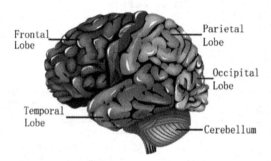

Fig. 2. Physiological Structure of the Cerebral Cortex.

Table 1. EEG characteristics of different bands.

Types	Area	Mental states and conditions
δ band (0.5–4 Hz)	Temporal lobe and parietal lobe	Deep sleep, unconscious
θ band (4–8 Hz)	Forehead position in adults and hindbrain position in infants	Intuitive, creative, recall, fantasy, imaginary, dream
α band (8–14 Hz)	Posterior part of the brain and both sides of the brain	Relaxed but not drowsy, tranquil, conscious
β band (14–30 Hz)	Both sides of the brain	Alert, thinking, and active concentration
γ band (>30 Hz)	In the sensory cortex of the body	Motor functions, higher mental activity

Acquiring EEG signals and accurately processing EEG information becomes the key to BCI. A complete EEG signal acquisition system consists of a signal acquisition cap, amplifier, and data storage device [10]. The electrodes of the signal acquisition cap can be divided into dry electrodes and wet electrodes. Dry electrodes are generally made of stainless steel as conductors, while the conductors of wet electrodes are usually made of silver and silver chloride materials. A comparison of dry electrode collection devices and wet electrode collection devices is shown in Table 2. Since both acquisition devices have their advantages and disadvantages, the appropriate device can be selected for EEG signal acquisition during the study according to the length of the experiment, laboratory environment, and other factors.

Table 2. Comparison table of dry electrode and wet electrode.

Name	Wet electrode	Dry electrode
Whether to add conductive media	Yes	No
Advantages	Stable acquired EEG signal, better signal-to-noise ratio, easy impedance drop, and high reliability. Less difficulty in subsequent EEG feature extraction	No need to add conductive media, the subject experience is good, easy to use and fast
Disadvantages	The conductive medium is easy to wear, becomes dry, and cannot collect signals for a long time, the subject experience is poor, and the experimental procedure of a wet electrode EEG cap is more complicated than that of a dry electrode	More sensors are needed, the quality of the acquired EEG signals is average, the reliability is poor, the impedance does not drop easily, there are artifact signals, and the subsequent EEG feature extraction is difficult

Table 3. Typical time domain feature extraction methods.

Reference	Method	Introduction
Rodríguez [19]	Auto-regressive (AR) modeling	AR models signal from each channel as a weighted combination of its previous samples and AR coefficients are used as features
Croz-Baron [20]	Adaptive autoregressive (AAR) modeling	As an extension of AR modeling, the coefficients in AAR are not constant and, in fact, vary with time
Adam [21] Yilmaz [22]	The peak-valley modeling	Represent the signal in terms of peaks (local maximum) and valleys (local minimum), various features points are extracted between neighboring peak and valley points

The current electrodes of EEG acquisition devices follow the international standard for placement of electrodes for the 10–20 system developed in 1958 [11], as shown in

Fig. 3. Where 10 represents the distance from the midpoint of the frontal pole to the root of the nose and the distance from the occipital point to the external occipital ridge each representing 10% of the total connecting distance, and 20 represents the distance between the remaining collection points representing 20% of the total distance. Since the EEG information collected by the EEG acquisition device is extremely weak, the collected signal needs to be amplified by an amplifier, which also reduces the effect of environmental noise and the weakening of the signal caused by cable movement. Finally, the collected EEG information is stored through storage devices such as mobile hard disks or Raspberry Pi.

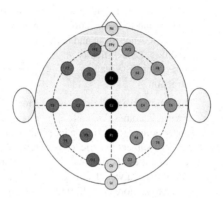

Fig. 3. International standard 10–20 EEG recording system electrode placement.

3   Preprocessing of MI-EEG Signals

To obtain effective EEG signals, signal processing usually consists of three parts: preprocessing, feature selection and extraction, and feature classification, which we will introduce in this section and the rest in the next two sections.

EEG signals collected with EEG acquisition equipment are usually mixed with many artifacts and noise. Artifacts are usually generated by the human body, such as eye artifacts, heart artifacts, muscle disorders etc. Noise is usually generated by equipment outside the human body, such as EEG acquisition equipment failure, poor electrode contact, electrode impedance, electromagnetic noise, power line interference etc. Noise and artifacts cause great obstacles to the analysis of EEG data, and the preprocessing of EEG signals based on MI-BCI system is to filter the original EEG signals mainly by using temporal filters and spatial filters to eliminate noise and artifacts to get signals with specific patterns [12, 13].

Temporal filters, which mainly include low-pass and band-pass filters, are the most commonly used in the preprocessing stage. Temporal filters mainly restrict the EEG signal to the frequency band where the neurophysiological information related to the cognitive task is located. For example, the signal will block the high frequency signal in the signal after passing through the low-pass filter (myoelectric or other noisy signals).

Signals in both the α band and the β band are usually closely related to the motor imagery task, so the band-pass filter is usually set in the MI task at a frequency of 8 to 30 Hz [14, 46].

The main function of the spatial filter is to extract the necessary spatial information related to the motion imagery task [15]. The common average reference (CAR) and the Laplacian spatial filter are two common spatial filters and are computationally inexpensive. The CAR mainly removes the common components from all channels, leaving only the channel-specific signals. The Laplace spatial filter is designed to remove the common components of adjacent signals, increasing the difference between channels.

4 Features Extraction and Analyses

Due to the multi-electrode and high sampling rate of EEG acquisition devices, a large amount of EEG data is generated every second species, but the vast majority of these data are non-valid. It is important to correctly distinguish the intentional neural activity (such as motor imagery task of a specific limb) and non-intentional neural activity (such as EEG, EMG) of the subjects to extract useful EEG information. Feature extraction is mainly the process of abstracting feature vectors that can strictly distinguish different thinking states from the pre-processed EEG signals, and removing non-valid data from the feature vectors to retain valid data. Feature extraction methods based on motion imagery can be broadly classified into: time domain methods, frequency domain methods, time-frequency domain methods, spatial domain methods, time-space domain methods, spatial spectrum methods etc. [16, 47].

4.1 Time Domain Methods

The EEG signal is an extremely weak and unstable signal, and its amplitude, frequency, period, and phase all change with the changes in the sensory motor rhythm, the EEG signal shows different characteristics at each moment. The time domain analysis method mainly extracts the EEG signal features at each time node from time, which is the earliest and most intuitive feature extraction method used, easy for people to understand, and can obtain both time domain and frequency-domain features. However, the algorithm is complex and computationally intensive, which is difficult to meet the real-time requirements of the BCI [17]. And the method is highly subjective, largely influenced by the analyst's thoughts, and it is often difficult to objectively evaluate EEG signals.

The time domain method first extracts and analyzes the EEG signals for every single channel, then fuses the features of all acquired channels into a large feature set and applies this feature set to a single motion imagery paradigm, Table 3 summarizes several commonly used methods employed for time domain feature extraction. To extract effective time domain features, the EEG signal needs to be digitally filtered to extract the values of the motor rhythm components in the frequency band of interest to the researcher, and then the energy values of the filtered frequency band power features are calculated. Mathematical statistical methods such as mean, root mean square, standard deviation, and variance are all widely used in MI task classification [18].

4.2   Frequency Domain Methods

Spectral Domain Methods (SDM) are used to extract frequency domain information from EEG signals. Some statistical methods in the time domain (such as mean, standard deviation, variance etc.) are also applicable in the frequency domain. Samuel [23] used 12 spectral domain descriptors (SDD) and 20-time domain descriptors (TDD) for a total of 32 EEG Feature extraction methods were used to decode the MI task for different limbs, and the results showed an average accuracy of 99.55% for a set of optimal SDD and 90.68% for a set of optimal TDD by a linear feature combination technique. The power of specific frequency bands, such as δ, θ, α, β, and γ bands, can be analyzed using the fast Fourier transform (FFT) [24].

The power spectral density method (PSD) is a frequency domain based method, PSD is a measure of how the power of a signal is distributed over frequency, it is performed by parametric or non-parametric methods, commonly used are Welch's averaged modified periodogram [25], Yule-Walker equation [26], Lomb-Scargle periodogram [27], Spectral entropy [28].

4.3   Time-Frequency Domain Methods

For EEG signals with more prominent time-frequency characteristics, this is generally analyzed by time-frequency methods, which means that the EEG signal can be extracted in both time and frequency domains simultaneously. Short Term Fourier Transform (STFT) [29] and Wavelet Transform [30] are the more commonly used analysis methods in the time-frequency domain. STFT first splits the EEG signal into overlapping time frames and then performs Fast Fourier Transformation (FFT) on the time frames by a fixed window function. FFT has the advantages of simple calculation and short computation time, so it has been widely used. Wavelet transform is a decomposition of the signal into wavelets, which is a finite harmonic function (sin/cos). The wavelet transform has a flexible time-frequency resolution, the signal is progressively refined using a variable time-frequency window, and the energy intensity or density of the signal can be represented in both the time and frequency domains [31].

Main formulas of STFT:

$$S(m, k) = \sum_{n=0}^{N-1} s(n + mN)\varpi(n)e^{-j\frac{2\Pi}{N}nk} \tag{1}$$

Main formulas of Wavelet Transform:

$$\psi_{s,\tau}(t) = \frac{1}{\sqrt{s}}\psi\left(\frac{t-\tau}{s}\right) \tag{2}$$

Empirical modal decomposition (EMD) is an analysis method similar to Wavelet Transform, but instead of decomposing the EEG signal into wavelet functions, it decomposes the EEG signal into intrinsic mode functions (IMF), which are simple oscillatory functions in mathematics, and the IMF capture the frequency signals in order from high to low.

Main formulas of EMD:

$$x(t) = \sum_{i=1}^{n} c_i(t) + r_n(t) \tag{3}$$

4.4 Spatial Domain Methods

Although the time domain method has been used earlier, only a single channel can be selected for EEG signal extraction and analysis at a time, and the algorithm is more cumbersome. The spatial domain method extracts features by combining multiple channels with certain feature relationships, and it can process multiple channels at a time, among which blind source separation (BSS) [32] is a widely used unsupervised feature extraction method. Cortical current density (CCD) and independent component analysis (ICA) are both good applications of the blind source separation method. The blind source separation method is an unsupervised feature extraction method in which there is no correspondence between classes and features.

Main formulas of BSS:

$$x(t) = As(t) \tag{4}$$

$$s^{'}(t) = Bx(t) \tag{5}$$

where x (t) is the vector of the mixed signals, s (t) is the vector of sources, and A is the unknown non-singular mixing matrix. They aim to find a matrix B that reverses the channels back into their sources.

Common Spatial Pattern (CSP) is a supervised feature extraction method based on classes and features, which can effectively detect event related desynchronization (RED), and the method has a high recognition rate and low computational complexity and is more widely used in BCI. The preprocessed EEG data are first subjected to wavelet transform, and then the wavelet transformed finite harmonic function is used as input for the common spatial mode transformation. This enables the transformation of EEG information into another new space that minimizes the variance of the class signal [33]. This spatial filtering algorithm can be considered as a data driven dimensionality reduction method to improve the variance difference between the two conditions. The common spatial frequency subspace decomposition (CSFSD) used by Ramoser [34] and Choi [35] method is an improvement of the CSP method.

Main formulas of CSP:

$$J(\omega) = \frac{\omega^T C_1 \omega}{\omega^T C_2 \omega} \tag{6}$$

where C_1 and C_2 represent the estimated covariance matrix of each MI class. The above equation can be solved while using the Lagrange multiplier method.

4.5 Spatio-Temporal Domain Methods

The combination of time domain feature extraction methods and space-domain feature extraction methods results in spatio-temporal domain feature extraction methods, and the more common spatio-temporal methods in the past were the Riemannian geometry based methods. Riemannian flow shape is formed by using EEG data with flow characteristics and sample covariance matrix (SCM) acting in symmetric positive definite (SPD) matrix space [36]. The distances of Riemannian manifolds are curves not straight lines, which can be calculated using the affine invariant Riemannian metric (AIRM) [37].

Most of the remaining spatio-temporal domain methods are based on deep learning. For example, the new method proposed by Echeverri [38] in 2019 uses a blind source separation (BSS) algorithm to separate the single channel signal into independent components of the estimated source signal, and then uses the continuous wavelet transform (CWT) for 2D representation of the separated independent components, and finally uses a convolutional neural network (CNN) method for classification. Yang [39] proposed a method using a long short term memory network (LSTM) and convolutional neural network to extract temporal and spatial features from the raw EEG signal, followed by extracting the spectral information of the EEG signal by discrete wavelet transform. Li [40] proposed an end-to-end EEG decoding framework by first extracting spatial and temporal features from the raw EEG signal, and then by using wave amplitude-scramble data enhancement assisted by channel-projection mixed-scale convolutional neural network (CP-MixedNet) technique to improve the decoding accuracy.

4.6 Spatio-Spectral Domain Methods

The combination of spatial domain feature extraction methods and spectral domain methods results in a spatio-spectral domain feature extraction method, and if temporal and spatial filters can be learned simultaneously, a unified framework can extract information from both spatial and spectral domains. For example, Wu [41, 48] proposed an iterative spatio-spectral patterns learning (ISSPL) algorithm that learns both spatio-temporal filters and spectral filters simultaneously. Suk [42, 49] used the interplay between particle filtering algorithms, feature vectors, and class labels information proposed a probabilistic method for optimizing spatio-temporal spectral filtering of BCI based on EEG. Zhang [43] proposed a structure based on deep recurrent and 3D convolutional neural networks (R3DCNNs) that enables simultaneous learning of EEG signal features from spatial, spectral, and temporal dimensions. Bang [44] proposed to superimpose the filtered spectral filters and construct a 3-D-CNN feature map, and by using this feature map, a layer-by-layer decomposition model of the framework was implemented and experimental accuracy was ensured.

5   Classification of MI EEG Signals

A feature classification algorithm is to classify the extracted feature vectors according to the target discriminant criterion to obtain the best classification result, which is the mapping from the feature space to the target space, and usually consists of three parts: the mapping function, the objective function, and the minimization/maximization algorithm. Among them, the mapping function determines the feature space and the approximation ability of the classifier, the objective function describes the problem to be solved by the classifier, and the minimization/maximization algorithm is to find the best mapping function to ensure the mapping of the data to the target space.

Algorithms such as Linear Discriminant Analysis (LDA), Support Vector Machine (SVM), Multilayer Perceptron (MLP), and Bayesian classifier are feature classification stage commonly used algorithms. In recent years, some deep learning-based feature classification algorithms have been proposed, but the feature classification stage of deep learning based on motion imagery is still difficult to be widely used due to noise, the correlation between channels, and small dataset of subjects [45].

6 Conclusions

This paper introduces the research of brain-computer interface based on motion imagery, which mainly involves the classification of brain-computer interface, an overview of EEG signal and signal acquisition, pre-processing of MI, feature extraction, feature classification methods etc.

With scientists' research on MI-BCI, various signal processing methods have made some progress and the performance of algorithms has improved substantially. However, the research on MI-BCI is far from over, and there are still some key issues waiting to be solved. For example, due to the extreme nonlinearity and non-smoothness of EEG itself, the target user often needs to conduct a large number of training experiments, which leads to a longer calibration period of a MI model. Current research on motor imagery is mainly focused on offline models, and research on MI in online models needs to be enhanced. Researchers should set a unified BCI criterion for algorithm evaluation, which in turn can better measure performance improvement.

Acknowledgments. This work is supported by The Chinese Society of Academic Degrees and Graduate Education under grant B-2017Y0002-170, Shaanxi Province Key Research and Development Projects under grant 2016GY-040, and Yulin City Science and Technology Project under grant CXY-2020-026.

References

1. Erp, J.V., Lotte, F., Tangermann, M.: Brain-computer interfaces: beyond medical applications. Computer **45**(4), 26–34 (2012). https://doi.org/10.1109/MC.2012.107
2. Nicolas-Alonso, L.F., Gomez-Gil, J.: Brain computer interfaces, a review. Sensors (Basel). **12**(2), 1211–1279 (2012). https://doi.org/10.3390/s120201211
3. Tello, R.M.G., Müller, S.M.T., Hasan, M.A., et al.: An independent-BCI based on SSVEP using figure-ground perception (FGP). Biomed. Sig. Process. Control. **26**, 69–79 (2016). https://doi.org/10.1016/j.bspc.2015.12.010
4. Banville, H., Falk, T.H.: Recent advances and open challenges in hybrid brain-computer interfacing: a technological review of non-invasive human research. Brain-Comput. Interf. **3**(1), 9–46 (2016). https://doi.org/10.1080/2326263X.2015.1134958
5. Bashashati, H., Ward, R.K., Bashashati, A., Mohamed, A.: Neural network conditional random fields for self-paced brain computer interfaces. In: 15th IEEE International Conference on Machine Learning and Applications (ICMLA), pp. 939–943 (2016). https://doi.org/10.1109/ICMLA.2016.0169
6. Kevric, J., Subasi, A.: Comparison of signal decomposition methods in classification of EEG signals for motor-imagery BCI system. Biomed. Sig. Proces. Control. **31**, 398–406 (2017). https://doi.org/10.1016/j.bspc.2016.09.007

7. Suma, D., Meng, J., Edelman, B.J., He, B.: Spatial-temporal aspects of continuous EEG-based neurorobotic control. J. Neu. Eng. **17**(6), 066006 (2020)

8. Ramadan, R.A., Vasilakos, A.V.: Brain computer interface: control signals review. Neurocomputing **223**, 26–44 (2016). https://doi.org/10.1016/j.neucom.2016.10.024

9. Gazzaniga, M.S., Mangun, G.R.: The cognitive neurosciences. Minds Mach. **25**(3), 281–284 (2015)

10. Wang, M., Ma, C., Li, Z., et al.: Alertness estimation using connection parameters of the brain network. In: IEEE Transactions on Intelligent Transportation Systems, pp. 1–10 (2021). https://doi.org/10.1109/TITS.2021.3124372

11. Jasper, J.J.: The ten-twenty electrode system of international federation in electroencephalography and clinical neurophysiology (1958)

12. Linassi, F., Zanatta, P., Tellaroli, P., et al.: Isolated forearm technique: a meta-analysis of connected consciousness during different general anaesthesia regimens. BJA Br. J. Anaesth. **121**(1), 198–209 (2018). https://doi.org/10.1016/j.bja.2018.02.019

13. Huang, Z., Wang, M.: A review of electroencephalogram signal processing methods for brain-controlled robots. Cogn. Robot. **1**, 111–124 (2021). https://doi.org/10.1016/j.cogr.2021.07.001

14. Pfurtscheller, G., Neuper, C.: Motor imagery and direct brain-computer communication. Proc. IEEE. **89**(7), 1123–1134 (2001). https://doi.org/10.1109/5.939829

15. Wang, T., Ke, Y., Wang, N., et al.: Application and research development of spatial filtering method in brain-computer interfaces. Chin. J. Biomed. Eng. **38**(5), 599–608 (2019). https://doi.org/10.3969/j.issn.0258-8021.2019.05.011

16. Singh, A., Hussain, A.A., Lal, S., Guesgen, H.W.: A comprehensive review on critical issues and possible solutions of motor imagery based electroencephalography brain-computer interface. Sensors. **20**(6), 2173 (2021). https://doi.org/10.3390/s21062173

17. Tang, Z., Li, C., Sun, S.: Single-trial EEG classification of motor imagery using deep convolutional neural networks. Int. J. Light Electron Optics (2017). https://doi.org/10.1016/j.ijleo.2016.10.117

18. Hamedi, M., Salleh, S., Noor, A.M., Mohammad-Rezazadeh, I.:Neural network-based three-class motor imagery classification using time-domain features for BCI applications. In: IEEE Region 10 Symposium, pp. 204–207 (2014). https://doi.org/10.1109/TENCONSpring.2014.6863026

19. Rodríguez-Bermúdez, G., García-Laencina, P.J.: Automatic and adaptive classification of electroencephalographic signals for brain computer interfaces. J Med Syst **36**, 51–63 (2012). https://doi.org/10.1007/s10916-012-9893-4

20. D'Croz-Baron, D., Ramirez, J. M., Baker, M., Alarcon-Aquino, V., Carrera, O.: A BCI motor imagery experiment based on parametric feature extraction and Fisher criterion. In: 22nd International Conference on Electrical Communications and Computers, pp. 257–261 (2012). https://doi.org/10.1109/CONIELECOMP.2012.6189920

21. Adam, A., Ibrahim, Z., Mokhtar, N., Shapiai, M.I., Cumming, P., Mubin, M.: Evaluation of different time domain peak models using extreme learning machine-based peak detection for EEG signal. Springerplus **5**(1), 1–14 (2016). https://doi.org/10.1186/s40064-016-2697-0

22. Yilmaz, C.M., Kose, C., Hatipoglu, B.: A Quasi-probabilistic distribution model for EEG Signal classification by using 2-D signal representation. Comput. Method Prog. Biomed. **162**, 187–196 (2018). https://doi.org/10.1016/j.cmpb.2018.05.026

23. Samuel, O.W., Geng, Y., Li, X., Li, G.: Towards efficient decoding of multiple classes of motor imagery limb movements based on EEG spectral and time domain descriptors. J. Med. Syst. **41**(12), 1–13 (2017). https://doi.org/10.1007/s10916-017-0843-z

24. Rashkov, G.V., Bobe, A.S., Fastovets, D.V., et al.: Natural image reconstruction from brain waves: a novel visual BCI system with native feedback (2019). https://doi.org/10.1101/787101

25. Virgilio, G.C.D., Sossa, A.J.H., Antelis, J.M, Falcón, L.E.: Spiking neural networks applied to the classification of motor tasks in EEG signals. Neural Netw. **122**, 130–143 (2020). https://doi.org/10.1016/j.neunet.2019.09.037

26. Lee, S.B., Kim, H.J., Kim, H., et al.: Comparative analysis of features extracted from EEG spatial, spectral and temporal domains for binary and multiclass motor imagery classification. Inf. Sci. **502**, 190–200 (2019). https://doi.org/10.1016/j.ins.2019.06.008

27. Chu, Y., Zhao, X., Zou, Y., et al.: A Decoding Scheme for Incomplete Motor Imagery EEG with deep belief network. Front. Neuro. **28**, 680 (2018). https://doi.org/10.3389/fnins.2018.00680

28. Zhang, R., et al.: Predicting Inter-session Performance of SMR-Based Brain–Computer Interface Using the Spectral Entropy of Resting-State EEG. Brain Topogr. **28**(5), 680–690 (2015). https://doi.org/10.1007/s10548-015-0429-3

29. Samiee, K., Kovács, P., Gabbouj, M.: Epileptic seizure classification of EEG time-series using rational discrete short-time Fourier transform. IEEE Trans Biomed Eng. **62**(2), 541–552 (2015). https://doi.org/10.1109/TBME.2014.2360101

30. Gao, Z., Wang, Z., Ma, C., Dang, W., Zhang, K.: A Wavelet time-frequency representation based complex network method for characterizing brain activities underlying motor imagery signals. IEEE Access. **6**, 65796–65802 (2018). https://doi.org/10.1109/ACCESS.2018.2876547

31. Wang, M., Huang, Z., et al.: Maximum weight multi-modal information fusion algorithm of electroencephalographs and face images for emotion recognition. Comput. Electr. Eng. **94**(107415), 1–13 (2021). https://doi.org/10.1016/j.compeleceng.2021.107319

32. Jung, T.P., Makeig, S., Humphries, C., et al.: Removing electroencephalographic artifacts by blind source separation. Psychophysiology **37**(2), 163–178 (2000)

33. Palumbo, A., Gramigna, V., Calabrese, B., et al.: Motor-Imagery EEG-based BCIs in wheelchairs movement and control. A systematic literature review. Sensors **19**(18), 6285 (2021). https://doi.org/10.3390/s21186285

34. Ramoser, H., Muller-Gerking, J., Pfurtscheller, G.: Optimal spatial filtering of single trial EEG during imagined hand movement. IEEE Trans. Rehab. Eng. **8**(4), pp. 441–446 (2000). https://doi.org/10.1109/86.895946

35. Choi, K.: Control of a vehicle with EEG signals in real-time and system evaluation. Eur J Appl Physiol. **112**(2), 755–766 (2012). https://doi.org/10.1007/s00421-011-2029-6

36. Barachant, A., Bonnet, S., Congedo, M., et al.: Classification of covariance matrices using a Riemannian-based kernel for BCI applications. Neurocomputing **112**, 172–178 (2013). https://doi.org/10.1016/j.neucom.2012.12.039

37. Horev, I., Yger, F., Sugiyama, M.: Geometry-aware principal component analysis for symmetric positive definite matrices. Mach. Learn. **106**(4), 493–522 (2016). https://doi.org/10.1007/s10994-016-5605-5

38. Ortiz-Echeverri, C.J., Salazar-Colores, S., Rodríguez-Reséndiz, J., Gómez-Loenzo, R.A.: A new approach for motor imagery classification based on sorted blind source separation. Contin. Wavelet Transf. Convolut. Neu. Netw. Sensors. **19**, 4541 (2019). https://doi.org/10.3390/s19204541

39. Yang, J., Yao, S., Wang, J.: Deep fusion feature learning network for MI-EEG classification. IEEE Access. **6**, 79050–79059 (2018). https://doi.org/10.1109/ACCESS.2018.2877452

40. Li, Y., Zhang, X., Zhang, B., et al.: A channel-projection mixed-scale convolutional neural network for motor imagery EEG decoding. IEEE Trans. Neural Syst. Rehab. Eng. **27**(6), 1170–1180 (2019). https://doi.org/10.1109/TNSRE.2019.2915621

41. Wu, W., Gao, X., Hong, B., Gao, S.: Classifying single-trial EEG during motor imagery by iterative spatio-spectral patterns learning (ISSPL). IEEE Trans. Biomed. Eng. **55**(6), 1733–1743 (2008). https://doi.org/10.1109/TBME.2008.919125

42. Suk, H.I., Lee, S.W.: A probabilistic approach to spatio-spectral filters optimization in Brain-Computer Interface. In: IEEE International Conference on Systems, Man, and Cybernetics, pp. 19–24 (2011). https://doi.org/10.1109/ICSMC.2011.6083636

43. Zhang, P., Wang, X., Zhang, W., Chen, J.: Learning spatial–spectral–temporal EEG features with recurrent 3D convolutional neural networks for cross-task mental workload assessment. IEEE Trans Neural Syst Rehab Eng **27**(1), 31–42 (2019). https://doi.org/10.1109/TNSRE.2018.2884641

44. Bang, J.S., Lee, M.H., Fazli, S., Guan, C., Lee, S.W.: Spatio-spectral feature representation for motor imagery classification using convolutional neural networks. In IEEE Transactions on Neural Networks and Learning Systems, pp. 1–12 (2021). https://doi.org/10.1109/TNNLS.2020.3048385

45. Schirrmeister, R.T., Springenberg, J.T., Fiederer, L.D.J., et al.: Deep learning with convolutional neural networks for EEG decoding and visualization. Hum Brain Mapp. **38**(11), 5391–5420 (2017). https://doi.org/10.1002/hbm.23730

46. Lu, H., Zhang, M., Xu, X.:. Deep fuzzy hashing network for efficient image retrieval. In: IEEE Transactions on Fuzzy Systems, https://doi.org/10.1109/TFUZZ.2020.2984991, 2020

47. Huimin, L., Li, Y., Chen, M., et al.: Brain Intelligence: go beyond artificial intelligence. Mob. Netw. Appl. **23**, 368–375 (2018)

48. Huimin, L., Li, Y., Shenglin, M., et al.: Motor anomaly detection for unmanned aerial vehicles using reinforcement learning. IEEE Internet Things J. **5**(4), 2315–2322 (2018)

49. Lu, H., Qin, M., Zhang, F., et al.: RSCNN: A CNN-based method to enhance low-light remote-sensing images. In: Remote Sensing, p. 62 (2020)

Lightweight 3D Point Cloud Classification Network

Zihao Xin, Hongyuan Wang$^{(\boxtimes)}$, and Ji Zhang

Changzhou University, Changzhou 213100, China
hywang@cczu.edu.cn

Abstract. In this paper, we propose a new lightweight neural network for point cloud classification that has only about 100 K parameters. Most of the current research focuses on aggregating network features through pooling layers and extracting abstract features of 3D point clouds using higher dimensions. In this work, we turn our attention to exploring the relationships between points at a deeper level, using a multilayer perceptron module with a residual structure to suppress the performance degradation problem that comes with increasing the number of network layers. On the ModelNet40 dataset, our method achieves an accuracy of more than 92.5%, which is the first of its kind in our knowledge for ultralight networks. Without using any techniques such as pruning and quantization, the model was trained at 1214 samples per second and inferred at a staggering 1956 samples per second.

Keywords: Point cloud classification · Lightweight neural network · Multilayer perceptron · Deep learning

1 Introduction

Two-dimensional images only have flat information but lack depth information, robots, self-driving cars and other devices cannot perceive real scenes accurately, and more and more research is now focused on three-dimensional scenes. With the development of LiDAR and binocular cameras, the cost of devices has also dropped significantly, and more and more consumer-grade products are equipped with LiDAR or binocular cameras to acquire 3D scenes. Among them, point cloud is the simplest and efficient 3D scene representation method, and it has been widely used in different fields, such as autonomous driving, 3D scene segmentation and virtual reality (VR). While 2D images are represented by dense regular pixels, point clouds are often represented by sparse points in 3D space. Therefore, the feature extraction network of 2D images cannot be directly used for 3D point cloud information extraction.

In this paper, we propose an efficient and lightweight network architecture which has only about 100K parameters. This novel neural network architecture is specifically tailored for mobile robots or portable VR devices that do not have powerful processors. Unlike recent state-of-the-art (SOTA) algorithms that search for semantic cues by using graphs, self-attentive mechanisms, etc., which introduce complex structures and a large

S. Yang and H. Lu (Eds.): ISAIR 2022, CCIS 1701, pp. 95–105, 2022.
https://doi.org/10.1007/978-981-19-7943-9_8

number of parameters to obtain higher scores, our method simply use a simple convolutional network with remaining blocks to learn salient geometric features in point clouds. Our approach not only far outperforms these SOTA models in terms of training and interface speed, but also achieves similar performance (see Fig. 1).

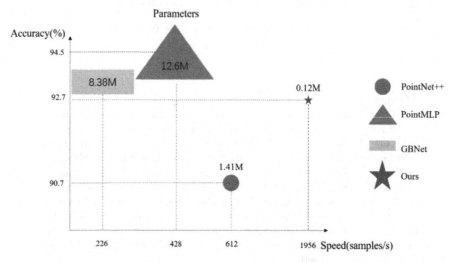

Fig. 1. Our method runs significantly faster than other 3D point cloud networks with comparable performance. And our model has a very small number of parameters.

We summarize the main contributions of our work as follows.

1. We propose a novel deep convolutional network with residual blocks that can substantially reduce the number of parameters for point cloud classification.
2. We show that the training and inference speed of the model exceeds that of other methods.
3. We report extensive experiments on multiple datasets. We perform ablation experiments and detailed comparisons, and point out the shortcomings of the SOTA models.

2   Related Work

2.1   Hand Crafted Features

Since point clouds are disordered and dispersed in 3D space, most 2D image processing methods do not work. Many methods use local feature descriptors to capture the geometric structure of the point cloud [1, 2, 5, 18], but these methods only work for specific data sets and fail if the point cloud density changes. To use 2D image processing methods in 3D point clouds, some methods project the points in the cloud onto the 2D plane through different angles [7, 8, 19, 21]. However, these methods rely heavily on the angle of the selected view, and different primary views should be chosen for different point cloud images, e.g., a top view angle is good for an airplane but not for a hat.

2.2 Point Cloud Classification

Point cloud classification is very challenging due to the disorderly nature of point clouds. VoxelNet [29] solves this problem by converting a set of points within each voxel into a uniform feature representation. Alternatively, there are approaches to classify point clouds by graph structure to represent the relationships between them. DGCNN [25] designs a novel neural network that captures potentially long-range semantic features in the original embedding. RGCNN [22, 30] defines the convolution of a graph via a Cheby-shev polynomial approximation to capture the structure of dynamic graphs adaptively. Recent work has shown that on standard datasets (e.g. ModelNet40), competitors and hardly distinguish between ranks. The difference between state-of-the-art methods such as PointMLP [11], CurveNet [13], GBNet [13] is less than 1% in object classification accuracy.

2.3 Deep Learning on Point Cloud

There are three main types of point cloud models based on deep learning: multi-view projections, voxel-based networks, and direct point cloud methods. Unlike images, 3D point clouds do not have neatly aligned pixel points and require another way to extract features from the point clouds. The most common way to overcome this problem is to project the point cloud onto a plane from different views, which is called multi-view projection method. MVCNN [19, 31] uses a convolutional network to extract features from the projected image from the point cloud, and then aggregates these features through a pooling layer to obtain global features for classification. Voxel-based networks [6, 12, 20] place points on a grid, each of which can be analogous to a pixel point, but generate a large amount of computation because the number of voxels grows in a cube. To reduce the computation, larger networks are often used, but local geometric details may be lost at lower resolutions, so these voxel-based networks cannot handle complex point cloud data. PointNet [15] is designed to be an efficient network for the direct point cloud method. PointNet is not only much faster than the view and volume representation-based methods, but also allows to obtain geometric features without loss of detail geometric features without loss of detail. To obtain more local structure, PointNet++[16, 33] introduces a layered neural network that learns more features as the contextual scale increases. Others [3, 9, 32] use graphs to connect the points and pass information on top of them.

3 Lightweight 3D Point Cloud Classification Network

We first briefly review how the SOTA method captures fine geometric structures from point clouds. Then, we describe the structure of our network and finally describe how the residual blocks can better extract local features and reduce the number of parameters at the same time. The entire pipeline of our network is given in Fig. 2.

3.1 Background

There are a number of different methods to extract features directly from point clouds, the most representative of which is PointNet. Let $\chi = \{x_i | i, ..., n\}$ be a set of feature

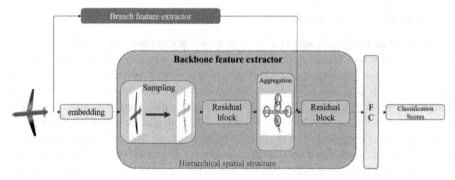

Fig. 2. Architecture of our Snowpoints for point cloud classification.

vectors, where n denotes the number of points. The core modules of the PointNet family are the multilayer perceptron network and the maximum set function, which can be expressed as:

$$y_{i,t} = \text{MaxPooling}(\text{MLP}(x_{i,j})|j = 1, ..., t) \qquad (1)$$

where y_i is the output after feature aggregation and $x_{i,j}$ is the j-th nearest neighbor point feature of the i-th centroid being sampled. The centroids are sampled by the farthest point sampling algorithm, which covers all points of the object compared to random sampling. PointNet++is the first method to build a hierarchical spatial structure to improve sensitivity to local geometric layout for efficient sampling of point clouds, and to develop multiple sampling strategies [4, 26]. The density adaptive layer is called multi-scale grouping (MSG) and can be expressed as follows:

$$y_i = y_{i,t_1} \oplus y_{i,t_2} \oplus y_{i,t_3}, \quad t_1 < t_2 < t_3 \qquad (2)$$

where $\oplus$ stands for the connection operation. This operation allows the network to group local regions and combine features of different scales. The point transformer, inspired by transformers and self-attentive mechanisms, assumes that the point transformer layer is used to encode location information and can be represented as follows:

$$y_i = \sum_{x_j \in \chi(i)} \rho(\gamma(\varphi(x_i) - \psi(x_j) + \delta)) \odot (\alpha(x_j) + \delta) \qquad (3)$$

where γ, ϕ, ψ and α are linear projections, $\odot$ is the Hadamard product, and ρ is a normalization function such as softmax. $\delta = \theta(x_i - x_j)$ is the position encoding function between the points x_i and x_j, and the encoding function θ includes the multilayer perceptron and the ReLU function. The point transformer compares the similarity of neighboring local regions in the point cloud by relative position encoding, which can find promising results. Unlike the point transformer, pointMLP [11] proposes a geometric affine module to normalize local points, which can make the model robust. The normalization formula is defined as follows:

$$x_{i,j} = \alpha \odot \frac{x_{i,j} - x_i}{\sigma + \epsilon} + \beta, \quad \sigma = \sqrt{\frac{\sum_{i=1}^{n} \sum_{j=1}^{k} (x_{i,j} - x_i)^2}{k \times n \times d}} \qquad (4)$$

where σ is a scalar describing the deviation of the features, α and β are learnable parameters, and ϵ is a small number used for numerical stabilization. By doing this, the local points will be mapped to a normal distribution, and the network can then be trained more easily.

Each method has its own advantages and disadvantages. Linear projections and ensemble structures like PointNet have limitations in obtaining fine geometric features, while the self-attention module in point transformers generates a large number of computations and is not applicable to lightweight networks. The geometric affine module can improve accuracy, but through experiments, we found a more general approach - batch normalization - that not only achieves the same results, but also reduces parameters and improves training speed.

3.2 Position Encoding

Location encoding plays an important role in point cloud classification, where the model must extract fine local geometric features, gradually expand the perceptual field, and finally obtain global features. To make an effective trade-off between inference latency and accuracy, we reduce the feature dimensionality of the embedding layer compared to other networks and use the residual structure to enhance message passing.

We constructed a residual location encoding block using a multilayer perceptron and maximum pooling, as shown in Fig. 3. Linear projection proved to be effective for extracting point cloud features in PointNet, but it had to extract deep features in high dimensions, such as 1024. This not only slowed down the network, but in the last block, multiple fully connected layers were used to classify the high-dimensional features, which greatly increased the number of parameters. Therefore, we look for an efficient way to encode the point cloud.

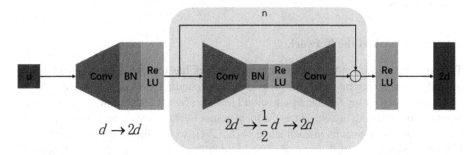

Fig. 3. Detail of the residual block.

Exploring the relationships between points within a local region of low dimensionality is the focus of the location coding layer. We must leave useful data and add dimensionality carefully. We divide the point features into backbone features and residual branch features. Backbone features contain deep point features that are representative of the local region and aggregate local features through maximum pooling. However, the maximum pooling layer loses a large number of effective features, and other networks add feature dimensions to reduce the loss. In our approach, we use residual branching features to bring the shallow neighborhood context into the backbone features, enhancing the ability of the features to describe local regions in low dimensions, as shown in Fig. 4.

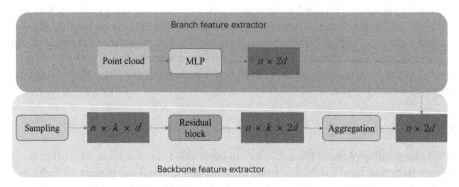

Fig. 4. Backbone feature extractor and branch feature extractor.

We replace the residual branch features with higher dimensional features, which can not only reduce the number of parameters, but also improve the training and inference speed. In the backbone network, we also propose a mini-residual block to extract local features. We use deeper layers rather than higher dimensions to extract better local features, but the degradation problem is exposed as the depth of the network increases. Simply increasing the number of network layers may result in failure to extract effective features, leading to worse results. Constant mapping layers can overcome this problem, and constant mapping branches can prevent the degradation problem due to too deep network layers.

3.3 Framework of the Network

The position encoder in the classification framework has four stages, where each stage has a down sampling rate of 2, for progressively expanding the local receptive field for extracting a larger range of local point cloud features. Select 1024 points as the network input and 64 centroids are chosen as the local point cloud feature centers. The expansion rate of feature dimensions in each stage is [2,2,2,1], so the dimensions of point cloud features generated in each stage are [2d,4d,8d,8d], where d is the feature dimension encoded by the embedding layer.

In detail, the centroid sampling method refers to [15]. The farthest point sampling (FPS) method can generate overlapping partitions of the point set at high speed. We visualize the sampling results in Fig. 5.

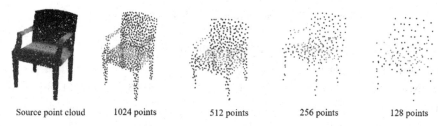

Source point cloud   1024 points   512 points   256 points   128 points

Fig. 5. Example result the point cloud sample.

4 Experiment

4.1 Detail Experimental Setting

We implemented our network in PyTorch [14]. We trained the model on four Nvidia 2080Ti GPUs with 200 epochs and a batch size of 128. we used the SGD optimizer with momentum and weight decay set to 0.9 and 0.0002, respectively. The learning rate was initially set to 0.2 and the cosine annealing scheduler [10] was used to adjust the learning rate. To better compare with other models, we use the same sampling method as the other models. For each sample in ModelNet40 and ScanObjectNN, 1024 points were sampled uniformly from the grid surface and rescaled to fit the unit sphere. Object classification is evaluated by accuracy.

4.2 Results in ModelNet40

There are forty classes of items in the ModelNet40 dataset [1], with a total of 9840 samples in the training set and 2468 samples in the test set. The results of the experiments are shown in Table 1.

Compared with current SOTA methods, our approach demonstrates excellent classification accuracy and fast training and inference speed.

Table 1. Classification results on ModelNet40 dataset.

Method	Accuracy(%)	Param.(million)	Train speed	Test speed
PointNet [15]	86.0	0.8		
PointNet++[16]	90.7	1.41	413.3	612.8
MVCNN [19]	90.1	138.0		
PointConv [26]	92.5	18.6	37.9	21.6
KPConv [23]	92.9	15.2	31.0	80.0
Point Trans. [27]	92.8			
PointMLP [11]	94.5	12.6	192.8	428.0
GBNet	93.8	8.39	35.2	226
VoxNet [12]	83.0	0.92		
LightNet [28]	86.9	0.30		
Ours	92.7	0.12	1214	1956

4.3 Results in ScanObjectNN

ScanObjectNN [24] is a point cloud benchmark dataset with 15 categories and 15,000 samples. The point clouds obtained from real-world 3D scans are significantly different from the CAD models in ModelNet40 due to the presence of noise from airborne dust. Unlike the ModelNet40 dataset, the density of the point clouds is heterogeneous due to the accuracy limitations of the acquisition equipment. Table 2 shows the quantitative results of the different methods.

Table 2. Classification results on ScanObjectNN dataset.

Method	Accuracy(%)
PointNet [15]	68.2
PointNet++ [16]	77.9%
PointCNN [26]	78.5
DGCNN [25]	78.1
PointMLP [11]	85.4
GBNet [17]	80.5
Ours	82.3

4.4 Ablation Study

We verified the effectiveness of the module by ablation experiments, which were designed to investigate the ablation of the dimensionality of the location coding layers,

Table 3. Ablation study: full connected layer.

FC layers	ModelNet40 Accuracy(%)	ScanObjectNN Accurancy(%)	Parameters
3	92.9	83.1	168960
2	92.7	82.6	141312
1	92.7	82.3	20480

and the number of fully connected layers. The experiments show that on two datasets, ModelNet40 and ScanObjectNN, the classification accuracy of the model is 92.9% and 83.1% if the commonly used three-layer fully connected layer classification network is followed, respectively. We also retrained the model with only two fully connected layers and one fully connected layer instead of pruning the three-layer fully connected layer model. The experiments show that the accuracy of using only one layer of fully connected layers is 92.7% and 82.3% in the two models, respectively, and the accuracy in the ModelNet40 dataset only decreases by 0.2%, while the number of parameters in the fully connected layers is only 12% of the original one.

5 Conclusion

We propose a lightweight point cloud classification network with residual blocks, which can reduce the width of the network while deepening the number of layers, thus significantly reducing the number of network parameters, and gradually expanding the local perceptual field by down sampling to obtain the global features of the point cloud. Compared with other methods, this network can better obtain high-dimensional global features, and we further reduce the number of fully connected layers and keep only one fully connected layer for classification, which significantly reduces the number of parameters and improves the training and inference speed. Compared with existing methods, our framework is able to obtain high-dimensional feature information with fewer parameters and extract local features of point clouds, and the training and inference speed is faster than all current methods.

Acknowledgements. This work is supported by the National Natural Science Foundation of China (61976028, 61572085, 61806026, 61502058).

References

1. Aubry, M., Schlickewei, U., Cremers, D.: The wave kernel signature: A quantummechanical approach to shape analysis. In: 2011 IEEE International Conference on Computer Vision Workshops (ICCV Workshops), pp. 1626–1633. IEEE, New Yorl (2011)
2. Bronstein, M.M., Kokkinos, I.: Scale-invariant heat kernel signatures for non-rigid shape recognition. In: 2010 IEEE Computer Society Conference on Computer Vision and Pattern Recognition, pp. 1704–1711. IEEE, New York (2010)

3. Gilmer, J., Schoenholz, S.S., Riley, P.F., Vinyals, O., Dahl, G.E.: Neural message passing for quantum chemistry. In: International Conference on Machine Learning, pp. 1263–1272. PMLR (2017)

4. Hu, Q., Yang, B., Xie, L., Rosa, S., Guo, Y., Wang, Z., Trigoni, N., Markham, A:Randla-net: Efficient semantic segmentationof large-scale point clouds. In: Proceedings of the IEEE/CVF Conference on Computer Vision and Pattern Recognition, pp. 11108–11117 (2020)

5. Johnson, A.E., Hebert, M.: Using spin images for efficient object recognition in cluttered 3d scenes. IEEE Trans. Pattern Anal. Mach. Intell. **21**(5), 433–449 (1999)

6. Klokov, R., Lempitsky, V.: Escape from cells: Deep Kd-networks for the recognition of 3d point cloud models. In: Proceedings of the IEEE International Conference on Computer Vision, pp. 863–872 (2017)

7. Lang, A.H., Vora, S., Caesar, H., Zhou, L., Yang, J., Beijbom, O.: Pointpillars: Fast encoders for object detection from point clouds. In: Proceedings of the IEEE/CVF Conference on Computer Vision and Pattern Recognition, pp. 12697–12705 (2019)

8. Li, B., Zhang, T., Xia, T.: Vehicle detection from 3d lidar using fully convolutional network. (2016)

9. Li, Y., Tarlow, D., Brockschmidt, M., Zemel, R.: Gated graph sequence neural networks. (2015)

10. Loshchilov, I., Hutter, F.: Sgdr: Stochastic gradient descent with warm restarts. (2016)

11. Ma, X., Qin, C., You, H., Ran, H., Fu, Y.: Rethinking network design and local geometry in point cloud: A simple residual mlp framework. (2022)

12. Maturana, D., Scherer, S.: Voxnet: A 3d convolutional neural network for real time object recognition. In: 2015 IEEE/RSJ International Conference on Intelligent Robots and Systems (IROS), pp. 922–928. IEEE, New York (2015)

13. Muzahid, A., Wan, W., Sohel, F., Wu, L., Hou, L.: Curvenet: Curvature-based multitask learning deep networks for 3d object recognition. IEEE/CAA J. Automat. Sin. **8**(6), 1177–1187 (2020)

14. Paszke, A., Gross, S., Massa, F., Lerer, A., Bradbury, J., Chanan, G., Killeen, T., Lin, Z., Gimelshein, N., Antiga, L., et al.: Pytorch: An imperative style, high performance deep learning library. Adv. Neural Inf. Proces. Syst **32** (2019)

15. Qi, C.R., Su, H., Mo, K., Guibas, L.J.: Pointnet: Deep learning on point sets for 3d classification and segmentation. In: Proceedings of the IEEE Conference on Computer Vision and Pattern Recognition, pp. 652–660 (2017)

16. Qi, C.R., Yi, L., Su, H., Guibas, L.J.: Pointnet++: Deep hierarchical feature learning on point sets in a metric space. Adv. Neural Inf. Process. Syst. **30** (2017)

17. Qiu, S., Anwar, S., Barnes, N.: Geometric back-projection network for point cloud classification. IEEE Trans. Multim. (2021)

18. Rusu, R.B., Blodow, N., Beetz, M.: Fast point feature histograms (fpfh) for 3d registration. In: 2009 IEEE International Conference on Robotics and Automation, pp. 3212–3217. IEEE, New York (2009)

19. Su, H., Maji, S., Kalogerakis, E., Learned-Miller, E.: Multi-view convolutional neural networks for 3d shape recognition. In: Proceedings of the IEEE International Conference on Computer Vision, pp. 945–953 (2015)

20. Tatarchenko, M., Dosovitskiy, A., Brox, T.: Octree generating networks: Efficient convolutional architectures for high-resolution 3d outputs. In: Proceedings of the IEEE International Conference on Computer Vision, pp. 2088–2096 (2017)

21. Tatarchenko, M., Park, J., Koltun, V., Zhou, Q.Y.: Tangent convolutions for dense prediction in 3d. In: Proceedings of the IEEE Conference on Computer Vision and Pattern Recognition, pp. 3887–3896 (2018)

22. Te, G., Hu, W., Zheng, A., Guo, Z.: Rgcnn: Regularized graph cnn for point cloud segmentation. In: Proceedings of the 26th ACM International Conference on Multimedia, pp. 746–754 (2018)

23. Thomas, H., Qi, C.R., Deschaud, J.E., Marcotegui, B., Goulette, F., Guibas, L.J. Kpconv: Flexible and deformable convolution for point clouds. In: Proceedings of the IEEE/CVF International Conference on Computer Vision, pp. 6411–6420 (2019)

24. Uy, M.A., Pham, Q.H., Hua, B.S., Nguyen, T., Yeung, S.K.: Revisiting point cloud classification: A new benchmark dataset and classification model on real-world data. In: Proceedings of the IEEE/CVF International Conference on Computer Vision, pp. 1588–1597 (2019)

25. Wang, Y., Sun, Y., Liu, Z., Sarma, S.E., Bronstein, M.M., Solomon, J.M.: Dynamic graph cnn for learning on point clouds. ACM Trans. Graph. 38(5), 1–12 (2019)

26. Wu, W., Qi, Z., Fuxin, L.: Pointconv: Deep convolutional networks on 3d point clouds. In: Proceedings of the IEEE/CVF Conference on Computer Vision and Pattern Recognition, pp. 9621–9630 (2019)

27. Zhao, H., Jiang, L., Jia, J., Torr, P.H., Koltun, V.: Point transformer. In: Proceedings of the IEEE/CVF International Conference on Computer Vision, pp. 16259–16268 (2021)

28. Zhi, S., Liu, Y., Li, X., Guo, Y.: Lightnet: A lightweight 3d convolutional neural network for real-time 3d object recognition. In: 3DOR@ Eurographics (2017)

29. Zhou, Y., Tuzel, O.: Voxelnet: End-to-end learning for point cloud based 3d object detection. In: Proceedings of the IEEE Conference on Computer Vision and Pattern Recognition, pp. 4490–4499 (2018)

30. Huimin, L., Zhang, M., Xing, X.: Deep fuzzy hashing network for efficient image retrieval. IEEE Trans. Fuzzy Syst. (2020). https://doi.org/10.1109/TFUZZ.2020.2984991

31. Huimin, L., Li, Y., Chen, M., et al.: Brain Intelligence: go beyond artificial intelligence. Mobile Netw. Appl. 23, 368–375 (2018)

32. Huimin, L., Li, Y., Shenglin, M., et al.: Motor anomaly detection for unmanned aerial vehicles using reinforcement learning. IEEE Internet Things J. 5(4), 2315–2322 (2018)

33. Huimin Lu, Mengjiao Qin, Feng Zhang, et al. RSCNN: A CNN-based method to enhance low-light remote-sensing images. Remote Sens. 62 (2020)

Unsupervised Domain Adaptive Image Semantic Segmentation Based on Convolutional Fine-Grained Discriminant and Entropy Minimization

Xiaohao Zhao, Lihua Tian[✉], and Chen Li

School of Software Engineering, Xi'an Jiaotong University, Xi'an, China
lhtian@xjtu.edu.cn

Abstract. Deep convolutional neural networks have made considerable progress in the field of semantic segmentation of images. However, due to inter-domain differences, even modern networks cannot segment test datasets from different domains very well. To reduce and avoid costly annotation of the source domain training data, unsupervised domain adaptation attempts to provide efficient information transfer from the source domain with detailed annotation to the target domain without annotation. However, most existing methods attempt to align the source and target domains from a holistic view, ignoring the underlying class-level structure in the target domain, along with large noise and ambiguity at the class junctions. In this work, we innovatively employ a fine-grained unsupervised domain adaptation semantic segmentation method with increased entropy certainty, and guide the model for finer-grained feature alignment by adversarial learning, while increasing the pixel certainty near the category boundaries. Our approach is easy to implement and we have achieved good results on both the urban road scene datasets GTA5->Cityscapes and SYNTHIA->Cityscapes.

Keywords: Semantic Segmentation · Unsupervised Domain Adaptation · Class-Level Alignment

1 Introduction

The goal of image semantic segmentation is to be able to assign the correct category labels to all pixels in an image, so it is suitable for complex image-based scene analysis, which is required for applications such as autonomous driving. The recently adopted convolutional neural networks (CNNs) offer various methods with the best performance for this task [1–3]. At the same time, there is a real problem that cannot be ignored, namely, all models depend on a well-trained dataset and its corresponding labels. If all images to be semantically segmented had a test dataset and its complete good label, this task would be a breeze. However, in practice there are two unavoidable problems: first, not all source domain datasets are easily available, e.g., some medical images are not publicly available per se or the number of samples is too small; second, the labels corresponding to the training data are too expensive to obtain, and these labels often require a large number of intensive pixel-level annotations that are done by expensive human labor, which is time-consuming and labor-intensive.

A potential solution to these two problems is to use simulated data, such as selected images from virtual scenes generated by computers or simulators [4–6] as source domain data, which has the advantage that a large number of source domain data samples can be easily obtained to solve the problem of insufficient data, while the labeling of these synthetic images is also done by computers, which is not only very complete and detailed but also fast to save time and cost. However, the models trained with simulated images, no matter how perfect they perform in the simulated data environment, often fail to achieve the expected or satisfactory results once they are replaced by real scene images, and even the accuracy drops drastically. The reason for this degradation is that the two domains (source and target) are taken from different datasets, which have independent data distributions and large inter-domain differences. This phenomenon is commonly referred to as domain drift or domain shift [7]. The cross-domain task [8] needs to overcome this problem and undoubtedly faces a great challenge.

In order to achieve the cross-domain task to solve the domain drift problem, we adopt a domain adaptive approach, i.e., we reduce the domain drift problem to some extent by adjusting the feature distribution of the source domain (virtual image data) and the target domain (real image data) to reduce the distribution difference between them. Specifically we use the idea of adversarial learning to design a segmentation network and a discriminator network as the main framework of the model, and a segmentation network and a discriminator network are designed as the adversarial sides to distinguish the target sample from the source sample by training the domain discriminator, while the segmentation network tries to deceive the discriminator [8–16] into making wrong judgments by generating domain invariant features, and the discriminator is responsible for trying its best to identify whether the generated image comes from the source domain or the target domain. As the adversarial training escalates, the images generated by the segmentation network become more and more deceptive closer and closer to the target domain images, which means that the distribution difference between the source and target domains is gradually shrinking and the consistency between the two is getting stronger and stronger, finally achieving the purpose of solving the domain drift.

Despite the impressive progress in domain-adaptive semantic segmentation, most of the previous work has been devoted to the complete global feature distribution without paying much attention to the underlying structure between classes, and there is still a large amount of noise at the junction between classes. This is one of the reasons why the current domain-adapted semantic segmentation is not yet effective enough. As discussed in recent works [17, 18, 36], matching the global feature distribution alone does not guarantee that the expected error on the target domain is reduced and the class conditional distributions should be aligned as well. This implies that class-level alignment plays an equally important role in domain-adapted semantic segmentation. Therefore, it is necessary to satisfy both the matching alignment of global features of the image and also to solve the problem about the alignment between semantic classes. The difference between global alignment and class alignment is shown in Fig. 1, where blue indicates the source domain samples and red indicates the target domain samples. Figure

(a) shows the results of global feature alignment, where the traditional discriminator can achieve good inter-domain discrimination, and the feature alignment between the two domains is basically good after domain adaptation, but some samples are still mixed together incorrectly. Figure (b) shows the semantic class level alignment by the fine-grained discriminator, which not only achieves the correct classification of the source and target domains but also distinguishes the different semantic classes in the source and target domains.

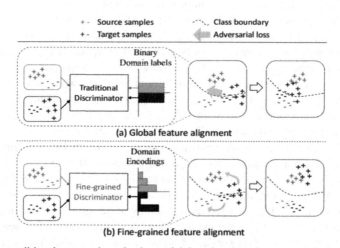

Fig. 1. The traditional approach and adversarial learning based on semantic category fine-grained are illustrated. Traditional adversarial learning pursues edge distribution alignment and ignores the inconsistency of semantic structure between domains. We propose to use fine-grained discriminators to achieve semantic class-level alignment.

There have been some inspiring works [11, 19, 37] to try to solve the problem of semantic class-level alignment.Chen et al. [19] proposed to use multiple independent discriminators for class-level alignment, but since each discriminator is independent and the effective information of the learned features is not further integrated and optimized, the model may still fail to capture the relationship between individual semantic classes. Luo et al. [11] introduced adaptive adversarial loss functions to roughly approximate class-level alignment by applying different weights to each region in the image. In practice, however, they do not explicitly incorporate semantic class information effectively into their approach, which may not facilitate class-level alignment.The work of Haoran Wang [20, 38] et al. is illuminating in that although the labels of the target domain are inaccessible in the unsupervised domain adaptive task, they find that the model predictions on the target domain also contain by semantic class information, and demonstrate that it is possible to use predictions on both domains to supervise the discriminator: i.e., merging semantic class information into the learning process of the adversarial network allows the model to model the semantic inter-class structure, thus enabling fine-grained semantic class-level feature alignment.

We follow this idea by introducing semantic class information in the adversarial learning process and aligning features according to specific classes. We find that this operation also offers the possibility of fine-grained classification, where we integrate semantic class information into the discriminator and encourage it to judge and align at the fine-grained semantic class level by means of an objective optimization function. In addition, we observe a more general problem in the semantic segmentation results between, i.e., different semantic classes always have a large noise at the intersection, or even a segmentation error. As shown in Fig. 2, in the Source only graph it can be seen that the sidewalk is incorrectly segmented into the road, and in the AdaptSegNet graph on the right it is seen that the edge segmentation of the building class and the vegetation class is also not accurate enough.

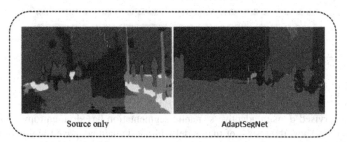

Fig. 2. It illustrates that the pixel certainty of previous domain adaptive semantic segmentation methods for boundary segmentation of semantic categories still needs to be improved.

The study [21]showed that there is some connection between pixel certainty and entropy and also demonstrated that if the model is trained only on the source domain then it tends to produce overconfident (i.e., low entropy) source-like image predictions and underconfident (i.e., high entropy) target-like image predictions. This phenomenon is shown in Fig. 2.

On the one hand the predicted entropy map of the scene from the source domain looks like the edge detection results, with only high entropy activations at the boundaries of each semantic category. On the other hand the prediction for the target domain image is uncertain, which leads to a large amount of noise in the image segmentation result, which is represented as some columns of high entropy output in the entropy map. It is easy to argue that one possible way to reduce the difference in distribution between the source and target domains is to reduce the entropy of the pixels in the prediction of the target image, thus increasing the confidence level of the predicted pixels, especially those near the boundaries. Thus, we decided to try to increase the degree of certainty that the target predicted pixels belong to that semantic category while ensuring semantic category alignment. Experiments show that our model outperforms some of the more advanced unsupervised domain-adaptive semantic segmentation methods, and we also tested it on a commonly used publicly available road scene dataset. (Fig. 3)

- We propose a new mechanism that introduces a target prediction pixel entropy minimization strategy during fine-grained adversarial learning at the semantic class level for images to achieve better semantic segmentation, which results in clearer semantic segmentation outputs and correct recovery of larger blurred regions in images.

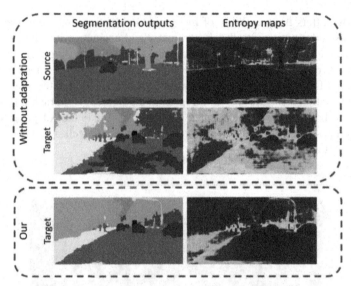

Fig. 3. Unsupervised domain adaptive semantic segmentation based on entropy minimization. The top two rows show the results of the model without domain adaptive training in the source and target domain scenarios. The bottom row shows the results of the model based on entropy minimization domain adaptive training in the same target domain scenario. The left and right columns show the visual semantic segmentation output and the corresponding predicted entropy mapping results, respectively.

- We evaluate our method by comprehensive experiments. Significant progress is achieved on popular domain adaptive semantic segmentation tasks compared to other state-of-the-art methods, including GTA5->Cityscapes and SYNTHIA->Cityscapes.

2   Related Works

2.1   Semantic Segmentation

Semantic segmentation is the task of predicting the unique semantic class label corresponding to each pixel of an input image, which can also be considered as a pixel-level classification task. With the development of deep convolutional neural networks, computer vision has made tremendous progress in this area. Many excellent models have emerged for the task of image semantic segmentation, which often perform well when sufficient training data and labels are available, but the models do not generalize well enough and show a sharp performance degradation when tested on other discrepant datasets. However, in real-world scenarios, it is not guaranteed that the model has a large amount of well-labeled training data under arbitrary conditions, especially in some unfamiliar and unknown scenarios, and it is also difficult to meet the consistency of the distribution between the source domain data when the model is trained and the target domain data when the model is actually working.

2.2 Domain Adaptation

Domain adaptation, as a representative approach to migration learning, aims to address various types of cross-domain tasks, i.e., for model performance degradation caused by different distributions of the source domain (training data) and the target domain (test data). In recent years, several studies have been proposed to address this problem in image classification tasks [12, 17]. Inspired by the existence of risk-theoretic upper bounds in the target domain [22], some pioneering works have suggested feature alignment by optimizing the inter-domain difference measure between the two domains [23, 24, 39]. Recently, adversarial training, driven by GAN networks [25], has attracted attention for its leading ability to align features [12, 13, 19].

2.3 Unsupervised Domain Adaptive Semantic Segmentation

The semantic segmentation of images can in fact be seen as a more detailed pixel-level image classification problem, so theoretically semantic segmentation domain adaptation can fully draw on the existing related research results in the field of image classification. Because the labels of the target domain images are inaccessible, the challenge of unsupervised domain adaptation (UDA) [26, 27] is enormous. The aim is to better perform the cross-domain task by transferring the effective information learned by the network model in the labeled source domain dataset to the unlabeled target domain images, thus improving the performance of the model on the target domain. Many UDA methods have been proposed to mitigate the domain drift problem. One common idea is to align the source and target domain distributions [28]. There are several ways to explore this idea in practice.CLAN [11] is an outstanding representative of this: it suggests applying different adversarial weights to different regions, but it does not directly and explicitly merge semantic class information into the model. AdaptSegNet [13] and Advent [21] mitigate domain drift. Another common direction to solve the problem is to align the input pixels of source and target domain images by generating adversarial networks [10] or Fourier transforms [29]. In recent years, especially in the field of UDA semantic segmentation, pseudolabel refinement in a self-training framework has achieved quite good results. By iteratively training the network with progressively improved target pseudolabels, the performance of the model in the target domain can be further improved. Driven by this motivation, CBST [16] also achieved good results by setting appropriate thresholds for different semantic categories to improve the performance of model self-training.

3   Method

In this section, we propose the domain adaptive semantic segmentation algorithm with convolutional fine-grained discrimination and entropy minimization. To better introduce our model, we will start with the existing convolutional fine-grained adversarial learning and then describe how to introduce the entropy minimization approach and the process of fusing the two.

3.1 Semantic Segmentation

The structure of the entire adversarial network can be divided into a generative network and a discriminator network. Traditional adversarial training seeks to align the feature distribution by confusing the binary discriminator; specifically, the generative network makes every effort to generate images that can deceive the discriminator in an attempt to make a wrong judgment; while the binary discriminator tries to correctly identify whether the input image comes from the source or target domain in an attempt to avoid being deceived by the generative network.. The limitation of the traditional binary discriminator is that it can only make simple judgments, i.e., whether the image has a higher probability of belonging to the source domain or to the target domain, which largely limits the segmentation accuracy of the model and falls far short of our requirements. In order to make the discriminator not only focus on the differentiation domain, our idea is to make the discriminator not limited to making simple binary judgments but also focus on the semantic class information, specifically, we use the convolutional fine-grained discriminator to optimize and upgrade the binary discriminator by expanding its original two output channels to K channels, and then encourage it to perform the semantic class level at a finer granularity. Adversarial training. Where, K denotes the number of semantic classes to be segmented in the source and target datasets. By this design, the discriminator can fully exploit the role of adversarial learning, so that the discriminator can not only distinguish the domain to which the feature image belongs, but also further distinguish the specific class to which the feature belongs, e.g., whether it is the sky class or the building class in the source domain or the row human class or the vegetation class in the target domain. In other words, the prediction confidence of both source and target domains are represented as confidence distributions over different semantic classes, which enables the new convolutional fine-grained discriminator to model a more complex underlying structure between semantic classes, and thus better perform semantic class-level alignment. After this operation is done, the corresponding binary domain labels of the traditional discriminators are correspondingly overwhelmed and need to be converted into a general form, i.e., domain encoding, to contain semantic class information as well. The domain labels traditionally used for training binary discriminators are the source domain [1,0] and the target domain [0,1], respectively. In contrast, the domain encoding is represented by vectors [a;0] and [0;a] for the two domains, where a is the feature extracted in classifier C, represented by a k-dimensional vector; and 0 is an all-zero k-dimensional vector. When the discriminator believes that an image feature belongs to the i-th class of the source domain with higher probability, it will set the i-th dimensional vector in [a;0] to 1 and the rest to 0. Similarly, when the discriminator makes a judgment that an image feature belongs to the j-th class of the target domain, it will set the j-th dimensional vector in [0;a] to 1. This achieves the transformation from the traditional binary discriminator to the convolutional fine-grained discriminator. Transformation. This allows the discriminator to not only correctly distinguish domains during adversarial learning, but will also learn to model class structure and be able to portray the semantic class-to-class relationships in more detail.

The network structure is shown in Fig. 4. We divide the whole network structure into three parts: the generative network or called semantic segmentation part, the adversarial learning network, and the entropy minimization network that increases the pixel certainty.

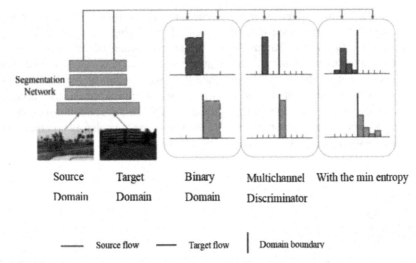

Fig. 4. Different strategies for generating domain labels, as shown in the figure, the traditional binary discriminator is only able to determine which domain the feature pixel comes from, while the updated multi-channel discriminator is able to perform a more fine-grained determination of semantic categories, and then when the entropy minimization strategy is added, it can be seen that the degree of certainty that each pixel belongs to its semantic category also increases significantly.

In which, the segmentation network G consists of feature extractor F and classifier C. Firstly, some images are randomly selected from the source and target domains and fed into the segmentation network. After the feature extraction and classification by the extractor and classifier, the feature maps of the source and target domains are obtained. On the one hand, the segmentation loss is calculated by comparing the source domain feature map with its corresponding source domain label, and the segmentation loss is continuously reduced in the process of adversarial training to help the segmentation network generate more deceptive images, i.e., the consistency of the source and target domain images in the generated images of the segmentation network is getting higher and higher, i.e., the gap between domains is decreasing.

On the other hand, after obtaining the feature maps, the semantic feature maps of the two domains are then input to the convolutional fine-grained discriminator and enter into the discriminator work part. At this point the discriminator uses the domain encoding processed from the sample prediction and tries to distinguish the domain information and class information of the features on the fine-grained semantic classes, calculates the probability that the feature pixel belongs to the domain and the class and makes a corresponding judgment, and calculates the loss of the discriminator by comparing the number of correct and incorrect judgments of the discriminator. In the adversarial training, the parameters are continuously iterated and updated to reduce the loss function, thus improving the ability of the discriminator to make correct judgments to continue the confrontation with the generative network. Also, to increase the degree of confidence of a pixel in the semantic class to which it belongs and to reduce the large amount of noise present in image segmentation, especially near the junction between semantic classes. We transform the hard-to-express degree of pixel certainty into pixel entropy that can quantify the output, by adding the process of calculating the target pixel entropy minimization for the feature output, so that it can be learned adversarially with the discriminator to compensate for the wrong judgments made by the convolutional fine-grained discriminator. Therefore, we integrate the loss function of the convolutional fine-grained discriminator with the loss function of entropy minimization, and during the iterative process of adversarial learning, as the adversarial loss is continuously reduced, our segmented images will become more and more accurate, and also avoid much noise in the segmentation, being the boundary more clear (Fig. 5).

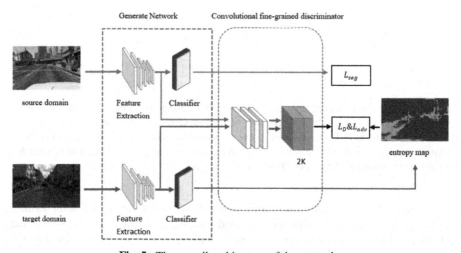

Fig. 5. The overall architecture of the network.

In order to better constrain the learning process of the network, we design three loss functions in the whole network structure, including: segmentation loss function L_{seg}, discriminator loss function L_D, and adversarial loss function L_{adv}.

The segmentation loss function is as follows.

$$L_{seg} = - \sum_{(h,w) \in n_s} \sum_{k=1}^{K} y_s^{(h,w)} log P_{x_s}^{(h,w)} \tag{1}$$

The main role of the segmentation loss function is to guide the segmentation network to generate semantic segmentation images with finer accuracy, which is achieved by training the reduction on the source domain dataset while training the reduced adversarial loss on the target domain dataset together with continuously updating the feature extractor and classifier. Where, is the source domain label, is the probability confidence that the segmentation network predicts that the source domain sample x belongs to the kth semantic class.

The loss function of the discriminator is as follows.

$$L_D = - \sum_{i=1}^{n_s} \sum_{k=1}^{K} a_{ik}^{(s)} log P(d = 0, c = k | f_i) - \sum_{j=1}^{n_t} \sum_{k=1}^{K} a_{jk}^{(t)} log P(d = 1, c = k | f_j) \tag{2}$$

During the training process, the discriminator not only tries to distinguish between source or target domains, but also will learn to model the semantic class structure. Where $a_{ik}^{(s)}$ and $a_{jk}^{(s)}$ is the kth class feature of sample i in the source domain and sample j in the target domain.

The adversarial loss function is as follows.

$$L_{adv} = -\sum_{j=1}^{n_t} \sum_{k=1}^{K} a_{jk}^{(t)} \log P(d = 0, c = k|f_j) \tag{3}$$

The main role of L_{adv} is to deceive the discriminator and guide the generative network to generate feature maps with consistent distribution between domains, in other words to maximize the probability of target domain features being used as source domain features without compromising the relationship between features and semantic classes.

3.2 Entropy Minimization

In unsupervised domain adaptive semantic segmentation, the target domain is unlabeled, and there is no way to use the labels to compute the segmentation loss function to guide the model training as in the source domain. So we propose to use a constrained model to make it produce high confidence predictions. Here we do not use high confidence pseudo-labeling based on the lack of memory capacity of the graphics card, because end-to-end training is not worth the memory occupied by pseudo-labeling. Instead, we generate semantic segmentation images with a high confidence level by minimizing the prediction pixel entropy. Specifically, we use Shannon entropy [30] to accomplish this task. Given a target domain input image x_t, the entropy mapping $E_{x_t} \in [0, 1]^{H \times W}$ consists of independent pixel-level entropies normalized to the range [0,1] as follows.

$$E_{x_t}^{(h,w)} = -\frac{-1}{\log(K)} \sum_{k=1}^{K} P_{x_t}^{(h,w,k)} \log P_{x_t}^{(h,w,k)} \tag{4}$$

Then, the entropy loss can be defined as the sum of all pixelated normalized entropies as follows.

$$L_{ent}(x_t) = \sum_{h,w} E_{x_t}^{(h,w)} \tag{5}$$

Similarly, in the training process, we jointly optimize the cross-entropy loss of the supervised segmentation of the source domain samples and the unsupervised entropy loss of the target domain samples. The loss function of minimum entropy can be obtained and expressed as:

$$\min_{G} \frac{1}{|x_s|} \sum_{x_s} L_{seg}(x_s, y_s) + \frac{\lambda}{|x_t|} \sum_{x_t} L_{ent}(x_t) \tag{6}$$

3.3 Fusion and Adversarial Learning

By carefully observing and studying the prediction results of semantic segmentation, we found that if only the adversarial learning of convolutional fine-grained discriminator is performed, although the modeling of semantic inter-class relations can be improved, the confidence of the pixels in the classes to which they belong still needs to be improved, and intuitively the semantic segmentation pixels in the target domain still have a large ambiguous part, especially at the locations where classes intersect with each other. Therefore, we introduce the entropy minimization of the predicted pixels on top of the convolutional fine-grained discriminator. The specific measures we take are as follows: first, to find the right time for the entropy minimization to be added, here we add it in the adversarial network, and the fine-grained discriminator piece by piece in the adversarial learning to continuously constrain the segmentation network to generate feature images with higher segmentation accuracy. We do not recommend adding this operation after the classifier in the segmentation network, as it has been found experimentally that the effect of entropy minimization in improving pixel confidence will be greatly reduced if the adversarial learning process is lost. In addition, since the adversarial network contains both the convolutional fine-grained discriminator and the entropy minimization, we also modify the adversarial loss. Then the adversarial loss function of the whole network becomes:

$$L_{adv} = -\sum_{j=1}^{n_t} \sum_{k=1}^{K} a_{jk}^{(t)} \log P(d = 0, c = k|f_j) + \lambda \sum_{h,w} E_{x_t}^{(h,w)} \tag{7}$$

where is the weight of the sum of all pixel-wise normalized entropies.

In the training process, we then jointly optimize the supervised segmentation loss of the source domain data samples and the unsupervised adversarial loss of the target domain data samples. The final optimization problem is formulated as follows.

$$\min_{G} L_{seg} + \lambda_{adv} L_{adv} \tag{8}$$

In this way, the entropy minimization of the predicted pixels can well compensate for the lack of pixel confidence in the fine-grained discriminator, and together with the convolutional fine-grained discriminator, through adversarial learning, continuously promote the improvement of the network segmentation image accuracy, and finally reach the effect that the model is trained in the source domain and can also achieve good performance in the target domain.

4 Experiments

4.1 Datasets

We performed a comprehensive evaluation of our proposed method on two popular unsupervised domain adaptive semantic segmentation datasets, GTA5->Cityscapes and SYNTHIA->Cityscapes.

Cityscapes Cityscapes [31] is a large-scale dataset for autonomous driving model training, focusing on some road scenes of urban life, with a high diversity of videos and images sampled from different urban centers, as well as in multiple seasons. Set contains 2975 images, the validation set 500 images and the test set 1525 images. Following standard protocols [8, 10, 13], we use 2975 images from the Cityscapes training set as the unlabeled target domain training set and evaluate our model on 500 images from the validation set.

SYNTHIA SYNTHIA [5] is a large synthetic dataset of images obtained from scene renderings of virtual cities. We selected its subset SYNTHIA-RAND-CITYSCAPES, which shares 16 semantic classes with Cityscapes, as the source domain. In total, 9400 images from the SYNTHIA dataset were used as the source domain training data for this task.

GTA5 GTA5 [4] is another synthetic dataset that shares 19 semantic classes with Cityscapes. The dataset was rendered from the modern computer game Grand Theft Auto V, which has labels fully compatible with Cityscapes. 24,966 images of urban scenes were collected and used as source training data.

4.2 Network Architecture

We use Deeplab-V2 [2] as the basic semantic segmentation architecture, and apply a void space pyramidal pooling (ASPP) on the feature output of the last layer in order to better capture the scene context. The sampling rate is fixed to {6,12,18,24}, similar to the ASPPL model in [2]. We perform experiments on the base deep CNN architecture ResNet-101 [32]. After [2], we modify the step size and expansion rate of the last layer to produce denser feature maps and larger perceptual fields. To further improve the performance of ResNet-101, we also adapt the multilevel outputs from the conv4 and conv5 features [13].

4.3 Implementation Details

We use the PyTorch [33] implementation. For a fair comparison, we used DeeplabV2, as the segmentation base network. All models are pre-trained on ImageNet [34]. For the convolutional fine-grained discriminator, we used a simple structure consisting of 3 convolutional layers with {256,128,2K} channels, 3 convolutional kernels, and a step size of 1. Each convolutional layer except the last one is followed by a Leaky-ReLU [35] parameter with a value of 0.2. To train the segmentation network, we use a stochastic gradient descent (SGD) optimizer, where the momentum is 0.9 and the weights decay to. The learning rate was initially set and decreased with a poly learning rate of power of 0.9. The discriminator is trained using the Adam optimization algorithm, $= 0.9$, $= 0.99$, with an initial learning rate of. The same poly learning rate strategy was used. It was set to 0.001. Regarding the training process, the network is first trained on the source data for 20k iterations and then fine-tuned for 40k iterations using our framework. The batch size is 2. One of them is the source image and one is the target image. Some data enhancement methods are used, including random flips and color changes, to prevent overfitting.

4.4 Experimental Results

Our approach is tested with respect to domain adaptation on both datasets, and the experimental results show that our algorithm achieves excellent results. The experiments use the mean intersection-to-merge ratio (mIoU) as an evaluation metric, which is the most important evaluation metric in semantic segmentation tasks. Our algorithm model achieves 49.5 mIoU in GTA5->Cityscapes experiments and 45.4 in SYNTHIA->Cityscapes experiments.

Table 1. GTAV-to-Cityscapes results.

Method	Road	Side	Building	Wall	Fence	Pole	Light	Sign	Vegetation	terrain	Sky	Person	Rider	Car	Truck	Bus	Train	Motor	Bike	mIoU
Source Only	75.8	16.8	77.2	12.5	21.0	25.5	30.1	20.1	81.3	24.6	70.3	53.8	26.4	49.9	17.2	25.9	6.6	25.3	36.0	36.6
Cycada	79.1	33.1	77.9	23.4	17.3	32.1	33.3	31.8	81.5	26.7	69.0	62.8	14.7	74.5	20.9	25.6	6.9	18.8	20.4	39.5
AdaptSeg	86.5	25.9	79.8	22.1	20.0	23.6	33.1	21.8	81.8	25.9	75.9	57.3	26.2	76.3	29.8	32.1	7.2	29.5	32.5	41.4
SIBAN	88.5	35.4	79.5	26.3	24.3	28.5	32.5	18.3	81.2	40.0	76.5	58.1	25.8	82.6	30.3	34.4	3.4	21.6	21.5	42.6
CLAN	87.0	27.1	79.6	27.3	23.3	28.3	35.5	24.2	83.6	27.4	74.2	58.6	28.0	76.2	33.1	36.7	6.7	31.9	31.4	43.2
CBST	86.8	46.7	76.9	26.3	24.8	**42.0**	**46.0**	**38.6**	80.7	15.7	48.0	57.3	27.9	78.2	24.5	49.6	17.7	25.5	45.1	45.2
DISE	**91.5**	47.5	82.5	31.3	25.6	33.0	33.7	25.8	82.7	28.8	82.7	**62.4**	30.8	85.2	27.7	34.5	6.4	25.2	24.4	45.4
ADVENT	89.4	33.1	81.0	26.6	26.8	27.2	33.5	24.7	83.9	36.7	78.8	58.7	30.5	84.8	**38.5**	44.5	1.7	31.6	32.4	45.5
PyCDA	90.5	36.3	84.4	32.4	28.7	34.6	36.4	31.5	**86.8**	37.9	78.5	62.3	21.5	85.6	27.9	34.8	**18.0**	22.9	**49.3**	47.4
Ours	90.8	**49.8**	**85.0**	**39.5**	28.7	33.3	35.5	18.1	86.7	**39.7**	**85.6**	61.1	**35.9**	**86.7**	31.8	49.9	0.0	**35.5**	46.8	**49.5**

As can be seen from Table 1, all domain adaptive methods significantly outperform Source Only methods, i.e., models trained on images of synthetic scenes are directly applied to images of real scenes. This shows that domain adaptive methods are necessary for semantic segmentation tasks with different feature distributions. Comparing some current more advanced unsupervised domain adaptation methods, the model designed in this paper is able to achieve optimal results with a mIoU of 49.5, which is a significant improvement of 12.9 over the Source Only model trained on the source domain. Firstly, for the baseline method AdaptSegNet, which uses a traditional unsupervised domain adaptation method based on adversarial discriminations from The disadvantage of AdaptSegNet is that matching the global distribution of source and target domains may lead to some classes whose distributions in the feature space are already matched being disrupted after migration instead, resulting in some classes not performing as well as the Source Only model, i.e., a negative migration phenomenon. Specifically, for the classes "fence", "pole" and "bike" in Table 1, the performance of AdaptSegNet method on these three classes is even The performance of the AdaptSegNet method on these three classes is not even as good as that of the model without the domain adaptation method (i.e., Source Only). In contrast, the algorithm model proposed in this paper aligns the joint distribution of classes in the source and target domains at the class level, so that it can handle each class well and significantly outperforms the baseline method AdaptSegNe by 8.1 mIoU. More specifically, the algorithm in this study outperforms the Source Only model for almost all classes, i.e., there is no negative migration phenomenon. It should be noted that the simulator-generated dataset GTAV is taken from the in-game city scenes, and for the "train" category, its effect on the model is not considered for the time being because of the low stability of the training samples in this category in the source and target domains. Then, the algorithm of this study outperforms the unsupervised domain-based adaptive method CBST by 4.3 mIoU, and outperforms ADVENT and PyCDA by 4 mIoU and 2.1 mIoU, respectively. Overall, the algorithm model proposed in this paper outperforms other models, and the effectiveness of the model is verified by rich comparison tests.

It is obvious from Table 2 that all unsupervised image semantic segmentation algorithms using domain adaptation outperform Source only methods, which means that domain adaptation methods play an important role in reducing the domain gap between the source and target domains and improving the performance of the model on the target domain. It can be seen that the algorithm designed in this paper even improves the mIoU by 11.9 compared to Source only. Because algorithms SIBAN, AdaptSegNet and CLAN have individual semantic classes that are not correctly identified and segmented, their mIoU results are not calculated and further compared. In addition, compared to algorithms AdaptPatch and ADVENT, the algorithms in this paper improved 5.4 mIoU and 4.2 mIoU, respectively.

Table 2. SYNTHIA-to-Cityscapes results.

Method	Road	SideWalk	Building	Wall	Fence	Pole	Light	Sign	Vegetation	Sky	Person	Rider	Car	Bus	Motor	Bike	mIoU
Source only	55.6	23.8	74.6	**9.2**	0.2	24.4	6.1	12.1	74.8	79.0	55.3	19.1	39.6	23.3	13.7	25.0	33.5
SIBAN	82.5	24.0	79.4	-	-	-	16.5	12.7	79.2	82.8	**58.3**	18.0	79.3	25.3	17.6	25.9	-
AdaptSegNet	84.3	**42.7**	77.5	-	-	-	4.7	7.0	77.9	82.5	54.3	21.0	72.3	32.2	18.9	32.3	-
CLAN	**88.5**	35.4	79.5	-	-	-	32.5	18.3	81.2	76.5	58.1	**25.8**	82.6	34.4	21.6	21.5	-
AdaptPatch	84.5	38.0	78.6	8.7	**0.6**	26.0	3.9	11.1	75.5	**84.6**	53.5	21.6	71.4	32.6	19.3	31.7	40.0
ADVENT	62.4	42.2	79.7	8.7	0.4	25.9	5.4	8.1	80.4	84.1	57.9	23.8	73.3	36.4	14.2	33.0	41.2
Ours	84.3	40.5	**82.2**	8.6	0.2	**31.3**	18.4	18.2	**85.5**	83.4	54.5	18.7	**85.1**	**47.8**	22.6	**44.8**	45.4

The results of the ablation experiments are shown in Table 3. The results of the semantic segmentation model trained on the source domain without domain adaptation and tested directly on the target domain, i.e., the Source Only method, are shown first. The model without domain adaptation method shows a relatively poor result of

Table 3. Ablation experiments.

GTAV → Cityscapes

Source Only	AdaptSegNet	Convolutional fine-grained discriminator	entropy minimization	mIou
√	√	√	√	36.6
	√	√		41.4
	√			48.4
				49.5

36.6 mIoU on the target domain data aggregation. Then the results of the unsupervised domain adaptation method based on traditional adversarial discrimination for semantic segmentation, i.e., the AdaptSegNet method, are shown. The global alignment of the traditional adversarial discriminant-based method is significantly improved compared to the unsupervised domain adaptive model, with a result of 41.4 mIoU. After that, the discriminant network is modified based on the AdaptSegNet method, i.e., the original traditional binary discriminator is transformed into a multi-category convolutional fine-grained discriminator. The binary discriminator can only distinguish the source domain or target domain, and further make the judgment that the features may belong to a semantic category in the source or target domain, so that each semantic category can be well aligned. Then, on top of this, the target prediction pixel entropy minimization method is introduced, and the entropy loss function and adversarial training are used to increase the certainty of the predicted pixels, especially the pixels near the category boundaries, by calculating the entropy map of the target domain prediction image, so that the boundary features of the semantic categories are clearer, and the final model is improved again by 1.1 mIoU, and finally the mIoU of the algorithm model in this paper reaches 49.5 on the validation set of the target domain data.

The results of some randomly selected visualized adaptive semantic segmentation are shown in Fig. 6. It is obvious from the figure that the visualization results of the algorithm model in this paper are closer to the real image semantic labels than the Source Only model without domain adaptation, which can not only identify some rare categories, such as "pole" and "street light" It can not only identify some rare categories, such as "pole" and "street light", but also has no significant noise for the intersection boundary of different semantic categories.

The comparison focuses on the traffic sign class within the white box in the target domain image. For the segmentation results of the model without any domain adaptation processing (Source Only), the traffic sign classes can be correctly segmented, although the global segmentation results are poor. This phenomenon indicates that some classes are initially aligned in the distribution of source and target domain data features even though they are not processed by any domain adaptation method. The adversarial discrimination-based domain adaptive method AdaptSegNet, as the baseline method in this paper, uses a global-level alignment of the distribution of the output features of the source and target domains after the semantic segmentation network, and although the overall segmentation effect of the adversarial learning-based domain adaptive method is better than that of the

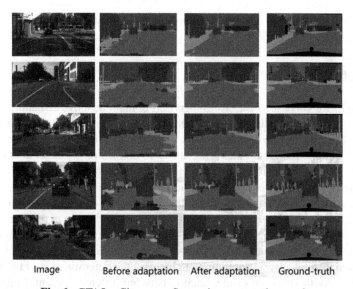

Image   Before adaptation   After adaptation   Ground-truth

Fig. 6. GTA5->Cityscapes Semantic segmentation results

model without any domain adaptation, the segmentation result for traffic signs is poor, even inferior to that of the model without any domain adaptive model. This is because the global alignment strategy favors some common classes with a large percentage of pixels and tends to make conservative predictions for the features. This results in some uncommon features being predicted to other common classes, causing a negative

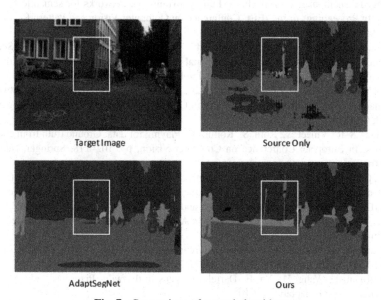

Target Image   Source Only

AdaptSegNet   Ours

Fig. 7. Comparison of several algorithms

migration phenomenon for those uncommon features, even though these classes are well aligned in the initial state (Fig. 7).

5   Conclusion

In this work, we solve the task of unsupervised domain adaptive semantic segmentation, and propose a convolutional fine-grained discriminant and entropy minimization algorithm. Specifically, the discriminant used in traditional confrontational training can only judge whether features come from the source domain or the target domain, which seriously damages the identification between semantic categories. Different from the traditional binary discriminator, the convolutional fine-grained discriminator expands the channel and keeps consistent with the number of semantic categories in the datasets of the target domain, so it can not only distinguish the source domain or the target domain, but also further make a judgment that the feature belongs to a class in the source domain or a class in the target domain. In addition, the entropy of the target pixel is calculated and reduced by adversarial training to increase the determination of the predicted pixel, especially the position of the junction between different semantic categories in the image. Finally, the effectiveness of the model in this task was verified by a large number of comparative experiments, and the contribution of each module to the model was verified by detailed ablation experiments. Our model achieves good results from two challenging synthetic datasets to real datasets.

References

1. Long, J., Shelhamer, E., Darrell, T.: Fully convolutional networks for semantic segmentation. In Proceedings of the IEEE Conference on Computer Vision and Pattern Recognition, pp. 3431–3440 (2015)
2. Chen, L.-C., Papandreou, G., Kokkinos, I., Murphy, K., Yuille, A.L.: Deeplab: Semantic image segmentation with deep convolutional nets, atrous convolution, and fully connected crfs. IEEE Trans. Pattern Analysis Mach. Intell. **40**(4), 834–848 (2018)
3. Luo, Y., Zheng, Z., Zheng, L., Guan, T., Yu, J., Yang, Y.: Macro-micro adversarial network for human parsing. In European Conference on Computer Vision, pp. 424–440. Springer, New York (2018)
4. Richter, S. R., Vineet, V., Roth, S., Koltun, V.: Playing for data: Ground truth from computer games. In European Conference on Computer Vision, pp. 102–118. Springer, New York (2016)
5. Ros, G., Sellart, L., Materzynska, J., Vazquez, D., Lopez, A.M.: The synthia dataset: A large collection of synthetic images for semantic segmentation of urban scenes. In Proceedings of the IEEE Conference on Computer Vision and Pattern Recognition, pp. 3234–3243 (2016)
6. Luo, Y., Guan, T., Pan, H., Wang, Y., Yu, J.: Accurate localization for mobile device using a multi-planar city model. In ICPR (2016)
7. Shimodaira, H.: Improving predictive inference under covariate shift by weighting the log-likelihood function. J. Stat. Plann. Inf. **90**(2), 227–244 (2000)
8. Hoffffman, J., Wang, D., Yu, F., Darrell, T.: Fcns in the wild: Pixel-level adversarial and constraint-based adaptation (2016)
9. Chen, Y., Li, W., Sakaridis, C., Dai, D., Van Gool, L.: Domain adaptive fast RCNN for object detection in the wild. In: Computer Vision and Pattern Recognition (CVPR) (2018)

10. Hoffffman, J., Tzeng, E., Park, T., Jun-Yan Zhu, a.P.I., Saenko, K., Efros, A.A., Darrell, T.: Cycada: Cycle consistent adversarial domain adaptation. In: International Conference on Machine Learning (ICML) (2018)
11. Luo, Y., Zheng, L., Guan, T., Yu, J., Yang, Y.: Taking a closer look at domain shift: Category-level adversaries for semantics consistent domain adaptation. In: The IEEE Conference on Computer Vision and Pattern Recognition (CVPR) (2019)
12. Saito, K., Watanabe, K., Ushiku, Y., Harada, T.: Maximum classififfier discrepancy for unsupervised domain adaptation (2017)
13. Tsai, Y.H., Hung, W.C., Schulter, S., Sohn, K., Yang, M.H., Chandraker, M.: Learning to adapt structured output space for semantic segmentation. In: IEEE Conference on Computer Vision and Pattern Recognition (CVPR) (2018)
14. Zhang, Y., David, P., Gong, B.: Curriculum domain adaptation for semantic segmentation of urban scenes. In: The IEEE International Conference on Computer Vision (ICCV), Vol. 2, p. 6 (2017)
15. Zhang, Y., Qiu, Z., Yao, T., Liu, D., Mei, T.: Fully convolutional adaptation networks for semantic segmentation. CoRR abs/1804.08286 (2018)
16. Zou, Y., Yu, Z., Vijaya Kumar, B.V.K., Wang, J.: Unsupervised Domain Adaptation for Semantic Segmentation via Class-Balanced Self-training. In: Ferrari, V., Hebert, M., Sminchisescu, C., Weiss, Y. (eds.) ECCV 2018. LNCS, vol. 11207, pp. 297–313. Springer, Cham (2018). https://doi.org/10.1007/978-3-030-01219-9_18
17. Chen, C., Xie, W., Huang, W., Rong, Y., Ding, X., Huang, Y., Xu, T., Huang, J.: Progressive feature alignment for unsupervised domain adaptation. In: The IEEE Conference on Computer Vision and Pattern Recognition (CVPR) (2019)
18. Kumar, A., et al.: Co-regularized alignment for unsupervised domain adaptation. In: Bengio, S., Wallach, H., Larochelle, H., Grauman, K., Cesa-Bianchi, N., Garnett, R. (eds.) Advances in Neural Information Processing Systems, vol. 31, pp. 9345–9356. Curran Associates, New York (2018)
19. Chen, Y., Chen, W., Chen, Y., Tsai, B., Wang, Y.F., Sun, M.: No more discrimination: Cross city adaptation of road scene segmenters. In: IEEE International Conference on Computer Vision, ICCV 2017, Venice, Italy, October 22–29, 2017, pp. 2011–2020 (2017)
20. Wang, H., Shen, T., Zhang, W., Duan, L., Mei, T.: Classes matter: A fiffine-grained adversarial approach to cross-domain semantic segmentation. In The European Conference on Computer Vision (ECCV) (2020)
21. Vu, T.H., Jain, H., Bucher, M., Cord, M., Perez, P.: Advent: Adversarial entropy minimization for domain adaptation in semantic segmentation. In: CVPR (2019)
22. Ben-David, S., Blitzer, J., Crammer, K., Kulesza, A., Pereira, F., Vaughan, J.W.: A theory of learning from different domains. Mach. Learn. **79**(1), 151–175 (2010). https://doi.org/10.1007/s10994-009-5152-4.
23. Long, M., Cao, Y., Wang, J., Jordan, M.I.: Learning transferable features with deep adaptation networks. In: Proceedings of the 32nd International Conference on International Conference on Machine Learning, ICML'15, Vol. 37, pp. 97–105. (2015), http://dl.acm.org/citation.cfm?id=3045118.3045130
24. Sun, B., Saenko, K.: Deep CORAL: Correlation Alignment for Deep Domain Adaptation. In: Hua, G., Jégou, H. (eds.) ECCV 2016. LNCS, vol. 9915, pp. 443–450. Springer, Cham (2016). https://doi.org/10.1007/978-3-319-49409-8_35
25. Goodfellow, I.J., Pouget-Abadie, J., Mirza, M., Xu, B., Warde-Farley, D., Ozair, S., Courville, A., Bengio, Y.: Generative adversarial nets. In: Proceedings of the 27th International Conference on Neural Information Processing Systems, NIPS'14, Vol. 2. pp. 2672–2680. MIT Press, Cambridge, MA, USA (2014). http://dl.acm.org/citation.cfm?id=2969033.2969125
26. Jialin Pan, S., Tsang, I.W., Kwok, J.T., Yang, Q.: Domain adaptation via transfer component analysis. IEEE Trans. Neural Netw. 22(2), 199–210 (2011)

27. Patel, V.M., Gopalan, R., Li, R., Chellappa, R.: Visual domain adaptation: A survey of recent advances. IEEE Sig. Proces. Mag. **32**(3), 53–69 (2015)
28. Ganin, Y., Lempitsky, V.: Unsupervised domain adaptation by backpropagation. In Proceedings of International Conference on Machine Learning (ICML), pp. 1180–1189 (2015)
29. Yang, Y., Soatto, S.: Fda: Fourier domain adaptation for semantic segmentation. In Proceedings of the IEEE/CVF Conference on Computer Vision and Pattern Recognition (CVPR), pp. 4085–4095 (2020)
30. Shannon, C.E.: A mathematical theory of communication. Bell Syst. Tech. J. (1948)
31. Cordts, M., Omran, M., Ramos, S., Rehfeld, T., Enzweiler, M., Benenson, R., Franke, U., Roth, S., Schiele, B.: The cityscapes dataset for semantic urban scene understanding. In: Proceedings of the IEEE Conference on Computer Vision and Pattern Recognition (CVPR) (2016)
32. He, K., Zhang, X., Ren S., Sun, J: Deep residual learning for image recognition. In CVPR (2016)
33. Paszke, A., Gross, S., Massa, F., Lerer, A., Bradbury, J., Chanan, G., Killeen, T., Lin, Z., Gimelshein, N., Antiga, L., Desmaison, A., Kopf, A., Yang, E., DeVito, Z., Raison, M., Tejani, A., Chilamkurthy, S., Steiner, B., Fang, L., Bai, J., Chintala, S.: Pytorch: An imperative style, high-performance deep learning library. In: Wallach, H., Larochelle, H., Beygelzimer, A., Alch´e-Buc, F., Fox, E., Garnett, R. (eds.) Advances in neural information processing systems, Vol. 32, pp. 8024–8035. Curran Associates Inc, New York (2019). http://papers.neurips.cc/paper/9015-pytorch-an-imperative-style-high-performance-deep-learning-library.Pdf
34. Deng, J., Dong, W., Socher, R., Li, L.J., Li, K., Fei-Fei, L.: ImageNet: A Large Scale Hierarchical Image Database. In: CVPR09 (2009)
35. Maas, A., Hannun, A., Ng, A.: Rectifier nonlinearities improve neural network acoustic models. In: Proceedings of the International Conference on Machine Learning, Atlanta, Georgia (2013)
36. Lu, H., Zhang, M., Xu, X.: Deep fuzzy hashing network for efficient image retrieval. IEEE Trans. Fuzzy Syst. (2020). https://doi.org/10.1109/TFUZZ.2020.2984991
37. Lu, H., Li, Y., Chen, M., et al.: Brain intelligence: go beyond artificial intelligence. Mob. Netw. Appl. **23**, 368–375 (2018)
38. Lu, H., Li, Y., Mu, S., et al.: Motor anomaly detection for unmanned aerial vehicles using reinforcement learning. IEEE Internet Things J. **5**(4), 2315–2322 (2018)
39. Lu, H., Qin, M., Zhang, F., et al.: RSCNN: A CNN-based method to enhance low-light remote-sensing images. In: Remote Sensing, p. 62 (2020)

Ensemble of Classification and Matching Models with Alpha-Refine for UAV Tracking

Zezhou Wang[1], Shuhao Chen[1], Chunjuan Bo[2(✉)], and Dong Wang[1]

[1] School of Information and Communication Engineering, Dalian University of Technology, Dalian, China
[2] School of Information and Communication Engineering, Dalian Minzu University, Dalian, China
bcj@dlnu.edu.cn

Abstract. Traditional single object tracking has has been well investigated in recent years. There are many excellent trackers including the offline tracker and the online updating tracker. However, few efforts were spent on drone-based object tracking because of its complexity. In this paper, a novelty ensemble of classification and matching model with alpha-refine (ECMMAR) method is proposed for drone-based object tracking. ECMMAR integrates two different types of trackers by a elaborate discriminator. This discriminator can combine the tracking results of the two trackers to judge the tracking credibility of the trackers and then choose a more reliable results.Experimental results on Visdrone-SOT 2020 benchmark for drone-based visual tracking demonstrate that our proposed method achieving a satisfactory tracking performance.

Keywords: Visual object tracking · Drone-based tracking · Ensemble of tracker

1 Introduction

Visual object tracking is a important task in computer vision. It models the appearance and motion information of the target to predict the motion state of the target with the context information of video and image sequences. Single object tracking aims to infer the location of an arbitrary target in a video sequence, given only its location in the first frame.In past decades, object tracking has made great progress and development, especially the deep learning methods [1, 11, 14, 15, 19–21, 26, 30] which achieved satisfactory results.However, existing tracking research mainly focused on the video sequences captured by normal cameras. In the recently years, drone-based object tracking has attracted the attention of the community due to its complexity. Compared to general object tracking challenges such as illumination variation and occlusion,drone-based tracking is more difficult because of extremely small targets, frequent view point change, and abrupt camera motion.

Presently, there are mainly two types of deep learning trackers. One [15, 29] based on siamese network extract the features of search image and template image from the same backbone network, then calculates the response map through the cross- correlation, and

S. Yang and H. Lu (Eds.): ISAIR 2022, CCIS 1701, pp. 125–135, 2022.
https://doi.org/10.1007/978-981-19-7943-9_10

uses region proposal network (RPN) [18] for regression. The other tracker combines discriminative localization model with a separate scale estimation model, such as DiMP [2] and ATOM [4]. Siamese trackers utilize the deep feature, and have simple model structure. But their shortcomings are obvious. They only utilize the target appearance without background information which is crucial for discriminating the target from similar objects. Aiming at the disadvantages of the siamese approach, DiMP utilizes the background information to designs a online-classifier, which improves the ability of model discrimination, and adopts a nice updating strategy. Even so, the possibility that drift frames can be used as a template for update can not be avoided in the DiMP. Besides, its long-term tracking capability is insufficient to cope with large shifts between frames and there is no mechanism to deal with occlusion.

In order to address the problems frequent occlusion, background clutter, and abrupt camera motion in the drone-based long-term object tracking, we propose a Ensemble of Classification and Matching Models with Alpha-Refine (ECMMAR) method, which combines DiMP and Siamese tracker. Our method mainly in- cludes a discrimination selection mechanism and a target redetection module, which are used for the interaction between two sub-trackers to improve tracking accuracy and credibility. In addition, there is a compensation strategy in our method for dealing with abrupt camera motion. We evaluated our tracker on the visdrone2020 dataset. Figure 1 demonstrates the improvement of our tracker.It always choose the right result from two sub-trackers, and correct the wrong result one in time. The results show that our tracking method has excellent performance in drone-based object tracking.In summary, the contributions of our work mainly include the following aspects: (1) We propose a method which can be used to automatically switch between two trackers and cooperate with each other to accurately judge the current tracking state; (2) We propose a redetection module to deal with the situation when target lost during long-term tracking; and (3) ECMMAR is applied to object tracking task of visdrone, which has excellent accuracy compared with other tracking methods.

GroudTrurh   SiamRPN++   DiMP   Ours

Fig. 1. Comparison result of DiMP, SiamRPN ++and our method on two challenging drone-based sequences. Our tracker is able to choose the right result from two sub trackers, and make the bounding box more tight with Alpha-Refine.The frame number is marked at the upper left corner of the image.

2 Related Work

In this section, we will review the single object tracking algorithms in recent years. The current tracking methods are mainly divided into two types.

2.1 Correlation-Filter-Based Methods

The earliest correlation filtering method MOSSE [3, 27] realizes the conversion from time domain to frequency domain through fast Fourier transform, which greatly improves the speed of the algorithm, so it has received widespread attention.Since then, there have been many related improved algorithms. CSK [12] and KCF [13] introduce circulant matrices and kernelized correlation, and utilize the improved features to achieve a significant performance improvement. DSST [6] regards object tracking as two independent problems: localization variation and scale change. It trains the translation filter and scale estimation separately. In SR-DCF [7], weight constraints are added to the filter coefficients, which effectively alleviates the boundary effect caused by the circulant matrix. Compared with methods based on deep learning, correlation filtering is computationally efficient but lacks accuracy.

2.2 Deep-Learning-Based Methods

With the development of deep learning technology, many deep learning based tracking algorithms have emerged, such as HCF [16], HDT [17], ECO [5], etc. Different from handcrafted features, they use CNNs to extract image features and merge them into the correlation filters to obtain good tracking performance. Other deep learning based tracking algorithms, such as SINT [19] and SiamFC [1], directly learn the matching function of target template and search image by using siamese network with offline-trained methods. However, they only use the target in the first frame as the template during the tracking, so these methods do not make accurate estimation of the target box and lack robustness. After that, the RPN (region proposal network) module is added to the SiamRPN, which significantly improves the accuracy of the predicted bounding box. Then DasiamRPN, SiameseRPN ++and SiamDW [25] and others have made improvements to solve the problems that the training samples of SiamRPN are unbalanced and the depth network break the translation invariance, which greatly improves the performance of the Siamese tracker. At the same time, trackers such as ATOM and DiMP divide the tracking task into a classification task and a target estimation task, and they all use online update classification modules, which improves the discriminative ability of the tracker and significantly improves the performance of the tracker.

Although great progress has been made in traditional single object tracking, these methods cannot cover problems in drone-based object tracking.In this work, we argue that our method can effectively improve the performance of the tracker in the field of drone-based object tracking.

3 Proposed Algorithm

In this section, we describe the proposed method in detail. First of all, we give the overview on the whole architecture of ECMMAR.And then we introduce the discriminator that judge the output result of the tracker and the method of redetection the tracking object after it is lost.

3.1 Overview

The structure of out tracker is shown in Fig. 2, including two sub trackers (Dimp and SiamPRN++), a discriminator, a refine module, and a redetection module. DiMP is a tracker whose filter can be updated online. It utilizes the background information to improve discrimination ability of the tracker. However, due to that, the cumulative error of online update increases gradually, which results in the incredible score of this tracker. SiamRPN ++is a offline-trained tracker, whose template will not be affected by the error accumulation caused by tracking frame offset during tracking. But it is easily interfered by similar objects. Our tracking algorithm is based on both of two trackers.

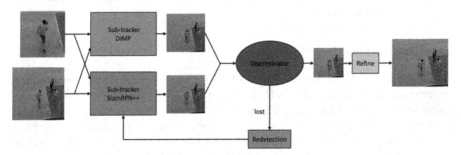

Fig. 2. Architecture of out tracker. It is composed of two sub-trackers (DiMP and SiamRPN++), discriminator, redetection and refine module.

First of all, the current frame image is sent to two sub trackers, then they give their tracking results and confidence scores respectively. Moreover, the output of DiMP includes a extra flag. It consists of *not_found, uncertain, hard_negative, normal,* which are set by preset different thresholds. The discriminator will give the tracker state with the results of two sub trackers, and make different selection and processing according to different states. After that, the result is send to the refine module. In the refine module, we will further modify the predicted bounding box to make it more compact. If the target state is loss given by discriminator, it will trigger the redetection mechanism to help tracker detect the target when it appears in the view again.

During the tracking, we also utilize camera motion compensation and image enhancement strategy. Camera motion compensation is to alleviate the target estimation drift caused by the rapid movement of the camera in a short time. The SIFT feature is utilized to help compensate the frame that the pixel difference between adjacent frames is greater than a certain threshold. Image enhancement is to improve the accuracy of the tracker at night. In the experiment (Sect. 4), we will explain the effect of both of strategies in detail.

3.2 Discriminator

Our discriminator will determine that the tracker is in the following three situations: (1) Normal tracking, that is, the output results of the two trackers are considered reliable. (2) One tracker drifts, and the other is normal. (3) Both tracking have drifted, and the target is lost.

Assume that in the current frame T_n we get the tracking result of DiMP (including the bounding box B_d and the current tracking state F_d) and the tracking result of SiamRPN ++(including the bounding box B_s and the current tracking confidence score C_s). First, we combine F_d and C_s to judge the current status of the tracker by calculating the ratio R_d and R_s. R_d is the proportion of F_d is lost in the T_{n-t+1} to T_n frame. R_s is the proportion of C_s is less than the threshold τ in the T_{n-t+1} to T_n frame.

For the condition

$$R_d > 0.9 \ and \ R_s > 0.5 \tag{1}$$

$$R_d > 0.5 \ and \ R_s > 0.9 \tag{2}$$

When neither of the above two conditions is satisfied, we believe that at least one of the two sub-trackers is correct, and further judgment will be made at this time. If the IOU(Intersection over Union) of B_d and B_s of the two sub-trackers is greater than 0, it is considered that both sub-trackers are in the normal tracking state. B_d is then selected as the tracking result and sent to Refine module. Moreover, we will update the (x_o, y_o) in the (5) with B_d. When the IOU is not satisfied, we calculate whether the IOU of B_d and B_s in the last 5 frames. If the IOUs from T_{n-4} to T_n frame are all 0, it is considered that one of the two trackers is abnormal. We will send the result of Dimp to SiamRPN ++tracker for scoring (the score of DiMP is not credible) and get a confidence score C_d. Then we compare it with confidence score C_s of SiamRPN++. Combining the tracking state F_d of DiMP to judge the following two situations:

$$C_s > 0.7 \ and \ C_s - C_d > 0.3 \tag{3}$$

$$C_d - C_s > 0.3 \ and \ F_s \neq' not\_found' \tag{4}$$

When condition (3) is true, the discriminator selects SiamRPN++, while condition (4) is true, the discriminator selects DiMP. When both of the above conditions are not true, we will calculate the Euclidean distance between the results of the two sub-trackers and the correct tracking position of the latest frame. As the (5), we select the tracking results of the sub trackers with smaller Euclidean distance.

$$\min \sqrt{(x_o - x_i)^2 + (y_o - y_i)^2}, \quad i \in \{1, 2\} \tag{5}$$

where (x_o, y_o) denotes the last credible location result of our tracker, and $(x_1, y_1) (x_2, y_2)$ denote the predicted locations of DiMP and SiamRPN ++separately. If either condition (1) or (2) is satisfied, the discriminator considers both sub-trackers are lost, and then the redetection model will be enabled. We will introduce the redetection module in detail.

3.3   Redetection Module

As described in Sect. 3.2, when the tracking target is determined to be lost, the redetection module is enabled. Specifically, in the drone-based object tracking, the UAV always moves with the target. When the target is severely blocked and disappears for a short time, the target is still near the center point of the picture. So it is considered that the target will not drift too far in the frames that determine the lost of the target. When target is lost, we change the center point of the search area of the current frame from the center of bounding box of the previous frame to the center of the picture, and utilize SiamRPN ++to redetect the target. Specifically, we expand the search area of SiamRPN ++to 36 times the size of the target. (the reason why we do not use DiMP to redetect the target is that the classification label used during DiMP training is Gaussian distribution, and the mismatch between the test search area and training search area will result in inaccurate response map). We assume that the change of scale is very small before and after the target disappears, so we update both of two sub trackers with the scale (width and height) of the target box before the t frame when target lost. In order to avoid that the loss ratio R_d and R_s in the first t frames are still large at the time when the tracker finds the target, we set a buffer time with deleting the first ten frames of the loss state flag.

4   Experiment

In this section, we use experiments to validate the performance of ECMMAR. Implementation details and results are also presented.We evaluate the proposed method on VisDrone-SOT2020 benchmark. Tracker performance is measured by Precision and Success. Our experiment was conducted on the basis of DiMP and SiamRPN++ pretrained models.Below we give a detailed analysis.

4.1   Dataset

The Visdron-SOT2020 dataset [9] is divided into three subsets, including the training set containing 70K frames of 86 videos, the verification set containing 7K frames of 11 videos, and the test set containing 145K frames of 95 videos. The VisDrone-SOT2020 dataset introduce more challenging drone sequences compared to VisDrone-SOT2018 dataset [22] of 132 videos and VisDrone-SOT2019 dataset [8, 28] of 167 videos. In order to reliably reflect the performance of tracking algorithms, the video sequences of the three subsets are captured from varying scenarios with various drone platforms under different conditions. In addition, there are 12 attributes to mark each video sequence, including aspect ratio change (ARC), background clutter (BC), camera motion (CM), fast motion (FM), full occlusion (FOC), partial occlusion (POC), illumination variation (IV), low resolution (LR), out-of-view (OV), similar object (SO), scale variation (SV) and viewpoint change (VC).

4.2   Implementation Details

The proposed method is trained on PyTorch deep learning framework with a 2080ti GPU.We use the training set of the Visdrone-SOT 2020 dataset to fine-tune the pretrained model of DIMP and AlphaRefine[24].We train DiMP with 35 EPOCH with optimization Adam. Parameters setting such as learning rate are the same as the [2]. We train Alpha-Refine based on pretrained model from epoch40 and iterated 20 epochs. The learning rate adopted a fixed step size 8, attenuation coefficient gamma is 0.5, and the remaining parameters are the same as the [24]. We use the long term version of SIAMRPN ++pretrained model without finetune. In the inference stage, because there are some videos at night in Visdrone-SOT 2020 dataset, low brightness will seriously affect the performance of the tracker, so we conduct light enhancement processing[10] for the video whose brightness is lower than the threshold.

4.3   Results and Analysis

In this section, we first evaluate our tracker on visdrone2020 *all testing* dataset, including *dev* and *test challenge* set, divided into short-term part and long-term part, and compare it with other tracking algorithms. After that, we carry out ablation experiments of our tracker.

We evaluate our tracker on the visdrone2020 *all testing* dataset. We compare it with 7 competitive methods, including Siamese network based algorithms and correlation filter based algorithms. The detailed comparison results are presented in Table 1, and the results on short-term part and long-term part are shown in Tables 2 and 3 respectively.

Table 1. Comparison results on VisDrone2020 *all testing* set with performance measures of Precision score (PRE) and Success score (SUC).

	SMILEv2	LTNMI	PrSiam RCNN	DIMP+ SiamRPN	DROL _ LT	DiMP _AR	ECO	**Ours**
PRE ↑	91.1	89.9	70.8	81.5	77.3	74.1	53.1	85.1
SUC ↑	66.0	66.0	54.7	60.3	58.2	56.0	38.3	63.0

Obviously, our tracker works well on the overall *all testing* dataset. Especially in Success score, our method achieves 63.0, which is very competitive to the state-of-the-art tracker SMILEv2 and LTNMI, and outperforms from the DiMP + SiamRPN with 60.3, The improvement mainly comes from the design of our Discriminator and Refine module, which could switch results between DiMP and SiamRPN ++automatically and make the predicted bounding box more strictly. As shown in Table 3, our tracker performs very well on long-term part. This is because that our redtection mechanism has played a important role. As for short-term part, our tracker is not robust enough, but our tracker outperform most of siamese network based trackers and correlation filter based trackers.

Following [23], we adopt precision (PRE) and success (SUC) scores in one- pass evaluation (OPE) to assess different tracking approaches.

Table 2. Comparison results on VisDrone2020 short-term part of *all testing* set.

	SMILEv2	LTNMI	PrSiam RCNN	DIMP+ SiamRPN	DROL_LT	DiMP_AR	ECO	**Ours**
PRE ↑	90.6	92.3	76.0	84.9	83.3	84.6	60.6	85.8
SUC ↑	73.4	76.5	65.2	68.7	70.7	70.8	47.9	69.1

Table 3. Comparison results on VisDrone2020 long-term part of *all testing* set.

	SMILEv2	LTNMI	PrSiam RCNN	DIMP+ SiamRPN	DROL_LT	DiMP_AR	ECO	**Ours**
PRE ↑	91.9	84.1	63.6	76.7	68.8	59.4	42.6	84.1
SUC ↑	55.5	51.3	39.9	45.6	43.6	35.2	24.9	54.4

To investigate the impact of each module in our tracker, we do the ablation study. We evaluate on VisDrone2020 *dev* set with each module in our tracker. "D" denotes *DiMP*, "S" denotes *SiamRPN++*, "AR" denotes *Alpha-Refine* module. Moreover, we evaluate our tracker on *test-challenge* set because *dev* set do not have enough sequences with attributes *camera motion, night* and *full occlusion*. "LLE" denotes *Low light enhancement*, "CMC" denotes *Camera motion compensation*. "REDE" denotes *redetection*. The results are presented in Tables 4 and 5. Experiment shows that results of each module in our tracker have obvious improvement, which further promotes the final tracking results more accurate and robustness.

As shown in Table 5, every module in our tracker has great contribution to the results. Especially the discriminator module (D + AR + LLE + S), is 11.3% higher than before. In addition, we find that UAV visual angle always jitter and the target is small, so it is not suitable to utilize search region 4 times than the template as traditional siamese based algorithms do. As a result, we do the experiment on VisDrone2020 *dev* set to explore the most suitable search region of different sizes. The results are presented in Table 6.

As shown in the results, it will reduce the tracker performance if we utilize search region 4 times than the template, and the SUC is only 59.2 with SiamRPN++. Search region size is very sensitive. If it is too small, the target is easy to get out the search region for the tracker in the current frame. In contrast, if the search region is too large, it is easy to get more distractors. Finally, we choose the search region 16 times larger than the template.

Table 4. Expected PRE and SUC results on VisDrone2020 *dev* set for different modules of our tracker.

	PRE ↑	SUC ↑
D	84.41	64.48
S	77.20	59.20
D + AR	85.19	66.97
D + S + AR	87.32	68.20

Table 5. Expected SUC results on VisDrone2020 *test-challenge* set for different modules of our tracker.

	SUC ↑
D + AR	65.78
D + AR + LLE	66.86
D + AR + LLE + S	74.44
D + AR + LLE + S + REDE	76.75
D + AR + LLE + S + REDE + CMC	78.95

Table 6. Comparison results on VisDrone2020 *dev* set with search region of different sizes of SiamRPN ++when normal tracking.

Search Region	PRE ↑	SUC ↑
4 times	77.2	59.2
9 times	82.4	62.9
16 times	83.0	63.3
25 times	79.9	60.9

5 Conclusion

In this work, we propose an method that combines an online tracker and an offline tracker named ECMMAR for drone-based object tracking. Specifically,we design a discriminator to switch between the two trackers and judge the tracking state of the two trackers.When the target lost, we use the redetection module to find it. And by employing brightness enhancement and motion compensation strategies, our approach can further improve the tracking accuracy.The experimental results demonstrate the superiority of our method.

Acknowledgement. This work was supported in part by the National Natural Science Foundation of China (NSFC) under Grant 62176041, in part by the Science and Technology Innovation

Foundation of Dalian under Grant 2020JJ26GX036, and in part by the Fundamental Research Funds for the Central Universities under Grant DUT21LAB127.

References

1. Bertinetto, L., Valmadre, J., Henriques, J.F., Vedaldi, A., Torr, P.H.: Fully-convolutional siamese networks for object tracking. In: European Conference on Computer Vision, pp. 850–865. Springer, New York (2016)
2. Bhat, G., Danelljan, M., Gool, L.V., Timofte, R.: Learning discriminative model prediction for tracking. In: Proceedings of the IEEE/CVF International Conference on Computer Vision, pp. 6182–6191 (2019)
3. Bolme, D.S., Beveridge, J.R., Draper, B.A., Lui, Y.M.: Visual object tracking using adaptive correlation filters. In: 2010 IEEE Computer Society Conference on Computer Vision and Pattern Recognition, pp. 2544–2550. IEEE, New York (2010)
4. Danelljan, M., Bhat, G., Khan, F.S., Felsberg, M.: Atom: Accurate tracking by overlap maximization. In: Proceedings of the IEEE/CVF Conference on Computer Vision and Pattern Recognition, pp. 4660–4669 (2019)
5. Danelljan, M., Bhat, G., Shahbaz Khan, F., Felsberg, M.: Eco: Efficient convolution operators for tracking. In: Proceedings of the IEEE Conference on Computer Vision and Pattern Recognition, pp. 6638–6646 (2017)
6. Danelljan, M., H¨ager, G., Khan, F., Felsberg, M.: Accurate scale estimation for robust visual tracking. In: British Machine Vision Conference, Nottingham, September 1–5, 2014. BMVA Press, Dundee (2014)
7. Danelljan, M., Hager, G., Shahbaz Khan, F., Felsberg, M.: Learning spatially regularized correlation filters for visual tracking. In: Proceedings of the IEEE International Conference on Computer Vision, pp. 4310–4318 (2015)
8. Du, D., Zhu, P., Wen, L., Bian, X., Ling, H., Hu, Q., Zheng, J., Peng, T., Wang, X., Zhang, Y., et al.: Visdrone-sot2019: The vision meets drone single object tracking challenge results. In: Proceedings of the IEEE/CVF International Conference on Computer Vision Workshops (2019)
9. Fan, H., Wen, L., Du, D., Zhu, P., Hu, Q., Ling, H., Shah, M., Wang, B., Dong, B., Yuan, D., et al.: Visdrone-sot2020: The vision meets drone single object tracking challenge results. In: European Conference on Computer Vision, pp. 728–749. Springer, New York (2020)
10. Guo, X., Li, Y., Ling, H.: Lime: Low-light image enhancement via illumination map estimation. IEEE Trans. Image Process. **26**(2), 982–993 (2016)
11. He, A., Luo, C., Tian, X., Zeng, W.: A twofold siamese network for real-time object tracking. In: Proceedings of the IEEE Conference on Computer Vision and Pattern Recognition. pp. 4834–4843 (2018)
12. Henriques, J.F., Caseiro, R., Martins, P., Batista, J.: Exploiting the circulant structure of tracking-by-detection with kernels. In: European Conference on Computer Vision, pp. 702–715. Springer, New York (2012)
13. Henriques, J.F., Caseiro, R., Martins, P., Batista, J.: High-speed tracking with kernelized correlation filters. IEEE Trans. Pattern Anal. Mach. Intell. **37**(3), 583–596 (2014)
14. Li, B., Wu, W., Wang, Q., Zhang, F., Xing, J., Yan, J.: Siamrpn++: Evolution of siamese visual tracking with very deep networks. In: Proceedings of the IEEE/CVF Conference on Computer Vision and Pattern Recognition, pp. 4282–4291 (2019)
15. Li, B., Yan, J., Wu, W., Zhu, Z., Hu, X.: High performance visual tracking with siamese region proposal network. In: Proceedings of the IEEE Conference on Computer Vision and Pattern Recognition, pp. 8971–8980 (2018)

16. Ma, C., Huang, J.B., Yang, X., Yang, M.H.: Hierarchical convolutional features for visual tracking. In: Proceedings of the IEEE International Conference on Computer Vision, pp. 3074–3082 (2015)

17. Qi, Y., Zhang, S., Qin, L., Yao, H., Huang, Q., Lim, J., Yang, M.H.: Hedged deep tracking. In: Proceedings of the IEEE Conference on Computer Vision and Pattern Recognition, pp. 4303–4311 (2016)

18. Ren, S., He, K., Girshick, R., Sun, J.: Faster r-cnn: Towards real-time object detection with region proposal networks (2015)

19. Tao, R., Gavves, E., Smeulders, A.W.: Siamese instance search for tracking. In: Proceedings of the IEEE Conference on Computer Vision and Pattern Recognition, pp. 1420–1429 (2016)

20. Valmadre, J., Bertinetto, L., Henriques, J., Vedaldi, A., Torr, P.H.: End-to-end representation learning for correlation filter based tracking. In: Proceedings of the IEEE Conference on Computer Vision and Pattern Recognition, pp. 2805–2813 (2017)

21. Wang, Q., Teng, Z., Xing, J., Gao, J., Hu, W., Maybank, S.: Learning attentions: residual attentional siamese network for high performance online visual tracking. In: Proceedings of the IEEE Conference on Computer Vision and Pattern Recognition, pp. 4854–4863 (2018)

22. Wen, L., et al.: VisDrone-SOT2018: The Vision Meets Drone Single-Object Tracking Challenge Results. In: Leal-Taixé, L., Roth, S. (eds.) ECCV 2018. LNCS, vol. 11133, pp. 469–495. Springer, Cham (2019). https://doi.org/10.1007/978-3-030-11021-5_28

23. Wu, Y., Lim, J., Yang, M.H.: Online object tracking: A benchmark. In: Proceedings of the IEEE Conference on Computer Vision and Pattern Recognition, pp. 2411–2418 (2013)

24. Yan, B., Zhang, X., Wang, D., Lu, H., Yang, X.: Alpha-refine: Boosting tracking performance by precise bounding box estimation (2020)

25. Zhang, Z., Peng, H.: Deeper and wider siamese networks for real-time visual tracking. In: Proceedings of the IEEE/CVF Conference on Computer Vision and Pattern Recognition, pp. 4591–4600 (2019)

26. Zhu, Z., Wang, Q., Li, B., Wu, W., Yan, J., Hu, W.: Distractor-Aware Siamese Networks for Visual Object Tracking. In: Ferrari, V., Hebert, M., Sminchisescu, C., Weiss, Y. (eds.) ECCV 2018. LNCS, vol. 11213, pp. 103–119. Springer, Cham (2018). https://doi.org/10.1007/978-3-030-01240-3_7

27. Lu, H., Zhang, M., Xu, X.: Deep fuzzy hashing network for efficient image retrieval. IEEE Trans. Fuzzy Syst. (2020). https://doi.org/10.1109/TFUZZ.2020.2984991

28. Lu, H., Li, Y., Chen, M., et al.: Brain Intelligence: go beyond artificial intelligence. Mob. Netw. Appl. 23, 368–375 (2018)

29. Huimin, L., Li, Y., Shenglin, M., et al.: Motor anomaly detection for unmanned aerial vehicles using reinforcement learning. IEEE Internet Things J. 5(4), 2315–2322 (2018)

30. Lu, H., Qin, M., Zhang, F., et al.: RSCNN: A CNN-based method to enhance low-light remote-sensing images. In: Remote Sensing, p. 62 (2020)

LayoutLM-Critic: Multimodal Language Model for Text Error Correction of Optical Character Recognition

Qinkun Xu[1]([⊠]) [iD], Lei Wang[2] [iD], Hui Liu[3] [iD], and Ning Liu[4] [iD]

[1] University of Electronic Science and Technology of China, Chengdu, Sichuan 611731, China
xu_qinkun@163.com
[2] Singapore Management University, Singapore 188065, Singapore
lei.wang.2019@phdcs.smu.edu.sg
[3] Beijing Rongda Technology Co., Ltd., Beijing 100166, China
[4] Beijing Forestry University, Beijing 100083, China
liuning0928@bjfu.edu.cn

Abstract. Recently, many approaches have been proposed to correct grammatical errors. Above them, LM-Critic. (Language model critic) achieved great success. It uses a language model to judge whether a sentence is grammatical and then uses Break-It-Fix-It (BIFI) framework to fix the broken sentence. However, it does not work in the scenario of multimodal, since the text is usually not a complete sentence and the errors are often not grammatical errors. Besides, because of the noise of scanned images, there always be inevitable recognition mistakes even though using the best Optical Character Recognition (OCR) engine. And some of those are intolerable, such as errors in receipt date, total amount, etc. Therefore, it's essential to introduce an error correction system to fix OCR results. Inspired by LayoutLMv2 (Layout Language Model version 2), which introduces a pretraining task to align the text and image, we present LayoutLM-Critic, a critic used to assess how much a sentence matches the bounding box and image for the visually-rich document.

Keywords: Error correction · Language model · Multimodal · OCR

1 Introduction

OCR error correction focuses on fixing noisy text in scene text recognition, such as character missing, case inconsistency, and character mismatch. For analyzing the error type of OCR engine output, we randomly sample 100 examples from scanned Chinese invoices and make a statistic for error types. The result shows that there are 5299 segment lines that are split by the image layout (both date and total amount are counted on one segment). However, 3796 segment lines contain errors. And among these 15.46% of lines have characters missing, 15.52% of which occur case inconsistency, and 69.02% of them are typos. If we dive deeper, we can see that there are almost 80% of segment lines with 1–10 characters differ from the ground truth text. These errors take challenges for

© The Author(s), under exclusive license to Springer Nature Singapore Pte Ltd. 2022
S. Yang and H. Lu (Eds.): ISAIR 2022, CCIS 1701, pp. 136–146, 2022.
https://doi.org/10.1007/978-981-19-7943-9_11

information extraction tasks. Even though obtaining correct labels for the text eventually, we can't get actual results since the broken text. So, if we have a preprocessing step to get clean data, then we have confidence in the inference based on the sequential labeling prediction results.

Haithem Afli [1] et al. use the statistical machine translation (SMT) model to post-process the OCR error text. Given an OCR sentence containing errors, the model maximizes the posterior probability $Pr(t|s)$. Although SMT has achieved some success in correcting French document OCR errors, it requires a large number of pairs of data, which is very costly. In addition, such a model does not have good transfer ability, that is, for documents in different languages and fields, the writing style will change greatly, so data need to be collected again and the model needs to be retrained. The costs are very large.

Other studies focus on the error correction approach based on the confusion set [14]. The confusion set is one of the key data in Chinese input error correction, which is used to store the possibility of each Chinese character's typo that may be confused. The data format of the confusion set is key-value format and the key is a commonly used Chinese character, and the value is the possible error form of the Chinese character. The quality of confusion sets largely determines the upper limit of Chinese error correction. There are mainly two strategies for direct confusion set substitution, total substitution, and single word substitution.

All Substitution. Assume that every word in the sentence is wrong, replace every Chinese character one by one with the construction set, generate all possible combinations, evaluate with the binary language model, and take the one with the highest probability as the correct answer [13]. This approach traverses most of the possibilities, but the disadvantages are performance issues and FAR being too low.

Word Replacement. Assume that every word in a sentence is wrong, using a confusion set to replace every single word after a word segmentation [5, 24]. This method achieved a good recall rate on error detection tasks but was not efficient in other aspects (a large number of normal sentences were considered as having clerical errors).

The replacement strategy for single words is too simple in the above two ways. Although a good recall rate can be achieved, a large number of normal sentences will be modified and the performance is poor. To solve the above problems, there are three main ways: one is to use rules to reduce the number of words substituted; one is to use word list templates or language models to filter correct expressions; the third is to use models to generate candidate text for revision.

Xiong [8] et al. use the idea of HMM error correction candidate generation. It considers that the traditional HMM has the following two problems in the text error correction task: first, the first-order Markov can't model the long-distance dependency; Another is that too many candidate entities can degrade the performance of the model and interfere with subsequent models. The error model in this paper uses edit distance estimation and the language model uses LM calculation. In the specific operation, firstly remove the parts that do not belong to Chinese in the original sentence, and then divide the original sentence according to punctuation marks to form clauses, which are the main unit of this paper. Construct a priority queue, express the clause as a single word, replace from the first word, replace the sentence as a candidate, calculate the score according to the channel noise model and add to the priority queue, if the priority queue is full, remove the lowest score, and repeat.

However, this approach is not able to solve the case where more than two consecutive words are wrong. To solve this situation, based on the first step set, all the words composed of two words are replaced (according to the performance and statistical results, more than two consecutive errors are relatively rare). Through the above steps, the error correction problem is transformed into a shortest path problem. Add the beginning and end tags before and after the statement, calculate the shortest path from the beginning to the end, and select the first several optimal error correction candidates.

Heafield et al. [16] proposed to train the Chinese n-gram language model based on Kenlm (Kenneth Language Model) statistical language model tool. Combining the rule method and confusion set, it can correct Chinese spelling errors. The method is fast and expansible, but the effect of text error correction is not good.

Ruiqing Zhang [15] et al. built a whole set of end-to-end Chinese text error correction models, including building a pre-trained language model MLM-Phonetics and fine-tuning downstream error correction tasks.

FASpell [17] was proposed by Yuzhong et al. in 2019 to correct Chinese spelling by training a BERT-based deep noise reduction encoder (DAE) and a confidence-word-word-line similarity-based decoder (CSD). In the DAE stage, BERT can dynamically generate candidate sets to replace the traditional confusion sets, while CSD can replace the traditional single threshold to select candidate sets by calculating the two dimensions of confidence and similarity of word, sound, and font, to improve the error correction effect and achieve a state-of-the ART (SOTA) effect. However, FASpell does not include few words and multi-word error correction, the training is not an end-to-end process, and the CSD boundary curve is generated by observation fitting.

Xingyi et al. present SpellGCN [18] in 2020, which mainly learns the relationship between the font and shape structure through Graph convolutional network (GCN), and integrates the font and shape vector into the embedding of the word. Error correction is more likely to predict words in the confusion set. Model training is an end-to-end process, and experiments show that there is a great improvement in the publicly available Chinese error correction dataset. However, the coverage of the confusion set used in the test set affects the effect evaluation.

Shaohua et al. divide the error correction task into two parts: The detection network and the Correction network [19, 22, 25]. In the error detection part, the BiGRU model is used to detect the error of each input character, and the error probability value of each input character is obtained and used to calculate the soft-masked embedding as the input vector of the error correction part, which reduces the overcorrection problem of the Bert model to a certain extent and improves the error correction accuracy. However, the model does not introduce the constraint of word, sound, and glyph similarity. Although the error detection module is introduced to reduce the correction problem through soft mask technology, it only relies on Bert's semantic recognition for error correction, which is not robust enough.

Yingbo et al. take error correction as a translation task [20], which can correct different types of error forms: wrong words, few words, many words, and so on. However, the model does not learn the similarity relation of word, sound, and shape, and the result after error correction is not constrained, so it is easy to have overcorrection and error correction problems.

Minh et al. learned hierarchical vectors of words through treeLSTM model [21, 23], which does not rely on fixed confusion sets, and made the model adaptively learn the features of glyph structure vectors. The confounding relation set can be expanded by learning the model, and it has better adaptability to new words and new fields. However, the pinyin similarity between characters is not used in model learning.

All of the above methods have a problem, that is, the sentences constructed by random substitution cannot fit the distribution of true errors well, thus limiting the correction ability of true error texts. Inspired by BIFI (Break-It-Fix-It [12]), they train the Breaker to produce the wrong text, gives a good approximation to the true wrong text, and then train fixers with the outputs of the Breaker.

Similarly, as Fig. 1 shows, we take the same ways. Firstly, we train a fixer f_0 and a breaker b_0 on synthetic paired data. Then, use the breaker to generate real error OCR text to feed the fixer. Cycle $K (K = 1, 2, \ldots, k)$ rounds.

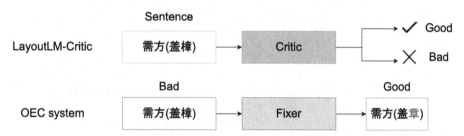

Fig. 1. The idea behind LayotLM-Critic: Local optimum criterion

2 Approach

The core component of OEC (OCR Text Error Correction) is a criterion, which gives a score for a sentence to show how much it is matched to the bounding box and image. Motivated by the large-scale pre-training multi-modal for visually-rich document understanding, such as LayoutLMv2 [9], we aim to decode the output of the LayoutLM encoder given a sentence, bounding box, and image. Specifically, we judge a sentence to be good if it has the highest probability within its local neighborhood.

2.1 Local Optimum Criterion of OCR Text

Because the LayoutLM assigns a higher probability to sentences that match the image and bounding box than mismatched ones. Based on this knowledge, a simple way to judge correction might be to obtain a threshold σ for the probability, and we have:

$$AbsThr - Critic(x) = \begin{cases} 1 \text{ if } p(x) > \sigma \\ 0 \text{ otherwise} \end{cases}. \tag{1}$$

However, we can't use this equation directly. As Fig. 2 shows, for example, "购消合同" (5th sentence) is mismatched and should have a lower probability (according to LayoutLM) than "陕西咸宁风险评估事务所有限公司" (1st sentence), which is matched. However, it contradicts reality. This is because the two sentences are not directly comparable.

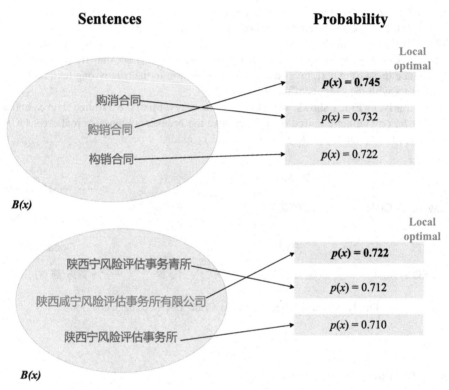

Fig. 2. The idea behind LM-Critic: Local optimum criterion

So, we should give some limitations that we can compare sentences with similar meanings.

Intuition 1 (Correlation of grammaticality and probability). For a correct sentence, x_{good}, and a broken version of it (with a similar meaning), x_{bad}, we have

$$p(x_{bad}) < p(x_{good}) \qquad (2)$$

Intuition 2 (Local neighborhood of sentences). Suppose that every sentence has only one good version of it (i.e., if the sentence matches with the image and bounding box, itself; if not, it's a corrected version). For each sentence x, there is a set of sentences, $B(x)$ (local neighborhood), that consists of the correct version and all other broken versions of x.

Based on the two intuitions, we get the following equation for judging whether a sentence is matching or not.

$$x \text{ is matching iff } x = \underset{x' \in B(x)}{\operatorname{argmax}} p(x') \tag{3}$$

2.2 Implementation of LayoutLM-Critic

Motivated by LM-Critic [10], we implement LayoutLM-Critic by approximating the local optimum criterion. First, for the sentence probability p(x), we train LayoutLM-Critic (by adding a dense layer to decode the output of LayoutLM encoder, as Fig. 3 shows) from synthetic paired data. Since obtaining the exact local neighborhood B(x) is nearly impossible, we consider to get an approximate, $\hat{B}(x)$; we implement a sentence perturbation function b, and let $\hat{B}(x)$ be samples from b(x). To check the correction of a sentence with a given bounding box and image, we apply the local optimum criterion (Eq. 4) using $\hat{B}(x)$:

$$\text{LayoutLM} - \text{Critic}(x,\ bbox,\ image) = \begin{cases} 1 \ if \ x = \underset{x' \in B(x)}{\operatorname{argmax}} p(x') \\ 0 \qquad otherwise \end{cases}. \tag{4}$$

LayoutLM-Critic. We fine-tune a critic based on the LayoutXLM using synthetic data (x_{bad}, x_{good}) pair. The dense layer of criteria will output a score range from 0 to 1 to represent the similarity between the target sentence and the correct one. And if the target sentence is correct, the score will be 1.0; otherwise, the score will be close to 0 if the sentence is totally mismatched with the bounding box and image.

Perturbation function. We study two strategies:

Word-level perturbation. Given a sentence, we randomly select a word from the confusing set to replace the current word.

Sentence-level perturbation. Given a sentence, we randomly select a sentence from the global document to replace it.

3 Experiment

3.1 LayoutLM-Critic

Figure 4 gives the distribution of log probability for pairs (x_{bad}, x_{good}) $(x_{bad} \neq x_{good})$ which randomly samples 600 sentences from SROIE [2] dataset. And Table 1 shows how often the LM gives larger scores to good samples than bad ones. From Tables 2 and 3, we can see that there are many uppercase words for fields company and address in ground truth texts. However, the OCR engine recognizes these words as normal sentences and only the first letter is capitalized. Besides, among of those the value of the amount maybe have missing characters in the OCR text, which leads the LM to give a larger score than the latter. For instance, the ground truth amount '559.53' gets a score of -20.830, and OCR text '59.53' get a score of -17.479. However, the LayoutXLM gives a higher divergence for bad samples and good samples. Table 4 shows the performance of LayoutLM-Critic.

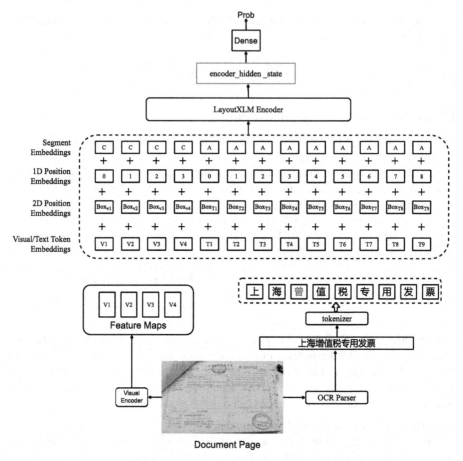

Fig. 3. The architecture of LayotLM-Critic

3.2 OEC

Setup and Data. Motivated by DrRepair [11], we get synthetic paired data by corrupting sentences from the analyzable PDF documents. Following the same steps, we learn a seq2seq model based on Transformer [7] to be our baseline fixer. We get 10M pairs of synthetic data.

Implementation details. We use traditional Transformer architecture with 12 hidden layers, 16 attention heads, and a hidden state size of 768. We use BART-base release to initialize our model parameters [4], and use the Adam algorithm as our optimizer [3], learning rate 0.00005, and gradient clipping 1.0 [6], on two GTX 3090 GPUs. In the step of generation, we use beam search with beam size 10. We run the BIFI algorithm for $K = 2$ rounds.

Results. Table 5 gives the results of the contract OCR text. The results show that the paired data generated by BIFI with LayoutLM-Critic is more realistic than the synthetic data. Figure 5 gives a sample of OCR error correction.

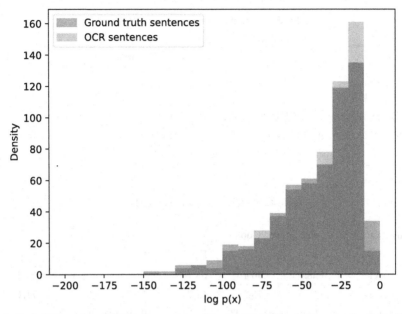

Fig. 4. Probability of ground truth sentence (blue) and OCR sentence (yellow) sentences, computed by a pre-trained LM (GPT2)

Table 1. How well OCR text probability returned by pre-trained LMs correlates with grammaticality empirically

Pretrained LM How often $p(x_{bad}) < p(x_{good})$?	
GPT2	83.53%
LayoutXLM	96.43%

Table 2. Examples when $p(x_{bad}) < p(x_{good})$

Ground truth	OCR output
DATE: 29/10/2017	Date: 29/10/2017
INPUT TAX CLAIMS, ON THE BASIC OF THE	input tax claims, on the basic of the
1 X 2.69	1 × 2.69
EXCHANGE ARE ALLOWED WITHIN	ExCHANGE ARE ALLONED WITHIN
CASH	SHO

Table 3. Examples when $p(x_{bad}) > p(x_{good})$

Ground truth	OCR output
3.60S	3.685
INV NO.: 1128507	o.:1128507
GOODS SOLD ARE NOT RETURNABLE. TQ	Goods Sold Are Not Returnable: TQ
STRICTLY NO CASH REFUND	R000115147
559.53	59.53

Table 4. Performance of LayoutLM-Critic

Perturbation	Recognize "Good"			Recognize "Good"		
	P	R	$F_{0.5}$	P	R	$F_{0.5}$
Word-Level	58.7	90.1	63.1	78.8	36.8	64.2
Sentence-Level	69.7	75.5	**69.7**	72.7	65.1	**71.1**
Perturbation	Recognize "Good"			Recognize "Good"		
	P	R	$F_{0.5}$	P	R	$F_{0.5}$
100	68.4	75.5	69.7	72.7	65.1	71.1
200	70.3	72.5	68.4	69.4	70.3	**73.8**
300	72.6	68.7	**71.8**	72.3	73.0	72.0

Table 5. OEC results

OEC system	CoNLL-2014(test)			Contract		
	P	R	$F_{0.5}$	P	R	$F_{0.5}$
Transformer	58.4	55.5	59.7	42.7	45.1	51.1
BIFI with no critic	59.3	62.5	58.4	59.4	50.6	63.6
BIFI (ours)	**63.0**	**67.6**	**62.3**	**65.4**	**67.1**	**73.2**

上海曾值税专用发票　⇨　上海增值税专用发票

Fig. 5. A sample of OCR error correction

4 Conclusion

We presented LayoutLM-Critic, an approach that uses a pretrained multimodal language model to assess how much the text, bounding box, and image match. With LayotLM-Critic and BIFI pipeline, we train an OCR error correction (OEC) by generating realistic paired data from unlabeled text. As a result, our way can be viewed as an unsupervised method to turn the LayoutLM into an actual OEC system.

References

1. Afli, H., Barrault, L., Schwenk, H.: Ocr error correction using statistical machine translation. Int. J. Comput. Linguist. Appl. **7**, 175–191 (2016)
2. Huang, Z., Chen, K., He, J., Bai, X., Karatzas, D., Lu, S., Jawahar, C.V.: Icdar2019 competition on scanned receipt ocr and information extraction (2021)
3. Kingma, D.P., Ba, J.: Adam: a method for stochastic optimization (2014)
4. Lewis, M., Liu, Y., Goyal, N., Ghazvininejad, M., Mohamed, A., Levy, O., Stoyanov, V., Zettlemoyer, L.: Bart: denoising sequence-to-sequence pre-training for natural language generation, translation, and comprehension (2019)
5. Lin, C.J., Chu, W.C.: NTOU Chinese spelling check system in SIGHAN Bake-off 2013. SIGHAN@IJCNLP 2013: 102–107
6. Pascanu, R., Mikolov, T., Bengio, Y.: On the difficulty of training recurrent neural networks (2012)
7. Vaswani, A., Shazeer, N., Parmar, N., Uszkoreit, J., Jones, L., Gomez, A.N., Kaiser, L., Polosukhin, I.: Attention is all you need (2017)
8. Xiong, J., Zhang, Q., Zhang, S., Hou, J., Cheng, X.: HANSpeller: a unified framework for Chinese spelling correction. Int. J. Comput. Linguistics Chin. Lang. Process. **20**(1) (2015)
9. Xu, Y., Xu, Y., Lv, T., Cui, L., Wei, F., Wang, G., Lu, Y., Florêncio, D.A.F., Zhang, C., Che, W., Zhang, M., Zhou, L.: LayoutLMv2: multi-modal pre-training for visually-rich document understanding. ACL/IJCNLP (1), 2579–2591 (2021)
10. Yasunaga, M., Leskovec, J., Liang, P.: LM-Critic: language models for unsupervised grammatical error correction. EMNLP (1), 7752–7763 (2021)
11. Yasunaga, M., Liang, P.: Graph-based, self-supervised program repair from diagnostic feedback (2020)
12. Yasunaga, M., Liang, P.: Break-It-Fix-It: unsupervised learning for program repair. ICML, 11941–11952 (2021)
13. Yu, L.C., Tseng, Y.H., Zhu, J., Ren, F.: Proceedings of the Seventh SIGHAN Workshop on Chinese Language Processing, SIGHAN@IJCNLP 2013, Nagoya, Japan, October 14–18, 2013. Asian Federation of Natural Language Processing 2013, ISBN 978-4-9907348-5-5 [contents]
14. Lin, C.J., Chu, W.C.A.: Study on Chinese spelling check using confusion sets and N-gram Statistics. Int. J. Comput. Linguist. & Chin. Lang. Process. **20**(1), June 2015-Special Issue on Chinese as a Foreign Language, 20(1) (2015).
15. Zhang, R., Pang, C., Zhang, C., Wang, S., He, Z., Sun, Y., Wu, H., Wang, H.: Correcting Chinese spelling errors with phonetic pre-training. ACL/IJCNLP (Findings), 2250–2261 (2021)
16. Heafield, K.: KenLM: faster and smaller language model queries. WMT@EMNLP, 187–197 (2011)
17. Hong, Y., Yu, X., He, N., Liu, N., Liu, J.: FASPell: a fast, adaptable, simple, powerful Chinese spell checker based on DAE-decoder paradigm. W-NUT@EMNLP, 160–169 (2019)
18. Cheng, X., Xu, W., Chen, K., Jiang, S., Wang, F., Wang, T., Chu, W., Qi, Y.: SpellGCN: incorporating phonological and visual similarities into language models for Chinese spelling check. ACL, 871–881 (2020)
19. Zhang, S., Huang, H., Liu, J., Li, H.: Spelling error correction with soft-masked BERT. ACL, 882–890 (2020)

20. Zhou, Y., Porwal, U., Konow, R.: Spelling correction as a foreign language. eCOM@SIGIR (2019)
21. Nguyen, M., Ngo, G.H., Chen, N.F.: Domain-shift conditioning using adaptable filtering via hierarchical embeddings for robust Chinese spell check. IEEE ACM Trans. Audio Speech Lang. Process. **29**, 2027–2036 (2021)
22. Lu, H., Zhang, M., Xu, X.: Deep fuzzy hashing network for efficient image retrieval. IEEE Trans. Fuzzy Syst. https://doi.org/10.1109/TFUZZ.2020.2984991 (2020).
23. Lu, H., Li, Y., Chen, M., et al.: Brain Intelligence: go beyond artificial intelligence. Mob. Netw. Appl. **23**, 368–375 (2018).
24. Lu, H., Li, Y., Mu, S., et al.: Motor anomaly detection for unmanned aerial vehicles using reinforcement learning. IEEE Internet Things J. **5**(4), 2315–2322 (2018).
25. Lu, H., Qin, M., Zhang, F., et al.: RSCNN: a CNN-based method to enhance low-light remote-sensing images. Remote Sens., 62 (2020)

Blind Image Deblurring Via Fast Local Extreme Intensity Prior

Dayi Yang[1,2] , Xiaojun Wu[1,2(✉)] , and Hefeng Yin[1,2]

[1] School of Artificial Intelligence and Computer Science, Jiangnan University, Wuxi, China
Wu_xiaojun@jiangnan.edu.cn
[2] Jiangsu Provincial Engineering Laboratory of Pattern Recognition and Computational Intelligence, Jiangnan University, Wuxi, China

Abstract. Blind image deblurring is a challenging problem in low-level computer vision, which aims to recover blur kernel and latent sharp image from a single blurry input. In recent years, channel priors such as dark channel prior and extreme channel prior have shown excellent results. However, the high computational cost and approximate solution of sub-problem limited the performance of these models. In this paper, a novel fast local extreme intensity prior (LEP) based on maximum a posterior (MAP) framework is presented for kernel estimation. The LEP is inspired by the observation that the blur will damage the local extreme intensity of an image patch. Moreover, we show the LEP is sparser in clear images than blurred ones, thus the change in sparsity of LEP motivated us to explore the kernel estimation model based on LEP. Then, unlike traditional half-quadratic splitting based optimization strategy, an effective and fast optimization algorithm is developed for this non-convex nonlinear problem. Experimental results on image sets show that the proposed algorithm is superior to state-of-the-art methods.

Keywords: Blind image deblurring · Local extreme intensity · Sparse

1 Introduction

As important processing technologies in the field of image and video analysis, blind image deblurring, image retrieval [1], semantic image segmentation [2], cross-modal common representations [3] and image-text matching [4] play an important role in various application scenarios of artificial intelligence [5], such as deep-sea visual monitoring system [6], autonomous driving [7], intelligent transportation system [8], routing registration system [9], etc. However, blind image deblurring is a highly ill-posed problem since both the blur kernel and latent sharp image are unknown. To make this problem well posed, plenty of image priors for kernel estimation have been developed. For example, sparsity prior [10–12], low-rank prior [13], weighted nuclear norm [14], structure prior [15], L_0 regularized [16], dark channel prior [17], extreme channel prior [18], local maximum gradient prior [19], local minimal intensity prior [20] and deep prior [21, 22]. Besides, patch prior [23, 24] has been widely used for kernel estimation, which is conducive for complex image structure extracting. In order to improve the effectiveness

© The Author(s), under exclusive license to Springer Nature Singapore Pte Ltd. 2022
S. Yang and H. Lu (Eds.): ISAIR 2022, CCIS 1701, pp. 147–158, 2022.
https://doi.org/10.1007/978-981-19-7943-9_12

of the MAP based method, edge selection step is often used for kernel estimation, such as strong edge prediction [25] and heuristic edge filtering [26–28]. With sufficient edge information, these methods can effectively achieve image deblurring; however, they are easy to cause increased noise and over-sharpening image. Since the model designed for natural images is less effective on special scenes, many priors are developed for special images, such as text [29, 30], face [31], and low-light [32].

Recently, the classical dark channel prior (DCP) has been proved effective for image deblurring [17]. But it is unlikely to help blur kernel estimation when the images have no zero pixels. To solve this problem, Yan et al. combined dark channel prior and bright channel prior (BCP) for kernel estimation [18]. However, the use of multiple priors significantly increases the computational cost.

In this paper, we present a fast local extreme intensity prior for blur kernel estimation from a single image. The prior is inspired by the observation that the local extreme intensity will be damaged by the blur processing, which is proved both mathematically and empirically. We develop a local extreme intensity approximation strategy to reconstruct the local extreme values. In addition, our local extreme intensity prior can improve low-level texture of intermediate latent image to strong edges and beneficial to kernel estimation. Moreover, we use a coarse-to-fine strategy to suppress noise and fit large kernel in the estimation process of blur kernel. It is worth noting that our prior only relies on internal patch information, but no other external statistical knowledge. Extensive experiments on different datasets demonstrate that our method is competitive compared to the state-of-the-art methods. The rest of this paper is organized as follows: In Sect. 2, we present the local extreme intensity approximation strategy and propose the new fast local extreme intensity prior. We outline our blind deblurring algorithms based on the MAP framework in Sect. 3. The experiment and further analysis of our proposed deblurring algorithm is given in Sect. 4. Finally, we present our conclusion in Sect. 5.

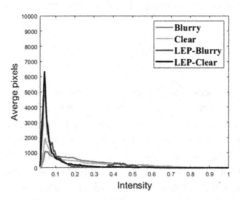

Fig. 1. Intensity histograms for local extreme intensity map of both clear and blurred images in the dataset [10]. Blurred images have far fewer extreme pixels than the clear ones

2 LEP: Local Extreme Intensity Prior

2.1 Building Local Extreme Intensity Collect Model

In a local image patch, the extreme value will be diminished after the blurring process. To formally describe this observation, we define an image $I \in \mathbb{R}^{m \times n \times c}$, and divided it into $K = \left\lceil \frac{m}{q} \right\rceil \cdot \left\lceil \frac{n}{q} \right\rceil$ non-overlapped patches with size $q \times q$. Let x and y denote the coordinates of the pixel in image I, respectively. Then, the local extreme intensity can be collected by:

$$\mathcal{L}(I)(i) = \begin{cases} min_{x \in \Omega^i}\big(min_{c \in (r,g,b)}(I^c(x))\big), & if \ u_i^b \geq u_i^d \\ max_{x \in \Omega^i}\big(max_{c \in (r,g,b)}(I^c(x))\big), & otherwise \end{cases} \tag{1}$$

where $i = 1,2,3,...K$, Ω^i denotes the i-th patch of image I, u_i^b and u_i^d denote the i-th distance between x and global brightness and darkness, respectively. I^c is the c-th color channel of image I. LEP is a collection of local extreme values on non-overlapping patches.

Previous methods have considered the intensities of pixels for blind image deblurring, such as L_0 norm of intensity and gradient for text image deblurring [16], dark channel [17] and bright channel [18] for natural image deblurring. The dark channel is defined as $D(I)(x) = min_{y \in \Psi(x)}\big(min_{c \in (r,g,b)}(I^c(y))\big)$ [8], where $\Psi(x)$ denotes the image patch centered at pixel x. Similarly, the bright channel is obtained by $B(I)(x) = max_{y \in \Psi(x)}\big(max_{c \in (r,g,b)}(I^c(y))\big)$ [9]. Note $\mathcal{L}(I) \in \mathbb{R}^K$, $D(I) \in \mathbb{R}^{m \times n}$, $B(I) \in \mathbb{R}^{m \times n}$, the proposed $\mathcal{L}(I)$ is much simpler than $D(I)$ and $B(I)$.

2.2 Fast Local Extreme Intensity Prior

Figure 1 plots the average intensity of clear and blurry images on dataset [10]. It can be seen that the LEP map of clear images have more zero pixels than those of blurry ones. And the histogram statistic of LEP map shows obvious sparsity. Therefore, LEP provides a point to distinguish clear image from blurred ones by sparsity.

Based on this characteristic, our algorithm enhance the sparsity of LEP during the process of deblurring to achieve a sparse solution of intermediate image. Let $\mathcal{L}(I)$ and $\mathcal{L}(b)$ denote the LEP map of clear image and blurred image respectively. If there exists zero pixels in the clear image, it will be greater than or equal to zero after blurred. We have:

$$\|\mathcal{L}(I)_0\| \leq \|\mathcal{L}(b)_0\| \tag{2}$$

This property can be directly derived via extending Property1 in [33]. In order to establish the relationship between the image pixel and its corresponding extreme value. We record the index when computing the LEP map of an image and use this index to map the solution to an image. The elements in M can be defined as:

$$M(I)(i) = \begin{cases} 1, & if \ u_i^b \geq u_i^d \\ 0, & otherwise \end{cases} \tag{3}$$

Let m_i denote the i-th elements of the mask M. When m_i equals to 1, the patch nearest neighbor extreme value is local minimal pixel, otherwise the patch nearest neighbor extreme value is local maximal pixel. Note that the matrix M maps an image to its LEP map and thus the transpose of M is its inverse operator.

3   Proposed Blind Deblurring Model

Local extreme function $\mathcal{L}(\cdot)$ is incorporated in our blind image deblurring model by regularizing optimization, which seeks an intermediate sparse representation I. The objective function is:

$$\min_{I,k} \|I \otimes k - b\|_2^2 + \mu \|\mathcal{L}(I)_0\| + \vartheta \|\nabla I_0\| + \gamma \|k\|_2^2 \qquad (4)$$

where μ, ϑ and γ are three non-negative regularization weights. Our model includes four terms. The data fidelity term $\|I \otimes k - b_2^2\|$ ensures the recovered image is consistent with the original image. $\|\mathcal{L}(I)_0\|$ is the new proposed prior. $\|\nabla I_0\|$ helps suppress ringing and artifacts. $\|k\|_2^2$ increases the sparsity of the blur kernel.

3.1   Estimating Latent Image

The objective function (4) can be solved directly by half-quadratic splitting method similar to [17, 18]. However, the computational cost of multiple priors optimization is expensive. Inspired by [20], in order to reduce the calculation cost, we adopt a new optimization method via alternating update the latent image and kernel. By convention, the estimation of blur kernel is performed in a coarse-to-fine manner. The results of coarse level is used as the initialization of next finer level. We elaborate the optimization process of the $(t + 1)$-th iteration in detail on the fine level, and other levels and different iterations have similar optimization.

We use a simple thresholding shrinkage step in the iteration procedure to impose sparsity inducing on the LEP of I. For an input image b, let I^{t+1} denote the latent image at the $(t + 1)$-th iteration, I_s^t and I_p^t denote the subset of $\mathcal{L}(I^t)$, we iteratively update I^{t+1} and g^{t+1} via the following steps. First, let $\in > 0$ and $0 < \omega < 1$ be threshold parameters. The LEP is thresholded as:

$$I_s^{t+1} = \begin{cases} 0, & if\ |I_s^{t+1}| < \in \\ I_s^{t+1}, & otherwise \end{cases} \qquad (5)$$

$$I_p^{t+1} = \begin{cases} 1, & if\ |I_s^{t+1}| > \omega \\ I_p^{t+1}, & otherwise \end{cases} \qquad (6)$$

Then the mask M is updated by:

$$M^{t+1}(i) = \begin{cases} 1, & if\ u_i^{t+1,b} \geq u_i^{t+1,d} \\ 0, & otherwise \end{cases} \qquad (7)$$

where $u_i^{t+1,b}$ and $u_i^{t+1,d}$ can be obtained according to Sect. 2.2. Finally, the I^{t+1} is updated as:

$$\tilde{I}^{t+1} = I_p^{t+1} \odot \left(1 - M^{t+1}\right) + I_s^{t+1} \odot M^{t+1} \tag{8}$$

where $\odot$ denotes the Hadamard product. $M(i)^{t+1}$ is determined by the index between the i-th patch and its corresponding extreme intensity. We record the index matrix M when computing the LEP map of an image and use this index to map the solution of I_p^{t+1}. and I_s^{t+1} to an image $\tilde{I}^{t+1}$.

Update g. With the given $\tilde{I}^{t+1}$, the ∇I is updated by:

$$\min_I \left\| \tilde{I}^{t+1} \otimes k - b \right\|_2^2 + \vartheta \left\| \nabla \tilde{I}^{t+1} \right\|_2^2 \tag{9}$$

Introducing an auxiliary variable g with respect to ∇I the problem can be approximated by

$$\min_g \left\| \tilde{I}^{t+1} \otimes k - b \right\|_2^2 + \lambda \left\| g - \nabla \tilde{I}^{t+1} \right\|_2^2 + \vartheta \| g \|_0 \quad s.t. \quad g = \nabla \tilde{I}^{t+1} \tag{10}$$

Note that the sup-problem about g in (10) is an element-wise minimization problem, thus the solution of g can be expressed as:

$$g^{t+1} = \begin{cases} \nabla \tilde{I}^{t+1}, \left| \nabla \tilde{I}^{t+1} \right| \geq \frac{\vartheta}{\lambda} \\ 0, otherwise \end{cases} \tag{11}$$

Update I. Finally, I is updated by solving the following formulation:

$$\min_I \| I \otimes k - b \|_2^2 + \lambda \nabla \left\| I - g^{t+2} \right\|_2^2 \tag{12}$$

Equation (12) contains all quadratic terms, and we can obtain its solution by the least square method. In each iteration, FFT (Fast Fourier Transform) is used to accelerate the computation process. Its closed form solution is given as follows:

$$I^{t+1} = \mathcal{F}^{-1} \left(\frac{\overline{\mathcal{F}(k)}\mathcal{F}(b) + \lambda \left(\overline{\mathcal{F}(\nabla_v)}\mathcal{F}\left(g_v^{t+1}\right) + \overline{\mathcal{F}(\nabla_h)}\mathcal{F}\left(g_h^{t+1}\right) \right)}{\overline{\mathcal{F}(k)}\mathcal{F}(k) + \lambda \left(\overline{\mathcal{F}(\nabla_v)}\mathcal{F}(\nabla_v) + \overline{\mathcal{F}(\nabla_h)}\mathcal{F}(\nabla_h) \right)} \right) \tag{13}$$

where $\mathcal{F}(\cdot)$ and $\mathcal{F}^{-1}(\cdot)$ are Fast Fourier Transform (FFT) and its inverse, respectively. $\overline{\mathcal{F}(\cdot)}$ denotes the complex conjugate operator of FFT, ∇_v, ∇_h are gradients in the vertical and horizontal directions, respectively.

3.2 Estimating Blur Kernel k

With given I^{t+1}, optimizing k becomes an independent sub-problem. To accelerate the convergence rate, we estimate k in the gradient space. Specifically, we obtain the solution to the blur kernel by minimizing the following problem:

$$k^{t+1} = \arg \min_k \nabla \left\| I^{t+1} \otimes k - b \right\|_2^2 + \gamma \| k \|_2^2 \tag{14}$$

where ∇ denotes the gradient operation. Note that solving k in the gradient space is beneficial to suppress the ringing and artifacts. Equation (14) is a classical least squares problem with respect to k. The closed form solution to Eq. (14) can be obtained directly by FFT method.

4 Experiment

We carry out experiments and compare with state-of-the-art approaches on four main-stream benchmark datasets [10, 16, 23, 34]. In all the experiments, the parameters are set as follows: $\mu = \vartheta = 0.004$, $\gamma = 2$, and the image patch size to compute the LEP is set to be 6.

4.1 Deblurring Images

Köhler et al.'s dataset. Firstly, we test our method on the synthetic non-uniform image dataset [34] for quantitative evaluations. This dataset includes 4 ground truth images and 12 different kernels. We compare our results with the state-of-the-art methods. Figure 2 presents visual comparison on one challenging example. For all the images in this dataset, we present the average Peak Signal to Noise Ratio (PSNR) and Structural Similarity (SSIM) value in Table 1. The PSNR and SSIM values of the restored images by our method are higher or not lower than those of the state-of-the-art algorithms [12, 17, 20, 27, 35, 36–38]. Our algorithm performs well compared with other methods on this benchmark dataset.

| (a) | (b) | (c) | (d) |

Fig. 2 Comparisons of state-of-the-art methods on one challenging image from the dataset [34]. The images (**a–d**) are groundtruth, Pan et al.'s [17] result, Yan et al.'s [18] result and our result, respectively

Levin et al.'s dataset. Then, we test our algorithm against the state-of-the-art methods [12, 17, 20, 27, 35, 36–38] on another benchmark dataset [10], which includes 4 original truth images blurred with 8 different kernels. One challenging example against the competing methods [17, 18] is shown in Fig. 3. For all the images in dataset [10], we report the PSNR and SSIM values of comparison methods in Table 2, our method performs better than the others. In addition, Fig. 4 plots the cumulative error ratios of

Table 1. Quantitative results (in PNSR and SSIM) on dataset [34]

Method	[27]	[12]	[36]	[35]	[37]	[38]	[17]	[20]	Ours
SSIM	0.87	0.76	0.77	0.70	0.81	0.81	0.88	0.89	0.89
PSNR	28.57	25.72	25.89	22.73	27.84	26.83	29.95	29.97	30.10

our method and the other competing methods. Note that our LEP based method outperforms state-of-the-art algorithms with 100% under error ratio 2. All the experimental results consistently show that our method is competitive compared with the competing methods.

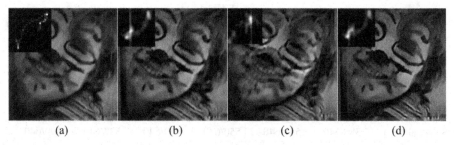

(a)   (b)   (c)   (d)

Fig. 3. A comparison of our method with state-of-the-art methods. The images (a-d) are groundtruth, Pan et al.'s [17] result, Yan et al.'s [18] result and our result, respectively

Table 2. The Average accuracy of the deblurred image (in PNSR and SSIM) for the Levin's dataset [10]

Method	[27]	[12]	[36]	[35]	[33]	[38]	[17]	[20]	Ours
SSIM	0.85	0.89	0.73	0.79	0.88	0.89	0.87	0.89	0.90
PSNR	28.29	31.72	26.86	26.33	30.10	30.53	29.33	32.23	32.39

Sun et al.'s dataset. To further explore the effectiveness of our method, we use the large image set introduced by Sun et al. [23], which contains 640 blurred images, and compare with state-of-the-art methods. For quantitative comparison, we record the success rates with different error ratio compared with the other methods on this image set in Table 3. According to the quantitative comparison results, our LEP based approach achieves the state-of-the-art performance.

Text image. We carry out experiments on text images against the state-of-the-art approaches [17, 18]. Figure 5 presents the recovered latent sharp images and estimated blur kernels of the two compared methods on two challenging samples in dataset [16]. It can be seen that the images restored by DCP [17] and ECP [18] still contain residual blur, and the blur kernel estimated by them is not as sparse as ours. In general, our proposed

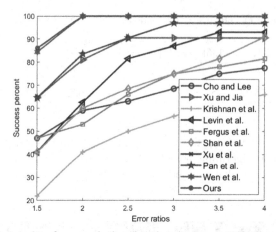

Fig. 4 Quantitative results of our method on benchmark dataset [10]. Error ratios comparison between our approach and the other methods

Table 3. Success rates of the state-of-the-art methods on dataset [23]

Error ratio	≤1.5	≤2	≤2.5	≤3	≤3.5	≤4
Sun et al. [23]	388/640	511/640	550/640	569/640	587/640	599/640
Pan et al. [17]	568/640	594/640	621/640	627/640	632/640	633/640
Yan et al. [18]	568/640	596/640	625/640	636/640	638/640	638/640
Ours	592/640	633/640	638/640	639/640	639/640	639/640

method helps to estimate the correct blur kernels and produce results with less ringing and artifacts.

4.2 Analysis and Discussion

Comparison with other related methods. Previous methods [11, 16] adopt L_0 norm priors for kernel estimation are less likely to perform well compared with the state-of-the-art approaches. Recently, some approaches enforce sparsity by L_0 regularized on the dark channel [17] and bright channel [18] of image pixel. We present the dark channel and bright channel maps compared to our LEP map for visual comparison in Fig. 6. Although the dark channel, bright channel and our LEP map of recovered image all have improvement than that in the corresponding blurry image, our LEP map improves more than the dark channel and bright channel. Moreover, our LEP map is more clearer than dark channel and bright channel in both blurry image and recovered image.

Ablation studies. To further explore the effectiveness of our LEP, we conduct ablation studies on dataset [10]. For fair comparison, we disable the LEP prior in the implementation. Figure 7a shows that our algorithm with LEP term performs better than that without LEP in terms of PSNR. Figure 7b plots the cumulation error ratio to further evaluate the

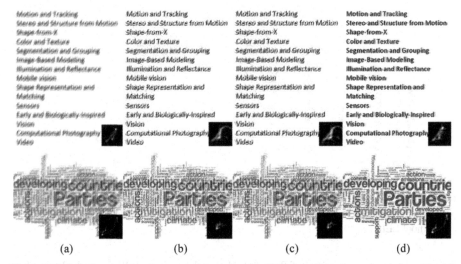

(a)   (b)   (c)   (d)

Fig. 5. Results of our method on text image dataset [16]. (**a**) blurry inputs and ground truth kernels. (**b**) results by Ref. [17]. (**c**) results by Ref. [18]. (**d**) Our results

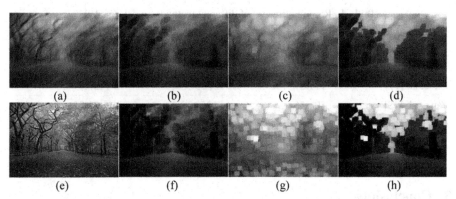

(a)   (b)   (c)   (d)

(e)   (f)   (g)   (h)

Fig. 6. Visual comparison of different maps. (**a**) is blurry sample. (**b**)–(**d**) are dark channel, bright channel and our LEP map of (**a**), respectively. (**e**) is recovered image. (**f**)–(**h**) are dark channel, bright channel and our LEP map of (**e**), respectively

effectiveness of LEP, our model with LEP is much better than that without LEP. Figure 7 validates the effectiveness of LEP.

Computational Complexity. Different from the traditional methods [17, 18], the proposed method adopt the new optimization strategy. We compare the running time of our algorithm with competitive methods. The method by Xu et al. [11] is implemented with C++ , and the method developed by Pan et al. [17] and Yan et al. [18] is optimized based on the half quadratic splitting algorithm. The experiment is conducted on a desktop PC with Intel Core i5-4590 CPU, 16 GB RAM. Table 4 shows the running time of relevant methods to deblur images with different sizes. It can be seen that the method of Xu et al.

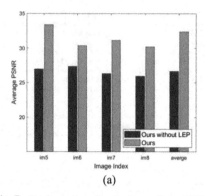 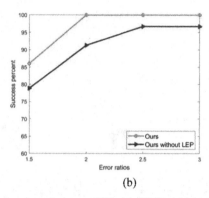

(a)   (b)

Fig. 7. Evaluate the effectiveness of our LEP on benchmark dataset [10]. (**a**) PSNR value comparison with and without LEP. (**b**) Quantitative evaluations on the benchmark dataset [10] with and without LEP

[11] is the fastest, the method of Pan et al. [17] and Yan et al. [18] is much slower than ours.

Table 4. Running time (s) of different methods on dataset [10]

Method	255×255	512×512	800×800
Xu et al. [11]	1.02	2.43	5.35
Pan et al. [17]	111.51	563.33	1150.17
Yan et al. [18]	306.56	1250.12	31.02
Ours	22.68	77.12	187.53

5 Conclusions

In this paper, a new fast local extreme intensity prior is proposed for single image deblurring. This prior is sparser on clear images over blurred ones. Then, we embed this prior into the MAP based blind deblurring framework for effective kernel estimation. To restore the latent sharp image regularized by the fast local extreme intensity prior, we present an effective optimization strategy based on the threshold shrinkage and alternating optimization method rather than the conventional half-quadratic splitting algorithm. Extensive experiments demonstrate that our method performs favorably and computational efficiency against state-of-the-art algorithms on mainstream benchmark datasets.

Acknowledgements. The research was funded by the National Natural Science Foundation of China (Grant No.62020106012, U1836218) and the 111 Project of Ministry of Education of China (Grant No. B12018).

References

1. Lu, H., Zhang, M., Xu, X., et al.: Deep fuzzy hashing network for efficient image retrieval. IEEE Trans. Fuzzy Syst. **29**(1), 166–176 (2021)
2. Nakayama, Y., Lu, H., Li, Y., et al.: WideSegNeXt: semantic image segmentation using wide residual network and NeXt dilated unit. IEEE Sens. J. **21**(10), 11427–11434 (2021)
3. Xu, X., Lin, K., Gao, L., Lu, H., et al.: Learning cross-modal common representations by private-shared subspaces separation. IEEE Trans. Cybern. **52**(5), 3261–3275 (2022)
4. Xu, X., Wang, T., Yang, Y., Zuo, L., et al.: Cross-modal attention with semantic consistence for image-text matching. IEEE Trans. Neural Netw. Learn. Syst. **31**(12), 5412–5425 (2020)
5. Lu, H., Li, Y., Chen, M., Kim, H., et al.: Brain Intelligence: Go beyond Artificial Intelligence. Mobile networks & applications Mobile Networks and Applications **23**(2), 368–375 (2018)
6. Ma, C., Li, X., Li, Y., Tian, X., et al.: Visual information processing for deep-sea visual monitoring system. Cogn. Robot. **1**, 3–11 (2021)
7. Zheng, Y., Li, Y., Yang, S., Lu, H.: Global-PBNet: a novel point cloud registration for autonomous driving. IEEE Trans. Intell. Transp. Syst. https://doi.org/10.1109/TITS.2022. 3153133 (2022)
8. Yang, S., Lu, H., Li, J.: Multifeature fusion-based object detection for intelligent transportation systems. IEEE Trans. Intell. Transp. Syst. https://doi.org/10.1109/TITS.2022.3155488 (2022)
9. Lu, H., Tang, Y., Sun, Y.: Drrs-bc: decentralized routing registration system based on blockchain. IEEE/CAA J. Autom. Sin. **8**(12), 1868–1876 (2021)
10. Levin, A., Weiss, Y., Durand, F., Freeman, W.T.: Understanding and evaluating blind deconvolution algorithms. In: 2009 IEEE conference on computer vision and pattern recognition, pp. 1964–1971. IEEE (2009)
11. Xu, L., Zheng, S., Jia, J.: Unnatural l0 sparse representation for natural image deblurring. In: Proceedings of the IEEE conference on computer vision and pattern recognition, pp. 1107–1114 (2013)
12. Krishnan, D., Tay, T., Fergus, R.: Blind deconvolution using a normalized sparsity measure. In: CVPR 2011. pp. 233–240. IEEE (2011)
13. Ren, W., Cao, X., Pan, J., Guo, X., Zuo, W., Yang, M.H.: Image deblurring via enhanced low-rank prior. IEEE Trans. Image Process. **25**(7), 3426–3437 (2016)
14. Gu, S., Zhang, L., Zuo, W., Feng, X.: Weighted nuclear norm minimization with application to image denoising. In: 2014 IEEE Conference on Computer Vision and Pattern Recognition. pp. 2862–2869 (2014). https://doi.org/10.1109/CVPR.2014.366
15. Bai, Y., Jia, H., Jiang, M., Liu, X., Xie, X., Gao, W.: Single image blind deblurring using multi-scale latent structure prior. IEEE Trans. Circuits Syst. Video Technol. (2019)
16. Pan, J., Hu, Z., Su, Z., Yang, M.H.: l_0-regularized intensity and gradient prior for deblurring text images and beyond. IEEE Trans. Pattern Anal. Mach. Intell. **39**(2), 342–355 (2016)
17. Pan, J., Sun, D., Pfister, H., Yang, M.: Deblurring images via dark channel prior. IEEE Trans. Pattern Anal. Mach. Intell. **40**(10), 2315–2328 (2018). https://doi.org/10.1109/TPAMI.2017. 2753804
18. Yan, Y., Ren, W., Guo, Y., Wang, R., Cao, X.: Image deblurring via extreme channels prior. In: Proceedings of the IEEE Conference on Computer Vision and Pattern Recognition, pp. 4003–4011 (2017).
19. Chen, L., Fang, F., Wang, T., Zhang, G.: Blind image deblurring with local maximum gradient prior. In: IEEE Conference on Computer Vision and Pattern Recognition, pp. 1742–1750 (2019). https://doi.org/10.1109/CVPR.2019.00184
20. Wen, F., Ying, R., Liu, Y., Liu, P., Truong, T.K.: A simple local minimal intensity prior and an improved algorithm for blind image deblurring. IEEE Trans. Circuits Syst. Video Technol., 1–1 (2020). https://doi.org/10.1109/TCSVT.2020.3034137

21. Ren, D., Zuo, W., Zhang, D., Xu, J., Zhang, L.: Partial deconvolution with inaccurate blur kernel. IEEE Trans. Image Process. **27**(1), 511–524 (2018). https://doi.org/10.1109/TIP.2017. 2764261

22. Li, L., Pan, J., Lai, W., Gao, C., Sang, N., Yang, M.: Learning a discriminative prior for blind image deblurring. In: 2018 IEEE/CVF Conference on Computer Vision and Pattern Recognition, pp. 6616–6625 (2018). https://doi.org/10.1109/CVPR.2018.00692

23. Sun, L., Cho, S., Wang, J., Hays, J.: Edge-based blur kernel estimation using patch priors. In: IEEE International Conference on Computational Photography (ICCP). pp. 1–8. IEEE (2013)

24. Michaeli, T., Irani, M.: Blind deblurring using internal patch recurrence. In: European Conference on Computer Vision. pp. 783–798. Springer (2014)

25. Joshi, N., Szeliski, R., Kriegman, D.J.: Psf estimation using sharp edge prediction. In: 2008 IEEE Conference on Computer Vision and Pattern Recognition, pp. 1–8. IEEE (2008)

26. Cho, S., Lee, S.: Fast motion deblurring. ACM Trans. Graph. (TOG) **28**(5), 145 (2009)

27. Cho, T.S., Paris, S., Horn, B.K., Freeman, W.T.: Blur kernel estimation using the radon transform. In: CVPR 2011, pp. 241–248. IEEE (2011)

28. Xu, L., Jia, J.: Two-phase kernel estimation for robust motion deblurring. In: Computer Vision—ECCV 2010, 11th European Conference on Computer Vision, Heraklion, Crete, Greece, September 5–11, 2010, Proceedings, Part I (2010)

29. Cao, X., Ren, W., Zuo, W., Guo, X., Foroosh, H.: Scene text deblurring using text-specific multiscale dictionaries. IEEE Trans. Image Process. **24**(4), 1302–1314 (2015)

30. Lee, H., Jung, C., Kim, C.: Blind deblurring of text images using a text-specific hybrid dictionary. IEEE Trans. Image Process. **29**, 710–723 (2019)

31. Pan, J., Hu, Z., Su, Z., Yang, M.H.: Deblurring face images with exemplars. In: European Conference on Computer Vision (2014)

32. Hu, Z., Cho, S., Wang, J., Yang, M.: Deblurring low-light images with light streaks. IEEE Trans. Pattern Anal. Mach. Intell. **40**(10), 2329–2341 (2018)

33. Pan, J., Sun, D., Pfister, H., Yang, M.H.: Blind image deblurring using dark channel prior. In: Proceedings of the IEEE Conference on Computer Vision and Pattern Recognition. pp. 1628–1636 (2016)

34. Köhler, R., Hirsch, M., Mohler, B., Schölkopf, B., Harmeling, S.: Recording and playback of camera shake: benchmarking blind deconvolution with a real-world database. In: European conference on computer vision, pp. 27–40. Springer (2012)

35. Fergus, R., Singh, B., Hertzmann, A., Roweis, S.T., Freeman, W.T.: Removing camera shake from a single photograph. In: ACM transactions on graphics (TOG). vol. 25, pp. 787–794. ACM (2006)

36. Shan, Q., Jia, J., Agarwala, A.: High-quality motion deblurring from a single image. Acm Trans. Graph. (tog) **27**(3), 73 (2008)

37. Whyte, O., Sivic, J., Zisserman, A., Ponce, J.: Non-uniform deblurring for shaken images. Int. J. Comput. Vis. **98**(2), 168–186 (2012)

38. Hirsch, M., Schuler, C.J., Harmeling, S., Schölkopf, B.: Fast removal of non-uniform camera shake. In: 2011 International Conference on Computer Vision, pp. 463–470. IEEE (2011)

STRDD: Scene Text Removal with Diffusion Probabilistic Models

Wentao Yang[1(✉)] ⓘ, Hui Liu[2] ⓘ, and Ning Liu[3] ⓘ

[1] University of Electronic Science and Technology of China, Chengdu Sichuan 611731, China
[2] Beijing Rongda Technology Co., Ltd., Beijing 100166, China
[3] Beijing Forestry University, Beijing 100083, China
liuning0928@bjfu.edu.cn

Abstract. Scene text removal (STR), which aims to erase text in the wild and fill with visually plausible content. Because text in the wild is often in a complex background, existing methods fail to replace the text regions with a visually plausible background. To tackle this challenge, it requires the model to learn the distribution of a large amount of data. Inspired by the successful adoptions of score-based diffusion models in image generation task, we proposed a new two-stage text erasing approach termed as STRDD. STRDD contains two modules: an autoencoder and an SDE. The autoencoder encodes the image into the features and reconstruct the image from the features. SDE learns the distribution of features encoded by the encoder and uses non-text regions in the image as conditions to turn text regions into background. The results of experiment on real-world dataset demonstrate that STRDD can remove the text in the wild well and achieve improvements on STR as compared to all baselines.

Keywords: Scene text removal · Diffusion model · Image inpainting

1 Introduction

Over the past few years, with the popularity of smart devices and streaming media, personal privacy is also more likely to be leaked. Specifically, text in natural images usually provides valuable private information such as name, address and mobile phone number. Therefore, scene text removal (STR), which aims to erase text in the wild and fill it with visually plausible content, has gained increasing attention in the optical character recognition community. Lately, many methods have been proposed to erase text in the wild [1–8]. These scene text removal methods can be roughly divided into two categories: one-step and two-step. The former is an end-to-end model that combines text region detection and background inpainting into one model. The relatively simple structure makes the one-step model lightweight and fast. EraseNet [4] is a GAN-based text erasure model that contains a text segmentation head and a coarse-to-fine network. The text segmentation head can enhance the perception of text regions. The coarse-to-fine network ensures sufficient receptive field and supervision information. Although the one-step model does not need to input text region information, this also makes the

© The Author(s), under exclusive license to Springer Nature Singapore Pte Ltd. 2022
S. Yang and H. Lu (Eds.): ISAIR 2022, CCIS 1701, pp. 159–170, 2022.
https://doi.org/10.1007/978-981-19-7943-9_13

model usually unable to accurately locate the text region and leave the remnants of text. The latter first detects text regions in the image, turns the text regions into holes, and then fills the holes into a visually reliable background. Zdenek et al. [5] applied a pretrained detector to predict bounding-box-level text region masks and used an image inpainting model trained on the Place2 [9], Paris Street View [10], ImageNet [11] datasets to replace text region masks with the background. However, because the training dataset used is different from the real world, the model will face the domain offset problem. Tang et al. [7] crop text instances from images using bounding box annotations and used a stroke mask prediction module to predict text strokes in cropped images. According to the text stroke masks and cropped images, use the background inpainting module to predict the text-erased images. Despite their success, there is the main challenge for scene text removal in general: text in the wild is often in a complex background. To replace the text region with a visually reliable background requires the model to learn the distribution of a large amount of data. Lately, the successful adoptions of score-based diffusion models in image editing [12], super resolution [13] and image segmentation [14] witness the power of score-based models in generative tasks. DDPM [15] and SMLD [16] ensure that the probability distribution of the images will not collapse to a low-dimensional manifold by adding discrete random noise in the diffusion process, so the score (i.e., the gradient of log probability density) will be well defined and score matching will provide a consistent score estimator. In the inference stage, the score-based model starts from a prior noise (i.e., standard gaussian noise), then progressively denoises the noise through Markov chains and score matching, and finally samples the high-quality images. SDE [17] unifies DDPM and SMLD into a time-continuous model based on stochastic differential equations. SDE considers the noise diffusion process as a stochastic process and uses stochastic differential equations to transform the data into a prior distribution. According to [18], an inverse SDE that reverses the diffusion process can be derived from the noise diffusion of SDE. Compared to GAN-based models, score-based model training is less unstable and does not suffer from mode collapse. Compared with other likelihood estimation-based models (e.g., autoregressive models, variational auto-encoders (VAEs), and normalizing flow), score-based models have less computational complexity and better image generation quality. In this work, we proposed a new text removal approach termed STRDD. STRDD contains two modules: an autoencoder and an SDE. The encoder first extracts features from the input images, then the SDE which has learnt the distribution of features uses features from non-text regions as condition to sample the features of text regions from noise and finally the image is reconstructed from the features by the decoder (Fig. 1).

The remainder of the paper is organized as follows. Section 2 presents related work about the task of scene text removal. Section 3 introduces the basic background of SDE. Section 4 illustrates the proposed STRDD during the training phase and inference phase. Section 5 presents the details of experiment and comparison between other scene text methods and STRDD. Finally, a summary of our study is provided in Sect. 6.

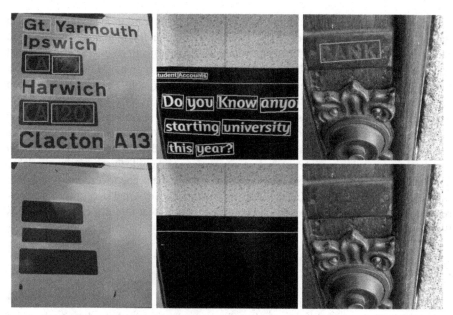

Fig. 1. Examples of scene text removal. Input an image with scene text and text regions, STRDD can remove the text fill with visually plausible content. From left to right, in each example, the top is the input image of IC13 and text regions labeled with polygons in green, while the down is the text-removed images generated by our method

2   Related Work

2.1   Scene Text Removal

Early text erasing research was mainly used to process born-digital text (such as watermarks, stamps and subtitles) in images or videos. These texts can be detected by using the binarization method [19] because the area, color and fonts are relatively fixed. And these text background textures are simple and can be inpainted using the smoothing method [20]. The diverse layout of texts in images, image degradation caused by blur and illumination conditions, and complicated background textures make removing text in scenes a challenging task. With the rapid development of deep learning, many text erasing methods have accomplished excellent results. Nakamura et al. [1] make the first try to use U-Net to erase text patch by patch. This method fails to locate text with complex shapes and inevitably damages the overall quality of the image. EnsNet [2] uses conditional GAN (cGAN) to erase the entire image. Both methods are one-step models, where the localization and erasure of text are performed at the same time. Such methods often result in inaccurate text localization and incomplete text erasure. To tackle this problem, MTRNet [3] uses auxiliary text masks to provide text position information, which is the main reason for outperforming previous methods. Zdenek et al. [5] used a weakly supervised approach to train on an unpaired dataset using a pretrained detector and an image inpainting model. Liu et al. [4] contributed a manually annotated dataset called SCUT-EnsText and proposed EraseNet which uses coarse-to-fine network structure and text segmentation head to enhance the perception of text regions. MTRNet++ [6] is a multi-branch network with the same structure for each branch. The structure between branches is also a coarse-to-fine network structure. Tang et al. [7] proposed a stroke-based model. The crop images which contain text are sent to the stroke mask prediction module to obtain the stroke-level text mask, and the background inpainting module is used to generate text-erased images. Compared with the previous model, the stroke-level text mask can provide more accurate text information and guide the inpainting model to generate higher quality images. PERT [8] decomposes the scene text removal task into multiple text remove stages. In each stage, it tries to take an equal step toward the text-removed image. The decomposed operation reduces the learning difficulty and makes the model more lightweight.

3 Background: SDE

SDE is a score-based generative model. Unlike other diffusion models (such as DDPM and SMLD), SDE uses an infinite number of noise scales to perturb the data. As the noise gradually increases, the distribution of the perturbed data changes as a random process. $t \in [0, T]$ is a continuous time variable, p_0 is the original distribution of the data, and p_T is a prior distribution (such as Gaussian distribution) independent of p_0. In this way, the diffusion process that converts $x_0 \sim p_0$ to $x_T \sim p_T$ by gradually adding noise can be modeled using an Ito SDE:

$$dx = f(x, t)dt + g(t)dw, \tag{1}$$

where $f(\cdot, t) : \mathbb{R}^d \to \mathbb{R}^d$ is a vector-valued function called drift coefficient of $x(t)$, and $g(t) : R \to R$ is a scalar function that does not depend on x known as the diffusion coefficient of $x(t)$, w is the standard Wiener process.

According to the result from Anderson [18], the reverse of the diffusion process is also a diffusion process, which can be modeled as an SDE:

$$dx = \left[f(x, t) - g(t)^2 \nabla_x p_t(x) \right] dt + g(t)dw \tag{2}$$

Therefore, if the score of marginal distribution ($\nabla_x p_t(x)$) can be accurately estimated for all t, we can obtain sample $x(0) \sim p_0$ from sample $x(T) \sim p_T$ by deriving the reverse diffusion process from Eq. (2).

4   Method

Training phase

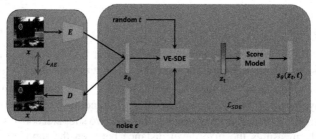

Inference Phase

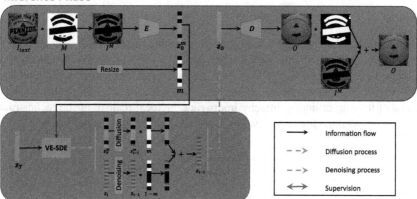

Fig. 2. Overview of our proposed STRDD during the training and inference process. The STRDD is composed of an autoencoder and a VE SDE

4.1   Overview

The overview of our scene text removal method termed STRDD is shown in Fig. 2. Fully convolutional networks with encoder-decoder structures are widely used in scene text removal, while diffusion models such as SDE have accomplish favorable results in various image generation tasks. Owing to the impressive results achieved by these two different models, STRDD first uses the encoder to extract the features of the images, and then let the SDE learn the distribution of the features, so that the SDE can gradually denoise the noise sampled from the prior distribution to obtain the real scene image features, and finally use the decoder to reconstruct high-quality scene images from the features. Unlike some diffusion models, the SDE of STRDD learns the distribution of images in feature space rather than pixel space. It can offer the following benefits:

- After the image is extracted by the encoder, SDE can directly learn important semantic representation information from the features, which reduces the data dimension and improves the capacity of the model.
- SDE is more efficient in learning and sampling in feature space than in pixel space.

4.2 Training

Autoencoder. The training process of the model is split into two stages. At first, We train a fully convolutional network autoencoder, given an input image $x \in \mathbb{R}^{H \times W \times 3}$, the encoder E encodes x into features $z_0 = E(x) \in \mathbb{R}^{\frac{H}{4} \times \frac{W}{4} \times c}$ by two down-sampling convolution layers and six residual connection blocks, and decoder D reconstructs the image $x\prime = D(z_0) = D(E(x))$ from features z_0 through two subpixel convolution blocks. L1 loss directly measures the pixel-level distance between the input image and the reconstruction result, which is used to guide the pixel-level reconstruction in this work.

$$\mathcal{L}_{pixel}(x, x') = ||x - x'||_1 = ||x - D(E(x))||_1 \tag{3}$$

But solely relying on the L1 loss makes the reconstruction result over-smooth and loses local detail. To avoid this, we add a perceptual loss and a style loss. Both perceptual loss and style loss use pre-trained VGG19 to capture semantic features at different levels on the image and constrain the difference between the features of the input image and the features of the output image, thereby improving the local realism of the reconstructed image. The perceptual loss is defined by Eq. 4 and the style loss is defined by Eq. 5:

$$\mathcal{L}_{perceptual} = \mathbb{E}[\sum_{i=1}^{5} ||\phi_i(x) - \phi_i(x')||_1 \tag{4}$$

$$\mathcal{L}_{style} = \mathbb{E}\left[\sum_{i=1} ||G_i^{\phi}(x) - G_i^{\phi}(x')||_1\right] \tag{5}$$

where ϕ_i denotes the i th activation maps from the first activation function of each layer in VGG19. $G_i^{\phi} = \frac{\phi_i \phi_i^T}{C_i H_i W_i}$ is the Gram matrix. C_i, H_i, W_i are the number of channels, width and height of the feature maps of ϕ_i, respectively. The loss of the autoencoder is

$$\mathcal{L}_{AE} = \mathcal{L}_{pixel} + \lambda_0 \mathcal{L}_{perceptual} + \lambda_1 \mathcal{L}_{style} \tag{6}$$

where the hyper-parameters λ_0 and λ_1 are set to 0.005 and 20, respectively. When the autoencoder is trained, we fix the parameters of the autoencoder so that the data distribution of z_0 is deterministic.

SDE. In this work, we use the VE SDE proposed by [17] to learn the data distribution of features. The perturbation kernel of VE SDE is as follows:

$$p_{0t}(z_t|z_0) = \mathcal{N}\left(z_t; z_0, \sigma_{min}^2 \left(\frac{\sigma_{max}}{\sigma_{min}}\right)^{\frac{2t}{T}} I\right) \tag{7}$$

Typically, σ_{min} is small enough such that $p_{\sigma_{min}}(z) \approx p_0(z)$ and σ_{max} is large enough such that $p_{\sigma_{max}}(z) \approx p_T(z)$. The input feature z_0, a random time variable t and a standard Gaussian noise $\in$ are taken as input, the output of VE SDE is perturbed feature $z_t = z_0 + \sigma_{min}\left(\frac{\sigma_{max}}{\sigma_{min}}\right)^{\frac{t}{T}} \in$. Then, z_t goes through the score model s_θ which is a time-condition U-Net to get the score prediction $s_\theta(z_t, t)$. To be able to sample data from noise, the score model needs to correctly estimate the gradient of log density distribution for all $t \in [0, T]$ and $z_0 \sim p_0(z)$. So, the optimization function of the score model can be derived as follows:

$$\mathcal{L}_{SDE} = \mathbb{E}_{t\sim[0,T]}\left[\lambda(t)\mathbb{E}_{z_0\sim p_0(z)}\mathbb{E}_{z_t|z_0}\left[s_\theta(z_t, t) - \nabla_{z_t}\log p_{0t}(z_t|z_0)\right]\right] \qquad (8)$$

where $\lambda : [0, T] \to \mathbb{R}_{>0}$ is a weighting function.

4.3 Inference

As shown at the bottom of Fig. 2, given an image with scene text I_{text} and corresponding text region mask M, we first get the masked image I^M by using mask M to fill the text regions with blank. I^M is encoded to masked feature z_0^m by encoder E. To make the most of the information provided by the mask, M is resized to the same size as the z_0^m denoted by m. In every step from z_t to z_{t-1}, the z_{t-1} does not solely depend on z_t, we use the masked feature z_0^m and the resized mask m as a condition to control the denoising process. Thus, we first diffuse z_0^m into z_{t-1}^m with the same noise scale as the z_{t-1} and then we denoise z_t into z_{t-1}. z_{t-1}^m has more semantic information of background than $m \odot z_{t-1}$, so z_{t-1}^m and z_{t-1} are combined to the new z_{t-1} by using the mask m.

$$z_{t-1} = z_t + \frac{g(t)^2}{N}s_\theta(z_t, t) + \sqrt{\frac{g(t)^2}{N}} \in \qquad (9)$$

$$z_{t-1}^m = z_0^m + \sigma_{min}\left(\frac{\sigma_{max}}{\sigma_{min}}\right)^{\frac{t-1}{T}} \in \qquad (10)$$

$$z_{t-1} = (1 - m) \odot z_{t-1} + m \odot z_{t-1}^m \qquad (11)$$

After the denoising process, the new features z_0' sampled from noise are decoded by decoder D. into the scene image $O\prime$. Finally, we combine I^M and $O\prime$ to the text-removed scene image O.

$$O = I^M + (1 - M) \odot O\prime \qquad (12)$$

5 Experiment

5.1 Datasets

SCUT-Syn [2] is a synthetic dataset generated by the Synthesis text engine [24]. There are 8000 training images and 800 test images in this dataset. all the training and test samples are resized to 512×512. This dataset has a paired image with text and its background image. We use the background images of the training set to train the STRDD.

SCUT-EnsText [4] is a challenging scene text removal dataset. It contains 2,749 images for training and 813 images for testing. All the images in this dataset are collected from several public real-word scene text datasets, including IC13 [21], IC15 [22], COCO-Text [25], SVT [26], MLT2017 [23], MLT2019 [27] and ArTs [28]. This dataset contains both Chinese and English text instances, which have diverse shapes, colors, fonts. To maintain the consistency of erased text regions and surrounding texture, the text instances were carefully erased and filled with a visually plausible background. The text-erased images of the training set are also used to train the STRDD, and the paired images of the test set are used for qualitative and quantitative evaluation.

5.2 Evaluation Metrics

To quantitate the ability of a model on how much text can be erased, an evaluation approach proposed by [1] that utilizes an auxiliary text detector to detect text on the text-erased images, then assesses the precision, recall, and F1-score under scene text datasets according to the ground truths for text localization. For a fair comparison with previous methods, we employ CRAFT [30] on the SCUT-EnsText. The above method only focuses on how much text is erased but disregard the local details and realism of the entire image. Therefore, in order to evaluate the final text removal results more comprehensively, we use some evaluation metrics commonly used in the image translation task as follows:

- MSE: The average squared difference between two images.
- PSNR: The square of the ratio of the maximum possible difference between the two images to the actual difference.
- MSSIM [31]: Multiscale structural similarity which evaluates the difference in illuminance, contrast and structure between two images.

A higher PSNR and MMSIM, or a lower MSE indicate the better results.

5.3 Comparison with Other Scene Text Removal Methods

To evaluate the effectiveness of STRDD, we compared it with some inpainting methods and scene text removal methods on the SCUT-EnsText. Firstly, we compared STRDD with state-of-the-art image inpainting method. The LBAM [32] and RFR-Net [29] were pretrained on the Pairs Street View dataset. We generated text region masks directly from the annotations provided by SCUT-EnsText. The resolution of the input image and masks are 512×512. The results on SCUT-EnsText are shown in Table 1, and these results prove that STRDD can surpass these inpainting methods on PSNR, MSSIM and MSE. But our model's inference speed is about 60 times slower than LBAM because STRDD requires multiple loops to sample the features from noise. From some samples presented in Fig. 3, the output of LBAM and RFR-Net contains obvious distortion. STRDD can a generate visually plausible background. To enable a fair comparison with other scene text removal methods, we utilize a pretrained scene text detector to produce text region labels instead of directly from annotations. In this experiment, we use CRAFT to detect

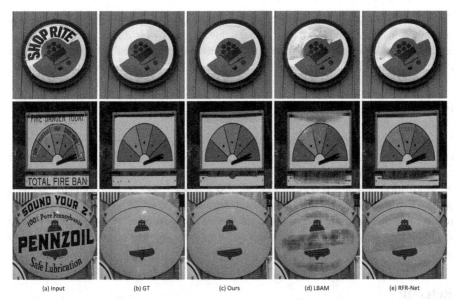

Fig. 3. Visual results of scene text removal methods on the SCUT-EnsText. From left to right: input image with bounding boxes, ground truth, output of STRDD, output of LBAM, output of RFR-Net

Table 1. Comparison between State-of-the-Art inpainting methods and STRDD on the SCUT-EnsText

Method	SCUT-EnsText			Inference speed
	PSNR↑	MSSIM (%)↑	MSE↓	
LBAM	33.0421	93.3275	0.0013	**25 ms**
RFR-Net	33.6560	93.9355	0.0012	193 ms
STRDD	**34.8403**	**94.7480**	**0.0010**	1600 ms

Table 2. Comparison between scene text removal methods and STRDD on the SCUT-EnsText

Method	Qualitative eval			Quantitative eval
	PSNR↑	MSSIM (%)↑	MSE↓	R↓
SceneTextEraser	25.47	90.14	0.0047	5.9
Pix2Pix	26.70	88.56	0.0037	35.4
EnsNet	29.54	92.74	0.0024	32.8
EraseNet	32.30	**95.42**	**0.0015**	**4.6**
STRDD	**32.60**	93.80	**0.0015**	5.9

the texts in the images and generate text region masks as the input of STRDD. The results are shown in Table 2. Overall, our model achieves the lowest PSNR and MSE values, which indicates that our model can generate reasonable backgrounds. However, due to the limited capabilities of the detector, the values of MSSIM and recall increase.

6 Conclusion

In this paper, we present a new scene text removal approach termed STRDD which consists of an autoencoder to extract features and reconstruct images, and an SDE to learn the data distribution of features. In the inference phase, our model can make full use of information of non-text regions in scene text images. Experimental comparisons with some scene text removal approaches on SCUT-EnsText show that STRDD can effectively remove text and generate reasonable background. In the future, we will explore how to speed up sampling for diffusion models and improve the performance of erasing scene text.

References

1. Nakamura, T., Zhu, A., Yanai, K., Uchida, S.: Scene text eraser. In: 2017 14th IAPR International Conference on Document Analysis and Recognition (ICDAR), vol. 1, pp. 832–837 (2017)
2. Zhang, S., Liu, Y., Jin, L., Huang, Y., Lai, S.: Ensnet: Ensconce text in the wild. Proc. AAAI Conf. Artif. Intell. **33**, 801–808 (2019)
3. Tursun, O., Zeng, R., Denman, S., Sivapalan, S., Sridharan, S., Fookes, C.: Mtrnet: A generic scene text eraser. In: 2019 International Conference on Document Analysis and Recognition (ICDAR), Los Alamitos, CA, USA, IEEE Computer Society, pp. 39–44 (2019)
4. Liu, C., Liu, Y., Jin, L., Zhang, S., Luo, C., Wang, Y.: Erasenet: end-to-end text removal in the wild. IEEE Trans. Image Process. **29**, 8760–8775 (2020)
5. Zdenek, J., Nakayama, H.: Erasing scene text with weak supervision. In: 2020 IEEE Winter Conference on Applications of Computer Vision (WACV), pp. 2227–2235 (2020)
6. Tursun, O., Denman, S., Zeng, R., Sivapalan, S., Sridharan, S., Fookes, C.: Mtrnet++: one-stage mask-based scene text eraser. Comput. Vis. Image Underst. **201**, 103066 (2020)
7. Tang, Z., Miyazaki, T., Sugaya, Y., Omachi, S.: Stroke-based scene text erasing using synthetic data for training. IEEE Trans. Image Process. **30**, 9306–9320 (2021)
8. Wang, Y., Xie, H., Fang, S., Qu, Y., Zhang, Y.: Pert: a progressively region-based network for scene text removal. arXiv preprint arXiv:2106.13029 (2021)
9. Zhou, B., Lapedriza, A., Khosla, A., Oliva, A., Torralba, A.: Places: A 10 million image database for scene recognition. IEEE Trans. Pattern Anal. Mach. Intell. (2017)
10. Doersch, C., Singh, S., Gupta, A., Sivic, J., Efros, A.: What makes Paris look like Paris? ACM Trans. Graph. TOG **31** (2012)
11. Russakovsky, O., Deng, J., Su, H., Krause, J., Satheesh, S., Ma, S., Huang, Z., Karpathy, A., Khosla, A., Bernstein, M., et al.: Imagenet large scale visual recognition challenge. Int. J. Comput. Vis. **115**, 211–252 (2015)
12. Meng, C., He, Y., Song, Y., Song, J., Wu, J., Zhu, J.Y., Ermon, S.: SDEdit: Guided image synthesis and editing with stochastic differential equations. In: International Conference on Learning Representations (2022)

13. Li, H., Yang, Y., Chang, M., Chen, S., Feng, H., Xu, Z., Li, Q., Chen, Y.: Srdiff: single image super-resolution with diffusion probabilistic models. Neurocomputing **479**, 47–59 (2022)
14. Amit, T., Nachmani, E., Shaharabany, T., Wolf, L.: Segdiff: Image segmentation with diffusion probabilistic models. CoRR abs/2112.00390 (2021)
15. Ho, J., Jain, A., Abbeel, P.: Denoising diffusion probabilistic models. In: Larochelle, H., Ranzato, M., Hadsell, R., Balcan, M.F., Lin, H. (eds.) Advances in Neural Information Processing Systems. Volume 33., Curran Associates, Inc., pp. 6840–6851 (2020)
16. Song, Y., Ermon, S.: Generative modeling by estimating gradients of the data distribution. In: Proceedings of the 33rd Annual Conference on Neural Information Processing Systems. (2019)
17. Song, Y., Sohl-Dickstein, J., Kingma, D.P., Kumar, A., Ermon, S., Poole, B.: Score-based generative modeling through stochastic differential equations. In: International Conference on Learning Representations. (2021)
18. Anderson, B.D.: Reverse-time diffusion equation models. Stoch. Process. Their Appl. **12**, 313–326 (1982)
19. Pnevmatikakis, E.A., Maragos, P.: An inpainting system for automatic image structure-texture restoration with text removal. In: 2008 15th IEEE International Conference on Image Processing, pp. 2616–2619. IEEE (2008)
20. Wagh, P.D., Patil, D.: Text detection and removal from image using inpainting with smoothing. In: 2015 International Conference on Pervasive Computing (ICPC), pp. 1–4. IEEE (2015)
21. Karatzas, D., Shafait, F., Uchida, S., Iwamura, M., Bigorda, L.G.I., Mestre, S.R., Mas, J., Mota, D.F., Almazàn, J.A., de las Heras, L.P.: Icdar 2013 robust reading competition. In: 2013 12th International Conference on Document Analysis and Recognition, pp. 1484–1493 (2013)
22. Karatzas, D., Gomez-Bigorda, L., Nicolaou, A., Ghosh, S., Bagdanov, A., Iwamura, M., Matas, J., Neumann, L., Chandrasekhar, V.R., Lu, S., Shafait, F., Uchida, S., Valveny, E.: Icdar 2015 competition on robust reading. In: 2015 13th International Conference on Document Analysis and Recognition (ICDAR), pp. 1156–1160 (2015)
23. Nayef, N., Yin, F., Bizid, I., Choi, H., Feng, Y., Karatzas, D., Luo, Z., Pal, U., Rigaud, C., Chazalon, J., Khlif, W., Luqman, M.M., Burie, J.C., Liu, C.l., Ogier, J.M.: Icdar2017 robust reading challenge on multi-lingual scene text detection and script identification - rrc-mlt. In: 2017 14th IAPR International Conference on Document Analysis and Recognition (ICDAR). Volume 1, pp. 1454–1459 (2017)
24. Gupta, A., Vedaldi, A., Zisserman, A.: Synthetic data for text localisation in natural images. In: Proceedings of the IEEE conference on computer vision and pattern recognition, pp. 2315–2324 (2016)
25. Veit, A., Matera, T., Neumann, L., Matas, J., Belongie, S.: Coco-text: Dataset and benchmark for text detection and recognition in natural images. In: arXiv preprint arXiv:1601.07140 (2016)
26. Wang, K., Belongie, S. In: Word Spotting in the Wild. Volume 6311 of Lecture Notes in Computer Science, pp. 591–604. Springer Berlin Heidelberg, Berlin, Heidelberg (2010)
27. Nayef, N., Patel, Y., Busta, M., Chowdhury, P.N., Karatzas, D., Khlif, W., Matas, J., Pal, U., Burie, J.C., Liu, C.l., et al.: Icdar2019 robust reading challenge on multilingual scene text detection and recognition—rrc-mlt-2019. In: 2019 International conference on document analysis and recognition (ICDAR), pp. 1582–1587. IEEE (2019)
28. Chng, C.K., Liu, Y., Sun, Y., Ng, C.C., Luo, C., Ni, Z., Fang, C., Zhang, S., Han, J., Ding, E., et al.: Icdar2019 robust reading challenge on arbitrary-shaped textrrc-art. In: 2019 International Conference on Document Analysis and Recognition (ICDAR), pp. 1571–1576. IEEE (2019)

29. Li, J., Wang, N., Zhang, L., Du, B., & Tao, D.: Recurrent feature reasoning for image inpainting. In: Proceedings of the IEEE/CVF Conference on Computer Vision and Pattern Recognition, pp. 7760–7768 (2020)
30. Baek, Y., Lee, B., Han, D., Yun, S., Lee, H.: Character region awareness for text detection. In: Proceedings of the IEEE/CVF Conference on Computer Vision and Pattern Recognition, pp. 9365–9374 (2019)
31. Wang, Z., Bovik, A., Sheikh, H., Simoncelli, E.: Image quality assessment: from error visibility to structural similarity. IEEE Trans. Image Process. **13**, 600–612 (2004)
32. Xie, C., Liu, S., Li, C., Cheng, M. M., Zuo, W., Liu, X., ... & Ding, E.: Image inpainting with learnable bidirectional attention maps. In: Proceedings of the IEEE/CVF International Conference on Computer Vision, pp. 8858–8867 (2019)
33. Lu, H., Zhang, M., Xu, X., et al.: Deep fuzzy hashing network for efficient image retrieval. IEEE Trans. Fuzzy Syst. **29**(1), 166–176 (2020)
34. Ma, Chunyan, et al.: Visual information processing for deep-sea visual monitoring system. Cogn. Robot. **1**, 3–11 (2021)
35. Lu, H., Li, Y., Chen, M., et al.: Brain intelligence: go beyond artificial intelligence. Mob. Netw. Appl. **23**(2), 368–375 (2018)
36. Nakayama, Y., Lu, H., Li, Y., et al.: WideSegNeXt: semantic image segmentation using wide residual network and NeXt dilated unit. IEEE Sens. J. **21**(10), 11427–11434 (2020)
37. Zheng, Y., Li, Y., Yang, S., et al.: Global-PBNet: a novel point cloud registration for autonomous driving. IEEE Trans. Intell. Transp. Syst. (2022)
38. Yang, S., Lu, H., Li, J.: Multifeature fusion-based object detection for intelligent transportation systems. IEEE Trans. Intell. Transp. Syst. (2022)
39. Xu, X., Lin, K., Gao, L., et al.: Learning cross-modal common representations by private-shared subspaces separation. IEEE Trans. Cybern. (2020).
40. Lu, H., Tang, Y., Sun, Y.: DRRS-BC: Decentralized routing registration system based on blockchain. IEEE/CAA J. Autom. Sin. **8**(12), 1868–1876 (2021)
41. Xu, X., Wang, T., Yang, Y., et al.: Cross-modal attention with semantic consistence for image–text matching. IEEE Trans. Neural Netw. Learn. Syst. **31**(12), 5412–5425 (2020)

Geometry-Aware Network for Table Structure Recognition in Wild

Baoyu Xu[1](✉) [iD], Hui Liu[2] [iD], and Ning Liu[3] [iD]

[1] University of Electronic Science and Technology of China, Chengdu Sichuan 611731, China
xubaoyu12@gmail.com
[2] Beijing Rongda Technology Co., Ltd., Beijing 100166, China
[3] Beijing Forestry University, Beijing 100083, China
liuning0928@bjfu.edu.cn

Abstract. Table is a common representation format used to record and summarize important data in our daily life. Table detection, cell detection and table structure recognition have been widely discussed in recent years. The recognition of table structure in clean and noiseless images or documents has achieved good results, but in the real world with distorted images containing noise disturbance, the existing methods cannot get good results. The reason for this problem is that the image in the real world contains various distortions, such as curve, which causes the model to fail to parse the table correctly. To solve this problem, we propose a network with geometry awareness, which can enhance the ability of the model when facing the real-world images containing distortion.

Keywords: Geometry awareness · Table structure recognition · Object detection

1 Introduction

Table is a format commonly used in our daily life to record and summarize important data. Tables can quickly visualize information and data, and can intuitively provide readers with compact and important information. Tables exist in a wide variety of formats, including but not limited to web pages, PDFs, word processors, and document images [1]. With the development of natural language processing technology, many table-based tasks have emerged, such as table-based question answering [2, 3], entity linking [4], etc., which have attracted extensive attention in academia. However, most of these existing studies only consider structured tabular data, relational tabular data, or clean document images in simple scenarios, which are far from real-world data in the wild. Therefore, it is an existing problem to automatically parse the unstructured noisy image data in the wild in the real world into a structured digital format. In addition, with more and more mobile camera devices such as smart phones, images containing tables are becoming very common. Therefore, this imposes a requirement on the automatic extraction and parsing of table structures from images in wild.

For an image, the purpose of table structure recognition (TSR) is to extract all tables, locate their cells, and obtain row and column information in the table. Early pioneering works, such as [5], usually use heuristic rules, which will first detect low-level cue units such as lines, boundaries, text regions, then combined these units in a bottom-up manner to complete TSR task. In recent years, with the development of deep learning and its wide application in various tasks, the deep learning method of developing end-to-end model is proposed to avoid heuristic grouping scheme design. However, previously this problem was mostly studied on document image. In this case, the table image is taken or scanned under good imaging conditions, or even extracted directly from a completely noise free PDF file, usually with a clean background and clear table structure aligned horizontally (and vertically). Limited by the training data set used for table structure parsing [6–9], these methods still solve this problem under the assumption that the table image is well aligned. For the more practical needs of parsing table structures from images taken from wild handheld cameras, the most advanced methods available [10, 11, 21–23] are prone to failure because common assumptions about table images in clean documents no longer hold. Specifically, in widely used data sets (such as ICDAR2013, Table-bank), table images usually have clear backgrounds and clear table structures. Due to this limitation, most of the existing TSR methods can only complete the TSR task by grouping low-level cues in clean and noise-free simple cases.

For the recognition of table structure in wild, this paper [24, 38] focuses on the important problem of cell boundary accuracy in text recognition and proposes a method based on key points detection. This method no longer has a priori assumptions of cell alignment and others, expanding the scope of the table structure recognition model from clean document images to real world images. However, if there is distortion in the image of the table, such as bending, blocking or blurring of the overall table line, and extreme ratio, existing methods don't perform very well on these images In order to solve the performance degradation caused by the distortion of the table image, we propose a geometry aware network GA-CenterNet based on Cycle-CenterNet, through which the model can obtain the ability of geometry deformation of the table and improve the recognition result in the face of the above situation. The experiment results show that the performance of the proposed method is better than that of the existing methods when there is a lot of distortion in real world.

The rest of the paper is structured as follows. In Sect. 2, we first present related work on table detection, table structure recognition, and spatial transformation networks. Second, in Sect. 3, we elaborate the proposed method, including the overall framework of the model, and the geometry-aware representation. We then show related experiments in Sect. 4.

2   Related Work

Table detection and table structure recognition have been widely studied in recent years. For simple structed documents such as PDF, the heuristic-based approach is popular and achieves good results. Typically, heuristic methods start from metadata to define various heuristic rules for documents, which means this approach fails when process image data. In addition, the generalization ability of heuristic methods is often limited by changes in table structure. In the survey [35, 39], methods and techniques for table detection and recognition from an earlier time were introduced. With the great success brought by deep neural networks in the field of computer vision, the research methods about table images are more universal [22, 25, 26]. With the great development of deep learning, deep learning-based solutions have become mainstream, and we focus more on deep learning-based models in this section.

2.1 Table Detection

Table detection and cell detection tasks generally appear as subtasks of table structure recognition. It has been discussed in many studies. The techniques of object detection and semantic segmentation are often used to solve the tasks of table detection and table structure recognition. Therefore, currently popular target detection schemes, such as Fast-RCNN [27], Mask-RCNN [36] and FCN [37, 40], have been widely applied in relevant studies. DeepDeSRT [17] is a method based on deep learning, which aims to detect tables and identify table structures. [28] proposed a multi-stage expansion Mask R-CNN deep learning network for table detection tasks. [29, 41] adopted a cascaded network structure model, which can cascade the tasks of table detection and table structure recognition, but this model is very dependent on complex data augmentation and transfer learning. [21] adopted a single model based on semantic segmentation to solve the tasks of table detection and table recognition. Methods for object detection and semantic segmentation have also been used in other studies. Most of these studies take a top-down approach to design or improve network architectures for different application scenarios. For better results, the transfer learning method be used to strengthen the model ability. In the top-down approach, the task of table detection and table structure parsing can be accomplished simultaneously, such as segmenting table cells. In the bottom-up method, table detection needs to be performed first, and then table structure recognition is performed on the basis of table detection.

2.2 Table Structure Recognition

Based on the granularity of the basic components, we have roughly divided the previous approaches into two categories: global object-based approaches and local object-based approaches.

Global Object-Based Approaches. Global object-based methods focus on important global elements, such as columns/rows, and usually detect or segment global elements. Study [22] uses a detection or segmentation model to obtain row and column regions, and then considers the intersection of the two regions as cells of the table. Region masks, including row masks and column masks, are learned in [21]. In this way, table detection and table recognition tasks are implemented in end-to-end way. Different from [22, 30] learns a region segmentation mask between rows/columns to split rows and columns, and then the intersecting regions outside the mask are considered as cells of the table. In addition, there is an end-to-end method. [8] serializes the information of the entire table, and outputs the table corresponding to the image as a text sequence through the encoder-decoder method. This method is relatively simple in model, and is an end-to-end way. However, these models require a large amount of labeled training data and usually are difficult to train.

Local Object-Based Approaches. The local object-based approaches start with the smallest base element cell. Due to cell-level text area annotation, it is easier to complete text detection tasks by using commonly used detection methods such as Yolo [31] and Faster RCNN [27]. Then, the relationships between cells are reconstructed through heuristic-based rules or algorithms. If the detected box is regarded as a node in the graph, and the relationship between the boxes is an edge, then the table structure can be predicted using the technology of the graph network. The relationship among three types of nodes (horizontal connection, vertical connection and connectionless) is predicted by using visual features, text location, word embedding and other features in. [9] augmenting the ability of graph networks with a graph attention mechanism improves the performance of the model. Since empty cells cannot be detected, local object-based methods are often ambiguous in the face of empty cells.

2.3 Transformation Learning Networks

The Spatial transformer networks (STN) [32] module performs a global affine transformation on the entire feature map, which is not flexible enough to adapt to local deformations. Inspired by the Instance Transformation Network (ITN) [34], through deformable convolutional networks [33], the transformations are embedded into the convolutional layers to generate geometry-aware representations. The STN module adopts an unsupervised end-to-end learning method, and the ITN module performs supervised learning for each instance.

3 Proposal Method

The difficulty of distortion table structure recognition lies in its rapidly changing geometry, including scale, direction, curve, and aspect ratio. The canonical representation learned in the standard CNN model does not encode the unique geometric distribution of table cells well. Therefore, in this study, we propose a transformation network to learn geometric aware representations detected for table elements with distortions. In this section, we will describe our approach in detail. Specifically, we first introduce the framework of GA-CenterNet, then introduce geometric aware representation.

Based on Cycle-CenterNet, the network proposed by us detects the center of the cell and the intersection points of the cell based on key point detection. Meanwhile, two branches are used for regression from the center of the cell to the intersection point of the cell and regression from the intersection point of the cell to the center of the cell respectively. On this basis, we utilize geometric representation network to explicitly aware the spatial distortion. All cells can be spliced together by common vertices between adjacent cells to get a complete table structure (Fig. 1).

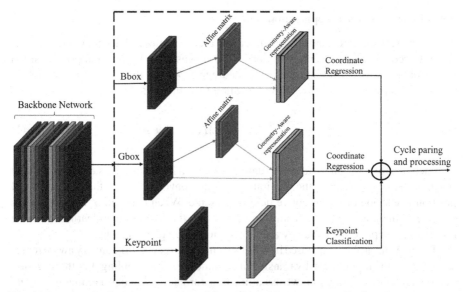

Fig. 1. Based on Cycle-CenterNet, the model consists of three parts: (1) The first part is the shared bottom which is a feature extraction backbone network, specifically using DLANet-34. (2) The second part contains three branches, from top to bottom, the coordinate regression of the center to the vertex, the coordinate regression of the vertex to the center, and the classification of the center points and the key points.

3.1 Framework

The model consists of three parts: a backbone composed of convolutions, which is used to extract features from images and fully fuse features of different scales; a geometry-aware transformation network that generates geometry -aware representations; three parallel downstream tasks. Specifically, the backbone is DLA-34. Then the geometric aware representation is generated by embedding module of transformation network. In this module, the parameter θ of affine transformation is generated by mapping feature map M with stacked 3×3 convolution layers.

Then GA-CenterNet performs multi-task learning, parallel three branches: classifying the center of the cells and the vertex of the cells, coordinate regression from the center of the cells to the vertex of the cells and coordinate regression from the vertex of the cells to the center of the cells. Taking a pixel position as an example, the geometric aware representation is used for classification, and coordinate regression. The sampling boundary of conventional convolution is a bounding box with a fixed shape (such as a 7×7 square). Inspired by STN network, the geometry-aware transformation network performs affine transformation on the bounding box of the fixed shape. The transformed boundary should cover the target to be detected as much as possible. So it can be considered as a rough estimate of detection. The model is trained in supervised strategy and has three outputs at each pixel location:(a) the prediction probability that the current position is key point; (b) vertex to center coordinate regression; (c) center to vertex coordinate regression.

3.2 Geometry-Aware Representation

Given an input feature map M generated by a convolutional backbone, we want to generate geometry-aware representations V for downstream tasks. Each pixel position in V is obtained by convolving the input feature map M with the convolution kernel W. The standard form of the convolution operation is defined as:

$$v_{xy} = \sum_{p=-k}^{k} \sum_{q=-k}^{k} w(p, q) M(x + p, y + q) \tag{1}$$

Each feature position v_{xy} after standard convolution is obtained by sampling the fixed shape of the feature map of the previous layer and convolution with the kernel. For all position, the shape of the receptive field is the same. When the ratio of target object is extreme or there is geometric distortion such as tilt, the features map learned by using this square receptive field strategy are difficult to be complete and clear.

To solve this problem, inspired by STN, we attempt to generate geometry aware representations of the input image by transforming guided feature sampling. For the selection of a particular transformation, we use affine transformation. We observe that in the real world most of the table distortion in the image is subject to projection transformation.

The projective transformation matrix consists of affine matrix and projection vector. Learning projective transformations directly in the network is difficult, and the transformation network is very parameter-sensitive and not differentiable. Similar to ITN, we choose to use affine transformations to encode geometric distortions, making the network geometry aware.

We estimate the affine transformation $T_{\theta_{xy}}$ of parameterized θ_{xy} at pixel positions (x, y) in V and embed it in the feature sampling stage to adaptively match the current receive field to the surrounding key points region. In particular, if the current location is not part of the key points region, we don't care about the transformation. Transform embedding is achieved by pixel-to-pixel alignment and by twisting the regular sampling boundary into an adaptive sampling boundary guided by $T_{\theta_{xy}}$:

$$v_{xy} = \sum_{p=-k}^{k} \sum_{q=-k}^{k} w(p, q) M\left(G_{\theta_{xy}}(x + p, y + q)\right) \tag{2}$$

where $G_{\theta_{xy}} = (\hat{x}, \hat{y})$, and

$$\begin{pmatrix} \hat{x} \\ \hat{y} \end{pmatrix} = A_\theta \begin{pmatrix} x \\ y \\ 1 \end{pmatrix} = \begin{bmatrix} \theta_1 & \theta_2 & \theta_3 \\ \theta_4 & \theta_5 & \theta_6 \end{bmatrix} \begin{pmatrix} x \\ y \\ 1 \end{pmatrix} \tag{3}$$

where A_θ is a 2D affine transformation matrix parameterized by a 6D vector.

3.3 Loss Function

The overall training loss is:

$$L = L_k + \lambda_{off} L_{off} + L_p + L_t$$

where L_k and L_{off} are consistent with keypoint branch and offset branch in CenterNet, L_p is dynamic cycle paring loss in Cycle-CenterNet and L_t is transformation loss defined as: $L_t(\theta_i, \theta_i^*) = smooth\_l1(\theta_i, \theta_i^*)$.

4 Experiments

4.1 Datasets

The WTW dataset is large-scale real world table dataset containing a large number of table images with geometric distortions. We conduct experiments on the WTW dataset to verify the effectiveness of the model.

4.2 Evaluation Metric

Reasonable evaluation metric is very important for quantitative comparison of different evaluation methods. The evaluation of table structure recognition consists of two parts, the correctness of the physical structure and the correctness of the logical structure. Specifically, the metrics on the physical structure are precision, recall and F1 score. Different from general object detection, table structure recognition requires higher precision and lower tolerance for table cells. Therefore, cells that detect an IOU below 0.9 are considered a false positive sample. For the correctness of logical structure, we follow the evaluation protocol used in the document image, and make use of the tree-editor-Distance-based Similarity (TEDS).

Table 1. Results on WTW dataset.

Model	Backbone	Prec.	Rec.	F1	TEDS
Split + Heuristic	–	3.2	3.6	3.4	26.0
CenterNet	DLA-34	74.2	72.1	73.1	58.7
CascadeTabNet	CascadeNet	–	–	–	11.4
Cycle-Centernet	DLA-34	78.0	**78.5**	**78.3**	83.3
GA-CenterNet	DLA-34	**78.2**	78.3	78.3	**83.5**

4.3 Evaluation Result

Table 1 shows the performance of existing models on the WTW real-world image in wild dataset. It can be seen that the Split+Heuristic method and the CascadeTabNet method, which perform well in processing undistorted tables, do not perform well in processing real wild world datasets. The reason is these models do not have the ability to process document images with distortion and geometric deformation. Our model outperforms Cycle-CenterNet by 0.2% on the logical structure metric TEDS, and by

0.2% in precision. Compared to Cycle-CenterNet, our model is close in F1, but has a small drop in recall.

Table 2 compares the performance of the models on each sub-category of distortion in detail. Existing models perform well on simple document images and are adequate for real-world images, but the performance still needs to be improved on sub-categories with distortion. Our model has different degrees of improvement in Curved, Occluded and Blurred, Extreme aspect ratio categories, close in Inclined category, and slight decline in Overlaid and Muti color and grid categories (Fig. 2).

Fig. 2. Results of model on WTW dataset.

Table 2. TEDS Results on distort categories of WTW dataset.

Model	Inclined	Curved	Occluded and blurred	Extreme aspect ratio	Overlaid	Muti color and grid
Cycle-Centernet	90.6	70	53.3	77.4	51.2	66.7
GA-CenterNet	90.6	70.3	53.9	77.8	50.8	66.6

5 Conclusion

In this paper, we propose a new model called GA-CenterNet, for the distortion problem of real-world wild images. The model perceives the distortion through the geometry-aware module, and predicts the coordinate in a geometry-aware manner in the face of instances with distortion and deformation. Comprehensive experiments show that the proposed method has improved performance in images with distortion.

References

1. Qiao, L., et al.: LGPMA: complicated table structure recognition with local and global pyramid mask alignment. ICDAR (1), 99–114 (2021)
2. Alon, T.: MultiModalQA: complex question answering over text, tables and images. ICLR (2021)
3. Svitlana, V.: TableQA: question answering on tabular data. SEMANTiCS Posters&Demos (2017)
4. Xusheng, L.: Cross-lingual entity linking for web tables. In: AAAI, pp. 362–369 (2018)
5. Katsuhiko, I.: Table structure recognition based on textblock arrangement and ruled line position. In: ICDAR, pp. 765–768 (1993)
6. Göbel, M.C.: ICDAR 2013 table competition. In: ICDAR, pp. 1449–1453 (2013)
7. Minghao, L.: Tablebank: a benchmark dataset for table detection and recognition. CoRR abs/1903.01949 (2019)
8. Xu, Z.: Image-based table recognition: data, model, and evaluation. ECCV (21), 564–580 (2020)
9. Zewen, C.: Complicated table structure recognition. CoRR abs/1908.04729 (2019)
10. Shah, R.Q.: Rethinking table recognition using graph neural networks. In: ICDAR, pp. 142–147 (2019)
11. Sachin, R.: Table structure recognition using top-down and bottom-up cues. ECCV (28), 70–86 (2020)
12. L Huimin 2021 Deep fuzzy hashing network for efficient image retrieval IEEE Trans. Fuzzy Syst. 29 1 166 176
13. Ma, C.: Visual information processing for deep-sea visual monitoring system. Cogn. Robot. 1, 3–11 (2021)
14. H Lu Y Li M Chen H Kim S Serikawa 2017 Brain intelligence: go beyond artificial intelligence Mob. Netw. Appl. 23 2 368 375 https://doi.org/10.1007/s11036-017-0932-8
15. Nakayama, Y.: WideSegNeXt: semantic image segmentation using wide residual network and NeXt dilated unit. IEEE Sens. J., 11427–11434 (2021)
16. Zheng, Y.: Global-PBNet: a novel point cloud registration for autonomous driving. Intell. Transp. Syst. (2022)
17. Yang, S.: Multifeature fusion-based object detection for intelligent transportation systems. IEEE Trans. Intell. Trans Syst. (2022)
18. X Xing 2022 Learning cross-modal common representations by private-shared subspaces separation IEEE Trans. Cybern. 52 5 3261 3275
19. L Huimin 2021 DRRS-BC: decentralized routing registration system based on blockchain IEEE CAA J. Autom. Sinica 8 12 1868 1876
20. X Xing 2020 Cross-modal attention with semantic consistence for image-text matching IEEE Trans. Neural Networks Learn. Syst. 31 12 5412 5425
21. Shubham S P.:TableNet: Deep Learning Model for End-to-end Table Detection and Tabular Data Extraction from Scanned Document Images. ICDAR 2019: 128–133
22. Sebastian, S.: DeepDeSRT: deep learning for detection and structure recognition of tables in document images. ICDAR, pp. 1162–1167 (2017)
23. Xinyi, Z.: Global Table Extractor (GTE): a framework for joint table identification and cell structure recognition using visual context. In: WACV, pp. 697–706 (2021)
24. Rujiao, L.: Parsing table structures in the wild. In: ICCV, pp. 924–932 (2021)
25. Nishida, K.: Understanding the semantic structures of tables with a hybrid deep neural network architecture. AAAI (2017)
26. Khan, S.A.: Table structure extraction with bi-directional gated recurrent unit networks. In: ICDAR, pp. 1366–1371 (2019)

27. Shaoqing, R.: Faster R-CNN: towards real-time object detection with region proposal networks. In: NIPS, pp. 91–99 (2015)
28. K Ertugrul 2020 Holistic design for deep learning-based discovery of tabular structures in datasheet images Eng. Appl. Artif. Intell. 90 103551
29. Devashish, P.: CascadeTabNet: an approach for end to end table detection and structure recognition from image-based documents. In: CVPR Workshops, pp. 2439–2447 (2020)
30. Chris, T.: Deep splitting and merging for table structure decomposition. In: ICDAR, pp. 114–121 (2019)
31. Joseph, R.: You only look once: unified, real-time object detection. In: CVPR, pp. 779–788 (2016)
32. Max, J.: Spatial transformer networks. In: NIPS, pp. 2017–2025 (2015)
33. Jifeng, D.: Deformable convolutional networks. In: ICCV, pp. 764–773 (2017)
34. Fangfang, W.: Geometry-aware scene text detection with instance transformation network. In: CVPR, pp. 1381–1389 (2018)
35. Z Richard 2004 survey of table recognition Int. J. Document Anal. Recognit. 7 1 1 16
36. He, K.: Mask r-cnn. In: Proceedings of the IEEE International Conference on Computer Vision, pp. 2961–2969 (2017)
37. S Evan 2017 Fully Convolutional networks for semantic segmentation IEEE Trans. Pattern Anal. Mach. Intell. 39 4 640 651
38. L Huimin M Zhang X Xing 2020 Deep fuzzy hashing network for efficient image retrieval IEEE Trans. Fuzzy Syst. https://doi.org/10.1109/TFUZZ.2020.2984991
39. L Huimin Y Li M Chen 2018 Brain Intelligence: go beyond artificial intelligence Mob. Netw. Appl. 23 368 375
40. L Huimin Y Li M Shenglin 2018 Motor anomaly detection for unmanned aerial vehicles using reinforcement learning IEEE Internet Things J. 5 4 2315 2322
41. Huimin, L., Qin, M., Zhang, F., et al.: RSCNN: a CNN-based method to enhance low-light remote-sensing images. Remote Sens. 13(1), 62 (2020)

A Differential Evolution Algorithm with Adaptive Population Size Reduction Strategy

Xiaoyan Zhang$^{(\boxtimes)}$, Zhengyu Duan, and Qianqian Liu

Xi'an University of Science and Technology, Xi'an 710000, China
zhangxy@xust.edu.cn

Abstract. Aiming at the problem that the differential evolution algorithm easily falls into a local optimum and results in premature convergence, a new differential evolution algorithm with an adaptive population size reduction strategy (APRDE) is proposed. Firstly, in the mutation and crossover operation, to balance the local exploitation and global exploration capabilities of the algorithm, a parameter adaptive tunning scheme based on the hyperbolic tangent function and Cauchy distribution is proposed to adaptively adjust the parameter factors. Secondly, an ordered mutation strategy is adopted to guide the direction of mutating and enrich the diversity of the population. Lastly, after each evolution iteration, adaptively reducing the population size according to the error between the fitness values of individuals and the current optimal. The proposed algorithm is compared with 5 other optimization algorithms on 8 typical benchmark functions. The results show that the algorithm has a great improvement in solution accuracy, stability and convergence speed.

Keywords: Adaptive differential evolution algorithm · Parameters tunning scheme · Ordered mutation strategy · Population size reduction strategy

1 Introduction

Coal has always been the main energy source in China, and accounts for more than 60% of consumption, it will remain be the main energy source in China until 2050. Coal intelligent mining is a new stage in the development of coal comprehensive mining technology, which is also an inevitable requirement for the technological revolution and upgrading development of coal industry [1]. Three-dimensional modeling of coal seams at the fully mechanized mining face is an important foundation for coal enterprises to realize "intelligent management and transparent mining".

Researchers often use kriging interpolation to interpolate unknown regions in space to build 3D models. For the problem that kriging interpolation is prone to overfitting or underfitting in the fitting process of variogram, this paper proposes a Differential Evolution algorithm with Adaptive Population size Reduction (APRDE) to optimize the kriging interpolation algorithm. After experimental verification, the adaptive differential evolution algorithm proposed in this paper has higher solution accuracy, faster convergence speed and better stability.

S. Yang and H. Lu (Eds.): ISAIR 2022, CCIS 1701, pp. 181–188, 2022.
https://doi.org/10.1007/978-981-19-7943-9_15

2 The APRDE Algorithm

The Differential Evolution (DE) algorithm [2] is an effective heuristic search algorithm that can be used to solve parameter optimization problems. This paper optimizes the DE algorithm by modifying the variation strategy, parameter adaptive adjustment mechanism, and population reduction strategy.

2.1 Variation Strategy

The mutation process and the crossover process are the core parts of the differential evolution algorithm, and the mutation formula is:

$$v_i = x_i + F\left(x_j - x_r\right) \tag{1}$$

where v_i is the individual after mutation, x_i, x_j, x_r are the random individuals in the current population and $i \neq j \neq r$, In the process of mutation, in order to enrich the diversity of the population and improve the local exploitation ability of the algorithm, this paper adopts an ordered mutation strategy [3], and the mutation equation is:

$$v_i = x_i + F(x_{best} - x_i) + F(x_{middle} - x_{worst}) \tag{2}$$

Three randomly selected individuals from the current population are sorted according to the fitness value to obtain $x_{best}, x_{middle}, x_{worst}$. With the current vector as the base vector, avoiding the algorithm from falling into a local optimal solution or stagnation. Combining the base vector and two ordered difference vectors, enriching the diversity of the population, and making the direction of variation gradually approach the optimal solution.

2.2 Parameter Adaptive Adjustment

In the variation process, the variation factor F controls the magnitude of the base vector change. To balance the global exploration and local exploitation abilities of the algorithm, the hyperbolic tangent curve between $[-4,4]$ [4] is used in this paper to control the variation of the mutation factor with the following variation equation.

$$F = \frac{F_{max} + F_{min}}{2} + \frac{\tanh\left(-4 + 8\frac{G_{max} - G}{G_{max}}\right)(F_{max} - F_{min})}{2} \tag{3}$$

where F_{min} is the minimum value and F_{max} is the maximum value of the variation factor. G_{max} is the maximum evolutionary generation and G is the current evolutionary generation. The hyperbolic tangent curve changes very little at the beginning and the end. The variation factor varies approximately linearly between the maximum and minimum values, striking a balance between global exploration and local exploitation ability. Besides, a variation factor based on normal distribution is used in this paper to enhance the diversity of the variation vector and jump out of the local optimal solution. The variation process of the variation factor is as follows:

$$F = \begin{cases} randn(0.5, 0.1), & \left| x_{best,g} - x_{best,g+1} \right| < 10^{-8} \\ equation(7), & otherwises \end{cases} \tag{4}$$

The crossover process of the differential evolution algorithm is as follows:

$$u_{i,j} = \begin{cases} v_{i,j}, & rand(0,1) < CR \text{ or } j = rand(1,D) \\ x_{i,j}, & otherwises \end{cases} \tag{5}$$

The crossover process is to operate on each variable in an individual, and D denotes the number of variables. The variables in the mutated individual are crossed with those in the initial individual by setting the conditions to obtain the crossover individual. To accommodate the crossover process, this paper changes the crossover factor in a linearly reduced manner with the evolutionary process, and the change equation is:

$$CR = CR_{max} - \frac{G(CR_{max} - CR_{min})}{G_m} \tag{6}$$

where the change range of the crossover factor is $[CR_{min}, CR_{max}]$. The adaptive differential evolution algorithm proposed in this paper adaptively changes the variance and crossover factors in evolutionary process, and balances the global exploration and local exploitation ability to some extent in the algorithm search process.

2.3 Population Reduction Strategy

Reduction of populations during evolution process of differential evolution algorithm can effectively capture useful individual information, reduce unnecessary computational resources, and improve convergence speed. This paper proposes a nonlinear population reduction strategy to control the reduction of population size according to the hyperbolic tangent function curve between $[-2.5,4]$. Through a predetermined maximum evolutionary generation G_{max}, the reduction function changes with the current evolutionary generation as the independent variable. The reduction equation is as follows:

$$F = \frac{NP_{max} + NP_{min}}{2} + \frac{\tanh\left(-2.5 + 4 \cdot \frac{G_{max} - G}{G_{max}}\right)(NP_{max} - NP_{min})}{2} \tag{7}$$

In the early stage of evolution, the size of population is large, and to ensure the diversity of population and to improve the global search ability of the algorithm. As the evolutionary process proceeds, the solved optimal individuals are closer and closer to the optimal solution. To save computational resources and improve the convergence speed, some individuals far from the optimal solution are removed. In the later stage of the evolutionary process, the population iterates around the optimal solution. To improve the local search ability, the population size is maintained at the small value and local search is performed carefully to ensure that the optimal solution in that range is found.

3 Numerical Experiment and Analysis

The experiments in this paper use a 64-bit Windows 10 operating system. The processor is an Intel(R) Core (TM) i5-5200U CPU @ 2.20 GHz with an Intel(R) HD Graphics 5500 GPU. Python 3.5.2 is selected as the experimental code language, and the experiment is run in PyCharm software to complete the experimental process.

3.1 Experiments Setup

In this paper, we choose five comparison algorithms, namely DE [2], LSHADE (Linear Success-History based Adaptive DE) [5], AGDE (Adaptive Guided Differential Evolution) [6], AMODE (a DE algorithm based on Adaptive Mutation Operator) [7] and ASVDE (modified DE algorithm based Adaptive Secondary Variation) [8]. The comparative analysis of the algorithms is performed on eight typical benchmark functions in CEC2014 [9], which are unimodal f_1, f_2, simple multimodal f_6, f_{12}, hybrid f_{17}, f_{22}, and composite functions f_{24}, f_{27}, as shown in Table 1. D is the dimensionality of the problem. The search space of these benchmark functions is [-100,100], with more local optima and function values greater than 0. Therefore, the fitness function is defined as f $= f(x) - f(x^*)$. $f(x)$ is the function value calculated by the algorithm, $f(x^*)$ is the known optimal value of the function. The closer the f is to zero, the closer the function value calculated by the algorithm is to the global optimum. The parameter variables set for the comparison experiments are shown in Table 2.

Table 1. Some benchmark functions of CEC2014

f	No.	Functions	$F_i^* = F_i(x^*)$
f_1	1	Rotated High Conditioned Elliptic Function	100
f_2	2	Rotated Bent Cigar Function	200
f_3	6	Shifted and Rotated Weierstrass Function	600
f_4	12	Shifted and Rotated Katsuura Function	1200
f_5	17	Hybrid Function 1 (N = 3)	1700
f_6	22	Hybrid Function 6 (N = 5)	2200
f_7	24	Composition Function 2 (N = 3)	2400
f_8	27	Composition Function 5 (N = 5)	2700

3.2 Comparison of Solution Accuracy and Stability

With the variable settings and experiments conducted in Table 2, the six comparison algorithms were run 21 times on the benchmark functions in the dimensions of D = 30., the average (avg) and standard deviation (std) of fitness function values were calculated and recorded in Tables 3, with the optimal values bolded in the table.

As shown in Table 3, the mean values solved by the APRDE algorithm on eight functions are 5.51E+02, 0.00E-00, 2.65E-01, 6.00E-01, 2.24E+02, 2.84E+01, 2.22E+02 and 3.20E+02, which are closer to the optimal solution than the mean values solved by other algorithms. The results obtained by the APRDE algorithm are closer to the optimal solutions compared with other algorithms, and also have better performance for solving high-dimensional optimization problems. The APRDE algorithm solves to the closest global optimal solution on 88% of the functions. The standard deviation range obtained by APRDE is 0.00E+00 to 3.85E+05, which has the smallest value compared with other algorithms, so the algorithm has the best stability.

Table 2. Parameter settings of comparison algorithms

DE	APRDE	AGDE	LSHADE	AMODE	ASVDE
$G_{max} = D * 100$ $NP = 100$					
$F = 0.75$	$F_{max} = 0.9$	$F = randn(0.1, 1)$	$F = 0.75$	$F = 0.75$	$F_{max} = 0.9$
$CR = 0.7$	$F_{min} = 0.2$	$F_{max} = 0.2$	$CR = 0.7$	$CR = 0.7$	$F_{max} = 0.2$
	$CR_{max} = 0.9$	$CR_2 = [0.9, 1.00]$	$p = 0.1$	$C = [0.05, 0.95]$	$Mr = 0.99$
	$CR_{min} = 0.2$		$H = 5$		$Max\_count = 5$
	$NP_{min} = 50$		$MF = MCR = 0.5NP_{min} = 10$		$CR = 0.7$

Table 3. Results of comparison algorithms on benchmark functions for D = 30

Function	Criterion	DE	AGDE	LSHADE	AMODE	ASVDE	APRDE
f_1	avg	5.46E + 07	1.97E+04	1.43E+04	2.91E+05	1.11E+06	**5.51E+02**
	std	1.57E+07	3.91E+03	3.45E+03	1.03E+05	1.05E+06	**3.91E+02**
f_2	avg	2.73E+07	9.86E+03	7.15E+03	1.46E+05	5.53E+05	**0.00E+00**
	std	2.95E+07	1.02E+04	7.55E+03	1.63E+05	9.27E+05	**0.00E+00**
f_3	avg	1.82E+07	6.57E+03	4.77E+03	9.70E+04	3.69E+05	**2.65E-01**
	std	2.73E+07	9.57E+03	7.03E+03	1.49E+05	8.00E+05	**5.29E-01**
f_4	avg	1.36E+07	4.93E+03	3.58E+03	7.28E+04	2.77E+05	**6.00E-01**
	std	2.49E+07	8.76E+03	6.43E+03	1.36E+05	7.11E+05	**8.26E-02**
f_5	avg	1.10E+07	4.03E+03	3.11E+03	6.11E+04	2.22E+05	**2.24E+02**
	std	2.29E+07	8.04E+03	5.82E+03	1.24E+05	6.46E+05	**1.44E+02**
f_6	avg	9.16E+06	3.37E+03	2.61E+03	5.10E+04	1.85E+05	**2.84E+01**
	std	2.13E+07	7.49E+03	5.43E+03	1.15E+05	5.95E+05	**6.82E+00**
f_7	avg	7.86E+06	2.92E+03	2.27E+03	4.37E+04	1.58E+05	**2.22E+02**
	std	2.00E+07	7.02E+03	5.10E+03	1.08E+05	5.55E+05	**2.65E-01**
f_8	avg	6.87E+06	2.60E+03	2.03E+03	3.83E+04	1.39E+05	**3.20E+02**
	std	1.89E+07	6.62E+03	4.81E+03	1.02E+05	5.22E+05	**4.02E+01**

3.3 Comparison of Convergence Speed

When D = 10, the convergence curves of the six compared algorithms on each function are shown in Fig. 1. From Figs. 1-a and 1-b, all algorithms show a single decreasing trend in the process of solving for unimodal functions, and the solution results are near the optimal solution. Compared with other algorithms, the APRDE algorithm converges the fastest, finds the global optimal solution first, and has the highest solution accuracy. In the simple multimodal functions f_3 and f_4, the fitness function values solved by

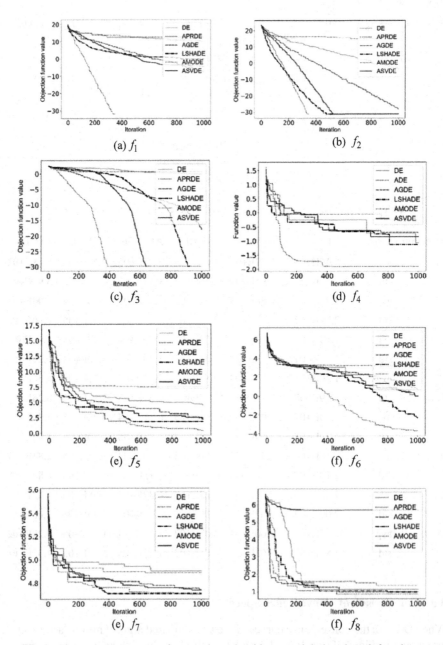

Fig. 1. The convergent curve of comparison algorithms on eight benchmark functions.

APRDE algorithm keep decreasing in the iterative process, the algorithm converges faster and first finds the global optimal solution first in the f_3 function, and in the f_4 function, the solved optimal is closer to the global optimal solution. Among the above four functions, compared with the ASVDE, LSHADE and AGDE algorithms, the APRDE algorithm not only finds the global optimal solution, but also converges faster and more efficiently. In the hybrid and composite functions $f_5 \sim f_8$, the functions have multiple local optimal solutions and larger local optimal values. The comparison results shows that the convergence curve of the APRDE algorithm is decreasing and the solved results are smaller and closer to the global optimal solution.

4 Conclusion

In the process of solving optimization problems, the differential evolution algorithm tends to converge prematurely and falls into a local optimal solution or stagnation state. In this paper, we propose a Differential Evolution Algorithm with Adaptive Population size Reduction (APRDE) strategy to remedy the shortcomings of traditional differential evolution algorithm. The APRDE algorithm proposes a parameter adaptive adjustment mechanism to balance the global exploration and local exploitation ability in the search process and adopts an ordered variation strategy to enrich the diversity of the population and improve the convergence speed and solution accuracy of the algorithm. In the evolutionary process, a nonlinear population reduction strategy is proposed to save computational cost and improve the quality of computational results at the same time. Compared with the other five optimization algorithms, the APRDE algorithm proposed in this paper has a fast convergence speed, the optimal solution is obtained in 88% of the tested functions, and the stability of the algorithm is relatively high.

References

1. Wang, G.F., Zhang, D.S.: Innovation practice and development prospect of intelligent fully mechanized technology for coal mining. J. China Univ. Min. Technol. **47**(3), 459–467 (2018)
2. Storn, R., Price, K.: Differential evolution—a simple and efficient adaptive scheme for global optimization over continuous spaces J. Global Optim. **11**(4), 341–359 (1997)
3. Mohamed, A.W., Hadi, A.A., Jambi, K.M.: Novel mutation strategy for enhancing SHADE and LSHADE algorithms for global numerical optimization. Swarm Evol. Comput. **50** 100455 (2019)
4. Yan, Q.M., Ma, R.Q., Ma, Y.X.: Adaptive simulated annealing particle swarm optimization algorithm Journal of Xidian University **48**(04), 120–127 (2021)
5. Mohamed, A.W., Mohamed, A.K.: Adaptive guided differential evolution algorithm with novel mutation for numerical optimization. Int. J. Mach. Learn. Cybern. **10**(2), 253–277 (2017)
6. Tanabe, R., Fukunaga, A.S.: Improving the search performance of SHADE using linear population size reduction. In: 2014 IEEE congress on evolutionary computation (CEC), pp. 1658–1665. IEEE (2014)
7. Liao, X., Li, J., Luo, Y.: Differential evolution algorithm based on adaptive mutation operator Comput. Eng. Appl. **54**(6), 128–134 (2018)

8. Hu, F., Dong, Q., Lv, L.: Modified differential evolution algorithm based on adaptive secondary variation and its application Comput. Eng. Appl. **38**(7), 271–280 (2021)
9. Liang, J.J., Qu, B.Y., Suganthan, P.N.: Problem definitions and evaluation criteria for the CEC 2014 special session and competition on single objective real-parameter numerical optimization. Computational Intelligence Laboratory, Zhengzhou University, Zhengzhou China and Technical Report, Nanyang Technological University, Singapore, 635: 490 (2013)

A Semi-supervised Road Segmentation Method for Remote Sensing Image Based on SegFormer

Tian Ma, Xinlei Zhou, Runtao Xi$^{(\boxtimes)}$, Jiayi Yang, Jiehui Zhang, and Fanhui Li

College of Computer Science and Technology, Xi'an University of Science and Technology,
Xi'an 710054, Shaanxi, China
jusadw@163.com

Abstract. Aiming at the problem that that pixel-level annotations of remote sensing images are difficult to obtain, a semi-supervised road segmentation method for remote sensing images is proposed. Firstly, an unsupervised network is designed to generate pseudo-labels of road images. In this module, a super-pixel segmentation method is used to pre-segment roads in remote sensing images, and then a lightweight convolutional neural network is used to extract road feature information, and to optimize the super-pixel segmentation result to generate the pseudo-label images. Secondly, the loss function of SegFomer is improved to solve the problem that, the difference between the number of front and rear pixels in the remote sensing road image is difficult to accurately segment. Finally, the pseudo-label image and the original image are combined and input to the improved SegFormer network for training. The experiment results show that, the segmentation effect of the proposed method is better than PSPNet, HRNet and other methods.

Keywords: Remote sensing image · Super pixel · Semi-supervised · SegFormer

1 Introduction

Remote sensing image is a synthesis of ground features. In order to identify and analyze the target, it is necessary to separate and extract the relevant area, and on this basis, the target can be further utilized, such as measurement and positioning. Remote sensing image segmentation refers to the technology and process of dividing the image into regions with different characteristics and extracting the target of interest. The characteristics here refer to the characteristics of remote sensing images, which can be targets such as grayscale, color, texture, etc., which can correspond to a single area or multiple areas. There is no general theory of remote sensing image segmentation so far. With the introduction of various disciplines and many new theories and methods, many image segmentation techniques combined with some specific theories and methods have emerged.

© The Author(s), under exclusive license to Springer Nature Singapore Pte Ltd. 2022
S. Yang and H. Lu (Eds.): ISAIR 2022, CCIS 1701, pp. 189–201, 2022.
https://doi.org/10.1007/978-981-19-7943-9_16

Due to the rapid development of remote sensing technology, the resolution of remote sensing images has been continuously improved, and the interference of noise on images has also increased. How to automatically extract high-precision road information from remote sensing images has become a hot and difficult research topic in recent years. At present, the remote sensing image segmentation method based on Convolutional Neural Network (CNN) is particularly outstanding. Compared with the traditional semi-automatic extraction method, this method can effectively suppress the noise generated in the process of road information extraction and reduce road detail information. Lost, which greatly improves the extraction effect. However, there are the following difficulties in automatically extracting road information from remote sensing images:

(1) The input image has a high resolution and a large amount of data, which requires a large enough receptive field;
(2) The roads in remote sensing images are slender and complex, and account for a small proportion of the entire image;
(3) The road has natural connectivity, that is, it has the topological characteristics of the image [1].

In recent years, a variety of methods have been proposed at home and abroad for the problem of how to automatically extract road information from high-resolution remote sensing images. The more common traditional remote sensing image road information extraction methods include pixel-based [2, 3], object-based [4, 5, 22], knowledge-based [6, 23] and machine learning-based methods. Das et al. [7] proposed to utilize the salient contrasting features of the spectrum and local linear trajectories to design a multi-level framework, while incorporating a probabilistic support vector machine to supplement the missing road information to obtain potential road targets. Chen [8, 24] et al. extracted the information of greenhouse cover in remote sensing images by fusing spectral features and texture features, and used confusion matrix to verify the classification results, which improved the recognition accuracy of greenhouse cover. With the rapid development of deep learning, Long et al. [9, 25] proposed a Fully Convolutional Network (FCN), which uses the skip connection structure to fuse the representation information of shallow and high layers to obtain accurate and fine segmentation results. Zhang et al. [10] combined residual learning and U-Net network structure to construct an algorithm for road region extraction, simplifying the training of deep networks through residual units, and the rich skip connections in the network can promote the dissemination of information, gradually recover road detail features in the image. Chen et al. [11] proposed the Atrous Spatial Pyramid Pooling (ASPP) module in the Deeplab series by combining multi-scale information and Dilated Convolution, which combined dilated convolutions with different dilation rates for feature fusion., which ensures that the feature receptive field is enlarged without sacrificing the feature spatial resolution.

Inspired by the self-encoder, Chaurasia et al. [12] proposed the LinkNet network structure, which improves the accuracy of road segmentation by directly connecting the encoder and the decoder, while retaining the encoded part information without adding additional parameters, learning efficiency. Since the feature resolution of the ASPP module is not dense enough on the scale axis and the acquired receptive field is not sufficient, Yang et al. [13] combined the dense connections in the Deeplab series of ASPP and DenseNet [14] to form Dense-ASPP. In order to better focus on key regions and suppress useless features, the PSANet proposed by Zhao et al. [15] obtains contextual information by learning self-attention feature maps at all locations, but introduces too many parameters and consumes a lot of memory. Fu et al. [16] proposed a Stacked Deconvolutional Network (SDN), which aims to capture more contextual information and gradually recover high-resolution predictions using progressively stacked networks.

However, deep learning is a data-driven technology. Manually labeling remote sensing images at the pixel level is expensive and difficult to obtain. Current existing semi-supervised learning methods train multiple networks to generate pseudo-labeled images, which is undoubtedly a heavy workload. In this paper, an unsupervised module is proposed for generating pseudo-labels of roads in remote sensing images and trained in an optimized SegFormer network.

2 Our Method

2.1 Training Strategy

At present, the mainstream semi-supervised remote sensing image road segmentation methods mainly use a pre-trained segmentation network to segment unlabeled images to obtain pseudo-labels, and then input the pseudo-labels into the semantic segmentation network for training, so as to obtain a good segmentation network. But such a method is very cumbersome, we have to train two networks or even more, and traditional methods are difficult to pre-segment complex images and generate pseudo-labels.

Our proposed method is divided into two stages for road segmentation, As shown in Fig. 1, the remote sensing image first generates pseudo-labels through a lightweight unsupervised module, and the pseudo-labels and the manually labeled pixel-level labels are input into the semantic segmentation network for training, so as to obtain the segmentation results. After boundary zing, the final pseudo-labels are obtained.

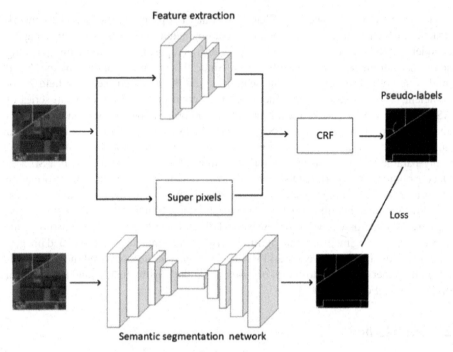

Fig. 1. General training strategy

2.2 Unsupervised Module Design

In this paper, an unsupervised method is used to generate pseudo-labeled images of remote sensing roads, which pre-segment remote sensing images through super pixel segmentation in machine learning algorithms to obtain preliminary segmentation results, and extract the features of remote sensing images through lightweight convolutional networks. The fine-grained pre-classification results of machine learning segmentation are processed. And in the iteration, the small blocks are gradually merged, and finally the expected semantic segmentation results are obtained, as shown in Fig. 2.

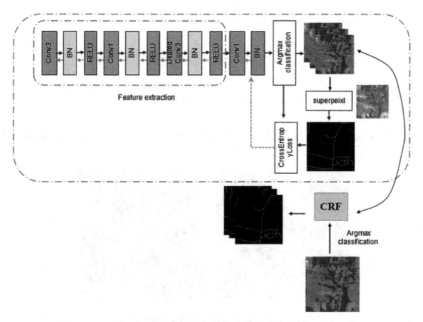

Fig. 2. Unsupervised Module Framework

3 Super Pixel Segmentation

Super pixel segmentation plays the role of pre-segmentation in the unsupervised module, and its segmentation effect determines the quality of pseudo-labels, so the selection of super pixel segmentation method is particularly important. In this paper, the Felzenszwalb [18] algorithm is selected as the super pixel segmentation algorithm.

The segmentation algorithm adopts a graph-based method, and the main steps are as follows:

(1) Calculate the dissimilarity between each pixel and its 8 neighbors
(2) Arrange the edges according to the dissimilarity from small to large to obtain $e_1, e_2, e_3 \ldots e_n$.
(3) Select e_n to perform a merge judgment on the currently selected edge. Let its connected vertices be (v_i, v_j), if the merging conditions are met;

- v_i, v_j belong to two different regions $Id(v_i) \neq Id(v_j)$;
- $w_{ij} \leq Mint(C_i, C_j)$, execute 4, otherwise execute 5;

(4) Update threshold and class number;

- Update the class label, $Id(v_i)$, $Id(v_j)$ are unified as $Id(v_i)$;

- The dissimilarity threshold w_{ij}, of the new class, the calculation formula:

$$w_{i,j} = \frac{K}{|C_i| + |C_j|} \tag{1}$$

(5) If $n \le N$, select the next edge in order, go to 4;

As can be seen from Fig. 3, the algorithm predicts the boundaries of the road well.

Fig. 3. Super pixel segmentation results

Feature extraction module

In this paper, a lightweight fully convolutional neural network is constructed to extract remote sensing image features. The module structure is shown in Fig. 2, mainly consists of using 3x3 alternating with 1x1, loss function, batch normalization. This lightweight structure enables the network to effectively extract features in a faster time, and calculate the cross-entropy loss function through the extracted features and the pre-segmentation result obtained by super pixel segmentation to optimize the result of road pre-segmentation, so as to obtain high-quality pseudo-labels. The cross-entropy loss function is shown in formula (2):

$$L = -\sum_{c=1}^{M} y_c \log(p_c) \tag{2}$$

Among them, M represents the number of categories, y_c is a one-hot vector, and the element has only two values, 0 and 1. If the category and the sample category are the same, it is 1, otherwise it is 0, and p_c represents the probability that the predicted sample belongs to c. Here, M is set to 2 to represent the background and foreground roads, respectively.

3.1 SegFormer Network Structure

The segmentation network is trained by combining the pseudo-labeled images obtained by the unsupervised module with the hand-labeled images.

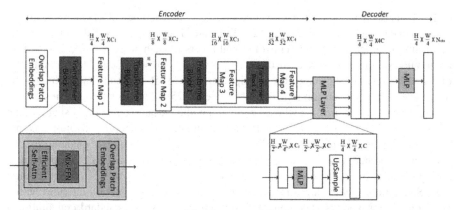

Fig. 4. The network structure of SegFormer, mainly the encoder-decoder structure

The Transformer module [20] inside the encoder MiT adopts the Overlap Patch Embeddings (OPE) structure to extract and downsample the input image, and then input the obtained features into the Efficient Multihead Self-Attention (Efficient Multihead Self-Attention). Attention, EMSA) layer and Mix Feed Forward (Mix-FFN) layer. Overlapping patch embeddings are computed using standard convolutional layers. After spatially flattening 2D features into 1D features, they are input to the EMSA layer for self-attention computation and feature enhancement. In order to replace the position encoding in the ordinary Transformer, a 3×3 convolutional layer is added between the two linear transformation layers of the ordinary feedforward layer to fuse the spatial position information (Table 1).

Table 1. Main parameters of MiT-B1

Embed dims	64
Num layers	[2,2,2,2]
Num heads	[1,2,5,8]
Mlp ratio	[7,3,3,3]
Sr ratios	[8,4,2,1]

Transformer Block employs multiple stacked EMSA and Mix-FFN to deepen the network depth to extract rich details and semantic features. Self-attention is calculated in EMSA at each scale. Compared with other previous networks based on convolutional neural networks that integrate information on all scales and then perform self-attention calculation, the self-attention at each scale purer.

According to the parameters of Fig. 1, embed dims is the encoding length of each feature point, Num layers represent the value of N in the Transformer Block in the first to fourth stages in Fig. 4, that is, the number of times to repeat EMA and Mix-FFN, and Num heads are the first to fourth stages, respectively. In the fourth stage, the number of heads in EMSA, multiplied by Embed dims, is the number of channels of output features in each stage, which are 64, 128, 320, and 512, respectively. Patch sizes are the convolution kernel sizes of the convolutional layers in each stage of OPE, and Strides is the OPE sampling step size. Sr ratios respectively represent the reduction multiples of K and V input in each stage. The multiplication of MLP ratio and Embed dims is the increased channel dimension in Mix-FNN, which is 256 in all four stages. The decoder of SegFormer is a feature map whose height and width output from the four stages of the encoder are 1/4, 1/8, 1/16, and 1/32 of the original image, and the input convolution kernel is a 1 × 1 volume. The product module uniformly adjusts the number of channels to 256, and adjusts the height and width of the feature map to 1/4 the size of the input image through bilinear interpolation upsampling, and then connects into a 1024-channel feature map. Semantic segmentation images are predicted by two convolution modules with 1 × 1 convolution kernels. The convolution module consists of standard convolutional layers, BN and ReLU. The characteristics of remote sensing road images are that the categories are unbalanced, and the pixels occupied by the background are much larger than those of the road. In view of this situation, the SegFormer loss function is designed as Dice Loss and Focal Loss, and its calculation formula is as follows:

$$DiceLoss = 1 - \frac{2|A \cap B|}{|A| + |B|} \tag{3}$$

In formula (3), Dice Loss is the degree of coincidence between the output result and the real label, A represents the output result; B represents the real label;

$$FocalLoss = -\frac{1}{N} \sum_{i=1}^{N} \left[\alpha y_i \left(1 - y_i'\right)^{\gamma} \log y_i' + (1 - \alpha)(1 - y_i)\left(y_i'\right)^{\gamma} \log\left(1 - y_i'\right) \right] \tag{4}$$

$$Loss = Diceloss + FoCalLoss \tag{5}$$

In formula (4): y_i represents the real sample label of pixel i, y_i' represents the prediction result of pixel i by the network, N represents the number of pixels, and γ represents the rate at which the sample weight decreases. In this paper, γ and α are respectively Take the value $\alpha = 0.1$, $\gamma = 2$. As shown in Eq. (5), the loss function is designed as the sum of the two.

4   Experiment

4.1   Datasets

This experiment uses the Massachusetts road data [21], which contains high-resolution images and corresponding real road labels, covering complex features such as cities and suburbs. We uniformly crop the dataset images to a size of 640*640 pixels, and collect a total of 700 images as the original training set. An example dataset is shown in Fig. 5.

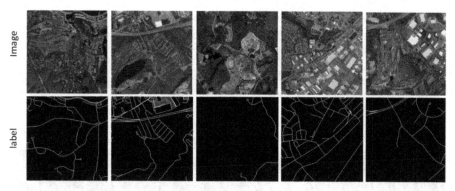

Fig. 5. Sample dataset

4.2 Experimental Setup

In order to verify the advantages of the method in this paper, three evaluation indicators, mIoU, MAP (accuracy) and F1-score, are used for comparative analysis, and the number of training rounds is 300 epochs. The experimental device runs on 3090Ti with 24G of memory.

Figure 6 shows the situation of the training process. Compared with SegFormer, our method has a faster convergence speed, and the loss function and mIoU are also better than SegFormer.

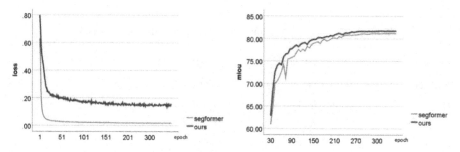

Fig. 6. The method in this paper is compared with the training process of segformer

4.3 Unsupervised Module Experiment

After many experiments, setting the number of iterations of the unsupervised module to 128 can get better segmentation results. Experiments show that under the 3090Ti device, the average time-consuming of images with different pixels is shown in Table 2.

The image of this experimental dataset is 640*640 pixels in size, and it only takes 5.69s on average to get a pseudo-label.

Figure 7 shows the segmentation results of the unsupervised module under different iteration times. It can be seen that the designed unsupervised module has a good effect on road segmentation.

Table 2. Time-consuming generation of pseudo-labels by unsupervised modules

Image size (iteration 128)	Time(s)
512*512	4.71
640*640	5.69
1024*1024	8.41

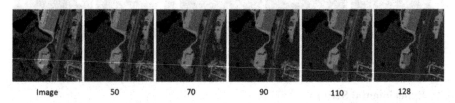

| Image | 50 | 70 | 90 | 110 | 128 |

Fig. 7. Segmentation results of unsupervised modules with different iterations

4.4 Comparative Test

First, we mix the pseudo-labeled images generated by the unsupervised module with the labeled images 1:20 to obtain 735 training sets, which are input to the improved SegFormer network for training. To verify the effectiveness of our method, our method is compared with the remaining four methods.

Table 3. Comparison of evaluation indicators of different algorithms

Method	MIoU	MAP	F1_score
PSPNet	51.44	52.64	54.1
HRNet	74.86	79.94	83.8
DeepLabv3+	78.61	85.30	85.0
SegFormer	81.16	86.52	98.04
Ours	**81.73**	**88.02**	**99.05**

It can be seen from Table 3 that the evaluation indicators of PSPNet are the lowest, which are 51.44, 52.64, and 0.541, respectively. Our method achieves the best indicators, which are 81.73, 88.02, and 99.05, respectively. Compared with SegFormer, our method has mIoU, MAP, The F1_score is increased by 0.57%, 1.5%, and 1.01%, respectively, indicating that our method can achieve better segmentation results when there is a large gap between front and back pixels.

Figure 8 shows the visualization of the segmentation results. It can be seen that the segmentation effect of PSPNet is the worst, and it is almost difficult to segment road images. Among the three convolutional neural networks, DeepLabv3+ has the best segmentation effect, but there is over-segmentation and under-divided; The segmentation

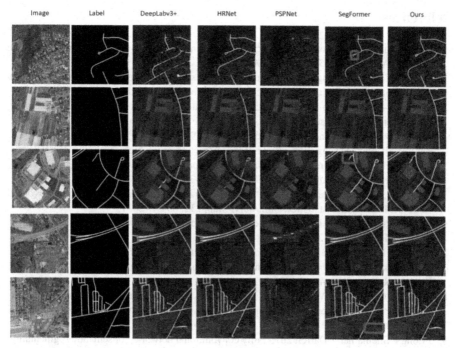

Fig. 8. Visualization of segmentation results under different algorithms

results of SegFormer are better than those of these three convolutional neural networks, but there are still cases of over-segmentation and under-segmentation, as marked in the red box in the figure, and our method is the best.

5   Conclusion

This paper designs a semi-supervised method for segmentation of remote sensing road images. In order to solve the problem that the pixel-level labels of remote sensing road images are difficult to obtain, a semi-supervised module is proposed to efficiently generate pseudo-labels of road images; it is used for the training of segmentation network; In remote sensing images, there is a large gap between foreground and background pixels. In this paper, a loss function that combines Dice Loss and Focal Loss is designed to optimize SegFormer. Compared with mainstream segmentation networks, our method has achieved advanced results. However, in terms of model performance, how to further design an efficient end-to-end semi-supervised segmentation model for remote sensing road images is a problem worthy of study.

Acknowledgments. This work was supported by the National Key Research and Development Program Topics (Grant No. 2021YFB4000905), the National Natural Science Foundation of China (Grant No. 62101432 and 62102309), and in part by Shaanxi Natural Science Fundamental Research Program Project (No. 2022JM-508).

References

1. Wang Xin.: Research on road extraction algorithm from remote sensing image. Autom. Technol. Appl. **37**(5), 65–67 + 72 (2018)
2. Sun Ke, Zhang Jun-ping: High-resolution remote sensing image road extraction based on local adaptive direction template matching. Opt. Precis. Eng. **23**(10), 509–515 (2015)
3. Lin Xiang-guo, Zhang Ji-xian, Li Hai-tao, et al.: Semi-automatic ex-traction of high-resolution remote sensing image strip roads based on T-type template matching. Journal of Wuhan University (In-formation Science Edition), **34**(3), 293–296 (2009)
4. Yu Jie, Yu Feng, Zhang Jing, et al.: Road extraction from high-resolution remote sensing images combining regional growth and road primitives. Journal of Wuhan University (Information Science Edition) **38**(7), 761–764 (2013)
5. Chu Heng, Li Hong-chuan, Liu Hong-bin: Road extraction from remote sensing images based on object histogram G statistics. Bull. Surv. Mapp. **12**, 63-67 (2017)
6. Tang Pu-xia, Shi Li-yi.: Image classification algorithm based on data mining. Mod. Electron. Technol. **40**(3), 54–57 (2017)
7. S Das TT Mirnalinee K Varghese 2011 Use of salient features for the design of a multistage framework to extract roads from highresolu-tion multispectral satellite images IEEE Trans. Geo-sci. Remote Sens. 49 10 3906 3931
8. Hasituya, Chen, Z.X., Wu, W.B., et al.: Monitoring plastic-mulched farmland using landsat-8 OLI imagery. In: International Conference on Agro-geoinformatics, pp. 292–301. IEEE (2015)
9. J Long E Shelhamer T Darrell 2015 Fully convolutional networks for semantic segmentation IEEE Trans. Pattern Anal. Mach. Intell. 39 4 640 651
10. Z Zhang Q Liu Y Wang 2017 Road extraction by deep residual U-net IEEE Geoenceand Remote Sens. Lett. 15 5 749 753
11. Chen, L.C., Papandreou, G., Schroff, F., et al.: Rethinking atrous con-volution for semantic image segmentation. arXiv preprint arXiv: 1706.05587 (2017)
12. Chaurasia, A., Culurciello, E.: LinkNet: exploiting encoder representations for efficient semantic segmentation. In: IEEE Visual Com-medications and Image Processing (VCIP), pp. 1–4. St. Petersburg, FL (2017)
13. Yang, M., Yu, K., Zhang, C., et al.: Dense-ASPP for semantic segmentation in street scenes. In: IEEE/CVF Conference on Computer Vision and Pattern Recognition, pp. 3684–3692. Salt Lake City, UT (2018)
14. Huang, G., Liu, Z., Laurens, V.D.M., et al.: Densely connected convolutional networks. arXiv preprint arXiv: 1608. 06993 (2016)
15. Zhao, H., Zhang, Y., Liu, S., et al.: Psanet: point-wise spatial attention network for scene parsing. In: Proceedings of the European Conference on Computer Vision, pp. 267–283. Springer, Cham (2018)
16. Fu, J., Liu, J., Wang, Y., et al.: Stacked deconvolutional network for se-mantic segmentation. arXiv preprint arXiv: 1708.04943 (2017)
17. Jiang, J., Zhang, Z., Huang, Y., et al.: Incorporating depth into both CNN and CRF for indoor semantic segmentation. In 2017 8th IEEE International Conference on Software Engineering and Service Science (ICSESS). IEEE (2017)
18. Felzenszwalb, P.F., Huttenlocher, D.P.: Efficient graph-based image segmentation. Int. J. Comput. Vis. **59**(2), 167–181 (2004)
19. Xie, E., Wang, W., Yu, Z., et al.: SegFormer: simple and efficient design for semantic segmentation with transformers (2021)
20. Liu, Z., Lin, Y., Cao, Y., et al.: Swin transformer: hierarchical vision transformer using shifted windows (2021)

21. Chen, J., Liu, X., Liu, C., et al.: A modified convolutional neural network with transfer learning for road extraction from remote sensing imagery. In: 2018 Chinese Automation Congress (CAC) (2019)
22. Huimin Lu, Ming Zhang, Xing Xu.: Deep fuzzy hashing network for efficient image retrieval. IEEE Trans. Fuzzy Syst. https://doi.org/10.1109/TFUZZ.2020.2984991 (2020)
23. Huimin Lu, Yujie Li, Min Chen, et al.: Brain Intelligence: go beyond artificial intelligence. Mob. Netw. Appl. **23**, 368–375, (2018)
24. Huimin Lu, Yujie Li, Shenglin Mu, et al.: Motor anomaly detection for unmanned aerial vehicles using reinforcement learning. IEEE Internet of Things J. **5**(4), 2315–2322 (2018)
25. Huimin Lu, Mengjiao Qin, Feng Zhang, et al.: RSCNN: a CNN-based method to enhance low-light remote-sensing images. Remote Sens., 62 (2020)

Cross-Layer Feature Attention Module for Multi-scale Object Detection

Haotian Zheng, Cheng Pang$^{(\boxtimes)}$, and Rushi Lan

School of Computer Science and Information Security, Guilin University of Electronic Technology, Guilin, China
`astrozhenght@163.com`, {`pangcheng3,rslan`}`@guet.edu.cn`

Abstract. Recent target detection networks adopt the attention mechanism for better feature abstraction. However, most of them draw feature attentions from merely one or two layers, failing to obtain consistent results for objects with different scales. In this paper, we propose a cross-layer feature attention module (CFAM) which can be plugged in any off-the-shelf architecture, and demonstrate that attentions obtained from multiple layers can further improve object detection. The proposed module consists of two components for cross-layer feature fusion and feature refinement, respectively. The former collects rich contextual cues by fusing the features from distinct layers, while the later calculates the cross-layer attention maps and applies them with the fused features. Experiments show the proposed module improves the detection rate by 2% against the baseline architecture, and outperforms recent state-of-the-art methods on the Pascal VOC benchmark.

Keywords: Attention · Feature fusion · Object detection

1 Introduction

Numerous works explore multi-scale object detection via advanced feature learning technologies [1–3], among which multi-level future fusion and refinement are most widely used [4–6]. For example, recent convolutional neural networks (CNNs) composite feature maps from different layers and coupled with anchor boxes, obtaining prominent results of detection. The power of these networks lies in their ability to discover objects with different scales and aspect ratios. To further promote the discrimination of fused features, the feature pyramid [7] and the attention mechanism [8–10] are introduced.

Features with distinct receptive fields depict an image in different scales: features with large receptive fields encode global information and semantic patterns, while features with small receptive fields carry local details and texture cues [11]. Either built from a sequence of pyramid images or generated from a CNN, detection methods based on feature pyramid concatenate feature maps depicting images in discrete scales to discover objects with different scales [12–15]. However, the concatenated feature maps contribute equally to the final results in these methods. As a comparison, the proposed module fuses the features in a weighted manner.

© The Author(s), under exclusive license to Springer Nature Singapore Pte Ltd. 2022
S. Yang and H. Lu (Eds.): ISAIR 2022, CCIS 1701, pp. 202–210, 2022.
https://doi.org/10.1007/978-981-19-7943-9_17

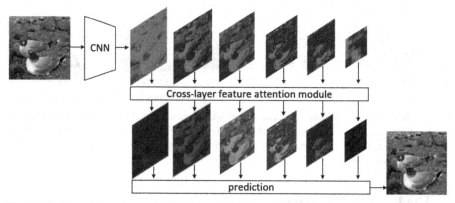

Fig. 1. Pipeline of the proposed CFAM: context information collection via cross-layer feature fusion, and feature refinement using channel attention.

The attention mechanism becomes increasingly prevalent in recent intricate deep networks [16, 17]. Motivated by the visual attention processing in the brain, researchers improve the performance of neural networks by selecting the information of interests while eliminating redundant information [18]. Two types of attentions are widely used in detection: the channel attention [8] and the spatial attention [9, 19]. The former supposes that different channels contribute partially to the final prediction, and explicitly models the importance of discrete feature channels by investigating the interdependencies between these channels. As a comparison, the spatial attention encourages regions in an image to have distinct importance to the prediction, which assigns optimal weights to the regions according to the current task [20]. Feature selection via attentions can be configured in a CNN handily, which benefits the learning process and domain transformation of the network [21–25].

Although the feature pyramid and attentions make great progress in fusing multi-level features, their symbiosis has not been extensively investigated. Most of the attention-based methods focus either spatial attentions or channel attentions in feature maps from one or two layers [26, 27], ignoring the multi-level context information of the feature pyramid obtained from multiple layers. However, the contextual cues encoding an object with distinct scales and abstraction levels could be essential to object detection [28]. As the size of an object may varies across numerous images, consistent detections of the object fundamentally rely on multi-level context cues in each of the image [29].

To explore the symbiotic feature pyramid and attention while further improve multi-scale object detection, we devise the CFAM module which explicitly model the interdependence of context cues at different level. The novelty of the proposed architecture lies in its combination of the feature pyramid and attention mechanism. Feature alignment and feature fusion are assembled in an unify pipeline which works with any backbone networks.

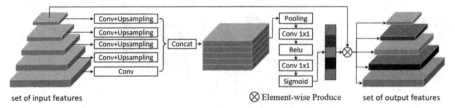

Fig. 2. The component of feature refinement multiplies the cross-layer feature maps with attention maps, collecting context cues from multiple layers and highlighting the detected objects of various scales. The attention map is obtained by summarizing activations in different channels of the cross-layer feature maps.

2 The Proposed Method

In this section, we introduce the proposed cross-layer feature attention module (CFAM). As illustrated in Fig. 1, the module consists of a cross-layer feature fusion component and a feature refinement component. An image is first fed into the backbone network, generating multiple feature maps in the convolutional layers. Then these cross-layer feature maps are aligned to have the same size via up-sampling before concatenation. After that, an attention map is calculated for fusing the aligned feature maps which highlights the detected objects with various scales.

2.1 Cross-Layer Feature Fusion

Extracting context information shows significant impact on multi-scale object detection, where the feature pyramid network (FPN) are commonly used. However, the up-sampling and fusion processes are alternated in the FPN, and no attention is incorporated in the pipeline. As shown in Fig. 2, the proposed cross-layer feature fusion component first aligns all the feature maps and then concatenate them, obtaining the cross-layer feature maps with rich contextual information.

Specifically, the feature fusion component takes the feature maps from convolutional layers as its input (Fig. 1). Firstly, 1×1 convolutions are applied to these features, reducing the dimension of the feature maps and summarizing the global information of each channel. After that, the number of channels of the feature maps is reduced to 256, which benefits the following feature learning and abstraction. At the same time, the network parameters are minimized, which accelerates the training process. Then, feature maps with smaller resolutions are up-sampled using bilinear interpolation, aligning themselves to the same size with the feature map with the largest resolution. Finally, the aligned feature maps after and concatenated to a single cross-layer feature map for the further refinement.

2.2 Feature Refinement

Conventional SSD networks utilize the feature pyramid to summarize feature maps at each scale with equal weights, incorporating no visual attentions. However, the attentions taking features differentially can be deterministic for multiscale object detection. Specifically, feature maps generated from layers close to the top usually have larger receptive field, and contain richer semantic information. On the other hand, feature maps generated from layers close to the bottom have smaller receptive field, which specify detailed information. As a result, highlevel features are commonly used to encode large objects while low-level features are used to encode small targets. The dependency between different features can be modeled through CFAM, and discrete weights can be assigned to the feature maps specifying objects with different abstraction levels. As shown in Fig. 2, the feature refinement is achieved by multiply the cross-layer feature map with an attention map.

In order to obtain the attention map, channel attention [8] is applied to calculate the weights for each feature in the cross-layer feature map, adjusting the contribution of each feature to multi-scale object detection. When calculating the attention map, the channel-based spatial information is obtained by global average pooling and global max pooling. Let O_c be the pooling result of the c-th channel in a $H \times W$ area R, for an input feature map $X \in \mathbb{R}^{C \times H \times W}$, it computes:

$$O_c = P(F_c) = \frac{1}{|R^{HW}|} \sum_{(a,b) \in R^{HW}} X_c(a, b) + \max_{(a,b) \in R^{HW}} X_c(a, b) \tag{1}$$

where P denotes the pooling function (global average pooling and maximum pooling), F_c denotes the input feature map. $|R^{HW}|$ represents the number of elements in the area R^{HW}, $X_c(a, b)$ represents the element at location (a, b) of the c-th channel.

Then, the attention map can be obtained by feeding O_c in two convolutional layers with kernel size 1×1, followed by a Relu layer and a sigmoid activation layer, respectively:

$$CA_c = Sigmoid(Conv(ReLU(Conv(O_c)))) \tag{2}$$

Finally, we multiply the attention map with the cross-layer feature map, producing the refined feature for multi-scale object detection:

$$F'_c = CA_c \otimes F_c \tag{3}$$

CFAM computes the attention map of each channel by considering the relationship between the feature maps specifying different scales. So that the important feature maps encoding objects are highlighted during detection, while feature maps specifying backgrounds are suppressed. CFAM works with stateof-the-art backbones, which further improves multi-scale object detection.

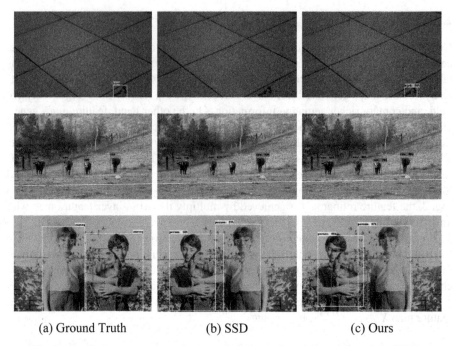

(a) Ground Truth   (b) SSD   (c) Ours

Fig. 3. Qualitative comparisons between the proposed module and the original SSD.

Table 1. Detection results of the entire VOC2007 and 20 categories obtained by different attention-based detection models.

Method	mAP	aero	bic.	bird	boat	bot.	bus	car	cat	cha.	cow	din.	dog	hor.	mot.	per.	pot.	she.	sofa	tra.	tv.
SSD	75.5	**81.2**	82.4	72.4	66.0	47.2	84.2	85.1	85.3	57.4	80.9	76.0	82.1	85.9	82.9	77.3	49.9	76.7	76.7	86.5	73.8
HyperNet	76.3	77.4	83.3	75.0	69.1	**62.4**	83.1	**87.4**	87.4	57.1	79.8	71.4	85.1	85.1	80.0	**79.1**	51.2	**79.1**	75.7	80.9	76.5
Ion	76.5	79.2	79.2	**77.4**	69.8	55.7	**85.2**	84.2	**89.8**	57.5	78.5	73.8	**87.8**	85.9	81.3	75.3	49.7	76.9	74.6	85.2	**82.1**
SSD+SE	76.9	80.4	83.4	75.2	69.5	50.1	83.0	85.3	87.9	59.9	81.6	77.6	85.6	86.5	**83.5**	77.4	**52.4**	77.1	78.7	87	75.9
SSD+CFAM	77.6	79.6	**84.6**	76.3	**71.8**	50.6	85.1	86.1	89.1	**62.4**	**84.6**	75.9	86.2	**87.6**	83.3	77.5	50.4	77.9	**79.3**	**87.8**	76.3

3   Experiments

3.1   Datasets and Settings

The proposed CFAM is extensively tested on the challenging Pascal VOC benchmark. We choose single shot multi-box detector (SSD) as the baseline architecture, conducting comparisons with several networks and modules for object detection. SSD uses vgg16 [30] as its backbone network, whose parameters are initiated with the model pre-trained on ImageNet [31]. Among the Pascal VOC dataset, VOC07+12 is used for training while the test set in VOC 2007 is used for validation. We take the layer Conv4_3, Conv7, Conv8_2, Conv9_2, Conv10_2, Conv11_2 in SSD to perform cross-layer fusion in CFAM. All the experiments run on a single NVIDIA Tesla P100 GPU. SGD optimizer is utilized for network training, with a batch size of 48, a learning rate of 1e-3 and a momentum of 0.9. The learning rate decreases to 1e-4 and 1e-5 when the training iteration approaches 130 and 220, respectively. 260 iterations of optimization are performed before convergence.

Table 2. Impact of the CFAM on the detection rate.

Method	CFAM on layers	mAP
SSD	w/o	75.50
SSD	Conv9,10,11	76.32
SSD	Conv4,7,8	77.55
SSD	Conv4,7,8,9,10,11	77.62

3.2 Comparison with State-of-the-Arts

Table 1 compares the mAP on the Pascal VOC dataset achieved by the proposed CFAM and some state-of-the-art attention modules backboned by SSD. To fairly investigate the performance of each attention module, we remain the training settings and hardware platform unchanged for all these modules. As shown in Table 1, the mAP is improved by 1.4% over the baseline SSD300 after incorporating the channel attention. The mAP is improved by 2.12% when the CFAM works with the baseline SSD300, demonstrating the proposed CFAM outperforms the channel attention on object detection. The power of the CFAM lies in its appropriate modeling of cross-layer feature attentions.

Comparisons of the detection accuracy of 20 categories in the Pascal VOC dataset are summarized in Table 1. As is shown, CFAM-SSD300 achieves consistently high accuracies among all categories, and makes great improvement in detecting small targets (cat, dog and sofa). Notice that, CFAM-SSD300 outperforms SSD300 in detecting most of the categories, demonstrating the effectiveness of the proposed module.

Qualitative comparisons between the proposed module and the SSD in object detection are illustrated in Fig. 3. The first row visualizes the detection results of single objects with small sizes, while the second and third row give the detection results of multiple targets with different sizes. As is shown, SSD network fails to detect some objects with small sizes and some overlapped targets. The proposed CFAM module achieves consistent detection results with regard to objects with various sizes and overlapped targets. Otherwise, the prediction scores for the ground-truth categories generated by CFAM are higher than that obtained by SSD.

3.3 Ablation Studies

To further investigate the benefits of the proposed CFAM to fuse different feature maps across network layers, three folds of experiments are conducted by removing some of the components from the original module. All modules are trained using the VOC 2007 and VOC 2012, and tested on the VOC 2007.

Table 2 shows the mAP scores obtained by the cross-layer feature fusion component under three different configurations, in which the CFAM is deployed in discrete layers in SSD300. (1) High-level feature maps from layer conv9_2, conv10_2 and conv11_2 are assembled to a cross-layer feature map, followed by feature refinement. In this case, the mAP score is 76.32%, which is a limited improvement over the original SSD300. (2) Low-level feature maps form layer conv4_3, conv7 and conv8_2 are fused, obtaining a mAP score of 77.55%. This is a significant improvement over the original SSD300; (3) Cross-layer fusion is performed on both high-level and low-level feature maps from layer conv4_3, conv7, conv8_2, conv9_2, conv10_2 and conv11_2. The final mAP score further goes up to 77.62%, suggesting that cross-layer feature fusion improves the detection performance of the network when CFAM is deployed. And the best result is obtained when both the high-level and low-level feature maps are fused together.

4   Conclusion and Future Work

This paper proposes a context-aware cross-layer feature attention module(CFAM) for multi-scale object detection. The module fuses cross-layer feature maps to collect context visual cues from both high-level and low-level features. When combined with the channel attention components, the module highlights the detected object disregard of their sizes, thus increase the detection robustness to scale variations. Otherwise, the proposed CFAM is feasible to deploy in any offthe-shelf architectures. Extensive experiments on the challenging Pascal VOC benchmark show the CFAM improves detection rate by a large margin over baseline architectures without additional costs. In our future works, CFAM will be modified to benefits more computer vision tasks like image enhancement, segmentation and visual tracking.

Acknowledgements. This work is partially supported by the National Natural Science Foundation of China (61962014) and the Guangxi Science and Technology Project (AD20159034 and 2021GXNSFBA220035).

References

1. Liu, W., Anguelov, D., Erhan, D., Szegedy, C., Reed, S., Fu, C.Y., Berg, A.C.: Ssd: single shot multibox detector. In: European Conference on Computer Vision, pp. 21–37. Springer (2016)
2. Lin, T.-Y. Goyal, P., Girshick, R., He, K., Dollár, P.: Focal loss for dense object detection. In: Proceedings of the IEEE International Conference on Computer Vision, pp. 2980–2988 (2017)
3. Redmon, J., Farhadi, A.: Yolov3: An incremental improvement. CoRR, vol. abs/1804.02767 (2018)
4. Jaderberg, M., Simonyan, K., Zisserman, A., et al.: Spatial transformer networks. In: Advances in Neural Information Processing Systems, vol. 28 (2015)
5. Kong, T., Yao, A., Chen, Y., Sun, F.: Hypernet: towards accurate region proposal generation and joint object detection. In: Proceedings of the IEEE Conference on Computer Vision and Pattern Recognition, pp. 845–853 (2016)

6. Liu, W., Rabinovich, A., Berg, A.C.: Parsenet: looking wider to see better. CoRR, vol. abs/1506.04579 (2015)
7. Lin, T.Y., Dollár, P., Girshick, R., He, K., Hariharan, B., Belongie, S.: Feature pyramid networks for object detection. In: Proceedings of the IEEE Conference on Computer Vision and Pattern Recognition, pp. 2117–2125 (2017)
8. Hu, J., Shen, L., Sun, G.: Squeeze-and-excitation networks. In: Proceedings of the IEEE Conference on Computer Vision and Pattern Recognition, pp. 7132–7141 (2018)
9. Woo, S., Park, J., Lee, J.Y., Kweon, I.S.: Cbam: convolutional block attention module. In: European Conference on Computer Vision, pp. 3–19 (2018)
10. Vaswani, A., Shazeer, N., Parmar, N., Uszkoreit, J., Jones, L., Gomez, A.N., Kaiser, Ł., Polosukhin, I.: Attention is all you need. In: Advances in Neural Information Processing Systems, vol. 30 (2017)
11. Nakayama, Y., Lu, H., Li, Y., Kamiya, T.: Widesegnext: semantic image segmentation using wide residual network and next dilated unit. IEEE Sens. J. 21(10), 11427–11434 (2020)
12. Xu, H., Yao, L., Zhang, W., Liang, X., Li, Z.: Auto-fpn: Automatic network architecture adaptation for object detection beyond classification. In: Proceedings of the IEEE International Conference on Computer Vision, pp. 6649–6658 (2019)
13. Ghiasi, G., Lin, T.Y., Le, Q.V.: Nas-fpn: Learning scalable feature pyramid architecture for object detection. In: Proceedings of the IEEE Conference on Computer Vision and Pattern Recognition, pp. 7036–7045 (2019)
14. Xu, X., Luo, X., Ma, L.: Context-aware hierarchical feature attention network for multi-scale object detection. In: 2020 IEEE International Conference on Image Processing (ICIP), pp. 2011–2015. IEEE (2020)
15. Yang, S., Lu, H., Li, J.: Multifeature fusion-based object detection for intelligent transportation systems. IEEE Trans. Intell. Transp. Syst. (2022)
16. Hou, Q., Zhou, D., Feng, J.: Coordinate attention for efficient mobile network design. In: Proceedings of the IEEE Conference on Computer Vision and Pattern Recognition, pp. 13713–13722 (2021)
17. Xie, R., Qiu, Z., Rao, J., Liu, Y., Zhang, B., Lin, L.: Internal and contextual attention network for cold-start multi-channel matching in recommendation. In: IJCAI, pp. 2732–2738 (2020)
18. Lu, H., Li, Y., Chen, M., Kim, H., Serikawa, S.: Brain intelligence: go beyond artificial intelligence. Mob. Netw. Appl., 23(2), 368–375 (2018)
19. Park, J., Woo, S., Lee, J.-Y., Kweon, I.S.: Bam: Bottleneck attention module. arXiv preprint arXiv:1807.06514 (2018)
20. Ba, J., Mnih, V., Kavukcuoglu, K.: Multiple object recognition with visual attention. arXiv preprint arXiv:1412.7755 (2014)
21. Xu, X., Lin, K., Gao, L., Lu, H., Shen, H.T., Li, X.: Learning cross-modal common representations by private-shared subspaces separation. IEEE Trans. Cybern. (2020)
22. Ren, H., Dai, H., Dai, Z., Yang, M., Leskovec, J., Schuurmans, D., Dai, B.: Combiner: full attention transformer with sparse computation cost. In: Advances in Neural Information Processing Systems, vol. 34 (2021)
23. Xu, X., Wang, T., Yang, Y., Zuo, L., Shen, F., Shen, H.T.: Cross-modal attention with semantic consistence for image–text matching. IEEE Trans. Neural Netw. Learn. Syst. 31(12), 5412–5425 (2020)
24. Zheng, Y., Li, Y., Yang, S., Lu, H.: Global-pbnet: a novel point cloud registration for autonomous driving. IEEE Trans. Neural Netw. Learn. Syst. (2022)
25. Lu, H., Tang, Y., Sun, Y.: Drrs-bc: Decentralized routing registration system based on blockchain. IEEE/CAA J. Autom. Sin. 8(12), 1868–1876 (2021)
26. Li, X., Wang, W., Hu, X., Yang, J.: Selective kernel networks. In: Proceedings of the IEEE Conference on Computer Vision and Pattern Recognition, pp. 510–519 (2019)

27. Dai, Y., Gieseke, F., Oehmcke, S., Wu, Y., Barnard, K.: Attentional feature fusion. In: Proceedings of the IEEE Winter Conference on Applications of Computer Vision, pp. 3560–3569 (2021)
28. Ma, C., Li, X., Li, Y., Tian, X., Wang, Y., Kim, H., Serikawa, S.: Visual information processing for deep-sea visual monitoring system. Cogn. Robot. **1**, 3–11 (2021)
29. Lu, H., Zhang, M., Xu, X., Li, Y., Shen, H.T.: Deep fuzzy hashing network for efficient image retrieval. IEEE Trans. Fuzzy Syst. **29**(1), 166–176 (2020)
30. Simonyan, K., Zisserman, A.: Very deep convolutional networks for large-scale image recognition. arXiv preprint arXiv:1409.1556 (2014)
31. Deng, J., Dong, W., Socher, R., Li, L.J., Li, K., Fei-Fei, L.: Imagenet: a large-scale hierarchical image database. In: Proceedings of the IEEE Conference on Computer Vision and Pattern Recognition, pp. 248–255. IEEE (2009)

Interact-Pose Datasets for 2D Human Pose Estimation in Multi-person Interaction Scene

Yifei Jiang and Hao Gao[✉]

Nanjing University of Posts and Communications, Nanjing, China
tsgaohao@gmail.com

Abstract. In recent years, several excellent works dealing with human pose estimation in complex multi-person scenes have focus on the problems of complex backgrounds and the multiplayer scene. However, when facing the scene of multi-person interaction, the results of current mainstream algorithms are still unsatisfactory and some common datasets are not suitable for coping with interaction problems. Therefore, we propose a new dataset named Interact-Pose for solving multi-person interactions problems. Firstly, We use the MSCOCO format to annotate Interact-Pose. Except that, we adopt the corresponding data augmentation scheme to exchange the background of the Interact-Pose Dataset to make it more complex and have better generalization performance. Then it is trained after being fused with the MSCOCO dataset. After training on HigherHRNet, the average AP value of our test results is 67.3% on the Validation set of COCO2017, which is higher than that of the test only being trained by MSCOCO.

Keywords: 2D human pose estimation · Multi-person interaction · Data augmentation · Multi-person interaction dataset

1 Introduction

In the past few years, human pose estimation has been a very popular issue in the field of computer vision. Due to the increasing demand in film shooting, motion analysis, behavior recognition, more and more scientific researchers begin to put their efforts on this issue. Early work focused on single-person human pose estimation tasks, such as Convolutional Pose Machines, Stacked Hourglass [9, 10]. The datasets used in these single-person human pose estimation tasks are usually relatively simple and mainly consists of single-person picture like LSP and FLIC [24, 29]. With the application of human pose estimation technology in many fields, the work of single-person human pose estimation is unable to meet the current demand. Therefore, researchers focus on multi-person human pose estimation based on deep learning methods. The task of human pose estimation tends to be much more complex than the task of single-person human pose estimation when facing multi-person interaction human pose. The difficulty of single-person human pose estimation research is that complex poses or diverse backgrounds may affect the results of pose estimation. The situation we face in multiplayer scenarios is more complicated. And Interactions between multiple people usually have a large impact on the results of pose estimation (Fig. 1).

S. Yang and H. Lu (Eds.): ISAIR 2022, CCIS 1701, pp. 211–223, 2022.
https://doi.org/10.1007/978-981-19-7943-9_18

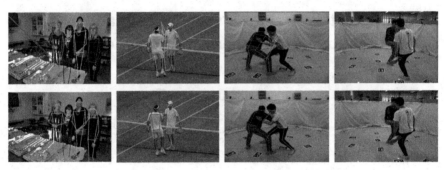

Fig. 1. After adding the Interact-Pose dataset and the MSCOCO dataset for fusion training, the performance in multi-person interaction scenarios has been significantly improved. The upper pictures are tested by the model trained by HigherHRNet with the MSCOCO dataset. The following line of pictures are tested by the backbone of HigherHRNet after adding the coco dataset and the interact-pose dataset for a new fusion dataset and for fusion training.

At present, there are many mainstream algorithms to solve the multi-person pose estimation problem, such as HRNet [3], HigherHRNet [12], Alphapose [16], and Open-Pose [1]. Currently, OpenPose is the most popular pose estimation algorithm, it uses the non-maximum suppression algorithm to detect all the joint points in the picture, and employs the Part Affinity Fields for Part Association method to combine joint points from different human bodies; HRNet [3] uses a parallel high-resolution network for human pose estimation, and the features of each resolution are retained in the whole process; HigherHRNet [12] adopts a bottom-up approach for pose estimation based on HRNet, and adds a deconvolution module to fuse Generate feature heatmaps at multiple resolutions [31]. These schemes all use the MSCOCO dataset as the evaluation index, and have achieved fine results on the MSCOCO dataset. At the same time, compared with other works (for example, CPM (Convolutional Pose Machines), Hourglass), these common algorithms are also better at solving some multi-person interaction scenarios. But the overall performance is still unsatisfactory, and from an intuitive point of view, its performance is still at a low level [32].

In the proposed training scheme which is proposed by us, a large amount of multi-person interactive data is used for training, and data augmentation is adopted to further improve the performance of pose estimation on the data. Besides, it not only improves the generalization performance of the model on the MSCOCO dataset, but also improves the accuracy of joint detection in multi-person interaction scenes (especially the accuracy of occluded joint detection during interaction). The contributions of our work could be summarized as follow:

- Our proposed Interact-Pose Dataset for solving multi-person interaction problems greatly makes up for the deficiencies of the current public datasets;
- The data augmentation programs on Interact-Pose Dataset can make traditional 2D human pose estimation backbone own better performance when facing multi-person scenes. Meanwhile this proposal can also boost the evaluation metrics in COCO2017;

2   Related Works

2.1   Datasets for 2D Human Pose Estimation

The current mainstream single-person datasets for 2D human pose estimation include LSP [24], FLIC [29], and so on. With market demands, advances in hardware performance, and improvements in algorithms, researchers pay their attention to multi-person human pose estimation. The datasets for multi-person human pose estimation include MSCOCO, CrowdPose, AI challenger. Although these datasets have been widely used in the field of human pose estimation, most of them are scattered multi-person scenes, and the interaction scenes involving multiple people are very limited. Therefore, it is not particularly helpful for us to solve the human pose estimation problem of multi-person interaction.

Fig. 2. The detection results of the HigherHRNet scheme and the DCPose scheme for the same group of pictures. The images are selected from the Interact-Pose dataset. The detection results of HigherHRNet (bottom-up scheme) (top) will not be missing the detection results of a single human body caused by multi-person interaction. In the same case, the DCPose (top-down) scheme we adopted will have a missing detection of a single human body. In this figure, it can be clearly found that there are human bodies that have not been detected at all in the detection results of DCPose.

2.2   Multi-person Human Pose Estimation

The multi-person human pose estimation task performed by the current mainstream deep learning-based solutions can usually be divided into two ideas: top-down; bottom-up; we use the Interact-Pose dataset to analyze the current mainstream algorithms. Due to the shortcomings of the object detection algorithm [6, 7, 23], most of top-down schemes do not have good performance when facing multi-person interaction. Specifically, when detecting samples with high IOU values, problems such as the bounding box error of human body detection and the number of human body errors often occur [33, 34], which will cause systematic defects in the subsequent pose estimation of a single human body. We can see from Fig. 2 that in most bottom-up schemes [1, 12, 15], we usually do not miss detection of all nodes of a single human body due to high IOU values.

Top-Down. The main procedure of this our method is to first detect a single person and obtain a bounding box through the target detection algorithm (usually the mainstream is to use YOLOv3, Faster RCNN) [6, 7]. Pose estimation is then performed for a single human body within each bounding box. It can be treated as transforming a multi-person problem into several single-person problems. Although in some scenarios with relatively low interaction between multiple people[35], the scheme achieves satisfactory accuracy. However, if it is in a multi-person interaction scenario, especially strong interaction, in the top-down solution may not be able to accurately detect the bounding box (as shown in the Fig. 3). Therefore, subsequent key point detection and skeleton connection work are meaningless. In addition, the detection time of this scheme will increase with the increase of the number of people to be detected, so the real-time performance is usually difficult to guarantee.

Fig. 3. All images tested are from the Interact-Pose dataset. (a), (c), (e) are the bounding-box of the human body detected in the DCPose algorithm; (b), (d), (f) are the results of the pose estimation; if there is a missing bounding-box detection, or the detection result of the bounding-box is not accurate enough, which will have a great impact on the subsequent human pose estimation results.

Bottom-Up. In this scheme, when estimating the human body pose, it first detects the key points of all the human bodies in the picture, then groups the key points, and finally assembles the skeletons of several completed human bodies. The proposal of Openpose makes the bottom-up scheme attract more and more researchers' attention. This scheme has certain advantages in studying the pose estimation problem in multi-person interaction scenarios. The resulting problem is that the human skeleton cannot be detected. At the same time, the detection efficiency of this solution in multi-person interaction scenarios is relatively considerable, and real-time effects can be achieved.

3   Method

Our training scheme is a fusion training scheme using the MSCOCO dataset and the Interact-Pose dataset. In this scheme, in order to ensure that the algorithm performs well on the COCO2017 validation set and the Interact-Pose test set, we need to perform data augmentation operations on the data set. The steps of data augmentation mainly include character background culling, background replacement, and reshaping the image (Fig. 4).

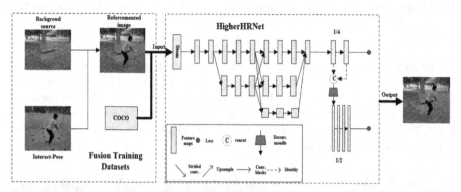

Fig. 4. The schematic diagram of our pipline. We take HigherHRNet as an example. We need to enhance the Interact-Pose dataset (the specific process will be explained in detail later). Better results are obtained by merging the two datasets together into the network for training.

3.1 Interact-Pose Dataset

We propose a brand new dataset, which is named Interact-Pose Dataset. This dataset was captured in a multi-camera laboratory setting (Fig. 5). The crew was wearing looser clothing when filming. Compared to existing datasets, we recorded in studio with green and white curtains to allow automatic segmentation and augmentation. There are a total of 12 actors (9Male+3Female) in this dataset, which contains many multi-person interaction scenes, including "intense" interaction scenes such as two-person boxing and wrestling. 90% of the pictures are interactive scenes of two or more people.

Fig. 5. The picture above shows the scene of the laboratory shooting. The scene consists of a solid color backdrop and 20 RBG cameras. Data can be collected from multiple angles.

To make poses as diverse as possible, we employ a real-time data acquisition system with up to 20 viewing angles. We can collect photos of people under the premise of ensuring good lighting to obtain an ideal posture. Each of the cameras is placed at a height of 1.8 m from the ground, maintaining a depression angle of about 15°. In this situation, the camera can ensure the integrity of the human body. Figure 6 shows some of the obtained images in the Interact-Pose dataset and their annotated results.

Data Collection. Given that our shooting scenes for the dataset are in laboratory scenes, we select the most representative 10,000 images from all shooting data. And divide the training set and the validation set according to the ratio of 9:1.

Image Annotations. At present, in the commonly used human pose estimation datasets, from the point of view of the number of joint points, MSCOCO has 17 joint points, MPII has 16 joint points, and CrowdPose has 14 joint points respectively. When we made our dataset, we used the same annotation method as the MSCOCO dataset, that owns 17 joints. Therefore, our data can be used for fusion training with the coco dataset to further improve the accuracy (Fig. 7).

Fig. 6. The figure shows some pictures in the Interact-pose dataset (the connection of the skeleton of the joint points is the labeled ground-truth). We can find that compared with public datasets such as MSCOCO, our annotation results pay more attention to the annotation results of occluded joints after multi-person interaction. The background of the laboratory scene is relatively simple, which is conducive to data enhancement work.

3.2 Multi-dataset Fusion Training

Due to the problems of different labels and different evaluation indicators between datasets, almost all the previous algorithms for 2D human pose estimation use the method of separating training data sets. We annotated the Interact-Pose in the same format as MSCOCO, and performed fusion training on the two datasets together with the MSCOCO dataset after data augmentation.

In our scheme, the training process requires alternating use of MSCOCO dataset and Interact-Pose dataset. The specific attempt is to first train the MSCOCO dataset. On this basis, continue to train the MSCOCO dataset and the Interact-Pose dataset to

Fig. 7. The figure shows the picture after data augmentation of the Interact-pose dataset (the connection of the joint points is the marked ground-truth). The background pictures are selected from the MSCOCO dataset. After the procedure of data augmentation, the background of our dataset is richer.

combine the fusion dataset. Based on the strong generalization ability of the MSCOCO dataset, when using the proposed scheme for training, we can fine-tune COCO dataset for multi-person interaction scenarios.

3.3 Data Augmentation Scheme

Although our dataset has more pose variations than other common 2D human pose estimation datasets, it meets our pose requirement for solving multi-person interactions. But appearance changes are still not comparable to wild images. Usually, when deep learning-based schemes are used for human pose estimation, many schemes [8, 12, 14, 15] perform data augmentation operations in the image preprocessing stage. The data augmentation scheme we adopt here is different from the traditional data augmentation. Since the data set we propose is collected in a laboratory scene, which means its action pose, shooting angle, clarity and the effect of multi-person interaction fully meet our needs, there is still a problem that its background is relatively monotonous. CSPNet [28] proposed to augment the data by horizontal flipping, changing the brightness, and changing the scale of the picture. The data augmentation method used in CSPNet is will also be reflected in many other works in the future [15, 20]. But for the data taken in the lab, the effect of the augmentation on the training effect is negligible. Therefore, here we propose a novel data augmentation scheme that can improve the training effect on our dataset. In the field of 3D human pose estimation, the MPI-INF-3DHP [2] dataset adds data augmentation processing for foreground and background to the dataset. The effect of data training has been significantly improved under the method. Inspired by this scheme, we perform a similar background augmentation replacement process on the Interact-Pose dataset. Our operation flow is shown in Fig. 8.

Fig. 8. Our process for data augmentation on the Interact-Pose dataset is shown in the figure. We first remove the background of the pictures in the original dataset, and then replace the background with pictures without people. Finally, generate our data-augmented picture. (a): Pictures selected from the Interact-Pose dataset; (b): The pixel value of the background of the characters is set to 0; (c): The pictures that do not contain the characters are selected; (d): The picture (b) is added to the (c) Figure. (At this time, the size of the image is the same as that of (c)); (e): Resize the image, making it share the same size with (a);

4 Experiments

In this section, we focus on the improvement of the training effect of the interact-pose dataset and the scheme of training in multiple datasets (MSCOCO dataset and Interact-Pose dataset).

4.1 Datasets

IN this section, We introduce some common datasets in detail.

MSCOCO Dataset: The size of the MSCOCO dataset is huge, and the scenes and annotations contained in it are rich. In the experiment, we use the COCO2017 dataset, which contains about 120k training sets and about 5k validation sets. It contains data of several people interacting with each other.

Interact-Pose: In our proposed dataset, we set a training set of 9000 images and a test set of 1000 images. We use the coco format to label the dataset, so the number of key points in this dataset and the connection method of key points are the same as that of the COCO.

The evaluation indicators in the experiment follow the evaluation indicators of the COCO dataset, that is, the average precision (AP) and the average recall (AR) are used. Object Keypoint Similarity (OKS) plays the same role as IoU, and AP/AR is used for keypoint detection. We consider mAP averaged over multiple OKS values (.50:.05:.95) as our primary metric.

This experimental framework is based on the deep learning framework of PyTorch. We utilized three 3090 GPUS as the hardware device, set the batch size to 18 and trained for 320 epochs.

Table 1. We use experiments to compare the experimental results before and after adding the Interact-Pose dataset, as well as before and after data augmentation. The data augmentation mentioned here is based on Interact-Pose.

	BackBone	Training datasets			mAP	AP.5
		MSCOCO	Interact-Pose	Reforcement data		
(a)	HigherHRNet-W32	✓			67.1	73.0
(b)		✓	✓		66.9	72.5
(c)		✓		✓	**67.3**	**73.6**

Table 2. The results of our testing on the test set of the Interact-Pose dataset. After adding the Interact dataset, the performance of the algorithm on the pose estimation problem of multi-person interaction has been significantly improved.

	BackBone	Training datasets			mAP	AP.5
		MSCOCO	Interact-Pose	Reforcement data		
(a)	HigherHRNet-W32	✓			4.5	17.8
(b)		✓	✓		11.9	40.5
(c)		✓		✓	**12.8**	**41.0**

4.2 Training

Following the requirements of the HigherHRNet framework and the Associative embedding [11], we need to preprocess the data before the experiment starts. The parameter of data augmentation is set as a random rotation within ($[-30°, 30°]$), a random scale within ($[0.75, 1.5]$), and a random translation within ($[-40, 40]$) respectively to crop the input patch of size 512×512 and Random flip, thus playing a role in data enhancement.

In the deep learning framework, we use the adam optimizer and set the initial learning rate at the beginning of the experiment to $1 * 0.001$. We reduce the learning rate by 0.0001 at the 100th epoch and 0.00001 at the 200th epoch.

In HigherHRNet, we train on different datasets and test on the validation set of COCO2017 and the Interact-Pose dataset, respectively. As shown in Table 1 and Table 2, it can be found that the test performance trained with our scheme is better than the test performance trained only with the COCO dataset.

In addition to HigherHRNet, we test the impact of the enhanced data of Interact-Pose on the test results on the OpenPose, PersonLab, PIFPAF, Hourglass algorithms. What we can find is that after adding the enhanced data of Interact-Pose and the MSCOCO dataset for fusion training, the test results are significantly improved on the test set of Interact-Pose. And most of the indicators of the results of the test on the val of the MSCOCO dataset have also been improved.

Ablation Experiment. We conduct experiments on HigherHRNet, OpenPose, Person-Lab, PIFPAF [1, 27, 30], which are bottom-up method. In the course of the experiment, we verified the effectiveness of our work through the following ablation experiments. In the experiment, we compared the impact of different datasets before and after the fusion training and the impact on the indicators before and after data augmentation respectively.

We can find that on the traditional COCO2017 training set for training, although the performance on the COCO2017 validation set is acceptable. But for the Interact-Pose dataset, which is more interactive with many people, it is difficult to satisfy only by training on the MSCOCO dataset. We can find from the table that only by training on the MSCOCO dataset, the mAP value tested on the Interact-Pose dataset is only 3.3. Even though the multi-person interaction scene of the Interact-Pose dataset is much more complex than the MSCOCO dataset, such performance is hardly satisfactory. In this section, we compare the results of training only on the MSCOCO dataset and testing on the MSCOCO test set and the Interact-Pose dataset. Through the experimental results, we can find that most of the indicators tested on the COCO dataset and all indicators tested on the Interact-Pose dataset have significantly improved. Our solution is very effective on mainstream bottom-up solutions. Table 3 and Table 4 show the test results at MSCOCO and Interact-Pose, respectively.

Table 3. We use the Interact-Pose dataset for data augmentation, and then perform fusion training with the coco dataset. We have tested numerous Bottom-up methods with good results.

Test on MSCOCO

Method	Backbone	Input size	AP	AP^{50}	AP^{75}	AP^M	AP^L	Training dataset
OpenPose	VGG-19	368	61.8	84.9	**67.5**	57.1	68.2	MSCOCO
			62.0	**85.2**	67.2	**57.6**	**68.7**	MSCOCO+ Interact-pose
PersonLab	ResNet-152	1401	66.5	**88.0**	72.6	62.4	**72.3**	MSCOCO
			67.1	87.6	**72.9**	**63.1**	72.1	MSCOCO+ Interact-pose
PifPaf	ResNet-50	–	50.0	73.5	52.9	35.9	69.7	MSCOCO
			50.2	**73.9**	52.9	**36.3**	**69.8**	MSCOCO+ Interact-pose
HigherHR-Net	HRNet-W32	512	67.1	86.2	73.0	61.5	**76.1**	MSCOCO
			67.3	86.2	**73.6**	**61.9**	75.8	MSCOCO+ Interact-pose

Table 4. We use the Interact-Pose dataset for data augmentation, and then perform fusion training with the Interact-Pose dataset. We have tested numerous Bottom-up methods with good results.

Test on Interact-Pose valset

Method	Backbone	Input size	AP	AP^{50}	AP^{75}	AP^M	Training dataset
OpenPose	VGG-19	368	2.9	14.1	0.5	10.1	MSCOCO
			10.1	**38.5**	**3.9**	**22.3**	MSCOCO+ Interact-pose
PersonLab	ResNet-152	1401	3.7	15.1	0.4	10.5	MSCOCO
			11.6	**39.1**	**3.9**	**23.4**	MSCOCO+ Interact-pose
PifPaf	ResNet-50	–	2.9	11.3	0.3	7.4	MSCOCO
			6.7	**31.4**	**2.3**	**19.5**	MSCOCO+ Interact-pose
HigherHRNet	HRNet-W32	512	4.5	17.8	0.5	10.9	MSCOCO
			12.8	**40.5**	**4.2**	**24.4**	MSCOCO+ Interact-pose

5   Conclusion

First, we introduce a new dataset named Interact-Pose, which focuses on complex multi-person interaction scenes. Furthermore, we adopt some mainstream 2D human pose estimation backbone frameworks, mainly including HigherHRNet, OpenPose, and PIFPAF based on the bottom-up scheme to use our proposed dataset. Second, the data augmentation method of our proposed Interact-Pose dataset is utilized in our paper, then fused our proposed dataset with the MSCOCO Dataset into a joint dataset for training. Compared with the traditional human joint detection framework, our human pose estimation system can better handle occlusion better in general. When our solution solves the problem of multi-person scene interaction, many algorithms have achieved satisfactory results. Among them, especially for the problem that several joint points between two or more people are blocked from each other or the human body interacts with each other, our scheme has achieved good results.

References

1. Cao, Z., Simon, T., Wei, S.-E., Sheikh, Y.: Realtime multi-person 2D pose estimation using part affinity fields. In: IEEE Conference on Computer Vision and Pattern Recognition (CVPR), pp. 1302–1310. IEEE (2017)
2. Mehta, D., Rhodin, H., Casas, D., Fua, P.: Monocular 3D human pose estimation in: the wild using improved CNN supervision. In: The 5th International Conference on 3D Vision (3DV), pp. 1751–1761 (2017)
3. Sun, K., Xiao, B., Liu, D., Wang, J.: Deep high-resolution representation learning for human pose estimation. In: IEEE Conference on Computer Vision and Pattern Recognition (CVPR), p. 1. IEEE (2019)

4. Li, J., Wang, C., Zhu, H., Mao, Y., Fang, H.-S., Lu, C.: CrowdPose: efficient crowded scenes pose estimation and a new benchmark. In: IEEE Conference on Computer Vision and Pattern Recognition (CVPR), pp. 2–8. IEEE (2019)

5. Lin, T.-Y., et al.: Microsoft COCO: common objects in context. In: Fleet, D., Pajdla, T., Schiele, B., Tuytelaars, T. (eds.) ECCV 2014. LNCS, vol. 8693, pp. 740–755. Springer, Cham (2014). https://doi.org/10.1007/978-3-319-10602-1_48

6. Redmon, J., Farhadi, A.: YOLOv3: an incremental improvement. In: IEEE Conference on Computer Vision and Pattern Recognition (CVPR), pp. 779–788. IEEE (2018)

7. Ren, S., He, K., Girshick, R., Sun, J.: Faster R-CNN: towards real-time object detection with region proposal networks. In: IEEE Transactions on Pattern Analysis & Machine Intelligence, pp.876–879. IEEE (2017)

8. Fang, H.-S., Xie, S., Tai, Y.-W., Lu, C.: RMPE: Regional multi-person pose estimation. In: IEEE International Conference on Computer Vision (ICCV), pp. 2353–2362. IEEE (2017)

9. Newell, A., Yang, K., Deng, J.: Stacked hourglass networks for human pose estimation. In: Leibe, B., Matas, J., Sebe, N., Welling, M. (eds.) ECCV 2016. LNCS, vol. 9912, pp. 483–499. Springer, Cham (2016). https://doi.org/10.1007/978-3-319-46484-8_29

10. Wei, S.-E., Ramakrishna, V., Kanade, T., Sheikh, Y.: Convolutional pose machines. In: IEEE Conference on Computer Vision and Pattern Recognition (CVPR), p. 1. IEEE (2016)

11. Newell, A., Huang, Z., Deng, J.: Associative embedding: end-to-end learning for joint detection and grouping. In: The Thirty-First Conference on Neural Information Processing Systems (NeurIPS), pp. 2277–2787 (2017)

12. Cheng, B., Xiao, B., Wang, J., Shi, H., Huang, T.S., Zhang, L.: HigherHRNet: scale-aware representation learning for bottom-up human pose estimation. In: IEEE Conference on Computer Vision and Pattern Recognition (CVPR), pp. 576–678. IEEE (2020)

13. Xiao, B., Wu, H., Wei, Y.: Simple baselines for human pose estimation and tracking. In: Ferrari, V., Hebert, M., Sminchisescu, C., Weiss, Y. (eds.) ECCV 2018. LNCS, vol. 11210, pp. 472–487. Springer, Cham (2018). https://doi.org/10.1007/978-3-030-01231-1_29

14. Chen, Y., Wang, Z., Peng, Y., Zhang, Z., Yu, G., Sun, J.: Cascaded pyramid network for multi-person pose estimation. In: IEEE Conference on Computer Vision and Pattern Recognition (CVPR), pp. 567–577. IEEE (2018)

15. Geng, Z., Sun, K., Xiao, B., Zhang, Z., Wang, J.: Bottom-up human pose estimation via disentangled keypoint regression. In: IEEE Conference on Computer Vision and Pattern Recognition (CVPR), p. 1. IEEE (2021)

16. Fang, H., Xie, S., Tai, Y.-W., Lu, C.: RMPE:regional multi-person pose estimation. In: IEEE. International Conference on Computer Vision (ICCV), pp. 2353–2362 (2017)

17. Toshev, A., Szegedy, C.: DeepPose: human pose estimation via deep neural networks. In: IEEE Conference on Computer Vision and Pattern Recognition (CVPR), pp. 1653–1660. IEEE (2014)

18. Peng, X., Tang, Z., Yang, F., Feris, R.S., Metaxas, D.: Jointly optimize data augmentation and network training: adversarial data augmentation in human pose estimation. In: IEEE Conference on Computer Vision and Pattern Recognition (CVPR), pp. 2652–2653. IEEE (2018)

19. McNally, W., Vats, K., Wong, A., McPhee, J.: Rethinking keypoint representations: modeling keypoints and poses as objects for multi-person human pose estimation. In: IEEE Conference on Computer Vision and Pattern Recognition (CVPR), pp. 2454–2471. IEEE (2021)

20. Liu, Z., et al.: Deep dual consecutive network for human pose estimation. In: IEEE Conference on Computer Vision and Pattern Recognition (CVPR), pp. 1786–1790. IEEE (2021)

21. Zhang, S.-H., et al.: Pose2Seg: detection free human instance segmentation. In: IEEE Conference on Computer Vision and Pattern Recognition (CVPR), pp. 1276–1301. IEEE (2019)

22. Liu, W., et al.: SSD: single shot multibox detector. In: IEEE Conference on Computer Vision and Pattern Recognition (CVPR), pp. 2101–2103. IEEE (2016)
23. Zheng, C., et al.: Deep learning-based human pose estimation: a survey. Tsinghua Sci. Technol., 99–110 (2019)
24. Johnson, S., Everingham, M.: Clustered pose and nonlinear appearance models for human pose estimation. In: British Machine Vision Conference, pp. 456–571 (2010)
25. Mehta, D., et al.: Monocular 3D human pose estimation in the wild using improved CNN supervision. In: 3D Imaging, Modeling, Processing, Visualization and Transmission (3DIMPVT), pp. 1542–1560 (2017)
26. Joo, H., et al.: A massively multiview system for social motion capture. In: IEEE. International Conference on Computer Vision (ICCV), pp. 3122–3132. IEEE (2015)
27. Papandreou, G., Zhu, T., Chen, L.-C., Gidaris, S., Tompson, J., Murphy, K.: PersonLab: person pose estimation and instance segmentation with a bottom-up, part-based, geometric embedding model. In: Ferrari, V., Hebert, M., Sminchisescu, C., Weiss, Y. (eds.) Computer Vision – ECCV 2018. LNCS, vol. 11218, pp. 282–299. Springer, Cham (2018). https://doi. org/10.1007/978-3-030-01264-9_17
28. Wang, C.-Y., et al.: CSPNet: a new backbone that can enhance learning capability of CNN. In: IEEE/CVF Conference on Computer Vision and Pattern Recognition Workshops (CVPRW), pp. 235–251. IEEE (2020)
29. Sapp, B., Taskar, B.: MODEC: multimodal decomposable models for human pose estimation. In: IEEE Conference on Computer Vision and Pattern Recognition (CVPR), pp. 1175–1181. IEEE (2013)
30. Kreiss, S., Bertoni, L., Alahi, A.: PifPaf: composite fields for human pose estimation. In: IEEE Conference on Computer Vision and Pattern Recognition (CVPR), pp. 11977–11986. IEEE (2019)
31. Huimin, L., Zhang, M., Xing, X.: Deep fuzzy hashing network for efficient image retrieval. IEEE Trans. Fuzzy Syst. (2020). https://doi.org/10.1109/TFUZZ.2020.2984991
32. Lu, H., Li, Y., Chen, M., Kim, H., Serikawa, S: Brain intelligence: go beyond artificial intelligence. Mob. Netw. Appl. 23(2), 368–375 (2018)
33. Lu, H., Li, Y., Mu, S., Wang, D., Kim, H., Serikawa, S: Motor anomaly detection for unmanned aerial vehicles using reinforcement learning. IEEE Internet Things J. 5(4), 2315–2322 (2017)
34. Hu, L., Qin, M., Zhang, F., Du, Z., Liu: RSCNN: a CNN-based method to enhance low-light remote-sensing images. Remote Sens. 13(1), 62 (2020)
35. Lu, H., Zhang, Y., Li, Y., Jiang, C., Abbas, H: User-oriented virtual mobile network resource management for vehicle communications. IEEE Trans. Intell. Transp. Syst. 22(6), 3521–3532 (2020)

Multimodal Breast Cancer Diagnosis Based on Multi-level Fusion Network

Mingyu Song[1], Xinchen Shi[1], Yonglong Zhang[1,2], and Bin Li[1(✉)]

[1] School of Information Engineering, Yangzhou University, Jiangsu, China
{ylzhang,lb}@yzu.edu.cn
[2] Jiangsu Key Laboratory of Zoonosis/Jiangsu Co-Innovation Center for Prevention and Control of Important Animal Infectious Diseases and Zoonoses, Yangzhou, China

Abstract. With the widespread application of artificial intelligence technology, deep learning algorithms have been extensively applied to the diagnosis and screening of breast cancer. However, the classification of breast cancer with the data from a single modality is still not accurate enough to meet clinical needs. This paper proposes a Multimodal breast cancer diagnosis based on Multi-level fusion network which integrates pathological images, structured data and medical description text. Specifically, we first construct a fully connected graph to extract the node and graph level feature representation of pathological images with graph attention layers. Second, we use the BERT model to extract the text features from the medical records. At last, the features of the above three modal data are fused using a multimodal adaption gate (MAG) for diagnosis. Experimental results indicate that the proposed method obtains superior performance (accuracy 93.62%) to most baseline methods on PathoEMR dataset.

Keywords: Deep learning · Graph neural network · Multimodal fusion · Breast cancer diagnosis

1 Introduction

Breast cancer is one of the most serious diseases which is threatens human life and health, and it is a medical and healthy problem of common concern all over the world. According to the data which released by the International Agency for Research on Cancer (IARC), a division of the World Health Organization (WHO) in 2020 [1], the number of new cases of breast cancer is over 2.26 million, exceeding the 2.2 million cases of lung cancer. Breast cancer had replaced lung cancer as the world's largest cancer. In clinical medicine, compared with Xray, MRI and other medical images, pathological images remain the best criteria for the diagnosis of breast cancer. Early identification of benign and malignant tumor pathological images of breast cancer is important for clinicians to develop individualized treatment plans. In earlier methods, the features of pathological image were extracted manually, based on support vector machine, random forest and other classifiers were used to complete the classification. This kind of methods has disadvantages such as high requirement expertise, features extraction is time-consuming, and it is difficult to extract high-quality features.

Deep learning methods have shown the increasing advantages in many medical image diagnosis tasks recently. Compared with manual-based pathological image classification, this kind of methods reduce the need for professional knowledge, and they can use the network to continuously learn image features and classify pathological images into benign and malignant [2–5]. This method not only improves diagnostic efficiency, but also provides physicians with more objective and accurate diagnostic results. But these methods still have some shortcomings: (1) A patient may contain multiple pathological images of various parts of breast cancer, and there are some consistent or compensative lesion information between these images. Using a single pathological image [3] will discard the existing image-to-image interaction. (2) Most of the existing studies use pathological images as the input of convolutional neural networks [2], but it is difficult to meet the requirements of clinical diagnosis. (3) There is a correlation between the data of different modalities, and the simple fusion method [4] will not give full play to the complementarity between the modalities.

For the above problems, we propose the following solutions: (1) We construct a fully-connected graph of the patient's pathological image set to extract the associations between the pathological images, and use a multi-level graph attention network (GAT) [6] to obtain high-level pathological image features, at last we concatenate the node and graph-level feature representation. (2) The electronic medical record (EMR) reflects some information of the patient's consultation, such as personal tumor history, family tumor history, orange peel and other information that cannot be displayed in the pathological image. We process the EMR according to certain medical rules and form a text description. Then, for the medical text description in the EMR data, we utilize the pretrained language model BERT [7] to extract the diagnostic text features of the patients. (3) Inspired by Multimodal Adaptation Gate (MAG) [8], we use an attention gating mechanism to fuse the various modalities which described above.The experimental results prove that the multimodal adaptation gate (MAG) model performs better.

The contributions of this paper can be summarized as follows:

- To the best of our knowledge, we are the first to fuse features from three modalities i.e., image, text and pathological to classify breast cancer. The proposed network structure outperforms significantly better than single modality methods.
- We construct a fully connected graph to extract the node and graph level feature representation of pathological images with graph attention layers. In this way, we can extract high-level feature of pathological images.
- We textually describe the structured electrical medical record and construct the medical record text according to the rules of clinical medicine. Then we use multimodal adaptation gate (MAG) to fuse image, text and pathological features.
- We conducted extensive experiments on PathoEMR dataset. It's showing that the model's classification accuracy can reach 93.62%, which is better than the most baseline methods. In addition, variant experiments are also performed to verify the validity of our proposed key components.

2 Related Work

As we known, the existing methods of classifying breast cancer are divided into the following four main categories: disease diagnosis based on manually extracted feature, disease diagnosis based on convolutional neural network (CNN), disease diagnosis based on electronic medical records, and disease diagnosis based on multimodality. In the following subsections, we briefly review previous work on computer-aided diagnosis of related diseases, respectively.

2.1 Disease Diagnosis Based on Manually Extracted Feature

Kowal et al. [9] had used various cell nucleus segmentation algorithms to classify the breast cancer pathological images. Nanni et al. [10] used local tristimulus patterns and local phase quantization histograms as image features to classify the masses as benign or malignant, respectively. Jagadeesh et al. [11] proposed two complex feature extraction methods, first using the Sech template method to select suspicious regions in the mammary gland for thresholding segmentation, and then using grayscale co-generation matrix and optical density features to extract information on local intensity relationships and discrete photometric distributions. Spanhol et al. [12] disclosed the breast cancer pathological image dataset BreaKHis. Based on this dataset, they used 6 feature descriptors such as Local Binary Pattern (LBP), Gray Level Co-occurrence Matrix (GLCM), and different classification algorithms such as Support Vector Machine and Random Forest for classification. The accuracy rate reached 80%–85%.

Most of the above classification algorithms are performed on different datasets. There is no uniform comparison standard between algorithms, and the accuracy rates are not comparable. More importantly, these algorithms use manual-based feature extraction methods, which not only require professional domain knowledge, but also consume a lot of time and energy to complete, and the results are highly susceptible to pathologists' subjective human factors. The limitation of these traditional machine learning algorithms for breast cancer pathological image classification is that some manually extracted features have poor generalization ability in the classification model. All these severely restrict the application of traditional machine learning algorithms in diagnosis of breast cancer.

2.2 Disease Diagnosis Based on Convolutional Neural Network (CNN)

Deep learning has made an important breakthrough in computer vision research. The major difference between deep learning and traditional machine learning methods is that its feature representation is automatically learned from a large amount of data, and it learns to obtain a distinguished target feature representation by constructing a learning model with multiple hierarchical structures and gradually extracting features from a large amount of training data from low-level edge and other features to high-level abstract semantic features. The complexity and limitations of manual feature extraction in traditional algorithms are avoided. Convolutional Neural Networks (CNN) as one of the widely used models in deep learning which have been widely used in natural language processing, computer version and other fields. CNN has achieved a series of achievements in the research of breast cancer pathological images.

Koné et al. [13] used the DenseNet50 model for the classification breast cancer pathological images which achieved 81% accuracy. Bayramoglu et al. [14]; Aresta et al. [15] utilized a multi-task magnification which is based on CNN architecture to distinguish benign from malignant breast cancer. Spanhol et al. [16] utilized AlexNet with different fusion strategies for classification. On BreaKHis dataset, Araújo et al. [17]; Rakhlin et al. [18] proposed a classification method which based on CNN and SVM for H&E stained breast cancer tissue images. Vang et al. [19]; Golatkar et al. [20] proposed a deep learning framework with the Inception-V3 model for multi-class breast cancer histology images. Awan et al. [21] utilized CNN to map the representation encoding of patches into a high-dimensional space, and uses support vector machine(SVM) to aggregate contextual information from high-dimensional features for breast cancer classification. Cao et al. [22] applied the RFSVM method to classify breast cancer data. Yan et al. [23] proposed a richer breast cancer classification fusion network based on pathological images and structured electrical medical record (EMR) data, and extract multi-level feature representations of pathological images. They further improved the accuracy of breast cancer classification by combining pathological images with structured data which extracted from EMR.

Although the method based on CNN not only can alleviate the complexity of extracting breast cancer pathological images, but also can overcome the defect of weak image feature extraction ability, and make the model achieve a good classification effect by deepening the network layers. But when the amount of data in the algorithm is not large enough, this method may find overfitting. What's more, only the features of single modality often have insufficient information, making it difficult to meet the requirements of clinical diagnosis of breast cancer.

2.3 Disease Diagnosis Based on Electronic Medical Records

EMR data includes structured attributes of patients. Compared with pathological images, electronic medical records can display features that cannot be reflected in images, such as patient age, gender, family tumor history and other consultation informations.

Liu et al. [24] utilized a graph-structured Transformer model to jointly learn statistical information from electronic medical records and medical knowledge graphs for performing diagnosis prediction tasks. Li et al. [25] used deep learning techniques to process gynecological electronic medical record texts to achieve better diagnostic results. Hazewinkel et al. [26] used text mining for psychiatric electronic medical records and assisted to give medical decisions. From the perspective of natural language, Gong et al. [27] used mining algorithms to mine the related information of breast cancer from clinical medical record texts to assist medical workers in making breast cancer staging decisions. Xu et al. [28] mined the feature of similar patients by using electronic medical records of breast cancer patients as research data.

However, it is difficult to directly reflect the actual status of the tumor from the description of the patient's symptoms based on the text of the medical record alone. When a patient is in the early stages of cancer, these symptoms are not very obvious, which has a significant influence on the accuracy of the classification.

2.4 Disease Diagnosis Based on Multimodality

Although existing deep learning models are powerful in learning visual and textual representations, and have achieved satisfactory performance in natural language process and medical image analysis [29], it is still a challenge to complementarily incorporate data from different modalities into a unified modality to improve the quality of disease diagnosis. A mainstream approach is to combine the features from different modalities and then performs multimodal learning with deep neural networks. Mobadersany et al. [30] combined histopathological features extracted from histological images using VGG-19 with genomic features of subjects by concatenation, and then input the concatenated features into a multilayer perceptron (MLP) for the classification of glioma cancer. Huang et al. [31] modeled the relationship between the patient's image data and non-image data through pairwise associative encoders, and they learned to construct fully connected graphs based on paired associative encoders adaptively, and improved the prediction performance.

On the one hand, in various diagnostic tasks, image data can provide the most intuitive features and ultimately determining the disease condition of a patient. On the other hand, non-image data (e.g., age, gender, tumor history) provides richer information about the patient. They can provide additional guidance for diagnosis, which is complementary to image data for the task diagnosis. Thus, it is important to study the ability of combining image data with non-image data for multimodal medical data which can lead to more comprehensive feature representation and more accurate disease prediction and diagnostic performance.

In this paper, we propose Multimodal breast cancer diagnosis based on Multi-level fusion network. Furthermore, in the face of the heterogeneous multimodal data fusion problem. Inspired by Rahman et al. [8], we used multimodal adaptation gates (MAG) with pathological images as the primary modality. The other two modalities are used as a complement to the image modal information for multimodal data fusion, and obtained the good results.

3   Methods

In this section, we describe the proposed method in detail. It includes three parts: image feature representation, text feature representation and multimodal fusion. The proposed method is shown in Fig. 1.

3.1   Image Feature Representation

With the development of deep learning in computer vision, different convolutional neural networks are used in various medical diagnostic tasks. Specifically, assuming that a breast cancer patient has k pathological images, the set of pathological images can be represented as $X = \{x_1, x_2, x_3, \ldots, x_k\}$. The node-level feature $V = \{v_i | i = 1, 2, 3, \ldots, k\}, v_i \in R^F$ of the pathological image is obtained through the DenseNet [32] model, and the dimension of the node-level features of each image is F.

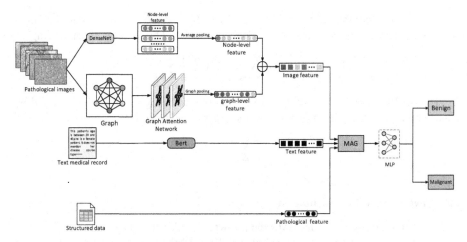

Fig. 1. The overall architecture of the proposed approach.

We construct the node-level feature $V = \{v_i | i = 1, 2, 3, \ldots, k\}, v_i \in R^F$ into a fully connected graph $G = (V, E)$ to obtain the correlation between pathological images. Each vertice in the graph is node-level feature, and we use the fully connected graph to compose the edge. This approach can assist the graph neural network to integrate and process the information between the images.

Here, we utilize Graph attention networks (GAT) to extract high-level features of patient images. The node-level feature $V = \{v_i | i = 1, 2, 3, \ldots, k\}, v_i \in R^F$ of the pathological image is used as the input of GAT. Through the multi-layer GAT model, we extracted the new node-level feature $V' = \{v_i' | i = 1, 2, 3, \ldots, k\}, v_i' \in R^{F'}$, F' is the dimension of the GAT output. The detailed process is as follows.

First, we apply $W \in R^{F' \times F}$ to each node to implement a parametric linear transformation. Then the attention coefficient e_{ij} indicates the importance of node j to node i:

$$e_{ij} = LeakyReLU\left(a^T[Wv_i || Wv_j]\right) \tag{1}$$

where $||$ is the concatenation operation, $a^T \in R^{2F'}$ is the parameterized weight vector, and $LeakyReLU$ is the nonlinear activation function. $E \in R^{t \times t}$ is the attention coefficient matrix; t is the number of patients; W is the parameter weight matrix.

Then, the coefficient e_{ij} is normalized with the *softmax* function to obtain the attention weight:

$$\alpha_{ij} = Softmax_j\left(e_{ij}\right) = \frac{exp(e_{ij})}{\sum_{k \in N_i} exp(e_{ik})} \tag{2}$$

where N_i is the neighborhood of node i in the graph. Finally, the normalized attention factor α_{ij} is used to calculate the weighted sum of the associated features. The output of the k-head attention is:

$$v_i' = ||_{k=1}^K ELU\left(\sum_{j \in N_i} \alpha_{ij} Wv_j\right) \tag{3}$$

where *ELU* is a combination of *Sigmord* and *ReLU*, which is a nonlinear activation function. The graph-level feature $\tilde{V}'$, $\tilde{V}' \in R^{F'}$ is obtained by V' after mean pooling:

$$\tilde{V}' = meanpool(\sum_{i=1}^{k} v_i') = \frac{1}{k} \sum_{i=1}^{k} v_i' \tag{4}$$

The final feature G, $G \in R^{F'+F}$ of the patient's pathological image is obtained by concatenating the node-level feature and the graph-level feature $\tilde{V}'$:

$$G = [\frac{1}{k} \sum_{i=1}^{k} v_i || \tilde{V}'] \tag{5}$$

3.2 Text Feature Representation

In this section, we use the PathoEMR dataset which collaborated by Yan et al. [23] with Peking University International Hospital. The PathoEMR dataset contains pathological images and structured EMR data for breast cancer classification. We textually describe these structured EMR data and construct the medical record text according to the rules of clinical medicine. As shown in Table 1 and Fig. 2, these are the electronic medical record text and 29 pathological features of patient S0000004 for textual description, respectively.

> This patient's age is between 20 and 40,she is a female patient.It does not mention her disease course type.She did not have any personal tumor history and any family tumor history.She did not receive any prophase treatment,and she did not receive any neoadjuvant chemotherapy.She did not have the dimple sign,and without the orange peel appearance.She did not have the symptom of redness and swelling of skin.She did not have the symptom of skin ulcers.She has the breast tumor without the symptom of breast deformation.She did not have any nipple change.She does not have any nipple discharge,such as bloody nipple discharge.She does not have axillary lymphadenectasis (AL).Her swelling of lymph nodes do not metastasize to distant sites.Her tumor position is in outer.Her breast has single tumor in unilateral breast.The size of her tumor is less than 20mm.Her tumor texture is soft.Her tumor border is clear.Her tumor is with smooth surface.Her tumor malignant masses exhibit regularity in shapes.Her tumor has good activity.Her tumors have enveloped capsules.She does not have any feeling of tenderness.She does not have skin adhesion.She does not have the symptom of pectoral muscle adhesion.

Fig. 2. Text medical record of patient S0000004

BERT has proved that it can achieve good performances in the text classification tasks. We use the BERT model to take the medical record text I as input, and extract the medical record text feature T, $T \in R^{F_1}$. F_1 is the dimension of the medical record text feature after BERT. The formula is as follows:

$$T = BERT_{base}(I) \tag{6}$$

In addition, 29 representative pathological features were selected from the patient's EMR, and defined as C.

Table 1. Structural features of patient S0000004, where "-" is the selected value, and "-" is followed by the description corresponding to the selected value

Age: 2-Between 20 and 40	*Gender: 2-Female*
Disease Course Type:0-Not mentioned	*Personal Tumor History:0-No*
Family Tumor History:0-No	*Prophase Treatment:0-No*
Neoadjuvant Chemotherapy:0-No	*Dimple Sign:0-No*
Orange Peel Appearance:0-No	*Redness And Swelling Of Skin:0-No*
Skin Ulcers:0-No	*Tumor:1-Yes*
Breast Deformation:0-No	*Nipple Change:0-No change*
Nipple Discharge:0-No	*Axillary Lymphadenectasis:0-No AL*
Swelling Of Lymph Nodes:0-No metastasize	*Tumor Position:1-Outer*
Tumor Number:1-Single-unilateral	*Tumor Size:1-Less than 20mm*
Tumor Texture:1-Soft	*Tumor Border:1-Clear*
Smooth Surface:1-Yes	*Tumor Morphology:1-Regular*
Activity:1-Moderate	*Capsules:2-Enveloped*
Tenderness:0-No	*Skin Adhesion:0-No*
Pectoral Muscle Adhesion:0-No	*Diagnosis:1-Benign*

3.3 Multimodal Fusion

In summary, we obtained the information consisting of three modalities of the patient: pathological image feature G, medical record text feature T and pathological feature C. Inspired by Multimodal Adaptation Gate (MAG) [8], we fuse three modalities with attention gate as shown in Fig. 3. The implementation of MAG was first studied by Wang et al. [33], we refer to the modality that is being adjusted as the primary modality and the other modalities as secondary modalities. For the medical classification task, we consider that the pathological image should be the main modality since the other two modalities are complementary to the image modality information. Essentially, the MAG unit receives three features as the input, such as image feature, text feature and pathological feature. Let the triplet (G, T, C) denote the patient's input in the sequence.

The formula of the attention gating in Fig. 3 is as follows:

$$g^t = ReLU\left(W_{gt}[G||T] + b_t\right) \tag{7}$$

$$g^c = ReLU\left(W_{gc}[G||C] + b_c\right) \tag{8}$$

where W_{gt} and W_{gc} are the weight matrices of text and pathological modalities, $||$ denotes the concatenation operation, and b_t and b_c are the bias vectors. *ReLU* is a nonlinear activation function.

Then, according to the above two weights, as well as the diagnostic text feature T and the pathological feature C, the vector H is obtained:

$$H = g^t \cdot (W_t T) + g^c \cdot (W_c C) + b_H \tag{9}$$

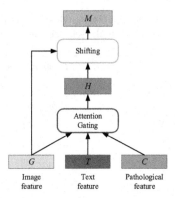

Fig. 3. Overall architecture of the MAG model. G, T and C are image features, text features, and pathological features, respectively. Displacement vectors derived from the image modality to adjust the representation of other modalities.

where W_t and W_c are the weight matrices for textual and pathological information, respectively, and b_H is the bias vector.

Finally, through the weighted summation of the pathological image feature G and the vector H, the final multimodal fusion feature M of the patient is obtained:

$$M = G + \alpha H \tag{10}$$

$$\alpha = min(\frac{\|G\|_2}{\|H\|_2}\beta, 1) \tag{11}$$

where β is the hyperparameter training with random initialization of the model. $\|G\|_2$ and $\|H\|_2$ denote the L_2 norm of G and H, respectively.

3.4 Classification Prediction

At last, we use the *Softmax* to predict the result of the breast cancer classification, i.e.:

$$\widehat{P} = softmax(Linear(M)) \tag{12}$$

where $\widehat{P} \in R^2$, M is the multimodal fusion feature, and *Linear* represents the output of the fully connected layer. We use cross-entropy to calculate the loss function:

$$L = -\frac{1}{t}\sum_{n=1}^{t} P_n log\left(\widehat{P}_n\right) + (1 - P_n log\left(1 - \widehat{P}_n\right)) \tag{13}$$

where t is the number of patients, $L \in R$ for binary classification problems, P_n and $\widehat{P}_n$ denote the actual and predicted values of the nth patient, respectively. We calculate the loss by replacing the ground truth label P and predicted label $\widehat{P}$.

4   Experiments

4.1   Dataset

The PathoEMR dataset is provided by the literature Richer fusion network for breast cancer classification based on multimodal data [23]. They obtained a new dataset PathoEMR from Peking University International Hospital, which contains pathological images and corresponding EMR data of each patient.

The dataset collected data from 185 breast cancer patients who were treated at Peking University International Hospital from March 2015 to March 2018, of which 82 patients were benign and 103 patients were malignant. Each patient included 2–97 pathological images for the study. Finally, there are a total of 3764 pathological images with size of 2048×1536 pixels, and each image is marked as benign or malignant (1332 benign, 2432 malignant).

In addition to the pathological images of patients, Yan et al. [23] also collected EMR data of patients. Electronic medical records (EMR) reflect some of the patient's consultation information. Yan et al. [23] also extracted 29 representative features from EMR.

4.2   Experimental Setup and Evaluation Metrics

We randomly selected 80% of the dataset as the train set to train the model and the remaining 20% as the test set for testing. Our proposed network is implemented using PyTorch, and using an ADAM optimizer with an initial learning rate of 0.0001 to minimize the cross-entropy loss during training with a batch size of 10 and epoch of 1000 on an NVIDIA RTX 3090 GPU. We resize each pathological image to 224×224, and extract the feature vector of pathological images from DenseNet with dimension $F = 1024$. We use a three-layer GAT, and the GAT hidden layer (the first layer) has 4 attention heads to calculate 256-dimensional features, the second and third layers with a single attention head to calculate $F' = 128$ dimensional features. The text of the medical record is extracted through BERT to extract the text features of $F_1 = 768$ dimensions. The pathological features were extracted from EMR with 29 dimensions.

In GAT, we set the depth as 60 nodes: if the number of nodes is less than 60, we will use the zero vector supplement. Please note that the supplemented zero vector here has no edges, so it has no effect on the experimental results. If the number of nodes is greater than 60, we take the middle 60 as the input, and truncate the more part. In the PathEMR dataset, there is only one case with more than 60 images, and 60 pathological images are enough to learn the image features of the patient, so it has no effect on the experimental results. For the evaluation of the proposed method, we compared our proposed model with previously proposed models for breast cancer classification. We evaluate the method in terms of classification accuracy (ACC), AUC, precision, recall and F1-score. The accuracy rate indicates the number of samples with correct predictions as a percentage of the total number of samples. Precision represents true positive samples rate of each positive samples. Recall represents the numbers of positive samples in the samples which predicted correctly. F1 score is a weighted average of accuracy and recall.

These metrics are calculated as follows:

$$ACC = \sum_{n=1}^{t} \frac{TN_n + TP_n}{TN_n + FP_n + FN_n + TP_n} \tag{14}$$

$$precision = \sum_{n=1}^{t} \frac{TP_n}{TP_n + FP_n} \tag{15}$$

$$recall = True\ positive\ rate = \sum_{n=1}^{t} \frac{TP_n}{TP_n + FN_n} \tag{16}$$

$$F_1 - score = 2 \cdot \frac{precision \cdot recall}{precision + recall} \tag{17}$$

$$FalsF\ positive\ rate = \sum_{n=1}^{t} \frac{FP_n}{FP_n + TN_n} \tag{18}$$

Among them, TP_n, TN_n, FP_n and FN_n denote the values of true positives, true negatives, false positives and false negatives respectively. t represents the number of patients in the dataset. The ROC curve and AUC were also used to further evaluate the performance of the classifier.

4.3 Comparative Experiment

We conduct extensive experiments to evaluate the performance of the proposed method. Few of the existing studies have used only clinical electronic medical record text to diagnose breast cancer, so we compared our method with several methods which are based on pathological images [14–23]. As shown in Table 2, the accuracy of our proposed model is higher than previous proposed methods.

Table 2. Comparison of the accuracy of different methods for breast cancer classification

Methods	Accuracy
Bayramoglu et al. (CNN) [14]	83%
Spanhol et al. (AlexNet) [16]	85%
Araújo et al. (CNN + SVM) [17]	83.3%
Rakhlin et al. (CNN) [18]	87.2%
Vang et al. (Inception-V3) [19]	87.5%
Golatkar et al. (Inception-V3) [20]	85%
Awan et al. (CNN + SVM) [21]	83%
Cao et al. (RFSVM) [22]	87.1%
Aresta et al. (CNN) [15]	87%
Yan et al. (VGG16 + denoising autoencoder) [23]	92.9%
Our proposed	93.62%

4.4 Model Analysis

Experimental Results

In order to verify the effectiveness of the proposed model, we conducted experiments on four variants of it: (1) Text: only use single-modality features which are based on text for classification; (2) Image-node only: only use node-level features for classification; (3) Image-graph: image features obtained by concatenating node-level features and graph-level features for classification; (4) Structured data: only from 29 representative structured pathological features for classification. Our experimental results are shown in Table 3 and Fig. 4. Figure 4(a) shows the classification performance of the different methods in each variant experiment. Based on the receiver operating characteristic (ROC) analysis, the area under the curve (AUC) using the variant experiment is shown in Fig. 4(b).

Table 3. Variant experiments for the proposed model. For classification tasks. We selected evaluation metrics such as ACC, Recall, Precision, F1-score, AUC, etc.

Methods	Accuracy	Recall	Precision	F1-score	AUC
Text	0.7447	0.7308	0.7917	0.7034	0.8077
Image-node only	0.8298	0.7692	0.8323	0.8163	0.8352
Image-graph	0.8723	0.8524	0.8275	0.8364	0.8936
Structured data	0.6596	0.7238	0.7456	0.6827	0.6807
Our proposed	**0.9362**	**0.8812**	**0.9013**	**0.8990**	**0.9476**

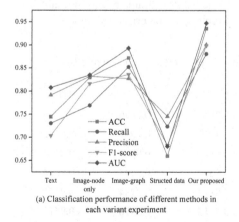

(a) Classification performance of different methods in each variant experiment

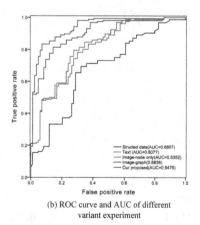

(b) ROC curve and AUC of different variant experiment

Fig. 4. The result of the classification performance.

It can be seen that only using the features of structured data have the lowest performance of classification tasks. The classification performance which is using Image-graph pathological image features is significantly better than Image-node only, although its Precision value is slightly lower than Image-node only by 0.0048, its values in ACC, Recall, F1-score and AUC are improved by 0.0425, 0.0832, 0.0201, 0.0584 respectively, and achieved the better performance. Because compared with Image-node only, Image-graph is GNN based. The graph structure provides a broader view and also includes interactions between individual node-level vectors. The graph structure method can model the structural continuity and interaction between individual pathological images of patients [34]. In contrast to convolutional neural network (CNN), graph neural networks (GNNs) are parameter efficient and also include the interactions that exist between images [35–37]. Our proposed method achieved the best performance, reaching the highest values in terms of ACC, Recall, Precision, F1-score, and AUC, which were 0.0639, 0.0288, 0.0738, 0.0626 and 0.0540 higher than the second best Image-graph method respectively. Although the performance of Text and Structured data alone is not good, but the features of these data can be used to fuse with image features, and the combination of multi-modal data fusion can make the fused feature representation richer. The complementarity between data can be fully exploited. The experimental results show that our proposed model achieves superior performance and makes the automatic breast cancer classification algorithms possible in medical diagnosis.

Fusion Strategy

We will change the components of the fusion model to explore their impact on performance. The results are shown in Table 4, Fig. 5(a). According to the ROC characteristic analysis, the area under the curve (AUC) using different fusion strategies is shown in Fig. 5(b). We selected evaluation indicators such as ACC, Recall, Precision, F1-score, and AUC to explore the influence of different fusion strategies. We enumerate some basic aggregation functions and compare them with our fusion strategy: (1) add:$x + y$; (2) concat:$x\|y$; (2) mlp:$x + tanh(W_y + b)$), where $tanh$ is the activation function; (3) att:$\alpha x + (1 - \alpha)y$, where α is a real-valued scalar parameterized by x and y; (4) gate:$\beta x + (1 - \beta)y$, where β is a real-valued vector parameterized by x and y.

Table 4. Influence of different fusion strategies on experimental results.

Methods	Accuracy	Recall	Precision	F1-score	AUC
add	0.8085	0.7783	0.7811	0.7856	0.7856
concat	0.8511	0.8359	0.8016	0.7962	0.8372
MLP	0.9149	0.8792	0.8614	0.8869	0.8777
att	0.8738	0.8503	0.8532	0.8693	0.8604
gate	0.9205	0.8705	0.8819	0.8784	0.9185
MAG	**0.9362**	**0.8812**	**0.9013**	**0.8990**	**0.9476**

In our proposed model, the MAG unit receives three feature inputs which are image feature G, $G \in R^{1152}$, text feature T, $T \in R^{768}$ and pathological feature C, $C \in R^{29}$.

During the variant experiment, we concatenate the text feature T and the pathological feature C to obtain the EMR feature $E, E \in R^{797}$. We reduce the image feature G and EMR feature E to 500 dimensions as the input of x and y to the fusion strategies except MAG for analysis. We can observe that the evaluation criterion value achieved by the MAG fusion strategy is significantly better than the performance of other fusion methods, and the classification accuracy of breast cancer is obviously improved.

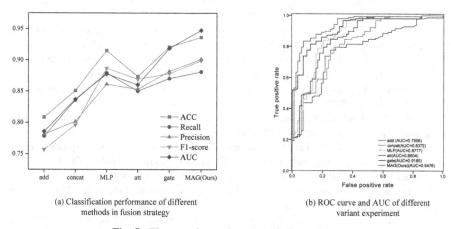

(a) Classification performance of different   (b) ROC curve and AUC of different
    methods in fusion strategy   variant experiment

Fig. 5. The experimental result of fusion strategy.

5 Conclusion

In this paper, we proposed Multimodal breast cancer diagnosis based on Multi-level fusion network. In the feature extraction stage, we used Graph Attention Network to extract node and graph level features to capture fine-grained features of pathological images. Besides, we processed the electronic medical record (EMR) and formed the medical text description, and we used the pre-trained model (BERT) to obtain diagnostic text feature extraction. To fuse the features by fully exploiting the correlation between different modalities, we fused the image, text and pathological features through a Multimodal Adaptation Gate (MAG).

Extensive experiments on PathoEMR datasets and compared with the other deep learning models for breast cancer diagnosis. It's prove that the performance of the proposed network is significantly better than that of the current state-of-the-art models, which demonstrates the validity and robustness of the method for the diagnosis of breast cancer.

Acknowledgements. This research was supported in part by the National Natural Science Foundation of China (No. 61972335 and 62002309), and supported by the Open Project Program of Jiangsu Key Laboratory of Zoonosis (No. R2017).

References

1. Cao, W., Chen, H.D., Yu, Y.W., Li, N., Chen, W.Q.: Changing profiles of cancer burden worldwide and in china: a secondary analysis of the global cancer statistics 2020. Chin. Med. J. **134**(07), 783–791 (2021)
2. Nawaz, W., Ahmed, S., Tahir, A., Khan, H.A.: Classification of breast cancer histology images using ALEXNET. In: Campilho, A., Karray, F., ter Haar Romeny, B. (eds.) ICIAR 2018. LNCS, vol. 10882, pp. 869–876. Springer, Cham. (2018). https://doi.org/10.1007/978-3-319-93000-8_99
3. Li, Y., Lu, H., Li, J., Li, X., Li, Y., Serikawa, S.: Underwater image de-scattering and classification by deep neural network. Comput. Electr. Eng. **54**, 68–77 (2016)
4. Zhao, W., Wang, M., Liu, Y., Lu, H., Xu, C., Yao, L.: Generalizable crowd counting via diverse context style learning. IEEE Trans. Circuits Syst. Video Technol. (2022)
5. Zhao, F., Lu, H., Zhao, W., Yao, L.: Image-scale-symmetric cooperative network for defocus blur detection. IEEE Trans. Circuits Syst. Video Technol. (2022)
6. Veličković, P., Cucurull, G., Casanova, A., Romero, A., Lio, P., Bengio, Y.: Graph attention networks. arXiv preprint arXiv:1710.10903 (2017)
7. Devlin, J., Chang, M.-W., Lee, K., Toutanova, K.: BERT: pre-training of deep bidirectional transformers for language understanding. arXiv preprint arXiv:1810.04805 (2018)
8. Rahman, W., et al.: Integrating multimodal information in large pretrained transformers. In: Proceedings of the Conference. Association for Computational Linguistics. Meeting, vol. 2020, pp. 2359. NIH Public Access (2020)
9. Kowal, M., Filipczuk, P., Obuchowicz, A., Korbicz, J., Monczak, R.: Computeraided diagnosis of breast cancer based on fine needle biopsy microscopic images. Comput. Biol. Med. **43**(10), 1563–1572 (2013)
10. Nanni, L., Brahnam, S., Lumini, A.: A very high performing system to discriminate tissues in mammograms as benign and malignant. Expert Syst. Appl. **39**(2), 1968–1971 (2011)
11. Jagadeesh, K., Jamunalaksmi, K., Muthuvidhya, P., Harris, S.M., Ganga, V.: Mammogram based automatic computer aided detection of masses in medical images. J. Telecommun. Study **3**(1), 4 (2018)
12. Spanhol, F.A., Oliveira, L.S., Petitjean, C., Heutte, L.: A dataset for breast cancer histopathological image classification. IEEE Trans. Biomed. Eng. (2015)
13. Koné, I., Boulmane, L.: Hierarchical ResNeXt models for breast cancer histology image classification. In: Campilho, A., Karray, F., ter Haar Romeny, B. (eds.) ICIAR 2018. LNCS, vol. 10882, pp. 796–803. Springer, Cham (2018). https://doi.org/10.1007/978-3-319-93000-8_90
14. Bayramoglu, N., Kannala, J., Heikkila, J.: Deep learning for magnification independent breast cancer histopathology image classification. In International Conference on Pattern Recognition (2017)
15. Gaa, B., et al.: Grand challenge on breast cancer histology images. Med. Image Anal. **56**, 122–139 (2019)
16. Spanhol, F.A., Oliveira, L.S., Petitjean, C., Heutte, L.: Breast cancer histopathological image classification using convolutional neural networks. In: International Joint Conference on Neural Networks (IJCNN 2016) (2016)
17. Teresa, A., et al.: Classification of breast cancer histology images using convolutional neural networks. PLoS ONE **12**(6), e0177544 (2017)
18. Rakhlin, A., Shvets, A., Iglovikov, V., Kalinin, A.A.: Deep convolutional neural networks for breast cancer histology image analysis. In: Campilho, A., Karray, F., ter Haar Romeny, B. (eds.) ICIAR 2018. LNCS, vol. 10882, pp. 737–744. Springer, Cham (2018). https://doi.org/10.1007/978-3-319-93000-8_83

19. Vang, Y.S., Chen, Z., Xie, X.: Deep learning framework for multi-class breast cancer histology image classification. In: Campilho, A., Karray, F., ter Haar Romeny, B. (eds.) ICIAR 2018. LNCS, vol. 10882, pp. 914–922. Springer, Cham (2018). https://doi.org/10.1007/978-3-319-93000-8_104

20. Golatkar, A., Anand, D., Sethi, A.: Classification of breast cancer histology using deep learning. In: Campilho, A., Karray, F., ter Haar Romeny, B. (eds.) ICIAR 2018. LNCS, vol. 10882, pp. 837–844. Springer, Cham (2018). https://doi.org/10.1007/978-3-319-93000-8_95

21. Awan, R. et al.: Context-aware learning using transferable features for classification of breast cancer histology images. In: International Conference Image Analysis & Recognition (2018)

22. Cao, H., Bernard, S., Heutte, L., Sabourin, R.: Improve the performance of transfer learning without fine-tuning using dissimilarity-based multi-view learning for breast cancer histology images. In: International Conference Image Analysis & Recognition (2018)

23. Yan, R., et al.: Richer fusion network for breast cancer classification based on multimodal data. BMC Med. Inform. Decis. Mak. 21(1), 1–15 (2021)

24. Liu, X., Wang, H., He, T., Gong, X.: Research on intelligent diagnosis model of electronic medical record based on graph transformer. In: 2021 6th International Conference on Computational Intelligence and Applications (ICCIA), pp. 73–78. IEEE (2021)

25. Hui, L., Li, X., Ramanathan, M., Zhang, A.: Identifying informative risk factors and predicting bone disease progression via deep belief networks. Methods 69(3), 257–265 (2014)

26. Hazewinkel, M.C., et al.: Text analysis of electronic medical records to predict seclusion in psychiatric wards: proof of concept. Front. Psychiatry 10, 188 (2019)

27. Lejun, G., et al.: Mining and decision-making of breast cancer medical record text based on decision tree. J. Nanjing Norm. Univ. (Nat. Sci. Ed.) 42(3), 10 (2019)

28. Xu, M., et al.: Visual analysis of cohorts and treatments of breast cancer based on electronic health records. J. Zhejiang Univ. (Sci. Ed.) 48(4), 391–401 (2021)

29. Khan, A., Sohail, A., Zahoora, U., Qureshi, A.S.: A survey of the recent architectures of deep convolutional neural networks. Artif. Intell. Rev. 53(8), 5455–5516 (2020). https://doi.org/10.1007/s10462-020-09825-6

30. Mobadersany, P., ET AL.: Predicting cancer outcomes from histology and genomics using convolutional networks. Proc. Natl. Acad. Sci. United States Am., 201717139 (2018)

31. Huang, Y., Chung, A.C.S.: Disease prediction with edge-variational graph convolutional networks. Med. Image Anal. 77, 102375 (2022)

32. Huang, G., Liu, Z., Van Der Maaten, L., Weinberger, K.Q.: Densely connected convolutional networks. In: Proceedings of the IEEE Conference on Computer Vision and Pattern Recognition, pp. 4700–4708 (2017)

33. Wang, Y., Shen, Y., Liu, Z., Liang, P.P., Zadeh, A., Morency, L.-P.: Words can shift: dynamically adjusting word representations using nonverbal behaviors. In: Proceedings of the AAAI Conference on Artificial Intelligence, vol. 33, pp. 7216–7223 (2019)

34. Zhou, Y., Zhou, T., Zhou, T., Fu, H., Shao, L.: Contrast-attentive thoracic disease recognition with dual-weighting graph reasoning. IEEE Trans. Med. Imaging PP(99), 1 (2021)

35. Sarah, P., et al.: Disease prediction using graph convolutional networks: application to autism spectrum disorder and Alzheimer's disease. Med.Image Anal., S1361841518303554 (2018)

36. Zhang, Y., Zhan, L., Cai, W., Thompson, P., Huang, H.: Integrating heterogeneous brain networks for predicting brain disease conditions. In: Shen, D., et al. (eds.) MICCAI 2019. LNCS, vol. 11767, pp. 214–222. Springer, Cham (2019). https://doi.org/10.1007/978-3-030-32251-9_24

37. Song, X., Li, H., Gao, W., Chen, Y., Lei, B.: Augmented multi-center graph convolutional network for covid-19 diagnosis. IEEE Trans. Ind. Inform. PP(99), 1 (2021)

Behavior Control of Cooperative Vehicle Infrastructure System in Container Terminals Based on Q-learning

Maopu Wu[1,2], Jian Gao[1(✉)], Le Li[1], and Yue Wang[2]

[1] Northwestern Polytechnical University, Room 127, Friendship West Road, Xi'an 710072, China
jiangao@nwpu.edu.cn

[2] The 716th Research Institute of China State Shipbuilding Corporation Limited, Room 18, Saint Lake Road, Lianyungang 222006, China

Abstract. Aiming at the problem of low intelligence of horizontal transport vehicles in container terminal, the research on cooperative vehicle infrastructure system is carried out combined with the characteristics of closure and low-speed for container terminals. The model for the behavior control and optimization of unmanned vehicles is designed based on Q-Learning, and the cooperative vehicle infrastructure system of container terminal is developed. A verification experiment is designed. Through sensor information recognition and behavior control training, the accuracy rate of driving behavior control of the system is more than 90%, which can effectively command vehicles, ensure traffic safety and improve traffic efficiency.

Keywords: Container terminal · Cooperative vehicle infrastructure system · Q-learning · Driving behavior

1 Introduction

The objective of horizontal transportation in container terminal is to dispatch and transport containers between the wharf and the yard by vehicles, and then realize the loading and unloading of containers in ships and yards. With the increase of global trade and the development of larger ships, driverless and intellectualization of vehicle will become the development trend in the future.

Based on the online learning algorithm, Li Jing studied the dynamic scheduling problem of horizontal transportation vehicles [1]. Kim J studied the multi-objective adaptive scheduling optimization of horizontal transport vehicles at the wharf [2]. Bian Zhan conducted research on vehicle task assignment [3]. Miyamoto t carried out the research on the route optimization of unmanned vehicles at the wharf [4]. Jamal shahrabi realized dynamic scheduling parameter optimization based on reinforcement learning [5]. Zhu l designed an on-line semi supervised learning algorithm for unmanned vehicle scheduling at the wharf [6].

© The Author(s), under exclusive license to Springer Nature Singapore Pte Ltd. 2022
S. Yang and H. Lu (Eds.): ISAIR 2022, CCIS 1701, pp. 240–246, 2022.
https://doi.org/10.1007/978-981-19-7943-9_20

Given all of that, it can be seen that most of the scholars pay attention to such issues as vehicle path planning, task allocation and equipment cooperative operation at the terminal, and pay little attention to the intelligent behavior of vehicles. In view of this problem, Cooperative Vehicle Infrastructure System in Container Terminals based on Q-Learning algorithm [7] is designed. Through many training and experiments, it is proved that the system can accurately identify environmental information and command vehicles to make correct behavior.

2 Design of Model

There are unmanned vehicles and traditional container trucks in terminal. There are more than a hundred of these two kinds of vehicles at the operation peak. Vehicles will accelerate, overtake, turn and turn around at road driving areas and intersections. Due to the limited number of roadways and the size of vehicles at the same time, there are overtaking collision, turning collision [8], U-turn collision, etc. on the shore, and there are overtaking collision, opposing collision, turning collision and complex conflict in the yard.

The information sources of the unmanned vehicle during driving mainly include radar and camera [9]. Information types mainly include location information, ground mark and obstacles. Ground marks mainly refer to straight ahead marks and turning marks. Random obstacles mainly refer to moving vehicles, random intruders and static objects. Unmanned driving can be realized only by recognizing environmental information and controlling driving behavior [10].

Q-learning is a model-free algorithm based on Q-value iteration. It is used to solve Markov decision problems and is widely used in the field of robotics [11, 12]. It is assumed that S is the state set of the environment, which refers to the set of driverless areas. S is a state. A is the action set of the agent. There are four actions of unmanned vehicle, including straight ahead, turning, stopping and overtaking. a is an action. A(s) is the set of all candidate actions in s state. R(s) is the return value of environmental feedback in s state. Q(s, a) is the Q value generated by executing the a action in the s state. Based on the Q-table, the Q-learning algorithm mainly update the Q value according to Eq. 1.

$$Q(s, a) \leftarrow (1 - \alpha)Q(s, a) + \alpha * [R(s) + \gamma * \max_{a'} Q(s', a')] \tag{1}$$

Here, s and s' are the current state and the lower state respectively. a is the effective action to make s to s'. α is called the learning rate, which is used to adjust the possible error in the learning process, $\alpha \in [0, 1]$. γ is the discount factor.

3 Design of Cooperative Vehicle Infrastructure System

Aiming at the problem of intelligent driving of unmanned vehicles in container terminal, Cooperative Vehicle Infrastructure System is designed. The system is composed of communication subsystem, dispatching control software and unmanned vehicle. The architecture is shown in Fig. 1. The communication subsystem can realize information communication between the dispatching control system and unmanned vehicles by wireless communication technology. The dispatching control software is equivalent to the control brain of the unmanned vehicle, and realizes the driving behavior control, traffic control, etc. Unmanned vehicles are equipped with high-precision maps and high-precision sensors, and have the functions of environmental perception, real-time scanning and uploading of road conditions, and intelligent driving.

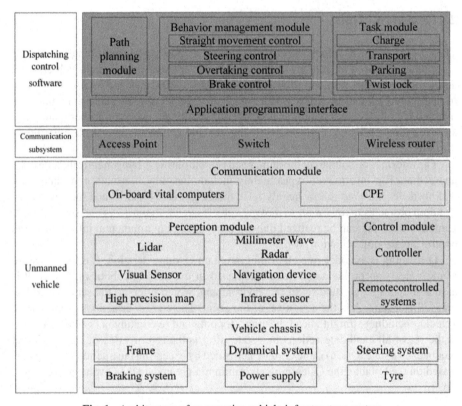

Fig. 1. Architecture of cooperative vehicle infrastructure system

The network topology of the cooperative vehicle infrastructure system mainly includes the on-board terminal, communication base station, communication link and central control center. The on-board host summarizes the environmental perception information of the on-board sensors, and sends information about vehicle and environmental to the dispatching software through the on-board terminal in combination with the high-precision map and the vehicle basic control module. The on-board terminal interacts with the base station by wireless communication. The base station sends the feedback information of the unmanned vehicle to the dispatching control software located in the central control center based on the communication link composed of the optical fiber and the switch. The scheduling control software integrates the Q-learning algorithm model and task scheduling rules, and can send the scheduling instructions to the unmanned vehicle host in reverse real time, so as to realize vehicle path planning, emergency response, task scheduling, etc. The network topology of the system is shown in Fig. 2.

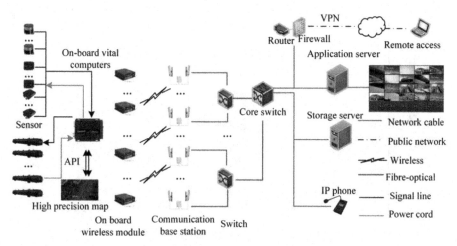

Fig. 2. The network topology of the system

4 Test Verification

4.1 Simulation Experiment

Based on Q-learning algorithm, the unmanned vehicle is controlled. The grid map is used to simulate the environment of the vehicle, and the map size is 40×80. The coordinate value of the vehicle position corresponds to a state of Q-table. S = {straight ahead area, turning area, parking area and obstacle area}. There are 4 types of vehicle actions. A = {straight ahead, turning, stopping and overtaking}. After the action selection is completed, the traveling road query will be conducted if a random obstacle is encountered. If there is an available road, enter the next state, that is, conduct obstacle avoidance operations, such as turning and overtaking. Otherwise, the vehicle is braked. After the action selection, while there is a running vehicle in the current side and there are other feasible roads, the vehicle which in straight ahead area will overtake. If there is a running vehicle on the front and there is no other feasible road, the vehicle shall keep a straight distance. There is no running vehicle on the front side, the vehicle accelerates. The starting position of the vehicle is at coordinates (3, 10) and the target position is at coordinates (78, 20). The main parameters in the experiment are set as follows. $\alpha = 0.2$, $\gamma = 0.99$, edge return value R1 $= -0.2$, target return value R2 $= 6$, obstacle return value R3 $= -1$. The velocity curve of unmanned vehicle is shown in Fig. 3.

It can be seen from the above figure that the unmanned vehicle can realize turning, emergency braking and other operations independently after many times of learning and training. Compared with manual remote control, the accuracy of vehicle behavior control based on machine learning algorithm can reach more than 90%.

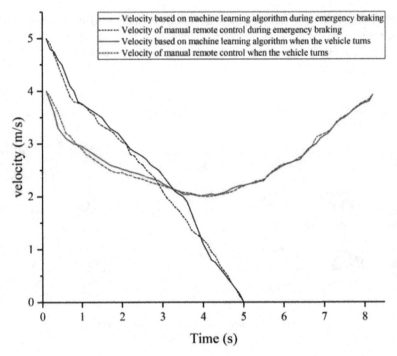

Fig. 3. Curve of velocity

4.2 Outdoor Experiment

The site is composed of a ring-shaped vehicle driving area and parking space area, and the site size is 200 * 100 m. People and trolleys are used as random obstacles. A port heavy-duty unmanned vehicle was independently developed. It is 15 m long, 3.2 m wide and 2.1 m high. The unmanned vehicle is equipped with camera, laser radar, millimeter wave radar, on-board map, etc. The maximum acceleration of the unmanned vehicle is 1 m/s^2, the maximum angular acceleration is 30°/s^2, the maximum operating speed is 8 m/s, the recommended no-load speed is 8 m/s, the full load velocity is 5 m/s, and the minimum external turning radius is 7.65 m. Some test results are shown in Fig. 4. It can be seen from the figure that the unmanned vehicle can recognize the obstacles of the trolley and brake the vehicle in time, which can keep a safe distance of 3 m from the obstacles. After arriving at the destination, the unmanned vehicle can realize accurate parking. The positioning accuracy can reach 2 cm.

a. Operation of avoid obstacles   b. Operation of parking

Fig. 4. Outdoor experiment results

5 Conclusion

In view of the low intelligence of the behavior control of unmanned vehicles in container terminals, this paper designs the behavior control model of unmanned vehicles based on Q-learning, and then develops the cooperative vehicle infrastructure system. The simulation results show that the algorithm model can effectively command the vehicle, and the accuracy rate is higher than 90%. Through outdoor experiments, it can be seen that the cooperative vehicle infrastructure system can identify obstacles, road signs and other surrounding environments, and effectively control the behavior of unmanned vehicles such as obstacle avoidance, turning and parking.

References

1. Li, J.: AGV scheduling method based on online learning on the automation container terminal. Dalian University of Technology, pp. 10–11 (2018)
2. Kim, J., Choe, R., Ryu, K.R.: Multi-objective optimization of dispatching strategies for situation-adaptive AGV operation in an automated container terminal. In: Research in Adaptive and Convergent Systems, pp. 1–6. ACM (2013)
3. Bian, Z., Jin, Z.: Truck assignment problem under different loading and unloading operation modes. Syst. Eng. **33**(12), 55–65 (2015)
4. Miyamoto, T., Inoue, K.: Local and random searches for dispatch and conflict-free routing problem of capacitated AGV systems. Comput. Ind. Eng. **91**(1), 1–9 (2016)
5. Shahrabi, J., Adibi, M.A., Mahootchi, M.: A reinforcement learning approach to parameter estimation in dynamic job shop dispatching. Comput. Ind. Eng. **110**(4), 75–82 (2017)
6. Zhu, L., Pang, S., Sarrafzadeh, A., et al.: Incremental and decremental max-flow for online semi-supervised learning. IEEE Trans. Knowl. Data Eng. **28**(8), 2115–2127 (2016)
7. Duan, Y., Xu, X.: Research on multi robot cooperation strategy based on multi-agent reinforcement learning. Syst. Eng. Theory Pract. **34**(5), 1305–1310 (2014)
8. Lu, H., Li, Y., Mu, S., Wang, D., Kim, H., Serikawa, S.: Motor anomaly detection for unmanned aerial vehicles using reinforcement learning. IEEE Internet Things J. **5**(4), 2315–2322 (2018)
9. Kang, S., et al.: Discrete-time predictive sliding mode control for a constrained parallel micropositioning piezostage. IEEE Trans. Syst. Man Cybern. Syst. **52**, 3025–3036 (2021)
10. Yang, X., et al.: Dynamics and isotropic control of parallel mechanisms for vibration isolation. IEEE/ASME Trans. Mechatron. **25**(4), 2027–2034 (2020)

11. Wang, T., et al.: Output bounded and RBFNN-based position tracking and adaptive force control for security tele-surgery. ACM Trans. Multimedia Comput. Commun. Appl. (2020). https://doi.org/10.1145/3394920

12. Wang, P., et al.: Numerical and experimental study on the maneuverability of an active propeller control based wave glider. Appl. Ocean Res. **104**,102369 (2020). https://doi.org/10.1016/j.apor.2020.102369

Backdoor Attack Against Deep Learning-Based Autonomous Driving with Fogging

Jianming Liu, Li Luo$^{(\boxtimes)}$, and Xueyan Wang

School of Computer Science and Information Security, Guilin University of Electronic Technology, Guilin, China
LiyiaLuo@163.com

Abstract. In recent years, deep learning is the main research direction of the autonomous driving industry. And security is the top priority in the research process of autonomous driving. Many studies show that the deep network neural is very vulnerable to be attacked by backdoor during training. The model affected by backdoor performs normally on the clean data, once it encounters the input with trigger designed by us, it will predict incorrect results which may be specially set by the attacker. Based on this, this paper proposes a new method for the vehicle autonomous driving fogging attack by fogging a small part of training data and implanting the back door into the victim model. We demonstrate on three deep neural network models and two data sets, which shows that we have a high attack success rate of 99 When the input image is fogged heavily enough.

Keywords: Autonomous driving · Deep neural network · Backdoor attack

1 Introduction

Deep neural network is a powerful deep learning model. With the rapid development of deep learning, it has made great achievements in the field of speech [2], image [3, 4], text [5] and other information processing [6]. It is promoting the development of various machine tasks such as machine translation [7], computer vision [8, 31] and speech recognition [9]. Of course, DNN is also applicable to a safety critical scenario: autonomous driving [10, 13, 15].

Autonomous driving is an area that most of us focus on. The whole autonomous driving is a process from image to action. It can be further divided into four steps: data acquisition [11], data processing [14, 16] and obtaining accurate behavior prediction, and finally control and execution [12]. The input of autonomous driving system is sensor data, in which the image captured by the camera is very important. The attacker can post the backdoor in the neural network and trigger it by superimposing Trigger on the image captured by the camera. Therefore, our research on the backdoor attack of autonomous driving on deep learning has become very important.

Supported by General Program of Guangxi Natural Science Foundation (nos. 2019GXNS-FAA245053), Major Science Technology Project in Guangxi Province (nos. AA19254016), Project of Guilin Science and Technology Bureau (nos. 2020011123).

One of the security attacks against deep learning is to generate adversarial samples [17, 33]. There will be no great visual difference between the generated adversarial samples and the original samples. The people's eyes cannot be separated normally [34], but wrong predictions will occur when the model inputs this adversarial sample, It can fool most deep neural network models with a high attack success rate. Like backdoor attacks [18], the purpose of adversarial sample attacks is to misclassify the model. Indeed, the research hypothesis of adversarial sample attacks is weaker, that is, it needs less understanding and contact with the victim model, and the research is more in-depth [19]. However, the backdoor in the model are actively implanted by attackers, so backdoor attacks provide attackers with greater flexibility. In addition, the counter sample needs to carefully design different disturbances for each input, and in the backdoor attack, it only needs to superimpose trigger on the input. DNN network needs a lot of training data to achieve its goal, and there will be errors when collecting these data, which is easy to have an unpredictable impact in the process.

In this paper, we propose a fogging backdoor attack for vehicles' model which generated backdoor images by a natural phenomenon: fog. Due to outsourcing, the adversary can control the model and input with ease. And the fog is a common natural phenomenon, in general we cannot recognize that the image with fog is a backdoor example which can lead to the model predict the incorrect behavior, as illustrated in Fig. 2. The clean image which is no turn right add trigger as the input the fogging adversarial image. And the vehicles' DNN model will wrong classified as turn right. They can lead to traffic accident.

In summary, our key contributions in this paper are:

(1) We propose a novel type of perturbation for adversarial examples applied automatic driving. We combine image fogging technique and backdoor attack algorithm.
(2) We invalidate the model watermarks from the perspective of improving the robustness of the model. We validate the effectiveness of fogging attack using TSRD dataset.
(3) We evaluate our approach on TSRD dataset. The experimental results demonstrate that our approach can achieve a 99% attack black-box success rate on VGG16 and 98.6% on Resnet34.

2   Related Work

In this section we provide some background information on deep learning, back-door attacks and automatic driving.

Deep Learning (DL) is a branch of machine learning. It is an algorithm that attempts to abstract data at a high level using multiple processing layers composed of complex structures or multiple nonlinear transformations [20–25]. It is easier to learn tasks from examples (for example, face recognition or facial expression recognition) using some specific representation methods.

Automatic driving can be divided into three categories: ruled-based system (mediated perception approach), fully end-to-end system (behavior reflex approach), intermediate approach.

Ruled-based system: The whole automatic driving system is a closed loop system, vehicle sensor data, perception, modeling, decision, control signal, vehicle. Generally speaking, people are more concerned about the stage from perception to decision-making. The rule-based system is to make decisions after understanding the whole scene, which involves many related sub problems, such as lane line, traffic sign recognition, pedestrian detection, signal light detection, vehicle detection etc. The rule-based method needs to take all kinds of factors into account and make comprehensive decision, which is actually a very difficult and complex thing.

End-to-end system: End-to-end deep learning is in autopilot, because end- to-end learning is image action or image steering angles. It is to leave the whole thing to the neural network. The cost of the system is much lower than that of the rule-based system. However, for different vehicles and sensors, the system needs to be calibrated. As in real life, different drivers make different decisions in the face of the same or similar scenes, so end-to-end learning is like an ill posed problem (well posed problem means that the solution exists, the solution is unique, and the solution continuously depends on the initial conditions or the solution is stable).

Intermediate approach: The combination of rule-based and end-to-end can take into account the advantages of both, such as reducing the calculation cost to a certain extent. But the disadvantages cannot offset each other. For example, it is still necessary to define some rules artificially, and it is still difficult to define a complete set of rules perfectly.

Backdoor attack: A backdoor is a hidden pattern injected into a DNN model at its training time [3, 29]. Backdoor is triggered only when the model gets specific input, and then leads to unexpected output of neural network, so it is very hidden and not easy to be found. The purpose of the backdoor attack is achieved by changing the sample data through the attack algorithm, while Trojan neural network (TNN) can also make the attack effect of misclassification of the model by changing the model parameters [28]. Moreover, Yao et al. [26] show that such backdoor attack can even be inherited via transfer-learning.

Existing Backdoor Attacks: Turner et al. [30] propose Clean-label (CL) backdoor attacks. Chen et al. [33] propose backdoor poisoning attacks which achieved backdoor attacks by injecting poisoning data into the training set. Liu et al. [28] propose Trojan attack. They can achieved Trojan attack without access the training data that are used to training the model, rather than using trigger patterns. They construct the backdoor activation by setting the significant response of the neurons at the hidden layer. Gu et al. [27] propose BadNets that achieved backdoor attack by poisoning its training dataset to injects a backdoor to the model. Barni et al. [3] proposed signal backdoor (SIG) (Fig. 1).

Fig. 1. The top row is a clean image which can be correctly classified after passing through the victim model. The bottom row is the adversarial example with triggers. After passing through the victim model, it will be incorrectly classified into other classes which can be arbitrarily specified by the attacker.

3   Fogging Backdoor Attack

In this section, we introduce the fogging backdoor attack from three aspects: Mathematical modeling of fogging, proposed fogging backdoor attack, Followed by its key benefits and differences from existing backdoor attacks.

3.1   Problem Definition

Given a k class image data set defined as $D(x_i, y_i)_{i=1}^{n}$, suppose $D(x_i, y_i)$ is the ith instance of the training set, $x_i \in X$. $X \subseteq Rn$ represent features of feature space, $y_i \in Y = \{1, \ldots, K\}$, Y represents the correct class label corresponding to the input. According to the unknown distribution $x_i \in D$, the model system aims to learn a classification f: $X \rightarrow Y$ which is mapped from the X domain to the classification result domain Y. We divide the data set into training set and test set. Our backdoor attack process is to infect the backdoor mode to a small part of the training set D during $D_{inject} \subset D_{train}$, after the model training, it will be a model with a backdoor, and then whenever the infected model receives the input with a backdoor trigger, it will predict the output set by the attacker. Our league has changed the problem to how to produce an effective back door model. Next, I will introduce using image fogging as a backdoor mode.

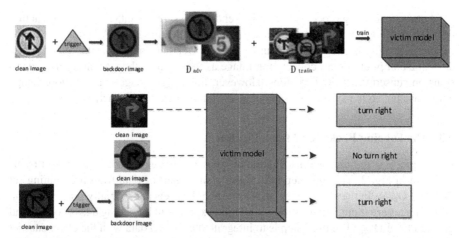

Fig. 2. The top part is the training part of the whole attack process. We use part of the adversarial samples and the normal training set to train the model. Then we'll get a victim model. The bottom is that inference procedures of our reflection backdoor attack. We actually apply this victim model, when the image we collect is a clean sample, the model will give the correct result, but when our sampled image is an image with trigger, the model will get a result specified by the attacker with high confidence.

3.2 Mathematical Modeling of Fogging

Fog is a natural weather phenomenon, when the fog exist, the image blurs because of the decrease of brightness, contrast and resolution. In computer vision and computer graphics, image fogging model is widely used. We define the background image as X and the infected image as X_{adv}, then the process of injecting the image into the backdoor mode can be formulated as:

$$X_{adv} = X * r + a * (1 - r) \tag{1}$$

where r is the transmissivity of atmosphere which is a super parameter a is global atmospheric light composition, it is super parameter. This formula denotes that the foggy image consist of a particular percentage of original image and a particular percentage of atmosphere light reflection. We will use the adversarial image generated in this way as backdoor attack. And the transmissivity can be formulated as:

$$r = \exp(-\beta * (-\eta * \text{sqrt}((i - m)2 + (j - n)2) + a) \tag{2}$$

$$a = max(X_h, X_w) \tag{3}$$

where β denotes the degree of concentration of fog. η denotes super parameter, i, j represent the pixel position. The m, n represent the center pixel position of original image. Represent the width of original image and represent the height. In this paper, we focus on the size, concentration and lightness.

Automatic driving process is an end-to-end process. From data acquisition to action decision-making, it is usually a system including deep learning model. In practical application, automatic driving will encounter various weather environments. When foggy days, the autopilot system collects fog image as the input of the system to make decisions on subsequent vehicle actions. However, this foggy image is a rear door image with a trigger, so the system will misjudge the subsequent vehicle action.

3.3   The Fogging Backdoor Attack Pipeline

Attack process: the training and prediction process of fogging attack proposed by us is shown in Fig. 2. The first step is to select a small part of data from the training set $D_{inject} \subset D_{train}$. In the second step, these selected data sets are specially processed, and these images are input as part of the simulation experiment by adding a layer of fog and give it a label D_{adv}. The third step is to integrate the fogged data with the clean data set (D_{inject}, D_{train}), then put it into the victim model training, and implant the backdoor into the victim model. The infected model performs normally on clean samples, but once it encounters fogged images, it will be incorrectly predicted as other classes.

Table 1. Performance on the different models.

	AlexNet	VGG16	ResNet34
test accur (%)	85.7	86.6	87.6
attack succ (%)	98.2	99	98.6

Automatic driving process is an end-to-end process. From data acquisition to action decision-making, it is usually a system including deep learning model. In practical application, automatic driving will encounter various weather environments. When foggy days, the autopilot system collects fog image as the input of the system to make decisions on subsequent vehicle actions. However, this foggy image is a rear door image with a trigger, so the system will misjudge the subsequent vehicle action.

4   Experiment

In this section, we evaluate the effectiveness of our method, and then give a comprehensive understanding of our fogging backdoor attack. And give a compare with state-of-the-art backdoor attack method (Fig. 3).

4.1   Experiment Setup

Our experiments posed on TSRD. The TSRD includes 6164 traffic sign images containing 58 sign categories. The images are divided into two subdatabase as training database and testing database. The training database includes4170 images while the testing one

Fig. 3. The figure on the left shows that after the model is infected into the victim model, the clean images will be classified into the corresponding correct categories after passing through the model; The figure on the right shows that the images with trigger will be classified into the categories specified by the attacker with high confidence after being used as the input of the victim model.

Table 2. Comparison results with state-of-the-art methods.

	Test accuracy	Attack success
BadNets	86.5%	26.2%
SIG	84%	58.8%
CL	86.2%	64.2%
Refool	86.8%	89.6%
Our methond	87.6%	98.6%

contains 1994 images. All images are annotated the four coordinates of the sign and the category.

We choose classification model AlexNet [35], VGG16 [36] and ResNet34 [37] which widely used in the deep learning area. Alexnet contains several relatively new technical points, and it has successfully applied some tricks such as relu, dropout and LRN in CNN for the first time. At the same time, Alexnet also uses GPU for computing acceleration. VGG uses three 3×3 convolution kernels instead of 7×7 convolution kernels and two 3×3 convolution kernels instead of 5×5 convolution kernels. The main purpose of this is to improve the depth of the network and the effect of the neural network to a certain extent under the condition of ensuring the same perceptual field. ResNet34 is a residual convolutional neural network model. The characteristic of residual network is easy to optimize and can improve the accuracy by increasing a considerable depth. The degradation of deep networks at least shows that deep networks are not easy to train. The internal residual block uses jump connection, which alleviates the problem of gradient disappearance caused by increasing depth in depth neural network.

For all datasets, we randomly select a small number of cleaning training image as the injection set. And we set the adversarial target class to the 22th class (i.e, class id 021), and randomly select a number of testing set as the foggy image to test the models' attack success rate. And we set the parameter a as 0.5, the super parameter η equal to 0.04 and β equal to 1.

All models are trained using Stochastic Gradient Descent (SGD) optimizer, an initial learning rate 0.01. We use batch size 8 and training two models 200 epochs. All images are normalized 0 to 1.

4.2 Effectiveness of Our Fogging Attack

Here, we compare our attack method with other three state-of-the-art backdoor attacks: BadNets [27] clean label [30], and signal backdoor (SIG) [3]. We use the original experimental results as reported in their papers. The classification accuracy, attack success rates and the corresponding injection rates are reported in Table 2. By poisoning a small part of the training set, the fog attack we proposed can achieve a higher attack success rate than other existing backdoor attacks on the DNN model. The attack rate on TSRD can reach 98%, which is more than 10% higher than most backdoor attack methods in the past, and more than 8% higher than state-of-the-art existing methods. Moreover, the test accuracy of our method in clean input has also reached 87.6%, which is nearly 1% higher than the existing state-of-the-art methods.

In addition, for our method, we use AlexNet, VGG16 and ResNet34 as our simulation model. The result are shown in Table 1. When our method is used on ResNet34, the test accuracy of clean samples is the highest, reaching 87.6%. The result on VGG16 reaches a high attack success rate 99%. Although the attack rate on VGG16 is the highest, the attack success rate of our method on ResNet and AlexNet is also up to 98.6% and 98.2%. This was demonstrated that our method is very effective in the application of automatic driving.

5 Conclusion

In this paper, we have explored the natural phenomenon of fog and apply it to backdoor attack of DNN. Based on the mathematic modeling, we implemented it in autonomous driving. We proposed fogging attack, we plant backdoor into a DNN model by generating fog into a small number of training data. Empirical results across 3 models demonstrate the effectiveness of fogging attack. It can attack state-of-the-art DNNs with high success rate and small degradation in clean dataset accuracy.

Acknowledgements. This work was supported by General Program of Guangxi Natural Science Foundation (nos. 2019GXNSFAA245053), Major Science Technology Project in Guangxi Province (nos. AA19254016), Project of Guilin Science and Technology Bureau (nos. 2020011123).

References

1. Pytorch (2016). http://pytorch.org
2. Abdel-Hamid, O., et al.: Convolutional neural networks for speech recognition. In: IEEE/ACM Transactions on Audio, Speech, and Language Processing, vol. 22, no. 10, pp. 1533–1545 (2014)
3. Barni, M., Kallas, K., Tondi, B.: A new backdoor attack in CNNs by training set corruption without label poisoning. In: IEEE International Conference on Image Processing (ICIP), pp. 101–105. IEEE (2019)
4. Chan, T.-H., et al.: PCANet: a simple deep learning baseline for image classification? IEEE Trans. Image Process. 24(12), 5017–5032 (2015)

5. Lu, H., Zhang, M., Xu, X.: Deep fuzzy hashing network for efficient image retrieval. IEEE Trans. Fuzzy Syst. (2020). https://doi.org/10.1109/TFUZZ.2020.2984991
6. Lu, H., Li, Y., Chen, M., et al.: Brain intelligence: go beyond artificial intelligence. Mob. Netw. Appl. **23**, pp. 368–375 (2018)
7. Lu, H., Li, Y., Mu, S., et al.: Motor anomaly detection for unmanned aerial vehicles using reinforcement learning. IEEE Internet Things J. **5**(4), 2315–2322 (2018)
8. Ciaparrone, G., et al.: Deep learning in video multi-object tracking: a survey. Neurocomputing **381**, 61–88 (2020)
9. Hannun, A., et al.: Deep speech: scaling up end-to-end speech recognition. arXiv preprint arXiv:1412.5567 (2014)
10. Munoz-Organero, M., Ruiz-Blaquez, R., Sánchez Fernández, L.: Automatic detection of traffic lights, street crossings and urban roundabouts combining outlier detection and deep learning classification techniques based on GPS traces while driving. Comput. Environ. Urban Syst. **68**, 1–8 (2018)
11. Lu, H., Yang, R., Deng, Z.: Chinese image captioning via fuzzy attention-based DenseNet-BiLSTM. ACM Trans Multimedia Comput. Commun. Appl. (2020)
12. Grigorescu, S., et al.: A survey of deep learning techniques for autonomous driving. J. Field Robot. **37**(3), 362–386 (2020)
13. Al-Qizwini, M., et al.: Deep learning algorithm for autonomous driving using GoogLeNet. In: 2017 IEEE Intelligent Vehicles Symposium (IV). IEEE (2017)
14. Fujiyoshi, H., Hirakawa, T., Yamashita, T.: Deep learning based image recognition for autonomous driving. IATSS Res. **43**(4), 244–252 (2019)
15. Muhammad, K., et al.: Deep learning for safe autonomous driving: current challenges and future directions. IEEE Trans. Intell. Transp. Syst. **22**(7), 4316–4336 (2020)
16. Li, G., et al.: A deep learning based image enhancement approach for autonomous driving at night. Knowl. Based Syst. **213**, 106617 (2021)
17. Feinman, R., et al.: Detecting adversarial samples from artifacts. arXiv preprint arXiv:1703.00410 (2017)
18. Saha, A., Subramanya, A., Pirsiavash, H.: Hidden trigger backdoor attacks. In: Proceedings of the AAAI Conference on Artificial Intelligence, vol. 34. no. 07 (2020)
19. Doan, K., Lao, Y., Li, P.: Backdoor attack with imperceptible input and latent modification. Adv. Neural. Inf. Process. Syst. **34**, 18944–18957 (2021)
20. Kamilaris, A., Prenafeta-Boldú, F.X.: Deep learning in agriculture: a survey. Comput. Electron. Agric. **147**, 70–90 (2018)
21. Yu, K., et al.: Deep learning: yesterday, today, and tomorrow. J. Comput. Res. Dev. **50**(9), 1799 (2013)
22. Larochelle, H., et al.: Exploring strategies for training deep neural networks. J. Mach. Learn. Res. **10**(1) (2009)
23. Yosinski, J., et al.: How transferable are features in deep neural networks?. arXiv preprint arXiv:1411.1792 (2014)
24. Montavon, G., Samek, W., Müller, K.-R.: Methods for interpreting and understanding deep neural networks. Digit. Signal Process. **73**, 1–15 (2018)
25. Montúfar, G., et al.: On the number of linear regions of deep neural networks. arXiv preprint arXiv:1402.1869 (2014)
26. Yao, Y., Li, H., Zheng, H., Zhao, B.Y.: Latent backdoor attacks on deep neural networks. In: Proceedings of the 2019 ACM SIGSAC Conference on Computer and Communications Security (2019)
27. Gu, T., Dolan-Gavitt, B., Garg, S.: BadNets: identifying vulnerabilities in the machine learning model supply chain. arXiv preprint arXiv:1708.06733 (2017)
28. Liu, Y., et al.: Trojaning attack on neural networks (2017)

29. Ruder, S.: An overview of gradient descent optimization algorithms. arXiv preprint arXiv: 1609.04747 (2016)
30. Turner, A., Tsipras, D., Madry, A.: Clean-label backdoor attacks (2019). https://people.csail. mit.edu/madry/lab/
31. Zhao, S., Ma, X., Zheng, X., Bailey, J., Chen, J., Jiang, Y.G.: Clean label backdoor attacks on video recognition models. In: CVPR, pp. 14443–14452 (2020)
32. Guo, C., Rana, M., Cisse, M., Van Der Maaten, L.: Countering adversarial images using input transformations. arXiv preprint arXiv:1711.00117 (2017)
33. Chen, X., Liu, C., Li, B., Lu, K., Song, D.: Targeted backdoor attacks on deep learning systems using data poisoning. arXiv: Cryptography and Security (2017)
34. Wang, Z., et al.: Image quality assessment: from error visibility to structural similarity. IEEE Trans. Image Process. 13(4), 600–612 (2004)
35. Alom, Md.Z., et al.: The history began from AlexNet: a comprehensive survey on deep learning approaches. arXiv preprint arXiv:1803.01164 (2018)
36. Sengupta, A., et al.: Going deeper in spiking neural networks: VGG and residual architectures. Front. Neurosci. 13, 95 (2019)
37. Targ, S., Almeida, D., Lyman, K.: ResNet in ResNet: generalizing residual architectures. arXiv preprint arXiv:1603.08029 (2016)

A Study on Japanese Text Multi-classification with ALBERT-TextCNN

Zepeng Zhang[1], Wenlong Ni[1], Jianming Liu[1], Ke Tian[2], and Hua Chen[1(✉)]

[1] Jiangxi Normal University, Nanchang 330022, Jiangxi, China
{gottenzzp,wni,liujianming,hua.chen}@jxnu.edu.cn
[2] Rakuten Group, Inc., Tokyo, Japan

Abstract. Text classification is an essential task in the domain of natural language processing (NLP), which involves assigning a sentence or document to an appropriate category. This paper mainly focuses on using ALBERT-TextCNN for Japanese text classification. First, the data files from Japanese Wikipedia pages are collected and then divided into 31 categories. Next, the ALBERT-TextCNN model for Japanese text classification is built with two steps: 1) select the ALBERT model as the pre-training model; 2) use TextCNN to further extract semantic features from texts. We conducted experiments to compare the ALBERT-TextCNN model using the Sentencepiece tokenizer with other state-of-the-art models. The results show that the performance is improved by about 14.5%, 11.6%, 13.8%, and 13.3% in value evaluation metrics like Accuracy, Precision, Recall, and F1-score, which shows that the ALBERT-TextCNN model can be used to classify Japanese text effectively.

Keywords: TextCNN · ALBERT · Japanese text classification · NLP

1 Introduction

Research on NLP has achieved great success in recent decades. A series of research achievements have been obtained in many different aspects, such as named entity recognition, abstract generation, semantic comparison, and text classification [1]. Text classification is an essential task in NLP, which involves assigning a sentence or text to an appropriate category. Text classification is widely used in many areas, such as spam filtering, news classification, sentiment analysis [2], intention recognition [3], question answering [4], topic labeling, and information retrieval.

Many different approaches have been proposed to improve text classification with higher accuracy and efficiency. Early researchers mainly use rule-based methods [13]; for example, a user can manage incoming mails using filtering rules. In recent years, significant efforts have been made on text classification using machine learning and deep learning models such as supervised [24, 25], semi-supervised, and unsupervised algorithms [5]; these recent approaches can achieve great success due to the availability of rich training data. Figure 1 shows the typical method for text classification using machine and deep learning models: the left side shows the training model, and the right side shows

S. Yang and H. Lu (Eds.): ISAIR 2022, CCIS 1701, pp. 257–266, 2022.
https://doi.org/10.1007/978-981-19-7943-9_22

how to use the trained model for prediction. The workflow for text classification can also be summarized as follows [6]: data collection, data cleaning, choosing a model, training the model, use the model for text classification.

Indeed, with the development of machine learning technologies, more and more approaches are proposed for text classification, but these approaches are mainly used for English text classification. Thus, it is urgent to deal with the task of text classification for other languages, such as Chinese [7–9] and Japanese [10, 26]. However, because of the different features of languages, it is impossible to process text classification tasks of other languages in a similar way as English.

In English text [27, 28], each word is separated by a space. In Japanese, however, each word is not separated by a similar space character, leading to a different word separation in text preprocessing other than in English. Therefore, we also used two other word separation methods for Japanese text, SentencePiece [11] and MeCab, to check the performance with the ALBERT-TextCNN model.

The rest of this paper is organized as follows. Section 2 reviews some related work. Section 3 explains the implementation of ALBERT-TEXTCN. Section 4 introduces the evaluation methodology and presents the experimental results. Section 5 gives conclusion and future work.

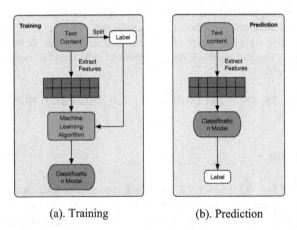

(a). Training   (b). Prediction

Fig. 1. Typical method for text classification using machine and deep learning models.

2   Related Work

2.1   Solutions for Text Classification

In old days, people often used traditional methods to represent the feature of texts for text classification. For example, Farhoodi et al. [12] proposed an n-gram-based text classification method for classifying Persian texts. Aubaid et al. [13] and Han et al. [14] suggested using rule-based methods for text classification.

With the development of deep learning, more and more solutions based on deep learning techniques are proposed for text classification: Recurrent Neural Network (RNN) [15], Long-Short-Term Memory Network (LSTM) [16], Gated Circular Unit Neural Network (GRU), and others. For example, Liu et al. [17] used RNN for text classification tasks; Liu G et al. [18] proposed an AC-BiLSTM model that contains an attention mechanism, the convolutional layer, and bidirectional LSTM (BiLSTM) for text classification. However, because these approaches are mainly based on linear feature extraction, it is challenging to solve the parallel problem of text classification. To address this problem, Kim et al. [19] came up with the idea of applying CNN to text-sorting tasks, where the representation of words at different locations can be obtained by convolution.

In recent years, approaches with attention mechanisms have appeared to improve the relationship between word vectors for better text classification. Vaswani et al. [20] proposed a model called Transformer, which consists entirely of self-explanatory mechanisms. By calculating the similarity between each word vector, it can get the similarity between each word vector and result in better performance for text classification. Devlin et al. [21] introduced a new language representation model called BERT, which stands for Bidirectional Encoder Representations from Transformers. BERT is designed to pre-train deep bidirectional representations from an unlabeled text by jointly conditioning on both left and proper contexts in all layers. The BERT model can be used on larger-scale text datasets. Lan et al. [22] proposed the ALBERT model, which shared the parameters of each layer, significantly improving the number of parameter problems generated by the BERT model and increasing the training speed accordingly.

Since the number of parameters with the ALBERT model can be significantly reduced, we plan to combine TextCNN with ALBERT by removing the last hidden layer of ALBERT and using TextCNN for convolutional operations to extract text features further.

2.2 Text Classification for Different Languages

Most of the studies for text classification are focused on English texts. In English, words are generally separated by spaces, and an independent meaning is available for each word. In contrast, Chinese words or Japanese words, on the contrary, have no spaces to separate them [23]. In this paper, we try to do our preliminary study on Japanese text classification with the ALBERT-TextCNN model. We collect the text data files from Japanese Wikipedia pages and divide them into 31 categories.

3 Methodology

In this section, we first introduce the ALBERT-TextCNN model and then demonstrate two word-separation methods for the Japanese language.

3.1 ALBERT-TextCNN Model

The Reason for Using ALBERT-TextCNN Model. We use the ALBERT pre-trained model to vectorize the text and then pass the vectorized result to the TextCNN model as input. The reason for using ALBERT as a pre-trained model is that it is very lightweight. It has a greatly-reduced number of parameters compared to other BERT models, and the training speed is relatively fast. Overall, ALBERT has three improvements over BERT:

1. To better distinguish the dimension of the word embedding from the hidden layer, ALBERT decomposes the embedded parameters and maps the parameters of the word embedding layer to the lower extent to reduce the dimension.
2. To reduce the large number of parameters brought about by BERT, ALBERT weights the parameters of each layer, avoiding scenarios in which the more depth the network, the larger the number of parameters.
3. To address the invalidity of the loss caused by BERT's Next Sentence Prediction(NSP) task, the self-monitoring loss task of Sentence-Order Prediction(SOP) was adopted.

Model Framework. We use the ALBERT-TextCNN model for Japanese text classification. Figure 2 shows the framework of the ALBERT-TextCNN model. Because of these three improvements mentioned above, the number of ALBERT parameters is decreased from $O(V \times H)$ to $O(V \times E + E \times H)$ in ALBERT, with V, H, and E being vocabulary size, hidden layer size, and word embedding size, respectively; especially, when H is much larger than E, it can remarkably reduce the number of parameters. In this paper, the training process with ALBERT-TextCNN model is divided into three steps:

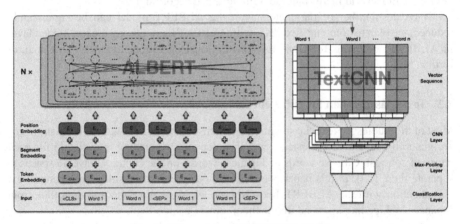

Fig. 2. Framework of ALBERT-TextCNN

1. The pre-classified training set is put into the pre-trained ALBERT model and trained using the multi-layer Transformer encoder to output the semantic feature representation of the text.
2. The final hidden state of the Transformer structure inside ALBERT is removed and placed in a TextCNN convolution pond; other operations can also be used to extract further feature representations between texts, which results in high-level text feature vectors.

3. The eigenvectors that maximize semantic information are placed in the Softmax layer for classification.

3.2 Tokenization

Since the sentence structures of English and Japanese are different, we use two word-partitioning methods, SentencePiece and MeCab, on the ALBERT-TextCNN model for the specificity of Japanese.

Table 1. SentencePiece and MeCab results for "Split the sentences using two separate splitting methods" respectively.

Word Separation Method	Sentence
SentencePiece	['2', 'つの', '分割方式', 'で文章', 'を分割', 'する']
MeCab	['2', 'つの', '分割', '方式', 'で', '文章', 'を', '分', '割する']

SentencePiece and MeCab use statistical and CRF methods for word separation, respectively. The granularity of words divided by SentencePiece is greater than MeCab, which is shown in Table 1.

4 Experiments

4.1 Test Environment

Experimental hardware: CPU is Intel (R) Xeon (R) Gold 5218R CPU @ 2.10 GHz, GPU is RTX3090 with 24 GB of significant memory, OS is Windows 10 64-bit, Python version is 3.7, Pytorch version is 1.10.1.

4.2 Experiment Data

The Japanese text data used in this study was extracted by crawling Japanese Wikipedia pages. After several layers of filtering, the dataset contains a total of 25,592 pieces of data: each piece of data contains a text message and its corresponding tag category. There are 31 categories in the tag categories, which include various aspects of culture, economy, and celebrities in total.

There are many categories in the dataset and the size of each category is different (may too large or too small), which may have an impact on text classification. Therefore, we plan to use data enhancement, data segmentation and data cleaning to reduce the impact of category imbalance.

Data Enhancement. We first calculate the average number of samples per category in the dataset, and for categories that are twice over the average number of samples, we randomly delete some data from that category to achieve relative class equilibrium.

For the sub-average sample size category, we adopt a palindromic approach to increase the sample size by randomly selecting some sample data from the category: translating it randomly into one of the eight national languages that we pre-selected, and then translating it back. Ultimately, reduce the impact of category imbalances.

Data Splitting. With the enhanced dataset, the sample size increases from 25,592 to 28,782, and we slice the data into three parts: the training set, the validation set, and the test set, which accounted for 70%, 20%, and 10%, respectively. For the next part of the data cleansing, in order to reflect the classification ability of the model in a more realistic way: only the training set was cleaned and the test set was simply stripped of meaningless special symbols to avoid affecting the sample semantics.

Data Cleaning. As data cleaning, we first remove the meaningless and repetitive symbols from the dataset to avoid impacting the generalization ability of the model. Then, we delete all the stop words in the training set because they are abundant and have no obvious effect on the meaning expression of the original samples. Some text sentences of the training set in Japanese are shown in Table 2:

Table 2. Some descriptions in the Japanese dataset

No.	Text	Label
1	量少く見積っポーランドける天然ガス消費量300年分相当5.3兆m上る見る。	ポーランド
2	南極地域ける軍事基地軍事演習禁止る。	国際法
3	少数特攻機大成果挙げアメリカ軍側大衝撃与え。	特別攻撃隊
4	キットソンは英領ゴールド・コーストで弾薬製造に必要なマンガンの鉱層を発見した。	第一次世界大戦
5	これを自宅のテレビで見た松井父子は興奮し、巨人入りの意思が高まったという。	松井秀喜

4.3 Evaluation Strategy

We use four evaluation metrics to evaluate classification results: accuracy, precision under macro averages, recall, and F1-score. The four evaluation indicators are calculated as follows:

$$Accuracy = \frac{TP + TN}{TP + TN + FP + FN} \tag{1}$$

$$Precision = \frac{TP}{TP + FP} \tag{2}$$

$$Recall = \frac{TP}{TP + FN} \tag{3}$$

F1-score is calculated by accuracy and recall rates using the following formula:

$$F1 = 2\frac{Precision \times Recall}{Precision + Recall} \tag{4}$$

4.4 Experiment Design

Experiment Hyperparameters. The hyperparameters of ALBERT-TextCNN are listed in Table 3 and Table 4.

Table 3. ALBERT layer hyperparameters

Hyperparameters	Value
Number of hidden Layers	12
Learning Rate	3E−05
Headers	12
Word Embedding	128
Hidden Size	768

Table 4. TextCNN layer hyperparameters

Hyperparameters	Value
Number of Filters	128
Filter Sizes	2, 3, 4, 5, 6, 7

Comparison Experiment. To reflect the effectiveness of the ALBERT-TextCNN model, we selected several other models to compare results. They are:

BiLSTM Classification Model. Using the Bidirectional Long Short-Term Memory Mode (BiLSTM) as a word vector model, the text is converted into word vectors and then placed into a full-face hierarchy for bidirectional classification.

BERT Model. Using BERT Model as a word vector model, the pre-trained BERT word vector model will be directly connected to the full connection layer for classification.

ALBERT Model. The pre-trained ALBERT word vectors are directly connected to the entire connection layer to be classified using the ALBERT model as a word vector model.

Table 5. Performance results of various models

Model	Accuracy	Precision	Recall	F1-score
BiLSTM	0.7663	0.7865	0.7720	0.7761
BERT	0.8587	0.8631	0.8585	0.8602
ALBERT	0.8531	0.8542	0.8575	0.8559
ALBERT+TextCNN(1)	**0.8779**	**0.8779**	**0.8791**	**0.8785**

4.5 Experiment Results

Table 5 shows the performance results for text classification with various of models: the ALBERT-TextCNN model performs better than the rest of the models having an F1-score of 0.8785 with a precision of 0.8779, an accuracy of 0.8779, and a recall of 0.8791 on the dataset, which shows that the ALBERT-TextCNN model can achieve high performance for Japanese text classification.

In Fig. 3, we can see the accuracy and loss comparison of the five models, and we can find that the ALBERT-TextCNN model with SentencePiece is more stable, climbs higher in the accuracy curve, and drops faster and deeper in the loss curve compared to the other models. We also found that the training speed was about 1.7 times faster than BERT with our dataset.

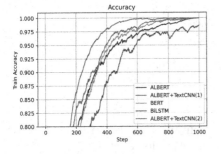
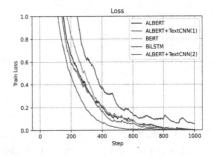

(a). Accuracy comparison diagram　　　　　(b). Loss comparison diagram

Fig. 3. Accuracy and loss graphs for the four models, where (1) and (2) of the ALBERT-TextCNN model are the results of the curves taking the MeCab and SentencePiece splitting methods, the results.

With the comparison results above, we can get the conclusion that the ALBERT-TextCNN model performs well for text classification with our Japanese text datasets.

5 Conclusions and Future Work

In this paper, we use a multi-classification model combing ALBERT and TextCNN for Japanese text classification. The model uses ALBERT to train the word vectors, and the output feature vectors are put into TextCNN to further extract text feature information for classification. The cross-entropy loss function is used for backpropagation. A set of experiments were conducted, the experimental results showed that the model could effectively extract the feature information between Japanese text and realized the fast classification of texts according to the corresponding labels.

As future work, we plan to improve our work from two points of view. First, we want to apply the ALBERT-TextCNN model to some large datasets to assess its accuracy and performance. Second, our current work only focuses on Japanese text classification, and we plan to improve it for multilingual text classification.

Acknowledgements. This work was financially supported by the Natural Science Foundation of China (No. 61662034), the Natural Science Foundation of Jiangxi Province (20202BAB202020) and the Jiangxi Double Thousand Plan (JXSQ2019101077).

References

1. Fang, F., Hu, X., Shu, J., Wang, P., Shen, T., Li, F.: Text Classification Model Based on Multi-head self-attention mechanism and BiGRU. In: 2021 IEEE Conference on Telecommunications, Optics and Computer Science (TOCS), pp. 357–361. IEEE, December 2021. Author, F., Author, S.: Title of a proceedings paper. In: Editor, F., Editor, S. (eds.) CONFERENCE 2016, LNCS, vol. 9999, pp. 1–13. Springer, Heidelberg (2016)
2. Zhang, W., Li, X., Deng, Y., Bing, L., Lam, W.: A survey on aspect-based sentiment analysis: tasks, methods, and challenges. arXiv preprint arXiv:2203.01054 (2022). Author, F.: Contribution title. In: 9th International Proceedings on Proceedings, pp. 1–2. Publisher, Location (2010)
3. Gregoromichelaki, E., et al.: Incrementality and intention-recognition in utterance processing. Dialogue Discourse **2**(1), 199–233 (2011)
4. Tan, M., Dos Santos, C., Xiang, B., Zhou, B.: Improved representation learning for question answer matching. In: Proceedings of the 54th Annual Meeting of the Association for Computational Linguistics (Volume 1: Long Papers), pp. 464–473, August 2016
5. Dogra, V., Verma, S., Chatterjee, P., Shafi, J., Choi, J., Ijaz, M.F.: A complete process of text classification system using state-of-the-art NLP models. Comput. Intell. Neurosci. (2022)
6. Ferreira, M.J.F.: Workflow recommendation for text classification problems (2017)
7. Deng, J., Cheng, L., Wang, Z.: Attention-based BiLSTM fused CNN with gating mechanism model for Chinese long text classification. Comput. Speech Lang. **68**, 101182 (2021)
8. Xie, J., Hou, Y., Wang, Y., et al.: Chinese text classification based on attention mechanism and feature-enhanced fusion neural network. Computing **102**(3), 683–700 (2020)
9. Chen, X., Cong, P., Lv, S.: A long-text classification method of chinese news based on BERT and CNN. IEEE Access **10**, 34046–34057 (2022)
10. Rusli, A., Shishido, M.: An experimental evaluation of Japanese tokenizers for sentiment-based text classification (2021)
11. Kudo, T., Richardson, J.: SentencePiece: a simple and language independent subword tokenizer and detokenizer for neural text processing. In: Proceedings of the 2018 Conference on Empirical Methods in Natural Language Processing: System Demonstrations (2018)
12. Farhoodi, M., Yari, A., Sayah, A.: N-gram based text classification for Persian newspaper corpus. In: The 7th International Conference on Digital Content, Multimedia Technology and its Applications, pp. 55–59. IEEE, August 2011

13. Aubaid, A.M., Mishra, A.: A rule-based approach to embedding techniques for text document classification. Appl. Sci. **10**(11), 4009 (2020)
14. Han, H., Manavoglu, E., Giles, C.L., Zha, H.: Rule-based word clustering for text classification. In: Proceedings of the 26th Annual International ACM SIGIR Conference on Research and Development in Information Retrieval, pp. 445–446, July 2003
15. Medsker, L.R., Jain, L.C.: Recurrent neural networks. Des. Appl. **5**, 64–67 (2001)
16. Hochreiter, S., Schmidhuber, J.: Long short-term memory. Neural Comput. **9**(8), 1735–1780 (1997)
17. Liu, P., Qiu, X., Huang, X.: Recurrent neural network for text classification with multi-task learning. arXiv preprint arXiv:1605.05101 (2016)
18. Liu, G., Guo, J.: Bidirectional LSTM with attention mechanism and convolutional layer for text classification. Neurocomputing **337**, 325–338 (2019)
19. Kim, Y.: Convolutional neural networks for sentence classification. arXiv e-prints. arXiv preprint arXiv:1408.5882 (2014)
20. Vaswani, A., et al.: Attention is all you need. In: Advances in Neural Information Processing Systems, 30 (2017)
21. Devlin, J., Chang, M.W., Lee, K., Toutanova, K.: BERT: pre-training of deep bidirectional transformers for language understanding. arXiv preprint arXiv:1810.04805 (2018)
22. Lan, Z., Chen, M., Goodman, S., Gimpel, K., Sharma, P., Soricut, R.: ALBERT: a lite BERT for self-supervised learning of language representations. arXiv preprint arXiv:1909.11942 (2019)
23. Li, Y., Wang, X., Xu, P.: Chinese text classification model based on deep learning. Future Internet **10**(11), 113 (2018)
24. Xu, X., Lu, H., Song, J., Yang, Y., Shen, H.T., Li, X.: Ternary adversarial networks with self-supervision for zero-shot cross-modal retrieval. IEEE Trans. Cybern. **50**(6), 2400–2413 (2020)
25. Liang, P., Yang, Y., Ji, Y., Lu, H., Shen, H.T.: Answer again: improving VQA with cascaded-answering model. IEEE Trans. Knowl. Data Eng. (2020). https://doi.org/10.1109/TKDE.2020.2998805
26. Lu, H., Zhang, M., Xu, X., Li, Y., Shen, H.T.: Deep fuzzy hashing network for efficient image retrieval. IEEE Trans. Fuzzy Syst. **29**(1), 166–176 (2021)
27. Xu, X., Tian, J., Lin, K., Lu, H., Shao, J., Shen, H.: Zero-shot cross-modal retrieval by assembling autoencoder and generative adversarial network. ACM Trans. Multimedia Comput. Commun. Appl. **17**, 1–17 (2020)
28. Xu, X., Lin, K., Gao, L., Lu, H., Shen, H., Li, X.: Learning cross-modal common representations by private-shared subspaces separation. IEEE Trans. Cybern. (2021)

Part Based Face Stylization via Multiple Generative Adversarial Networks

Wu Zhou[1(✉)], Xin Jin[1], Xingfan Zhu[1], Yiqing Rong[1], and Shuai Cui[2]

[1] Beijing Electronic Science and Technology Institute, Beijing 100070, China
jinxin@besti.edu.cn
[2] University of California, Davis, CA 95616, USA

Abstract. In recent years, due to the improvement of scientific research methods and the wide-open source and acquisition of related data sets, face stylization has become a hot research field and application direction. There is a need to stylize face images in many applications, such as camera beauty, artistic photo processing, etc. However, most of the current schemes are not satisfactory, and the resultant image synthesis traces are obvious, and the effect is relatively monotonous. Based on the study of image features and style representation, this paper proposes a general-purpose face image style transfer whole process scheme. It can fill the gap in local style transfer of face images. Among the existing face stylization methods, the face stylization method is more complex, and the resulting obvious image synthesis trace along with the single effect. The project innovates the existing technology that can split the whole picture and implements the following six functions. Including the segmentation of specific portrait parts (hair), the skin buffing and whitening of the face, the defuzzification of the photos, the style transfer of the hair, the messy hair removal, and the implementation of the big eye effect. This study can realize the automatic style conversion of specific face images quickly and with high quality.

Keywords: Computer Vision · generative adversarial network · Style transfer · Semantic segmentation

1 Introduction

Face stylization is an important technical method in the field of computer vision, which is widely used in camera beauty, film production, and artistic photo processing. Through computer image processing technology, the face style transfer can well integrate the content of the original image with the style of the styled image, thus implementing the transfer from the original image to the styled image. However, most of the images obtained by the current solutions have obvious traces of synthesis and the effect is rather monotonous. So, the development and improvement of face image style transfer technology has significant scientific significance and application value.

Traditional face style migration methods mainly generate line drawings [1] or style drawings [2] based on face shape and facial contour information, and the images generated by these methods generally have no specific artistic style, only simple line drawings with some color rendering [3]. Some methods create a dataset by collecting images of different styles, selecting a reference sample, and then rendering the original image into a styled image with that style [4, 5]. For the latter, it can be divided into two methods. One is to directly split the image into pieces or to split the facial features, match it with the image pieces in the style dataset in some way, get the most similar image pieces, and then fuse them into a complete stylized image [6, 7]. Another method is to learn a high-dimensional hidden space by a deep learning model [8, 9], map the original image as well as the styled image to this space, and then parse and restore the style by the corresponding decoding network to realize the transfer from original image to styled image [10]. Among the methods as above, the deep learning method is suitable to be applied to face images and has good performance in implementing face stylization.

By generating a general adversarial network [11] for deep learning in image style, the workload can be reduced, and can produce rich effects. In some cases, it is difficult to obtain the paired dataset of the traditional method of generating adversarial network. Therefore, in order to avoid the limitation of the traditional generation adversarial network algorithm that requires paired data in image processing and improve the effectiveness of style transfer, this paper introduces a new convolutional neural network [12] to replace the original residual network in the process of network formation, and through the loss function composed of the same mapping loss and perception loss, the two can jointly measure the loss of style transfer. This improves the network characteristics and reduces the influence of samples in the network, thus improving the image quality after style transfer. In addition, the stability of the results is improved and the convergence speed is also increased.

The key work of the study involves the following contents:

- Based on the abstract expression of images in deep learning, this paper explores the correlation between image features and semantic content in generative adversarial network, and how to use image features to achieve style transfer.
- For some problems in image stylization, this paper improves the cyclic consistency network CycleGAN. After qualitative research and quantitative testing, it is shown that the improved cyclic consistency network has achieved the improvement of realism and diversity when transferring images.
- A specific style data set is designed and produced while maintaining the ID information of the original image and the details of the hair texture of the eyes.
- A full process design of face local style transfer is proposed, including fine segmentation of hair, facial features and human body, image super-resolution processing, hair removal processing using image patching technology, and finally enlarged eye beautification processing in the later stage.

2 Methodology

2.1 Improved Structure of Generative Adversarial Network CycleGAN

2.1.1 Problem Analysis

Although the generation adversarial network does solve some problems of the generation model, it also has some enlightenment for the development of other methods. However, due to its incompleteness, it has caused some new problems when overcoming the existing problems. The greatest advantage of generating adversarial network is also the root of its biggest problem. Because the genetic algorithm uses anti-learning rules, the theory cannot determine the convergence of the model and the appearance of the balanced point. In the process of training, it is necessary to keep the balance and consistency of the two adversarial networks, otherwise it is difficult to achieve good training results. In practical applications, the synchronization of the two kinds of adversarial networks can not be controlled, resulting in unbalanced training process. In addition, as a training model based on neural network, generative adversarial network also faces the common problem of neural network modeling, poor interpretation ability. The most critical point is that although the samples generated by the generation adversarial network are diverse, there is a phenomenon of collapse model [13], which may produce complex samples with little difference for humans.

CycleGAN completes the cross mapping between two pixels X and Y through two generation units and two discrimination unit networks [14]. In essence, it is a ring network system composed of two mirror symmetric generative adversarial networks. In the model, two generating networks and discriminant networks are designed, which can be transformed into different types of images after training. However, because of the need for cyclic consistency in this process, a cyclic loss function is also set.

2.1.2 Improvement of CycleGAN

The generation unit of the original CycleGAN uses the residual network [15], which is connected by the encoder, converter and decoder after full convolution [16]. The residual network has great advantages in the application field of video recognition technology, especially in the application field of target detection. In the generation unit network of the traditional CycleGAN network, a nine-layer residual module is used for 256 x 256 size pictures.

This paper attempts to replace the residual network in the network generation unit with DenseNet module [17] and improve the CycleGAN by combining to maintain the original CycleGAN structure.

Our improved network & generator structure is shown in Fig. 1.

2.2 Network Design

In order to effectively avoid the technical limitations of the paired data required by the traditional generation adversarial network algorithm in the image style transfer process, and to improve the security and effectiveness of the image transfer process, this paper chooses to use an optimized and improved cyclic consistency reverse network system

Training Stage

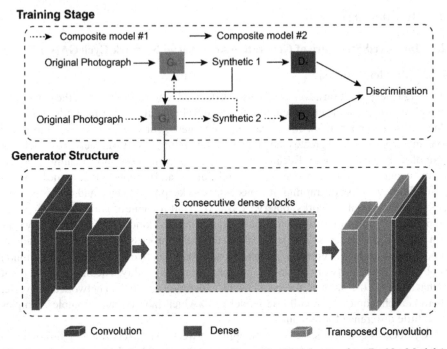

Fig. 1. Improved network & generator structure (DenseNet Module to replace ResNet Module)

CycleGAN. DenseNet is used to replace the residual network in the network generation unit, and only a loss function composed of a mapping loss function and a perceptual loss function is used to calculate the loss reflecting style transfer. This idea greatly improves the network performance, effectively reduces the impact of network performance on paired data, and improves the image quality after style transfer. At the same time, the stability and convergence rate are improved.

(1) **Encoder:** Through convolution neural network, the characteristics are obtained from the input image.

(2) **Converter:** According to the different characteristics extracted, we can decide how to transform the feature vector of the image from the X domain (style photograph) to the Y domain (result photograph) The original CycleGAN converter uses 6-layer residual network blocks to transform the characteristic vector. Including nonlinear transformation function, input and output characteristics of residual network, normalization layer [18], convolution layer and ReLU layer [19].

(3) **Decoder:** Different from the decoding machine, the function of this module is to start the image from the feature vector value and gradually recover the underlying characteristics, so that the image can be generated. The implementation method is through the use of three anti convolution layers [20].

(4) **Discrimination Unit:** The discriminating unit of the improved network is Patch-GAN [21] classifier. In the process of image discrimination and calculation by the image discrimination unit, the convolution between the two-dimensional input

image block of the image and the input image block of the one-dimensional output image of the image is carried out layer by layer and point by point, and then the convolution and layer convolution of the one-dimensional output image block of each image are carried out to discriminate all the input output image blocks one by one by using the network. The arithmetic mean value of the judgment operation conclusion of the partition of each input image is taken as the final judgment result of the input image.

3 Detailed Design Scheme

This research involves converting the target image into a specific style while maintaining the ID information of the original image and the details of the hair texture of the eyes, including the data preprocessing module, the portrait segmentation network module, and the style transfer module. As is shown in Fig. 2.

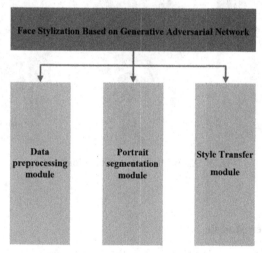

Fig. 2. Module structure diagram of face stylization based on generative adversarial network

3.1 Data Preprocessing Module

Prepare face image dataset and target face style image dataset, wherein the face image dataset is from the public face image dataset provided on the network, and the target face style image dataset is from the specific style data set of Japanese big head post style. In order to better train the network in pairs, preprocessing such as image clipping and data enhancement is carried out for the network, including detecting the face and key points, correcting the face according to the rotation of the key points, expanding the boundary box of the key points in a fixed proportion and clipping the face area, and using the portrait segmentation model to set the background white.

3.2 Portrait Segmentation Module

Innovate the existing technology that can segment the whole picture and realize the segmentation of specific portrait parts (hair). First, the image of the preprocessed data set is input into bisenetv2. Secondly, the input image is represented by two branches (detail branch and semantic branch). Thirdly, through the enhanced training strategy like booster, the auxiliary segmentation header is inserted into different positions of the semantic branch, which further improves the segmentation accuracy of the image without increasing any inference cost. Again, two types of feature representation are enhanced by the designed guided aggregation layer. Finally, output the image after semantic segmentation. An example of segmentation training is shown in Fig. 3.

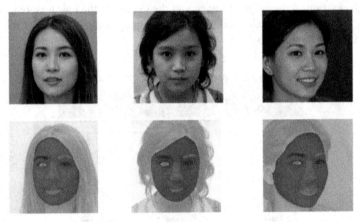

Fig. 3. An example of segmentation training

3.3 Style Transfer Module

Image style transfer is a subjective and exploratory design method. It is a method to design image changes according to the physiological characteristics of human visual system. However, most of the methods of degraded image restoration, including super-resolution image reconstruction, are based on an objective mechanism, so they can try to overcome it by trying to reproduce degraded images through reconstruction technology or using any prior knowledge in the process of image degradation, or by trying to use the completely opposite process of degraded images and images through image restoration technology or the technical model of image reconstruction. In addition, two technologies, excess hair removal and face authentication, are also applied.

It can be seen from Fig. 4 that the results of this process are good, the hair style is obviously transferred, the facial features are preserved, and the later beauty treatment is carried out.

Fig. 4. Face beautification with style transfer processing effect

4 Experiment Results

WGAN, CycleGAN and the modified CycleGAN were used to complete the image style transfer experiment independently. The results of the experiment are also shown in Fig. 5 below. In Fig. 5, the first column is the original drawing, the second column is the style drawing, the third column is the WGAN model result, the fourth column is the CycleGAN model result, and the fifth column is the improved CycleGAN result.

Fig. 5. Comparison results (Improved CycleGAN is our method)

Compared with the experimental results, we can further find that under the same number of iterations, all the schemes can complete the style transfer faster and better, and thus can obtain a more natural and real style transfer effect. The improved CycleGAN introduces a cyclic consistency loss function, which makes more effective use of the network bidirectional mapping model and prevents the collapse of the modeling itself to a certain extent. The improved CycleGAN provided in this paper also introduces the same perceptual loss function and mapping loss function. The flow of image style information transmission is relatively stable, but the modeling is not easy to collapse.

The whole process experiment of face local style is based on the Pytoch framework [22]. The experiment and test implementation are mainly divided into model part, training strategy part and evaluation index part.

It can be seen from Fig. 6 that the effect of the whole process of face stylization is very good.

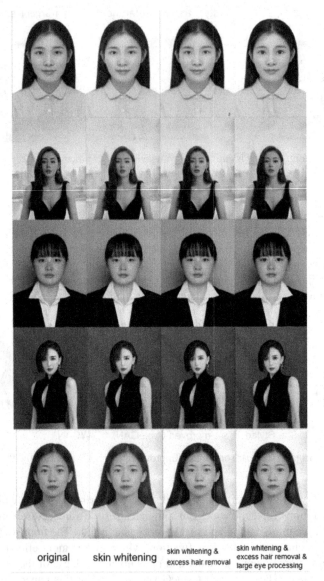

original   skin whitening   skin whitening & excess hair removal   skin whitening & excess hair removal & large eye processing

Fig. 6. The effect of the whole process of face stylization

5   Conclusion

This paper introduces semantic segmentation and combines it with other image processing technologies to solve the problem that local style transfer is not possible, which fills the gap in local style of face. Through the training experiment on the specific style dataset, a good local face style effect is obtained, which fully shows the performance of the model.

References

1. Brennan, S.E.: Caricature generator: the dynamic exaggeration of faces by computer. Leonardo **18**(3), 170–178 (1985)
2. Li, Y., Kobatake, H.: Extraction of facial sketch based on morphological processing. In: 1997 IEEE International Conference on Image Processing, pp. 316–319 (1997)
3. Kaneko, M., Meguro, M.: Synthesis of facial caricature using Eigenspaces and its applications to humanlike animated agents. In: International Workshop of Lifelike Animated Agents – Tools, Affective Functions, and Applications, Tokyo, pp. 58–63 (2002)
4. Lu, H., Yang, R., Deng, Z., Zhang, Y., Gao, G., Lan, R.: Chinese image captioning via fuzzy attention-based DenseNet-BiLSTM. ACM Trans. Multimed. Comput. Commun. Appl. **17**(1s), 1–18 (2021)
5. Zheng, Q., Zhu, J., Tang, H., Liu, X., Li, Z., Lu, H.: Generalized label enhancement with sample correlations. IEEE Trans. Knowl. Data Eng. (2021)
6. Liang, L., Chen, H., et al.: Example-based caricature generation with exaggeration. In: 10th Pacific Conferenceon Computer Graphics and Applications, Beijing, pp. 386–393 (2003)
7. Wang, X., Tang, X.: Face photo-sketch synthesis and recognition. IEEE Trans. Pattern Anal. Mach. Intell. **31**(11), 1955–1967 (2009)
8. Liu, J.F., Chen, Y.Q., Gao, W.: Mapping learning in eigenspace for harmonious caricature generation. In: 14th ACM International Conference on Multimedia, pp. 683–686 (2006)
9. Zhang, C., Liu, G., Wang, Z.: Cartoon face synthesis based on markov network. In: International Symposium on Intelligent Signal Processing and Communication Systems, pp. 1–4 (2010)
10. Lu, H., Li, Y., Chen, M., Kim, H., Serikawa, S.: Brain intelligence: go beyond artificial intelligence. Mob. Netw. Appl. **23**(2), 368–375 (2017). https://doi.org/10.1007/s11036-017-0932-8
11. Xu, F., Xu, F., Xie, J., Pun, C., Lu, H., Gao, H.: Action recognition framework in traffic scene for autonomous driving system. IEEE Trans. Intell. Transp. Syst. (2022)
12. Goodfellow, I., Bengio, Y., Courville, A.: Deep Learning. MIT Press, Cambridge, UK (2016)
13. Goodfellow, I.: NIPS 2016 tutorial: generative adversarial networks. arXiv:1701.00160 (2016)
14. Zhu, J.Y., Park, T., Isola, P., Efros, A.A.: Unpaired image-to-image translation using cycle-consistent adversarial networks. In: Proceedings of the IEEE international Conference on Computer Vision, pp. 2223–2232 (2017)
15. He, K., Zhang, X., Ren, S., Sun, J.: Deep residual learning for image recognition. In: Proceedings of the IEEE Conference on Computer Vision and Pattern Recognition, pp. 770–778 (2016)
16. Long, J., Shelhamer, E., Darrell, T.: Fully convolutional networks for semantic segmentation. In: Proceedings of the IEEE Conference on Computer Vision and Pattern Recognition, pp. 3431–3440 (2015)
17. Huang, G., Liu, Z., Van Der Maaten, L., Weinberger, K.Q.: Densely connected convolutional networks. In: Proceedings of the IEEE Conference on Computer Vision and Pattern Recognition, pp. 4700–4708 (2017)
18. Ioffe, S., Szegedy, C.: Batch normalization: accelerating deep network training by reducing internal covariate shift. In: International Conference on Machine Learning, pp. 448–456. PMLR (2015)
19. Glorot, X., Bordes, A., Bengio, Y.: Deep sparse rectifier neural networks. In: Proceedings of the Fourteenth International Conference on Artificial Intelligence and Statistics. JMLR Workshop and Conference Proceedings, pp. 315–323 (2011)
20. Zeiler, M.D., Krishnan, D., Taylor, G.W., Fergus, R.: Deconvolutional networks. In: 2010 IEEE Computer Society Conference on Computer Vision and Pattern Recognition, pp. 2528–2535. IEEE (2010)

21. Isola, P., Zhu, J.Y., Zhou, T., Efros, A.A.: Image-to-image translation with conditional adversarial networks. In: Proceedings of the IEEE Conference on Computer Vision and Pattern Recognition, pp. 1125–1134 (2017)
22. Paszke, A., et al.: Pytorch: an imperative style, high-performance deep learning library. Advances in neural information processing systems **32** (2019)

Network Intrusion Detection Method Based on Optimized Multiclass Support Vector Machine

Yuancheng Li, Shaofa Shang, Na Wang, and Mei Wang[✉]

College of Computer Science and Technology, Xi'an University of Science and Technology, Xi'an, China
`wangm@xust.edu.cn`

Abstract. With the popularization of network applications and the great changes in the international political, economic and military situations, network security is becoming more and more important. As an important part of network security, network intrusion detection (NID) is still facing the problem of low detection rate and difficulty to meet the real-time demand with the rapid increase of network traffic. Therefore, for the requirement of fast and accurate detection in real-time applications, this paper proposes a NID method based on optimized multiclass support vector machine (SVM). Firstly, the *ReliefF* feature selection algorithm is introduced to extract features with heuristic search rules based on variable similarity, which reduces the complexity of features and the amount of calculation; Secondly, a SVM training method based on data block method is proposed to improve the training speed; Finally, a multiclass SVM classifier is designed for typical attack types. Experimental results show that the proposed optimization method can achieve a detection rate of 96.9% and shorten the training time by 13.2% on average.

Keywords: Network intrusion detection · Support vector machine · Data block · Multiclass

1 Introduction

With the vigorous development of Internet technology, it has penetrated into people's daily life, not only completely changed the operation mode of the information industry, but also will have a profound impact on most other industries, and eventually lead to a new industrial revolution. However, due to the openness of the internet and the objective existence of system security vulnerability, there are inevitably some security vulnerabilities in operating system, application software and hardware equipment. Meanwhile, there are also some security risks in the design of the network protocol itself, which provide an opportunity for hackers to invade the system. Furthermore, with the discovery of more and more computer system vulnerabilities, especially with the current complex national political, economic and military situation, the network security has become more and more severe. More effective NID methods [1–3] have become one of the key issues to solve network security problem.

NID has received a lot of in-depth research and achieved fruitful results. In recent years, with the prosperity of deep learning technology, NID based on deep learning has made great progress. Facing the decreasing levels of detection accuracy, [4] proposed an intrusion detection method based on deep learning technique by introducing non-symmetric deep auto-encoder in which deep and shallow unsupervised feature can be effectively learned, then the accuracy and speed of detection can be significantly improved. For effectively fusing the benefits of typical deep learning model to large scale IDS, [5] presented a high accurate IDS model by adopting a unified model of Optimized CNN and Hierarchical Multi-scale LSTM to effectively extract and learn the spatial–temporal features. [6] detailed a bidirectional *BIDLSM* intrusion detection system to improve the low detection accuracy especially for the U2R and R2L attacks, and then to solve the problem that it is difficult to detect multiclass attacks, especially for unbalanced data sets in the existing deep learning methods.

For NID system, [7] pointed that the attacks are the minority classes compared to normal traffic, and there are still many challenges such as that the performance of NID is undermined because of the inherent defect of datasets which are collected from simulated environments rather than real networks. Since quickly network traffic behavior would yield low detection accuracy rate, by analyzing the large scale of network traffic in high-speed network, [5] proposed a scalable long-lasting detection framework and reliable ML-based NID model which can achieve up to 10Gbps of detection throughput. [8] described a data-driven NID system based on deep learning framework to extract the traffic data features with backpropagation algorithm.

The problems of imbalance data and overfitting can seriously affect the performance of identification. Fortunately, the SVM model has some computation advantages, such as suitability to finite samples and irrelevance between the complexity of algorithm and the sample dimension. For overcoming the limitation of overfitting problem, [9] proposed an AE-SVM-GO model in which the instances of minority classes can be generated to balance the dataset. [10] applied the SVM into intrusion detection for vehicular ad-hoc networks in which many optimization algorithms are introduced including genetic algorithm, particle swarm optimization and ant colony optimization. For detecting intrusions on large datasets with multiple attributes, [11] discussed an adaptive window SVM in which adaptive window can be used to identify the sudden generation of drift and SVM can be used to classify the normal and attack data.

Although the above methods have achieved good performance, there some problems such as that, the NID methods based on deep learning are generally suitable for processing large amounts of data which can lead high computational overhead. Additionally, for the special types of attack with small number of samples, the detection accuracy is still difficult to meet the real-time requirements. Therefore, this paper proposes a NID method based on optimized multiclass-SVM model. By introducing the *ReliefF* feature selection algorithm and heuristic search rules based on variable similarity, the amount of calculation can be significantly reduced. And the proposed SVM training method based on data block method is adopted to improve the training speed.

The main contributions of this work are:1) an optimization feature selection method is proposed to eliminate irrelevant feature and redundant feature based on the *ReleifF* algorithm and heuristic search rules using variable similarity; 2) describes an optimized training method based on data block to improve the training speed; 3) constructs a multiclass SVM classifier to detect the four attacks.

2 Optimized Feature Selection Method

In order to verify the effectiveness of the proposed method, this paper carries out relevant research based on KDD dataset [12] in which 41 features are extracted for each connection. Although the more features, the greater the amount of category information, too many features will lead to more calculation and may conversely reduce the recognition performance. Therefore, it is important to reduce the feature dimension as much as possible while keeping the classifier performance acceptable. In practice, feature extraction and feature selection are the main methods to reduce the dimension of features. In this paper, we propose an optimized feature selection method to reduce the calculation amount while with the acceptable classifier detection performance. In this method, *ReleifF* algorithm [13] is used to eliminate features irrelevant to classification and the heuristic search rules using variable similarity is used to eliminate the redundant features. The flow chat of feature selection is shown in Fig. 1.

Fig. 1. Flow chat of feature selection

2.1 Eliminating Irrelevant Feature Based on *ReleifF* Algorithm

The relevance of attributes is mainly evaluated based on the ability of attribute values to distinguish adjacent samples. Therefore, firstly we randomly select one sample R from the training data, and then find k nearest neighbor samples in the same class as the sample R in the training data, and call these K samples *nearHits*. Then, the k samples that are not in the same class as sample R are found in the training data, and these K samples are called *nearMisses*. The update of the weight of each attribute a depends on the randomly selected sample R in which the contributions of all *nearHits* and *nearMisses* are averaged. The specific *ReliefF* algorithm is shown in Fig. 2.

2.2 Eliminating Redundant Feature Based on Heuristic Search Rules Using Variable Similarity

After removing the irrelevant features, for compressing the redundancy of features, we introduce the maximum information compression criterion [14] in Eq. 1 and 2. For

ReliefF(D,N,M,K)
D is the training set, N is the number of features, M is the number of repetitions, and K is the number of nearest neighbors. First, initialize all attribute weights to 0, w [A] = 0;
For *i*=1 to M
    {randomly selects one sample neighbor R from D;
    Find K nearest neighbors *nearhits* in R and K neighbors *nearmisses* not in R;
    For A=1 to N
        { W[A]=W[A]-Avg(diff(A,R,nearMiss)); }
    }
    Return all the weight W[A].

Fig. 2. ReliefF algorithm flow chat

random variables x and y, ρ_{xy} is the correlation coefficient and the $(\lambda_2)_{xy}$ is the maximum information compression criterion.

$$\rho_{xy} = \frac{\sum\limits_{i=1}^{m} (x_i - \bar{x})(y_i - \bar{y})}{\sqrt{\sum\limits_{i=1}^{m} (x_i - \bar{x})^2 \sum\limits_{i=1}^{m} (y_i - \bar{y})^2}} \tag{1}$$

$$(\lambda_2)_{xy} = \frac{(var(x) + var(y)) - \sqrt{(var(x) + var(y))^2 - 4var(x)var(y)(1 - (\rho(x, y))^2)}}{2} \tag{2}$$

For the feature vector $X_m = \{X_1, X_2, \cdots, X_m\}$ and redundancy threshold as θ, the specific steps of using the maximum information compression criterion to remove redundant features are shown in Fig. 3. When a $< \theta$, it indicates that the value of the maximum information compression criterion between the features X_i and X_j is less than a preset minimum threshold, which indicates that one of the X_i and X_j is redundant and should be removed.

For i=1 to m-1
{for j=i+1 to m
    { Calculate the $(\lambda_2)_{xy}$;
    }
    A= min$(\lambda_2)_{xy}$;
    If (A $<\theta$)
    Remove the features X_i or X_j which with smaller weights.
}

Fig. 3. Flow chat of redundant feature elimination

After the hybrid feature selection including irrelevant feature elimination and redundant feature elimination, we can achieve a feature set that is related to classification and has little redundancy and the NID system based on this feature set will be more efficient.

3 Optimized Training Based on Data Block Method

For SVM classifier, usually all samples are trained at once in traditional training method while the training time is often very long for large-scale training samples. Especially for the training samples containing various types of attack information which are often gradually obtained and accumulated, the training time of SVM classifier is a critical issue for real-time processing. In this paper, we attempt to adopt an improved training method for SVM called data block training method. In this method, the training set firstly divided into several subsets, and then the SVM is trained on these subsets one by one. Additionally, the samples that do not meet the *KKT* [15] conditions in the previous training subset are added to the next subset until all training subsets are processed.

When the training samples in the previous training subset that do not meet the *KKT* conditions are added to the next training subset to train SVM, the hyperline of SVM will be changed under certain conditions. Although this change cannot guarantee the reduction of the classification error rate, it will make the SVM approach the theoretical hyperplane faster and thus the training speed can be improved.

The proposed training process based on data block can be described as follows:

Step1: Divide the training set into several subsets;
Step2: Taking the first subset as the training set;
Step3: Training SVM on the training set;
Step4: End the training if there are no more unprocessed subsets; Otherwise, execute step 5.
Step5: Select the training samples that do not meet the *KKT* conditions in the training subset and add them to the next training set to form a new training set;
Step6: Repeat the above steps from step 3.

4 Multiclass SVM for Intrusion Detection

The SVM method perfectly solves the binary classification problem, and gives the maximum interval classification plane for separable cases and the soft interval classification plane for non-separable cases. But for the multiclass classification problem of intrusion detection system, we need to construct an effective multiclass classifier based on SVM. SVM based multiclass classifier mainly include one-against-the-rest, one-against-one methods. Considering the efficiency and simplicity of the classifier, this paper adopts the one-against-the-rest method in which the five types of data are decomposed into five binary classification, and five binary SVM classifiers are constructed. According to the one-against-the-rest strategy, the four attacks can be effectively detected.

For an n ($n > 2$) class classification problem, n binary SVM classifiers are constructed, and the i-th classifier is used to separate the samples of the i-th class from those of other classes. In order to construct the i-th classifier, the class label of the i-th sample is set as 1, and the other samples are set as -1. Then the training is performed according to data set with class label. Finally, discriminate functions can be obtained just described in Eq. 3.

$$f_1 = (w_1 \bullet \phi(x)) + b_1$$
$$\cdot$$
$$\cdot \qquad\qquad (3)$$
$$\cdot$$
$$f_N = (w_N \bullet \phi(x)) + b_N$$

For any sample X without class label, inputs the sample into the N discriminant functions, and compares the output values of the discriminant functions. Then the class label can be determined according to the value. The discriminate function can be described as Eq. 4.

$$\text{Class of } x \equiv \arg \max_{i=1,\cdots,N} (w_i \bullet \phi(x) + b_i) \qquad\qquad (4)$$

5   Experiment and Results Analysis

5.1   Experiment Dataset

In this paper, we select the training subset and testing subset of KDD'99 dataset as our experimental dataset. Furthermore, in order to demonstrate the effectiveness of this method for a small number of sample set, we construct a mini training subset based on the training set to train our multiclass SVM classifier. Additionally, for reducing the negative impact result from imbalance of dataset, the sample proportions of several attack types are adjusted according to testing set in training set. Table 1 shows the details of the both training set and testing set. There are 311029 testing samples and only 5000 training samples.

Table 1. Attacks type distribution of dataset

Types of attack	Serial number	Percentage of types in training dataset	Percentage of types in training dataset
Normal	0	30.58%	19.48%
Probe	1	31.32%	1.34%
DOS	2	32.86%	73.90%
U2R	3	1.04%	0.07%
R2L	4	4.20%	5.20%

5.2 Experimental Results and Analysis

Because the classifier adopts data block training method, this paper divides 5000 subsets into two subsets of the same size. Due to the good performance of radial basis function [16] in intrusion detection applications, the radial basis function is selected as the kernel function to design the classifier for each attack type. For the misclassification penalty factor C and control factor G of kernel function, we adopt the heuristic rules [17] to explore and determine the final optimal parameter combination of C and G. Let DR denotes the detection rate just like Eq. 5. In Table 2, we present the training results of classifiers for four attacks and the *normal* type based on the optimal parameter combination.

$$DR = \frac{N_{output\_abnormal\&\&abnormal}}{N_{abnormal}} \times 100\% \qquad (5)$$

Table 2. The training results of classifiers for four attacks and the normal type

Parameter	Type of classifier	Data block training method		Original training method	
		Training time	DR	Training time	DR
$C = 10000, G = 0.5$	Dos	0.65 s	99.96%	0.74 s	99.84%
$C = 10000, G = 1$	Probing	0.64 s	99.51%	0.73 s	99.01%
$C = 10000, G = 0.5$	Normal	0.58 s	99.95%	0.69 s	99.79%
$C = 20000, G = 0.5$	U2R	0.73 s	89.4%	0.85 s	88.7%
$C = 20000, G = 1$	R2L	0.71 s	70.3%	0.80 s	69.2%

From Table 2, it is obviously that, the training method using data block needs less time than the traditional training method, and the detection rate is also slightly improved. This fully demonstrates the effectiveness of the optimized training strategy proposed in this paper, and provides a possibility for application in the actual network environment. Next, for easy comparison with the KDD'99, we adopt the Confusion Matrix (CM) to show the experimental results [18]. In Table 3, the comparison of performance between multiclass classifier composed of these classifiers and KDD'99 is shown in which the CM of KDD'99 optimal scheme is shown in brackets.

Furthermore, let ASC denotes average sample cost, FPR denotes the false positive rate, FNR denotes the false negative rate, CR denotes the correct recognition rate which described in Eq. 6, 7, 8 and 9. Then, the performance comparison between our multiclass SVM with the BP neural network method and the KDD'99 is presented in Table 4.

$$ASC = \frac{1}{N} \sum_{i=1}^{5} \sum_{i=1}^{5} CM(i,j) * C(i,j) \qquad (6)$$

$$FPR = \frac{N_{output\_normal\&\&abnormal}}{N_{out\_normal}} \times 100\% \qquad (7)$$

Table 3. The comparison of CM between the multi-SVM and KDD'99

Attack type	Normal	Probing	DoS	U2R	R2L	Correct %
Normal	60142 (60262)	241 (243)	198 (78)	8 (4)	4 (6)	99.3 (99.5)
Probing	513 (511)	3498 (3471)	163 (184)	2 (0)	0 (0)	84.0 (83.3)
DoS	4925 (5299)	879 (1328)	224088 (223226)	1 (0)	0 (0)	97.5 (97.0)
U2R	97 (168)	21 (20)	3 (0)	101 (30)	6 (10)	44.3 (13.2)
R2L	1626 (14527)	560 (294)	275 (0)	12 (8)	13723 (1360)	84.7 (8.4)

$$FNR = \frac{N_{output\_normal\&\&abnormal}}{N_{out\_abnormal}} \times 100\% \tag{8}$$

$$CR = \frac{N_{correct\_classified}}{N_{test}} \times 100\% \tag{9}$$

From Table 3 and Table 4, it can be seen that the multiclass classifier based on SVM can greatly improve the detection performance of *U2R* and *R2L* attacks. Meanwhile, compared with KDD'99 and BP neural network classifier, it also has good performance in other performance indicators. This fully shows the effectiveness of the proposed method in this paper.

Table 4. Performance compare of BP NN, Multi-SVM and KDD'99

Method	ASC (%)	FPR (%)	FNR (%)	DR (%)	CR (%)
KDD'99	0.23	34.0	0.1	91.8	92.7
BP NN	0.25	37.3	0.19	91.0	92.6
Multi-SVM	0.20	11.9	0.11	96.4	96.9

In addition, it also can be seen that the detection rates of *U2R* and *R2L* attacks are still not ideal. This is mainly because these two types of attacks take advantage of system vulnerabilities to obtain the access rights of the target host to realize the attacks. Their main features are concentrated in the contents of network data packets, but the 21 features selected in the experimental data can not fully reflect this information. Therefore, it is difficult to separate these two types of data from normal data according to the existing features. In the future, in order to further improve the detection performance of intrusion detection, especially for the latter two attacks, it is also necessary to provide more detailed content features, or combine other detection results such as intrusion detection results based on host data.

6 Conclusion

As an important approach to ensure network security which is the one of key issues in network application, NID technology is still facing the problem of low detection rate and difficulty to meet the real-time requirement with the rapid increase of network traffic. In order to tackle the problem, by optimizing the feature selection and training method, this paper proposes an intrusion detection method based on multiclass SVM. The *ReliefF* based feature selection algorithm is used to reduce the complexity of features and reduce the amount of calculation. And the optimized SVM training method based on data block method can be used to improve the training speed. Experimental results show that the proposed multiclass SVM classifier can achieve a detection rate of 96.9% and shorten the training time by 13.2% on average. And the work can provide a useful guidance for the design of effective NID for real-time network applications.

Acknowledgment. This research was partially supported by the Scientific and Technological Innovation 2030 - Major Project of New Generation Artificial Intelligence (2020AAA0104603), Science and technology plan of Shaanxi Province (2021JQ-576) and the Yulin Science and Technology Plan Projects (CXY-2020-026).

References

1. Aldweesh, A., Derhab, A., Emam, A.Z.: Deep learning approaches for anomaly-based intrusion detection systems: a survey, taxonomy, and open issues. Knowl.-Based Syst. **189**, 105124 (2020)
2. Zheng, Q., Zhu, J., Tang, H., Liu, X., Li, Z., Lu, H.: Generalized label enhancement with sample correlations. IEEE Trans. Knowl. Data Eng. (2021)
3. Lu, H., Li, Y., Chen, M., Kim, H., Serikawa, S.: Brain intelligence: go beyond artificial intelligence. Mobile Networks and Applications **23**(2), 368–375 (2017). https://doi.org/10.1007/s11036-017-0932-8
4. Xu, F., Xu, F., Xie, J., Pun, C., Lu, H., Gao, H.: Action recognition framework in traffic scene for autonomous driving system. IEEE Transactions on Intelligent Transportation Systems (2022)
5. Viegas, E., Santin, A.O., Abreu, V., Jr.: Machine learning intrusion detection in big data era: a multi-objective approach for longer model lifespans. IEEE Trans. Netw. Sci. Eng. **8**(1), 366–376 (2021)
6. Imrana, Y., Xiang, Y., Ali, L., Abdul-Rauf, Z.: A bidirectional LSTM deep learning approach for intrusion detection. Expert System and Applications **185**, 115524 (2021)
7. Chou, D., Jiang, M.: A survey on data-driven network intrusion detection. ACM Comput. Surv. (CSUR) **54**, 1–36 (2021)
8. Nie, L., Ning, Z., Wang, X., Hu, X., Cheng, J., Li, Y.: Data-driven intrusion detection for intelligent internet of vehicles: a deep convolutional neural network-based method. IEEE Trans. Netw. Sci. Eng. **7**(4), 2219–2230 (2020)
9. Chikkalwar, S.R., Garapati, Y.: Autoencoder-support vector machine-grasshopper optimization for intrusion detection system. Int. J. Intell. Eng. Syst. **15**(4), 406–414 (2020)
10. Ponmalar, A., Dhanakoti, V.: An intrusion detection approach using ensemble support vector machine based chaos game optimization algorithm in big data platform. Appl. Soft. Comput. **116**, 108295 (2022)

11. Rajesari, P.V.N., Shashi, M., Pao, T.K., Rajya Lakshmi, M., Kiran, L.V.: Effective intrusion detection system using concept drifting data stream and support vector machine. Concurrency and Computation-Practice & Experience **34**, e7118 (2022)
12. http://kdd.ics.uci.edu/databased/kddcup99/kddcup99.html (2001)
13. Zhang, B.S., Li, Y.Y., Chai, Z.: A novel random multi-subspace based ReliefF for feature selection. Knowl.-Based Syst. **252**, 109400 (2022)
14. Li, Y., Lu, H., Li, J., Li, X., Li, Y., Serikawa, S.: Underwater image de-scattering and classification by deep neural network. Comput. Electr. Eng. **54**, 68–77 (2016)
15. Zhao, W., Wang, M., Liu, Y., Lu, H., Xu, C., Yao, L.: Generalizable crowd counting via diverse context style learning. IEEE Trans. Circuits Syst. Video Technol. (2022)
16. Beitollahi, H., Sharif, D.M., Fazeli, M.: Application layer DDoS attack detection using cuckoo search algorithm-trained radial basis function. IEEE Access **10**, 63844–63854 (2022)
17. Modjtaba, R., Dawood, S.J.: Two fast and accurate heuristic RBF learning rules for data classification. Neural Netw. **75**, 150–161 (2016)
18. Elkan, C.: Results of the KDD'99 classifier learning. ACM SIGKDD Explorations Newsl. **1**(2), 63–64 (2000)

Face Recognition Based on Inverted Residual Network in Complex Environment of Mine

Yuancheng Li[1], Yufei Bao[2], Shaofa Shang[1], and Mei Wang[1(✉)]

[1] Xi'an University of Science and Technology, Xi'an 710054, China
wangm@xust.edu.cn
[2] Nubian Technology Limited Company, Shenzhen 518000, China

Abstract. The recognition of personnel entering and leaving the mine is an important link to ensure safe production. As an effective identity recognition technology, face recognition has been widely and deeply studied while facing the problem that the recognition rate is not high in the complex and harsh environment of mine such as facial expressions, pose variation, and low-resolution of face images. For effectively improving the face recognition rate of miners in uneven illumination environment, a face recognition method based on inverted residual network is proposed. In this method, through the optimization of the activation function, the amount of calculation can be greatly reduced while keeping the almost equivalent performance. And by the fusion of inverted residual network, the problem of partial feature information loss in face image recognition model training is effectively solved, which greatly improves the accuracy of recognition. The experimental results show that the accuracy of the inverted residual face recognition model is 81.4%, which is 5.7% higher than the residual network algorithm with additional 4.3% of time overhead, and 9.9% higher than the MTCNN model with only the 1/13 recognition time of MTCNN.

Keywords: Face recognition · Inverted residual network · Uneven illumination environment · Activation function optimization

1 Introduction

For the safety of coal mine production, especially the safety of personnel, it is very important to identify the personnel entering and leaving the mine. In recent years, with the rapid development of coal mine intelligence, many recognition technologies [1, 2] such as fingerprint recognition [3], radio frequency identification(RFID) [4] and face recognition have been introduced to identify personnel. However, since RFID is as a non-biometric technology, cheating is inevitable during in signing in. Additionally, because the fingerprints of the miners may be contaminated, fingerprint recognition may fail to identify correctly. As a contactless biometric recognition technology, face recognition can avoid the disadvantages of the both technologies discussed previously and has been widely and deeply studied. Unfortunately, the environment under the mine are very complex, such as uneven illuminations, facial expressions, pose variation, and low-resolution of

© The Author(s), under exclusive license to Springer Nature Singapore Pte Ltd. 2022
S. Yang and H. Lu (Eds.): ISAIR 2022, CCIS 1701, pp. 287–298, 2022.
https://doi.org/10.1007/978-981-19-7943-9_25

face images which will lead to low recognition rate and slow speed. Therefore, it is urgent to study a face recognition method suitable for complex and harsh conditions in coal mine [5–7]. For overcoming these disadvantages, many approaches have been deeply discussed and achieved some results in which mainly from the perspective of facial feature description and recognition network.

[8] proposed a *GroupFace* framework which can utilize multiple group-aware representations. Their main purpose is to solve the problem of recognition inefficiency with fewer dimensional embedding features for conventional model that has only a single branch. By providing self-distributed labels used to balance the large-scale samples belonging to each group, the proposed method can learn the group-aware representations and then improve the quality of the face features. For tackling the problem of loss of facial identity information result from decomposing facial feature into age-sensitive components, [9] originally constructed a multi-feature fusion and decomposition framework with multi-head attention mechanism. Their framework can be used to capture and extract contextual information of facial feature series, and learn more discriminative and robust features to reduce the intra-class variants. In order to overcome the lack of detailed annotations on attributes such as pose and expression caused by label noise and privacy issues of face images, [10] proposed a *SynFace* method to control different factors of synthetic face generated by *SynFace* framework. Then, by the performance comparison between typical face recognition models with the proposed synthetic and real face images, the great potentials of synthetic face data for face recognition with complex factors are well demonstrated.

For the extracted face features, an effective recognition network can further improve the accuracy and speed of recognition. In [11], an adaptive curriculum learning loss called *CurricularFace* is introduced into loss function for deep face recognition network. The margin-based loss functions can be used to increase the difference of feature margin between different classes and enhance the discriminability. To balance the performance difference of typical face recognition method between different races, [12] proposed a race balance network based on reinforcement learning. The margins information between different races can be easily extracted according to the adaptive margin policy in which the *Markov* decision process is introduced to adaptively obtain the optimal margins information for non-Caucasians. For cross age face recognition problems, [13] proposed a parallel multi-path age distinguish network model to respond to the challenges such as similarity score in some age groups may affect final classification results, inconsistency among the aging pattern of many individuals caused by the linear combination of identity information and age information. Their model can effectively realize cross age identification by the two cascading networks including the age distinguish mapping network and the cross-age feature recombination network.

Although these methods have achieved good performance on open datasets such as CASIA-WebFace [14], MS-Celeb-1M [15] and VGGFace2 [16], it is still difficult to meet the accuracy and speed requirements of real-time recognition especially for the complex environment under coal mine. In this paper, aiming to the specific identity recognition of underground personnel in coal mine, we propose a face recognition method based on inverted residual network. Through the optimization of the activation function, the amount of calculation can be greatly reduced while keeping the almost equivalent performance. And by the fusion of inverted residual network, the problem of partial feature information loss in face image recognition model training is effectively solved, which greatly improves the accuracy of recognition. Based on the real data set established according to coal mine, the experimental results show that, compared with the residual network algorithm and MTCNN algorithm, our method can achieve a better recognition accuracy and higher recognition speed. Our main contributions can be summarized as the two aspects: 1) propose an optimized activation function to reduce the calculation while keep the equivalent recognition accuracy. 2) fuse an inverted residual network into recognition network to overcome the problem of partial feature information loss.

2 Inverted Residual Face Recognition Algorithm

2.1 Analysis of Typical Face Recognition Framework

For the face recognition of personnel in special underground scenes, a typical face recognition model based on traditional methods is shown in Fig. 1. The model is composed of multiple convolutional neural networks and mainly includes three stages such as feature extraction stage, construction stage of feature pyramid network (FPN) [17] and prediction and result output stage.

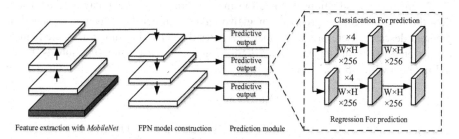

Fig. 1. Schematic diagram of a typical face recognition model

In feature extraction stage, the *mobilenet* [18] feature extraction network is mainly used as the backbone feature extraction network to extract the features of the face image in the coal mine. *Moblienet* adopts depthwise convolution to realize lightweight calculation, but the *ReLU* function will cause information loss for low dimensional data processing. Meanwhile, because of its own computing characteristics, it has no ability to change the number of channels and only output as many channels as the previous layer gives it. Therefore, if the number of channels provided by the previous layer is very small, depthwise can only extract features from low dimensional space resulting in poor performance.

In the construction stage of FPN, the FPN can build high-level semantic feature maps at all scales and then avoid the information loss of small object with a small amount of calculation increases. For the face image of personnel under coal mine, the quality of the image is poor and the proportion of face feature information is relatively small. Therefore, FPN is very suitable for face recognition applications in the scenarios mentioned in this paper.

Finally, in prediction and result output stage, due to the inherent defect of depthwise convolution in which low dimensional data information may be lost, the residual network structure [19] is introduced to increase the dimension of the low channel input before the depthwise convolution. And then the depthwise convolution can work in the high dimension space and improve the speed and accuracy of feature extraction. However, for the specific face images in complex coal mine, when the input is a low channel, the convolution kernel of the deep convolution layer tends to be inoperative in which most of the parameters of the convolution kernel are 0.

Therefore, based on the above analysis, this paper proposes a face recognition based on inverted residual network to overcome the problems analyzed above. By utilizing the inverted residual network, the input of the low channel can be processed to increase the dimension before the depthwise convolution. And then the depth convolution can work in high dimension space and effectively improve the speed and accuracy of face feature extraction.

2.2 Activation Function Optimization

The activation function used by the facial feature extraction network is the *ReLU* function, which is effective when the number of input channels is large. However, for the *ReLU* function, the situations that neurons may die and the gradient may become 0, and then the function cannot produce a negative value to affect the convergence speed of gradient descent. Therefore, this paper optimizes the activation function of the feature extraction network and introduces *swish* function as a new activation function, as shown in Eq. (1) in which β is a trainable parameter.

$$f(x) = x \bullet sigmoid(\beta x) \tag{1}$$

If $\beta = 0$, the *swish* becomes a linear function $f(x) = x/2$; and if $\beta = \infty$, the *swish* will becomes 0 or x which is equivalent to the *ReLU*. The gating mechanism in function makes it more flexible. The *swish* activation function curve with different β is shown in Fig. 2.

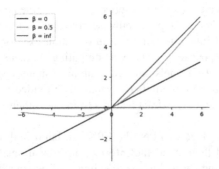

Fig. 2. Swish curve with different β

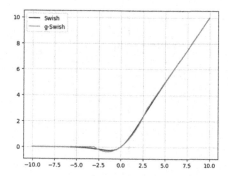

Fig. 3. Comparison between *g-swish* and *swish*.

Although this function inherits the advantages of *ReLU*, the problems such as the disappearance of gradient and the death of neurons can be effectively avoided. However, the calculation scale of *swish* activation function is still relatively large, and it is still difficult to meet the really requirements of rapid recognition in real-time application scenarios. For this reason, an optimized *swish* activation function named *g-Swish* to significantly reduce the calculation scale is introduced in this paer. In *g-Swish*, the *sigmod* function is replaced by *ReLU6* function and the optimized function is shown in Eq. (2).

$$g - Swish[x] = x \bullet \frac{ReLU6(x + 3)}{6} \tag{2}$$

Furthermore, the comparison curve between *g-swish* and *swish* is shown in Fig. 3. From Fig. 3, it can be seen that the curves of the two activation functions are almost identical. Since *SIGMOD* has a much larger amount of computation than *ReLU6*, the improved function greatly reduces the amount of computation with little impact of performance, and is applicable to almost all frameworks.

2.3 Fusion of Residual Networks

With the increase of convolutional neural network layers, the loss of the training set will gradually decrease and then tend to saturation. Nevertheless, if we continue to increase the network depth, the loss of the training set will increase. Fortunately, residual network can solve this problem effectively by using direct mapping to connect different layers of the network. In Fig. 4, a typical residual network structure is presented. The number of channels is reduced from 256 to 64 by 1 × 1convolution, and then the number of channels is restored to 256 by 3 × 3 convolution and 1 × 1 convolution orderly. Unfortunately, for the specific face images in complex coal mine, the convolution kernel of the deep convolution layer tends to be inoperative described in Sect. 2.1. Therefore, an inverted residual network is proposed to mitigate the impact of this problem shown in Fig. 5.

For face recognition using the extraction network with inverted residual network, if input the high channel information, the face recognition model still extracts feature according to the original network. Meanwhile, if input the high channel, the face recognition model will extract feature according to the inverted residual network. Low

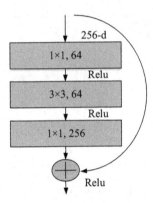

Fig. 4. Typical residual network structure

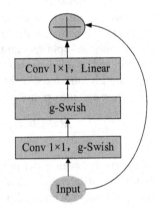

Fig. 5. Inverted residual network

dimensional features are extended to high dimensions by inverted residual network, and then the features are projected to a low dimensional compressed representation through a linear bottleneck. The improved face feature extraction network is shown in Fig. 6 and the improved face feature extraction network parameters are shown in Table 1.

3   Experiment and Result Analysis

3.1   Experimental Setup

The experiments in this paper are implemented on the pytorch1.2.0-GPU and the specific software and hardware parameters are as follows in Table 2.

Additionally, the public data set Wider Face Val (WFV) [20] is adopted as the basic training data of the face recognition model. Furthermore, different types of face images under the real mine were collected to expand the dataset just shown in Table 3. In Table 3 the types 1–8 respectively represent: subset 1 of WFV (*WFV-1*), clean miner's face under uniform illumination conditions(*Uni_Cln_M*), contaminated miner's face under uniform

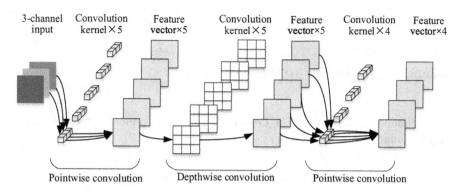

Fig. 6. Improved face feature extraction network

Table 1. The improved face feature extraction network parameters

Input	Operator	Extension factor	Number of output matrix channels	n	Step
$224^2 \times 3$	2D Conv	-	32	1	2
$112^2 \times 32$	Improved residual network	1	16	1	1
$112^2 \times 16$	Improved residual network	6	24	2	2
$56^2 \times 24$	Improved residual network	6	32	3	2
$28^2 \times 32$	Improved residual network	6	64	4	2
$28^2 \times 32$	Improved residual network	6	96	3	1
$14^2 \times 96$	Improved residual network	6	160	3	2
$7^2 \times 160$	Improved residual network	6	320	1	1
$7^2 \times 320$	2D 1 × 1 Conv	—	1280	1	1
$7^2 \times 1280$	Average pooling 7 × 7	—	—	1	—
$1 \times 1 \times k$	2D 1 × 1 Conv	—	k	—	—

illumination conditions(*Uni_Contam_M*), clean miner's face under uneven illumination conditions(*Un_Cln_M*), subset 2 of WFV(*WFV-2*), contaminated miner's face under

Table 2. Experimental environment configuration

OS	CPU	GPU	Memory	CUDA
Win10	i5-10400F	GTX 1660Super 8G	16G	CUDA10.0

uneven illumination conditions(Un_Contam_M), uniform illumination face(Uni_Face), uneven illumination face(Un_Face).

Table 3. Classification and description of face dataset

Environment	Type	Face image size	Number of face image
Uniform illumination	$WFV\text{-}1$	1280 × 1280	10000
	Uni_Cln_M	1280 × 1280	300
	Uni_Contam_M	1280 × 1280	300
	Uni_Face	1280 × 1280	300
Uneven illumination	$WFV\text{-}2$	1280 × 1280	10000
	Un_Contam_M	1280 × 1280	300
	Un_Cln_M	1280 × 1280	300
	Un_Face	1280 × 1280	300

3.2 Performance Analysis

For accurately evaluate the performance of the face recognition based on reverted residual network proposed in this paper, the average precision (AP), mean average precision (MAP) and average recognition time (ms) are selected as the evaluation indicators. The AP is used to evaluate the recognition performance of the model for different types of images, and the MAP represents the strength of the overall performance of the model which is obtained by calculating the average value of the APs of all classes. The higher the resolution of the input face image, the richer the feature information and detail information contained in the image, and the more face features extracted by the face recognition model. But the face image with too high resolution will increase the parameter value of the recognition model and increase the amount of calculation. In Table. 4, we present the comparisons of APs and MAPs of the face images with different resolutions. In Fig. 7, we give the trend comparison between the MAP and the average recognition time with the improvement of the resolution of the input face image.

From the Fig. 7, we can see that the resolution of the input image increases from 480 × 480 to 608 × 608, the average accuracy is increased by 2%, but the average recognition time of the model is increased by 56.2%. When the resolution reaches 480 × 480, with the increase of resolution, the average accuracy is not significantly improved, but the average recognition time is significantly increased. Therefore, the face image with 480 ×

Table 4. APs and MAPs of face images with different resolutions

Resolution	1AP	2AP	3AP	4AP	5AP	6AP	7AP	8AP	MAP
352 × 352	0.725	0.737	0.663	0.752	0.743	0.755	0.613	0.741	0.716
384 × 384	0.737	0.745	0.667	0.761	0.757	0.761	0.676	0.752	0.732
416 × 416	0.754	0.776	0.724	0.813	0.768	0.778	0.689	0.769	0.759
446 × 446	0.785	0.792	0.757	0.835	0.780	0.784	0.717	0.771	0.778
480 × 480	0.856	0.854	0.792	0.866	0.827	0.789	0.742	0.785	0.814
512 × 512	0.861	0.859	0.709	0.889	0.832	0.791	0.774	0.792	0.813
608 × 608	0.873	0.852	0.727	0.895	0.856	0.805	0.789	0.795	0.824

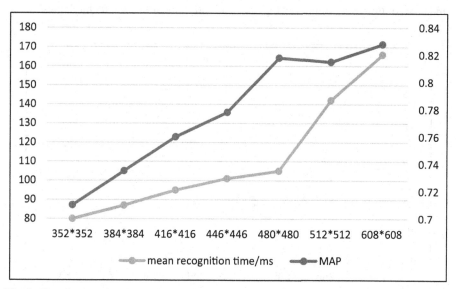

Fig. 7. Trend comparison between the MAP and the average recognition time with the improvement of the resolution of the input face image

480 resolution is selected as the input image for face recognition model. Then for 480 × 480 face image of in Table 4, the performance comparison of different face recognition models for 8 kinds of face images is presented in Fig. 8. It can be seen that, compared with residual network model and MTCNN model, our method has better performance of accuracy especially for *Uni_Contam_M* and *Un_Cln_M* images.

Finally, in Table 5, the comparison of MAP between our method with MTCNN and residual network method is presented to illustrate the effectiveness of the method in this paper. According to the Table 5, we can find that the accuracy of the inverted residual face recognition model is 81.4%, which is 12% higher than the residual network algorithm with additional 4.3% of time overhead, and 9.9% higher than the MTCNN model with only the 1/13 recognition time of MTCNN.

4   Conclusion

Face recognition is an effective technology for the identification of personnel entering and leaving the mine, while facing the problem that the recognition rate is not high in the complex and harsh environment of mine such as facial expressions, pose variation, and low-resolution of face images. Therefore, we introduce a face recognition method based on inverted residual network to effectively improve the recognition rate of miners in uneven illumination environment. Through the optimization of activation function and fusion of inverted residual network, we can obtain better recognition accuracy while maintaining a relatively fast speed. The experimental results show that the accuracy of the inverted residual face recognition model is 81.4%, which is 5.7% higher than residual network algorithm with additional 4.3% of time overhead, and 9.9% higher than MTCNN model with only 1/13 recognition time of MTCNN. It can provide useful guidance for the safety of miners together with other identification technologies.

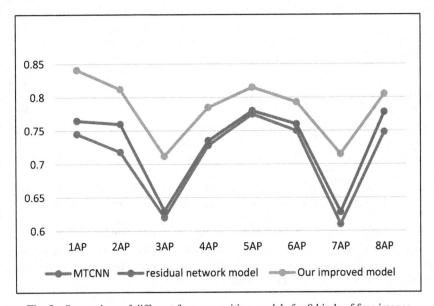

Fig. 8. Comparison of different face recognition models for 8 kinds of face images

Table 5. Comparison of MAP between our method with MTCNN and residual network

Recognition model	MAP	Recognition time/ms
MTCNN	0.741	1742.3
Residual network	0.770	102.4
Our recognition method	0.814	106.8

Acknowledgment. This research was partially supported by the Scientific and Technological Innovation 2030 - Major Project of New Generation Artificial Intelligence (2020AAA0104603), Science and technology plan of Shaanxi Province (2021JQ-576) and the Yulin Science and Technology Plan Projects (CXY-2020-026).

References

1. Chang, J., Lan, Z., Cheng, C., Wei, Y.: Data uncertainty learning in face recognition. In: Proceedings of the IEEE/CVF Conference on Computer Vision and Pattern Recognition, pp. 5710–5719 (2020)
2. Meng, Q., Zhao, S., Huang, Z., Zhou, F.: Magface: a universal representation for face recognition and quality assessment. In: Proceedings of the IEEE/CVF Conference on Computer Vision and Pattern Recognition, pp. 14225–14234 (2021)
3. Priesnitz, J., Rathgeb, C., Buchmann, N., Busch, C.: Deep learning-based semantic segmentation for touchless fingerprint recognition. In: Del Bimbo, A., Cucchiara, R., Sclaroff, S., Farinella, G.M., Mei, T., Bertini, M., Escalante, H.J., Vezzani, R. (eds.) ICPR 2021. LNCS, vol. 12668, pp. 154–168. Springer, Cham (2021). https://doi.org/10.1007/978-3-030-68793-9_11
4. Mezzanotte, P., Palazzi, V., Alimenti, F., et al.: Innovative RFID sensors for Internet of Things applications. IEEE J. Microwaves **1**(1), 55–65 (2021)
5. Li, C., et al.: A hybrid feature selection algorithm based on an discrete artificial bee colony for Parkinson's diagnosis. ACM Trans. Internet Technol. **21**, 1–22 (2020)
6. Chen, Z., et al.: Construction of a hierarchical feature enhancement network and its application in fault recognition. IEEE Trans. Industr. Inf. **17**(17), 4827–4836 (2021)
7. Lu, H., Yang, R., Deng, Z., Zhang, Y., Gao, G., Lan, R.: Chinese image captioning via fuzzy attention-based DenseNet-BiLSTM. ACM Trans. Multimed. Comput. Commun. Appl. **17**(1s), 1–18 (2021)
8. Kim, Y., Park, W., Roh, M.C., et al.: Groupface: learning latent groups and constructing group-based representations for face recognition. In: Proceedings of the IEEE/CVF Conference on Computer Vision and Pattern Recognition, pp. 5621–5630 (2020)
9. Yan, C., et al.: Age-invariant face recognition by multi-feature fusion and decomposition with self-attention. ACM Trans. Multimedia Comput. Commun. Appl. (TOMM) **18**(1s), 1–18 (2022)
10. Qiu, H., Yu, B., Gong, D., et al.: Synface: face recognition with synthetic data. In: Proceedings of the IEEE/CVF International Conference on Computer Vision, pp. 10880–10890 (2021)
11. Huang, Y., Wang, Y., Tai, Y., et al.: Curricularface: adaptive curriculum learning loss for deep face recognition. In: Proceedings of the IEEE/CVF Conference on Computer Vision and Pattern Recognition, pp. 5901–5910 (2020)
12. Wang, M., Deng, W.: Mitigating bias in face recognition using skewness-aware reinforcement learning. In: Proceedings of the IEEE/CVF Conference on Computer Vision and Pattern Recognition, pp. 9322–9331 (2020)
13. Wu, Y., Du, L., Hu, H.: Parallel multi-path age distinguish network for cross-age face recognition. IEEE Trans. Circuits Syst. Video Technol. **31**(9), 3482–3492 (2021)
14. Yi, D., Lei, Z., Liao, S., et al.: Learning face representation from scratch (2014). arXiv:1411.7923
15. Guo, Y., Zhang, L., Hu, Y., He, X., Gao, J.: Ms-celeb-1m: a dataset and benchmark for large-scale face recognition. In: Leibe, B., Matas, J., Sebe, N., Welling, M. (eds.) ECCV 2016. LNCS, vol. 9907, pp. 87–102. Springer, Cham (2016). https://doi.org/10.1007/978-3-319-46487-9_6

16. Cao, Q., Shen, L., Xie, W., et al.: Vggface2: a dataset for recognising faces across pose and age. In: 2018 13th IEEE International Conference on Automatic Face & Gesture Recognition (FG 2018), pp. 67–74. IEEE (2018)
17. Lin, T.Y., Dollár, P., Girshick, R., et al.: Feature pyramid networks for object detection. In: Proceedings of the IEEE Conference on Computer Vision and Pattern Recognition, pp. 2117–2125 (2017)
18. Howard, A., Sandler, M., Chu, G., et al.: Searching for mobilenetv3. In: Proceedings of the IEEE/CVF International Conference on Computer Vision, pp. 1314–1324 (2019)
19. He, K., Zhang, X., Ren, S., et al.: Deep residual learning for image recognition. In: Proceedings of the IEEE Conference on Computer Vision and Pattern Recognition, pp. 770–778 (2016)
20. Yang, S., Luo, P., Loy, C.C., et al.: Wider face: a face detection benchmark. In: Proceedings of the IEEE Conference on Computer Vision and Pattern Recognition, pp. 5525–5533 (2016)

Automated Cobb Angle Measurement Using MVIE-Net Combined with Vertebral Segmentation and Landmarks Detection

Caijun Gan, Xuqing Wang[✉], and Huadeng Wang

Guilin University of Electronic Technology, Guilin, China
dants2231111@gmail.com

Abstract. The Cobb angle is the most widely used measurement to quantify the magnitude of scoliosis. Accurate automated measurement of the Cobb angle can improve the efficiency of scoliosis diagnosis. The existing direct estimation of Cobb angle cannot extract structural information of the spine and lacks interpretability. Curvature-based Cobb angle estimation rely on vertebral feature information tend to focus on a single landmark or segmentation information and cannot provide robust vertebral feature information for post-processing of curvature calculations. In this paper, we propose a novel curvature-based method to automatic Cobb angle measurement. The proposed Multi-task Vertebra Information Extraction network (namely MVIE-Net) is used to predict vertebra contour and keypoint confidence map simultaneously. And we pair the vertebral corner points based on the positional relationships contained in the vertebral contours and calculate the Cobb angle accordingly. The performance on the public AASCE Challenge dataset proves the efficiency of the proposed method. Experimental results on external datasets demonstrate the more generalizability of the proposed method.

Keywords: Scoliosis · Multi-task learning · Segmentation · Cobb angle

1 Introduction

Adolescent idiopathic scoliosis (AIS) causes lateral curvature of the spine and rotation of the thorax and usually occurs in adolescents at or around puberty [1]. The diagnosis of AIS is based on accurate measurement of the Cobb angle. The Cobb angle refers to the angle between the upper and lower endplates of the end vertebrae. Manually measuring the Cobb angle clinically requires the radiologist to measure the angle of inclination of each vertebra on the patient's anterior and posterior radiographs, which is time-consuming, and the accuracy is affected by factors such as end vertebra selection, intra-observer and inter-observer variation, and so on. Therefore, it is necessary to propose an accurate and robust automatic Cobb angle measurement method.

With the development of deep learning, many methods for automatic Cobb angle measurement have been proposed. We roughly classify these methods into two categories: (1) Direct estimation of the Cobb angle, these methods regress Cobb angle [2–5] from the original image [5] or coarse processing results of the original image such as

© The Author(s), under exclusive license to Springer Nature Singapore Pte Ltd. 2022
S. Yang and H. Lu (Eds.): ISAIR 2022, CCIS 1701, pp. 299–312, 2022.
https://doi.org/10.1007/978-981-19-7943-9_26

coarse segmentation results [2, 3], spine centerline [4], etc., which achieve end-to-end Cobb angle measurement, but ignore the importance of vertebral structures and lack interpretability. (2) Curvature-based Cobb angle estimation methods that rely on verte-bral features [6–11]. These methods first extract vertebral feature information through neural networks, and then perform curvature calculation post-processing based on the extracted features. For example, some works detect landmarks and thus calculate Cobb angles by the landmarks [6–8, 10]. Some works calculate Cobb angle by segmenting the vertebrae and finding the upper and lower end plates of the vertebrae [9, 11]. These methods can obtain richer information about the spine structure for the subsequent treat-ment of scoliosis, but they often focus on a single vertebral feature and cannot meet the accuracy requirements of vertebral features for post-processing of curvature calculations.

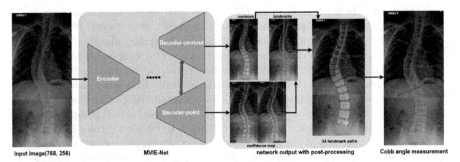

Fig. 1. An overview of the proposed method.

In this study, in order to obtain interpretable Cobb angle calculation results, we dis-card the end-to-end regression angle approach and choose the post-processing approach to calculate Cobb angle. Given the advantages and disadvantages of the landmarks detec-tion and contour segmentation, we combine the two approaches through the proposed MVIE-Net. We use the more robust confidence map to locate landmarks, since the direct landmark regression approach is vulnerable to accuracy and robustness. we generate confidence maps at landmark locations and obtain the coordinates of landmarks by seg-menting and parsing the confidence maps. The proposed MVIE-Net adopts a dual-task codec structure, where two tasks share the same encoder and have independent decoders, and the tasks interact with each other through a jump connection. We pair landmarks based on the location information obtained from vertebral contour segmentation.

In summary, the main contributions of this study are as follows:

- We use confidence maps to locate landmark coordinates, transforming the traditional points regression task into a confidence map segmentation task.
- We propose the simple and efficient multi-task learning framework MVIE-Net to simultaneously segment the vertebral contour and the confidence maps of landmarks.
- We combine vertebral contour information and landmarks information and match the landmarks of vertebrae by the relative position relationship between contours.

2 Method

As shown in Fig. 1, the spine X-ray images are input to the proposed MVIE-Net to generate segmentation results for vertebral contours and landmark confidence maps, respectively. Next, landmarks are resolved in the confidence map and paired left and right according to the relative configuration of vertebrae. Finally, Cobb angles are calculated from the paired landmarks.

2.1 Confidence Map of Landmarks

The vector $T = (t_1, t_2, \ldots, t_{34})$, $B = (b_1, b_2, \ldots, b_{34})$, $C = (c_1, c_2, \ldots, c_{34})$ represents the set of upper landmarks, lower landmarks and centers of mass of 12 thoracic and 5 lumbar vertebrae in the spine, respectively, where $t_{2j-1} = (t_{(2j-1,x)}, t_{(2j-1,y)})$, $b_{2j-1} = (b_{(2j-1,x)}, b_{(2j-1,y)})$, $c_{2j-1} = (c_{(2j-1,x)}, c_{(2j-1,y)})$, $j = 1, \ldots, 17$ denotes the coordinates of the four corner points along the clockwise direction and the centroid of the j-th vertebra, respectively.

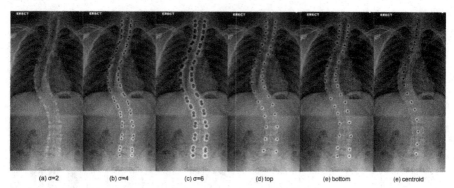

(a) σ=2   (b) σ=4   (c) σ=6   (d) top   (e) bottom   (e) centroid

Fig. 2. Confidence maps. (a)–(c) show the confidence maps generated at 68 landamrks for σ = 2, 4, 6. σ = 2 is not conducive to the segmentation of the confidence maps, and σ = 6 radiative range intersects, so we set σ = 4. However, integrating all key points into one confidence map makes the resolution of the segmented points difficult, so as shown in (d)–(f), three confidence maps are generated at the upper landmarks, the lower landmarks, and the centroid the vertebrae confidence maps.

To estimate the locations of 85 key points (68 landmarks and the 17 centroids of the vertebra), we employ confidence maps [12, 13] to represent the belief of each pixel location $x = (x', y')$, $x \in I$ with respect to the landmark and centroid. Considering the interference of intersecting confidence maps at different key points to parse the landmarks, we generate three confidence maps at the upper landmarks, lower landmarks, and form center of the vertebrae as the segmentation labels for landmark detection, which is defined by Eq. (1), Eq. (2), Eq. (3) respectively:

$$\Psi_t(x) = (exp(-\frac{\|x - t_1\|^2}{2\sigma^2}), \ldots, exp(-\frac{\|x - t_{34}\|^2}{2\sigma^2})), \tag{1}$$

$$\Psi_b(x) = (exp(-\frac{\|x - b_1\|^2}{2\sigma^2}), ..., exp(-\frac{\|x - b_{34}\|^2}{2\sigma^2})), \tag{2}$$

$$\Psi_c(x) = (exp(-\frac{\|x - c_1\|^2}{2\sigma^2}), ..., exp(-\frac{\|x - c_{17}\|^2}{2\sigma^2})), \tag{3}$$

where σ is the radiation radius of the confidence map generated by the key points. We tested the effect of different σ and finally set $\sigma = 4$, as shown in Fig. 2.

2.2 The Proposed MVIE-Net

As shown in Fig. 3, the hard parameter sharing structure [14] is used in our multi-task learning framework taking into account the similarity of vertebral contour segmentation and keypoint detection tasks. The two tasks share encoders with unique symmetric decoders. The basic convolution module consists of two 3×3 convolutions. ELU activation function and Batch Normalization are used to optimize the model parameters. The codec side uses jump connections to fuse low-level spatial location features with high-level semantic features [15].

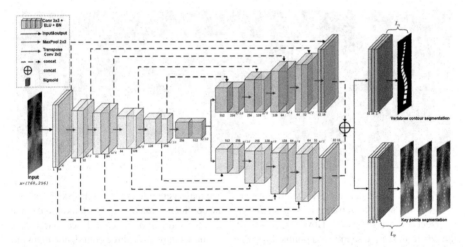

Fig. 3. MVIE-Net architecture. The proposed MVIE-Net is designed to perform vertebral contour segmentation and key points detection tasks at the same time.

On the encoder side, we extract the features of the image using the base convolution modules, and each base module is followed by a max pooling to halve the image size, and finally, we reduce the size of the feature map to 1/32 of the original size by down-sampling 5 times.

On the decoder side, we halve the channels and double the feature map size using a 2×2 transposed convolution. The feature information of the last layer of the two decoders is fused together byconcatenation, which allows the two tasks to interact with each other. At the end of the two decoders, we use two binary cross entropy losses L_c, L_p as the loss functions for the two tasks.Then the loss function of the whole network is $L = \lambda L_c + L_p$, and by experiment, we set $\lambda = 0.3$.

2.3   Cobb Angle Measurement

Given the lack of interpretability of regressing the Cobb angle directly from the model, we calculate the Cobb angle by mathematical modeling. We first extract the information needed to calculate the Cobb angle from the network segmentation results, and then model and calculate the Cobb angle based on the Cobb angle definition.

Post-processing Contour Segmentation Results

As shown in Fig. 4, we binarize the vertebral segmentation results and then calculate the minimum bounding rectangle of the vertebral contour. A line passing through the centroid of the vertebra and parallel to the MBR intersects the left and right midpoints of the vertebral contour. Intercept the middle 2/3 of the line connecting the left and right midpoints and make a vertical line through the two endpoints of the intercepted line. By fitting a straight line to the set of upper and lower boundary points of the vertebrae intercepted by two vertical lines, we obtain the upper and lower end plates similar to those manually labeled by the physician.

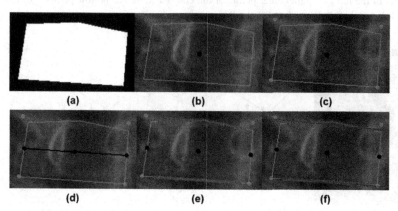

Fig. 4. Post-processing process of vertebral contour segmentation results. (a) vertebral contour segmentation results (b) vertebral contour point set (green) and the centroid of vertebra (red) (c) the four points of the minimum bounding rectangle (yellow) (d) Contour left and right midpoints (darkred) (e) vertebra upper and lower endplate point set (purple) (f) results of linear fitting of the upper and lower edge point sets (blue) (Colour figure online)

Post-processing Key Points Segmentation Results

As shown in Fig. 5, we parse the coordinates of the corresponding key points by finding the maximum value of the confidence region generated by each point. After obtaining the upper landmarks and lower landmarks of the vertebrae, the two upper and lower vertices belonging to the same vertebrae are paired according to the left and right midpoints of the vertebrae contours.

Methods of Calculating the Cobb Angle

We learned that the label of the Cobb angle used by the public AASCE Challenge dataset

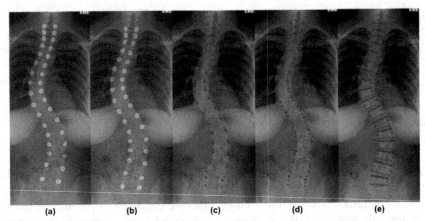

(a)   (b)   (c)   (d)   (e)

Fig. 5. Post-processing process of key points segmentation results. (a) upper landmarks confidence map segmentation result (b) lower landmarks confidence map segmentation result (c) coordinates paresd out from the two confidence map (green is the upper, red is the lower) (d) the position of the left and right center points of the contour (dark red hollow points). (e) results of landmark matching (Colour figure online)

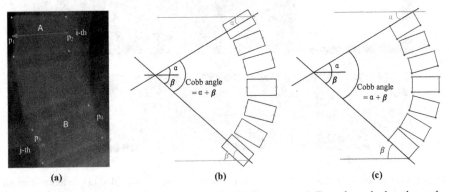

(a)   (b)   (c)

Fig. 6. Cobb angle measurement using landmarks. (a) the vectors A, B used to calculate the angle. (b) Calculating angles using the parallel property (c) Simulate the upper and lower end plates using the upper and lower landmarks connections

[16, 17] is calculated by Eq. (4):

$$angle = \arccos(\frac{A \cdot B}{\|A\| \cdot \|B\|}) \qquad (4)$$

As shown in Fig. 6 (a), the vectors $A = p_2 - p_1$, $B = p_4 - p_3$ represent the vectors of any two different vertebrae pointing from the midpoints of the two landmarks on the right to the midpoints of the two landmarks on the left.

We found that the algorithm given in the dataset uses the line connecting the midpoints of the left and right landmarks to simulate the vertebral endplates, which is different from the upper and lower endplates selected by physicians in clinical practice.

To investigate the effect of using different information on the Cobb angle measurements, we propose the following three ways to calculate the Cobb angle:

1. **Midpoint**: To obtain the angle of inclination of each vertebra, we let $k_a = y2 - y1/x2 - x1$, $k_b = y4 - y3/x4 - x3$, $\alpha = \arctan(k_a)$, $\beta = \arctan(k_b)$, (see Fig. 6(b)), then the angle between vertebrae $angle = \alpha + \beta$. Since the midpoint of the landmark is used, the results obtained by this method are the same as the method Cobb angle measurements given in the dataset.
2. **Endpoint**: As shown in Fig. 6(c), we follow more closely the way the clinician looks for the endplate, using the upper landmark connection of the vertebra above to simulate the upper endplate the lower landmark connection of the vertebra below to simulate the lower endplate.
3. **Straight-line fit**: In order to fully simulate the way physicians clinically mark the upper and lower endplates, we use the contour information alone to calculate the Cobb angle. We consider the straight lines fitted to the upper and lower boundaries of the contour as the upper and lower endplates of the vertebrae and calculate the Cobb angle from this.

3 Experimental Details

3.1 Dataset

The public AASCE Challenge dataset used for the experiment contained a total of 609 anterior-posterior radiographic images with labels. The dataset is divided by the provider into 481 images for training and 128 images for testing. Each image was manually labeled by a clinician with 68 landmarks in 12 thoracic and 5 lumbar vertebrae. These images are of varying sizes ($\sim 2500 \times 1000$).

3.2 Implement

We manually labeled 17 vertebrae as our contour segmentation labels using the labeling tool labelme, and generated key point segmentation labels by Eq. (1), Eq. (2), Eq. (3). To alleviate the overfitting problem of small datasets, we expanded the dataset through rotation, mirroring, and gamma transform (see Fig. 7).

We trained the proposed MVIE-Net in a Tesla T4 GPU using the pytorch framework. We resize the image to a fixed size of 768×256 while keeping the width and height of the image constant. The network was trained 500 epochs using the SGD optimization and stopped when the verification loss was not significantly reduced.

3.3 Evaluation Metrics

We qualitatively evaluated the vertebral segmentation results using the Dice Coefficient and the Intersection over Union (IoU) metrics which are defined as Eq. (5) and Eq. (6):

$$Dice = 2\frac{|V_{seg} \cap V_{gt}|}{|V_{seg}| + |V_{gt}|} = \frac{2TP}{FP + 2TP + FN}, \tag{5}$$

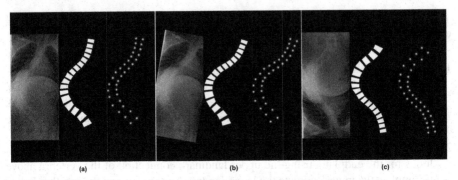

Fig. 7. Data augmentation. (a) resized image with its corresponding contour segmentation labels and upper landmarks confidence map (b) after rotating (c) after vertical mirroring

$$IoU = \frac{|V_{seg} \cap V_{gt}|}{|V_{seg} \cup V_{gt}|} = \frac{|V_{seg} \cap V_{gt}|}{|V_{seg}| + |V_{gt}| - |V_{seg} \cap V_{gt}|} = \frac{TP}{FP + TP + FN}. \quad (6)$$

Following the AASCE Challenge, we use Symmetric Mean Absolute Percentage Error(SMAPE) and mean absolute error (MAE) to evaluate the accuracy of the Cobb angle measurements which can be computed as Eq. (7) and Eq. (8):

$$SMAPE = \frac{1}{N} \sum_{i=1}^{N} \frac{\sum_{j=1}^{3} |X_{ij} - Y_{ij}|}{\sum_{j=1}^{3} |X_{ij} + Y_{ij}|} \times 100\%, \quad (7)$$

$$MAE = \frac{1}{N} \sum_{i=1}^{N} (\frac{1}{3} \sum_{j=1}^{3} |X_{ij} - Y_{ij}|), \quad (8)$$

where the X_{ij} and Y_{ij} is the estimation of the $j-th$ Cobb angle and corresponding ground truth for the test image i. N is the number of testing images.

4   Results and Analysis

To evaluate the proposed method, we tested the segmentation results of the proposed network and explored the effect of different Cobb angle calculation methods on the Cobb angle measurement results.

4.1   Segmentation Results of MVIE-Net

We compare the segmentation results of the two tasks of MVIE-Net separately with some efficient medical image segmentation networks. Table 1 shows the qualitative results of the proposed model on vertebral segmentation. Compared with the results of U-Net and U-Net++, the proposed model obtains better vertebral segmentation results. Although the proposed model has a larger number of parameters, it handles two tasks simultaneously. When using U-Net and U-Net++ to process two tasks simultaneously, the number of parametres would be twice as large as it is now, which means that our model reduces the

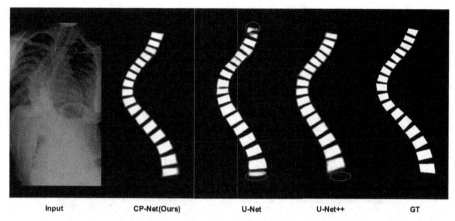

Fig. 8. Qualitative results of vertebrae segmentation. GT refers to the ground-truth landmarks. The red circle in U-Net marks the wrong segmentation, and the red circle in U-Net++ marks the missed vertebrae. (Colour figure online)

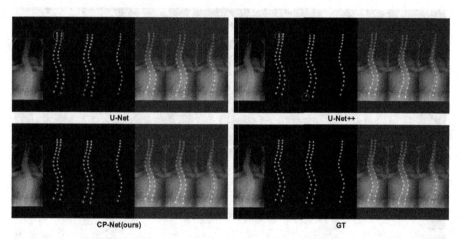

Fig. 9. Qualitative results of keypoints segmentation. The 7 images from left to right are the input image, the confidence map of the upper landmark, the confidence map of the lower landmark, the confidence map of the shape center, and the visualization of the confidence map on the original image. The red circle in U-Net shows the case where two points are connected, and the red circle in U-Net++ shows the segmentation anomaly of the points. (Colour figure online)

number of parametres by 4.71M compared to U-Net which also implements two tasks. Figure 8 shows the quantitative results for vertebral segmentation, and it can be seen from the red circles that the proposed network shows a significant improvement over U-Net and U-Net++ segmentation results, reducing the number of false segmentations that occur. Table 2 shows the qualitative results of the proposed model on keypoint segmentation. The qualitative metrics are generally low because the confidence maps generated by the key points are small relative to the images, but as can be seen in Fig. 9, the segmentation of the network can achieve the desired results, and as can be seen from the red circles, the proposed network has clearer and non-adhesive confidence map segmentation results.

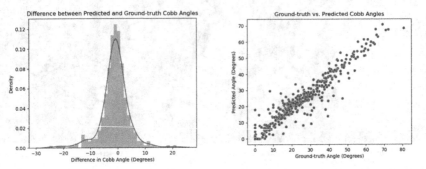

Fig. 10. Comparison and differences between the Cobb angle estimations and Cobb angle ground truth.

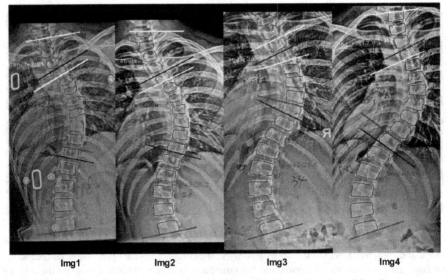

Fig. 11. Visualization of the straight-line fit method for estimation of four images.

4.2   Cobb Angle Measurement Results

We tested three Cobb angle calculation methods (midpoint method, endpoint method, and straight-line fit method), and the results are shown in Table 3. The Midpoint method achieved the best results because it is consistent with the Cobb angle labels in the dataset, which all pass through the vertebral The left and right midlinks simulate the endplates of the vertebrae.

Table 1. Qualitative vertebral segmentation results

	Dice	IoU	Params (M)
U-Net [15]	81.567	69.166	7.78 × 2
U-Net++ [18]	82.422	70.12	9.04 × 2
MVIE-Net	85.323	74.573	10.85

Table 2. Qualitative keypoints segmentation results

	Upper points		Lower points		Centroids	
	Dice	IoU	Dice	Iou	Dice	IoU
U-Net	33.029	20.815	31.412	19.686	42.329	25.346
U-Net++	38.783	24.128	37.709	23.308	42.715	27.235
MVIE-Net	**40.292**	**25.283**	**39.496**	**24.678**	**45.029**	**29.094**

Table 3. Cobb angle calculation results of 3 methods

	Midpoint	Endpoint	Straight-line fit
MAE (degree)	**3.31**	3.75	7.03
SMAPE (%)	**7.59**	8.54	16.15

Table 4. Comparison with the state-of-the-art methods

	MAE (degree)	SMAPE (%)	w/calculate
Landmark Net [19]	10.48	26.94	
Seg4Reg [2]	3.96	7.64	
Seg4Reg+ [3]	3.73	7.32	
AEC-Net [19]	4.90	23.59	✓
SLSN [7]	4.28	9.712	✓
Vertebra-focused [6]	4.07	9.53	✓
VF [20]	3.51	7.84	✓
Ours	3.31	7.59	✓

In order to show the accuracy of the proposed method in Cobb angle estimation, we compared the results of Cobb angle estimation with those of other methods, and the comparison results are shown in Table 4. The proposed method obtains the best results among all curvature post-processing methods for calculating Cobb angles, with MAE metrics reaching SOTA. Although the direct regression Cobb angle method [4] reaches SOTA in SMAPE metrics, the approach focused only on the Cobb angle calculation results and was unable to obtain information on the the end vertebrae, which is equally important for the diagnosis of scoliosis. Figure 10 shows the histogram of the difference and scatter plot between the Cobb angle estimation of the proposed method and the Cobb angle groud truth.

Table 5. Cobb angle estimations for 4 scoliosis radiographs

Cobb Angle	Img1		Img2		Img3		Img4	
	Upper	Lower	Upper	Lower	Upper	Lower	Upper	Lower
GT	39°	18°	39°	28°	49°	34°	60°	49°
Midpoint	44.2°	15.9°	47.4°	**28.8°**	52.9°	43.7°	61.5°	51.6°
Endpoint	45.2°	15.1°	48.5°	25.4°	**51.8°**	43.7°	**60.4°**	**49.9°**
Straight-line fit	**42.1°**	**17.4°**	**42.4°**	25.2°	**51.8°**	**29.6°**	62.1°	54.5°

It is important to note that we also tested our method on four scoliosis radiographs with the Cobb angle manually marked by the physician (see Fig. 11). The test results are shown in Table 5, where the straight-line fit method has the smallest SMAPE (3.88, compared to 5.51 for the midpoint method and 5.98 for the endpoint method), due to the fact that the method is more similar to the way clinicians determine the endplates. Therefore, we concluded that although the midpoint method showed better results on the public AASCE challenge dataset, the estimations of the straight-line fit method were more similar to the physician's manually labeled Cobb angle.

5   Conclusion

This paper presents a new method for automatic measurement of the Cobb angle of sco-liosis, using a network to extract scoliosis information and post-processing to calculate the Cobb angle, which can obtain more comprehensive vertebral contour information for visualization of the spine than direct Cobb angle regression. First, the proposed multi-task learning network MVIE-Net can simultaneously perform vertebral contour and key points detection, and the MVIE-Net network adopts a single encoder and dual decoder structure, and the symmetric structure and jump connection between the dual decoders improve the generalization ability of the network. Then, we proposed and tested three angle calculation methods based on the definition of the Cobb angle, namely the mid-point method provided by the public AASCE Challenge dataset, as well as the extended endpoint method, and the straight-line fit method that simulates the physician's position-ing of the endplate. MVIE-Net with midpoint method achieved SOTA in MAE metrics and the best SMAPE metrics among the known methods using post-processing on this dataset. The SMAPE of all three methods was lower than 6 on the physician manually labeled Cobb angle image processing, indicating that the proposed method can be used as an adjunct to the physician's clinical scoliosis Cobb angle measurement.

References

1. Seifert, J., Thielemann, F., Bernstein, P.: Adoleszente idiopathische Skoliose. Orthopade **45**(6), 509–517 (2016). https://doi.org/10.1007/s00132-016-3274-5
2. Lin, Y., Zhou, H.-Y., Ma, K., Yang, X., Zheng, Y.: Seg4reg networks for automated spinal curvature estimation. In: Cai, Y., Wang, L., Audette, M., Zheng, G., Li, S. (eds.) CSI 2019. LNCS, vol. 11963, pp. 69–74. Springer, Cham (2020). https://doi.org/10.1007/978-3-030-39752-4_7
3. Lin, Y., Liu, L., Ma, K., Zheng, Y.: Seg4reg+: Consistency learning between spine segmentation and cobb angle regression. In: de Bruijne, M., Cattin, P.C., Cotin, S., Padoy, N., Speidel, S., Zheng, Y., Essert, C. (eds.) MICCAI 2021. LNCS, vol. 12905, pp. 490–499. Springer, Cham (2021). https://doi.org/10.1007/978-3-030-87240-3_47
4. Huo, L., Cai, B., Liang, P., Sun, Z., Xiong, C., Niu, C., Song, B., Cheng, E.: Joint spinal centerline extraction and curvature estimation with row-wise classification and curve graph network. In: de Bruijne, M., Cattin, P.C., Cotin, S., Padoy, N., Speidel, S., Zheng, Y., Essert, C. (eds.) MICCAI 2021. LNCS, vol. 12905, pp. 377–386. Springer, Cham (2021). https://doi.org/10.1007/978-3-030-87240-3_36
5. Fu, X., Yang, G., Zhang, K., Xu, N., Wu, J.: An automated estimator for cobb angle measurement using multi-task networks. Neural Comput. Appl. **33**(10), 4755–4761 (2021)
6. Yi, J., Wu, P., Huang, Q., Qu, H., Metaxas, D.N.: Vertebra-focused landmark detection for scoliosis assessment. In: 2020 IEEE 17th International Symposium on Biomedical Imaging (ISBI), pp. 736–740. IEEE (2020)
7. Zhang, C., Wang, J., He, J., Gao, P., Xie, G.: Automated vertebral landmarks and spinal curvature estimation using non-directional part affinity fields. Neurocomputing **438**, 280–289 (2021)
8. Chen, K., Peng, C., Li, Y., Cheng, D., Wei, S.: Accurate automated keypoint detections for spinal curvature estimation. In: Cai, Y., Wang, L., Audette, M., Zheng, G., Li, S. (eds.) CSI 2019. LNCS, vol. 11963, pp. 63–68. Springer, Cham (2020). https://doi.org/10.1007/978-3-030-39752-4_6
9. Huang, C., et al.: Fully-automated analysis of scoliosis from spinal x-ray images. In: 2020 IEEE 33rd International Symposium on Computer-Based Medical Systems (CBMS), pp. 114–119. IEEE (2020)
10. Sun, Y., Xing, Y., Zhao, Z., Meng, X., Xu, G., Hai, Y.: Comparison of manual versus automated measurement of cobb angle in idiopathic scoliosis based on a deep learning keypoint detection technology. Eur. Spine J. **31**(8), 1969–1978 (2022)
11. Kuok, C.-P., Fu, M.-J., Lin, C.-J., Horng, M.-H., Sun, Y.-N.: Vertebrae segmentation from x-ray images using convolutional neural network. In: Proceedings of the 2018 International Conference on Information Hiding and Image Processing, pp. 57–61 (2018)
12. Cao, Z., Simon, T., Wei, S.-E., Sheikh, Y.: Realtime multi-person 2d pose estimation using part affinity fields. In: Proceedings of the IEEE Conference on Computer Vision and Pattern Recognition, pp. 7291–7299 (2017)
13. Payer, C., Štern, D., Bischof, H., Urschler, M.: Integrating spatial conguration into heatmap regression based CNNs for landmark localization. Med. Image Anal. **54**, 207–219 (2019)
14. Ma, J., Zhao, Z., Yi, X., Chen, J., Hong, L., Chi, E.H.: Modeling task relationships in multi-task learning with multi-gate mixture-of-experts. In: Proceedings of the 24th ACM SIGKDD International Conference on Knowledge Discovery & Data Mining, pp. 1930–1939 (2018)
15. Ronneberger, O., Fischer, P., Brox, T.: U-net: convolutional networks for biomedical image segmentation. In: Navab, N., Hornegger, J., Wells, W.M., Frangi, A.F. (eds.) MICCAI 2015. LNCS, vol. 9351, pp. 234–241. Springer, Cham (2015). https://doi.org/10.1007/978-3-319-24574-4_28

16. Wu, H., Bailey, C., Rasoulinejad, P., Li, S.: Automatic landmark estimation for adolescent idiopathic scoliosis assessment using boostnet. In: Descoteaux, M., Maier-Hein, L., Franz, A., Jannin, P., Collins, D.L., Duchesne, S. (eds.) MICCAI 2017. LNCS, vol. 10433, pp. 127–135. Springer, Cham (2017). https://doi.org/10.1007/978-3-319-66182-7_15

17. Wang, L., et al.: Evaluation and comparison of accurate automated spinal curvature estimation algorithms with spinal anterior-posterior x-ray images: the aasce2019 challenge. Med. Image Anal. **72**, 102115 (2021)

18. Zhou, Z., Rahman Siddiquee, M.M., Tajbakhsh, N., Liang, J.: Unet++: a nested u-net architecture for medical image segmentation. In: Stoyanov, D., Taylor, Z., Carneiro, G., Syeda-Mahmood, T., Martel, A., Maier-Hein, L., Tavares, J.M.R.S., Bradley, A., Papa, J.P., Belagiannis, V., Nascimento, J.C., Lu, Z., Conjeti, S., Moradi, M., Greenspan, H., Madabhushi, A. (eds.) DLMIA/ML-CDS -2018. LNCS, vol. 11045, pp. 3–11. Springer, Cham (2018). https://doi.org/10.1007/978-3-030-00889-5_1

19. Chen, B., Xu, Q., Wang, L., Leung, S., Chung, J., Li, S.: An automated and accurate spine curve analysis system. IEEE Access **7**, 124596–124605 (2019)

20. Kim, K.C., Yun, H.S., Kim, S., Seo, J.K.: Automation of spine curve assessment in frontal radiographs using deep learning of vertebral-tilt vector. IEEE Access **8**, 84618–84630 (2020)

Emotion-Sentence-DistilBERT: A Sentence-BERT-Based Distillation Model for Text Emotion Classification

Haoyu Wang, Xin Kang$^{(\boxtimes)}$, and Fuji Ren

Faculty of Engineering, Tokushima University, 2-1 Minamijyousanjima-cho, Tokushima 770-8506, Japan
c612035050@tokushima-u.ac.jp, {kang-xin, ren}@is.tokushima-u.ac.jp

Abstract. Text emotion classification is a hot research area in natural language processing, aiming to classify the human emotion into positive and negative categories based on words. As a well-established and widely used neural model, BERT has achieved many state-of-the-art results in various natural language processing tasks, including text emotion classification. However, the embedding of sentences from BERT has been proved to be insufficient in semantic representation, which we believe is especially crucial for building the emotion classification models. Another issue about employing BERT in text emotion classification is the model complexity, which has limited its training and application in natural human-computer interaction for emotional robotics. In this paper, we propose a novel Emotion-Sentence-DistilBERT (ESDBERT) model, which explores the rich emotional representation in sentences via a Siamese Network based Sentence-BERT module and further reduces the model complexity through a Knowledge Distillation process. Experimental results suggest that the proposed model can learn a rich emotional representation and to render a promising accuracy for text emotion classification compared with the undistilled BERT-based models.

Keywords: Sentence-BERT · DistilBERT · Text emotion classification · SST2

1 Introduction

With the rapid development of computer technology and the "explosion" of data size and form, text data mining techniques have developed rapidly since 2000 [1] and are now a popular direction at the intersection of natural language processing and data mining, while emotion analysis is a fundamental problem in text mining. BERT is a linguistic representation model released by Google in October 2018 [2]. When using BERT, good results can be obtained by modifying the output layer and fine-tuning the model according to downstream tasks. When BERT was released, it achieved better results than then on GLUE [3], MultiNLI [4], SQuAD [5], and other evaluation benchmarks and datasets. The BERT model has been shown to perform well on a variety of NLP tasks. The task of semantic text similarity is no exception. However, as specified by the BERT model,

© The Author(s), under exclusive license to Springer Nature Singapore Pte Ltd. 2022
S. Yang and H. Lu (Eds.): ISAIR 2022, CCIS 1701, pp. 313–322, 2022.
https://doi.org/10.1007/978-981-19-7943-9_27

two sentences need to be fed into the model for information interaction at the same time, which leads to a significant computational overhead. For example, given 10,000 sentences, we want to find the most similar sentence pair, which requires (10,000 * 9999/2) computations and about 65 h [6]. The BERT model is constructed in such a way that it is neither suitable for semantic similarity search nor for unsupervised tasks, such as clustering.

To address the shortcomings of the BERT model, Reimers et al. proposed the Sentence-BERT network architecture [7]. Briefly, referring to the framework of Siamese network model [8], different sentences are fed into two BERT models to generate Sentence Embedding vectors with semantics. The final generated sentence representation vectors can be used for semantic similarity computation and unsupervised clustering tasks. For the same 10,000 sentences, we want to find the most similar sentence pair, which takes only 10,000 computations [9] and takes about 5 s to complete. 5 s is a big difference from 65 h. However, Sentence-BERT is still a gap in the field of text emotion classification.

As the technology evolves, the amount of code for large NLP models like BERT or RoBERTa [10] is huge and the process of training such models is very lengthy. Due to their large size, training such models can last for days. When it comes to running them on small devices, we obviously pay a huge memory and time cost for the ever-increasing performance. There are ways to alleviate this pain with little impact on the performance of the model, and the technique is called distillation. When we want to port a model to smaller hardware, such as a limited laptop or cell phone, the benefits of knowledge distillation [11] are obvious, as the distilled model has fewer parameters, runs faster, and takes up less space while maintaining performance.

As a result, we decide to use Sentence-BERT for the text emotion classification task and further refine it to reduce its size. The target model body consists of two different DistilBERT models. After extracting features of the same sentence by two different DistilBERTs, the two outputs are brought together using the last layer of the hidden layer. In this paper, We tested taking CLS [12–14] vectors directly and average pooling. We crossed the sentence vectors of the two features obtained after pooling. Reimers et al. tried various crossover methods and it worked best in classifying $|u - v|$, so We chose this method as well. Finally, the results of $|u - v|$ were classified by the SoftMax layer.

The rest of this paper is organized as follows. We review related work in Sect. 2. In Sect. 3, we describe the construction of Sentence-BERT-based distillation models for text emotion classification. Section 4 describes the experimental setup and analyzes the results of text emotion classification. Section 5 provides our conclusions and future work.

2   Related Works

Reimers et al. 2019 proposed the Sentence-BERT model in their paper [7]. Sentence-BERT follows the structure of the Siamese network, and the text Encoder part is processed by the same BERT. Afterwards, Reimers et al. experiment with CLS-Token and two Pooling strategies (AVG-pooling and mean-pooling) and further extract and compress the character vectors of the BERT output to obtain u and v. Regarding the integration of u and v, Reimers et al. 2019 provide three strategies.

- For the classification task, u and v are spliced, connected to the fully connected network, and classified by SoftMax. The loss function uses cross entropy.
- Calculate and output cosine similarity directly. The training loss function uses the root mean square error.
- Ternary (triplet) objective function. Given an anchor sentence (a), a positive example sentence (p) and a negative example sentence (n), the ternary loss is used to adjust the network so that the distance between a and p is smaller than the distance between a and n.

In general, Sentence-BERT is directly initialized with BERT's original weights and fine-tuned on specific datasets, and the training process is not much different from the traditional Siamese Network. However, this training method can make BERT better capture the relationship between sentences and generate better sentence vectors. Instead, in the testing phase, Sentence-BERT directly uses cosine similarity to measure the similarity between two sentence vectors, thus improving the inference speed.

BERT is a 12-layer transformer encode, and Distilled BERT is a 6-layer trans-former encode. Distilled BERT does not conduct its own pre-training. Instead, some parameters of BERT are loaded directly into the Distilled BERT structure as initialization. The first paper on BERT distillation is the one that inspired us, Sanh et al. 2019 [15]. Apart from that there are some good other methods, such as [16] or [17], so it was natural to wonder why we restricted ourselves to DistilBERT. The answer is threefold, first, it is very simple and a good introduction to distillation; second, it gives good results; third, it also allows to refine other BERT-based models. BERT is primarily based on a series of attention layers stacked on top of each other. This therefore means that the "hidden knowledge" learned by BERT is contained in these layers. We won't care how these layers work, here we can treat the attention layer as a black box, it doesn't matter to us [18]. DistilBERT alternates between a full replicated layer and an ignored layer, according to the method of [16], which tries to replicate the top or bottom layer in preference. Thanks to the deformation module of Hugging-Face and some knowledge of the inner workings of BERT, this replication step can be easily implemented. If a BERT-based model is used for a specific task, such as time series classification, the head of the Teacher model needs to be copied into the Student model. However, in general, the head size of BERT is very small compared to the size of the attention layer and can be negligible.

We wanted to obtain a student model. However, the distillation process is not a classical fitting process. Our aim is not to teach the student model to learn the model as usual, but to imitate the teacher. And we want to set up two different DistilBERTs instead of using the same DistilBERT. Therefore, we will have to adjust the training process, especially our loss function.

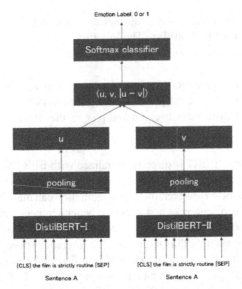

Fig. 1. Proposal model, Emotion-Sentence-DistilBERT.

3 Emotion-Sentence-DistilBERT

3.1 Model Structure

We choose a basic BERT model and build a two-tower model with two different distillation strategies, and input the output word vectors into pooling, and perform feature cross-validation on the two sentence vectors obtained after pooling to
improve the accuracy of text emotion classification calculation. We named this model
Emotion-Sentence-DistilBERT (ESDBERT).

The model run process. First, we input the sentences into two DistilBERT model
towers separately to get the word vectors, then we get the sentence vectors by pooling
strategy, then we stitch the two sentence vectors together and multiply them by a weight
W, i.e., $W_t(u, v, |u - v|)$. Finally, after SoftMax, we obtain the binary classification
probability function. We train the above network by minimizing the cross-entropy loss
while updating the weights W_t [19]. In this way, we can use SBERT for the task of
classifying sentence pairs.

SoftMax [25] is a very common and important function in machine learning, especially deep learning, especially in the context of multi-class classification. It [26] maps
some of the inputs to real numbers between 0 and 1, and the normalization guarantees
that the sum is 1, so the multi-class probabilities also sum to exactly 1.

Given an n-dimensional vector, the SoftMax function maps it to a probability
distribution [27]. The standard SoftMax function $\sigma: \mathbb{R}^n \to \mathbb{R}^n$ is defined by Eq. (3)

$$\sigma(X)_i = \frac{\exp(x_i)}{\sum_{j=1}^{n}\exp(x_j)}; \, i = 1, \ldots, n; \quad X = [x_1, \ldots, x_n]^T \in \mathbb{R}^n \qquad (1)$$

In classification problems, the SoftMax function is often used with the cross-entropy loss function.

$$Loss = -\sum_i t_i \ln y_i \tag{2}$$

3.2 ESDBERT for Sentence Pair Emotion Classification Tasks

We have a dataset containing sentence emotion labels, and the binary emotion labels indicate whether the sentence is positive (1) or negative (0), as shown in Table 1. The text input is formatted so that label 1 is positive and label 0 is negative.

We see how to use the above dataset to fine-tune a pre-trained BERT model for a sentence emotion classification task based on conjoined network. Let's start by looking at one of the sentences in the dataset.

- Sentence A oh, look at that clever angle!

We need to decide whether a given sentence pair is similar (1) or dissimilar (0):

- Tokens A = [[CLS], oh, look, at, that, clever, angle, [SEP]]

Then, we feed these labels into the pre-trained DistilBERT model to obtain a vector representation of each label. We then fed these labels into the pre-trained DistilBERT model to obtain a vector representation of each label. We learned that SBERT uses the Siamese network. Siamese network is essentially two identical networks that share weights. And our model uses two different DistilBERTs, so we input the list of labels for sentence A into the first DistilBERT-I, and then input the list of labels for sentence A into the other DistilBERT-II, and then calculate the feature vectors for both sentences. To compute the feature vectors for the sentences, we use the average pool here. After applying the pooling strategy, we have a sentence feature for the given sentence, as shown in Fig. 1.

This section focuses on the individual functions from input to output. The process is shown in Fig. 1. u represents the sentence representation of the DistilBERT-I output and v represents the sentence representation of the DistilBERT-II output. After obtaining the features u and v, a feature vector for matching the relationship between the two is constructed based on u and v, and then an additional model is used to learn a generic text relationship map.

Now, we concatenate them and the difference between their elements and multiply it by a weight W, as follows, $W_t(u, v, |u - v|)$. Note that the dimension of the weight W is $W_t \in R^{3n*k}$, where n is the dimension of the sentence embedding. k is the number of categories. Next, we feed this result into a SoftMax function that returns the given emotion probability.

$$o = Softmax(W_t(u, v, |u - v|)) \tag{3}$$

We train the above network by minimizing the cross-entropy loss while updating the weights W. In this way, we can use ESDBERT for the task of emotion classification

Table 1. Text input format, label 1 is positive, label 0 is negative

Sentence A	Label
The film is strictly routine	0
This is a stunning film, a one-of-a-kind tour de force	1
Marinated in cliches and mawkish dialogue	0
A visual spectacle full of stunning images and effects	1

sentence pairs. After feature extraction of two sentences via DistilBERT, the hidden layers of the last layer should be pooling. The feature crossover is performed on the two sentence vectors obtained after pooling. Finally, through the SoftMax layer.

3.3 Distillation Method

The purpose of model distillation is to inherit the effects of the model with fewer parameters. The model distillation is commonly used in the way of Teacher-Student model distillation. The whole idea is to let the Teacher model learn the large parameters of the model. Let the Student model inherit from it. Distill stands for distillation, and we can literally guess that we're going to Distill from a large model into a smaller model, or we can think of it in a way that we're going to have the large model as the Teacher of the small model, and the small model, the Student, is just going to try to learn everything that the Teacher outputs [20]. BERT is a 12-layer transformer encode, and Distilled BERT is a 6-layer trans-former encode. Distilled BERT does not conduct its own pre-training. Instead, some parameters of BERT are loaded directly into the Distilled BERT structure as initialization.

On the method of setting T and ∂ in distillation. The hyperparameter mainly controls the loss ratio of soft label and hard label [21]. In the experiment, Distilled BiLSTM [22] found that only using soft label would get the best results. We suggestion are to make soft label account for more. On the one hand, it is to force Students to have more Teacher knowledge. On the other hand, the experiment proves that soft target can play a regularization role and make the Student model converge more stably.

The hyperparameter T mainly controls the smoothness of the prediction distribution. TinyBERT [23] experiments show that T = 1 is better, and the search space of BERT-PKD is {5, 10, 20}. Therefore, it is recommended to try several times between 1 and 20, and the larger T is, the more generalization information of the Teacher model can be learned. For example, when MNIST [24] classifies the handwritten picture of 2, it may assign a confidence of 0.9 to 2, and 3 is 1E−6 and 7 is 1E−9. It can be seen from this distribution that 2 and 3 have a certain similarity. In this case, T can be increased to make the probability distribution smoother and show more generalization ability of Teacher.

Table 2. The Stanford Emotion Treebank (SST-2) dataset

SST-2	Label
A stirring, funny and finally transporting reimagining of beauty and the beast and 1930s horror films 1	1
Apparently reassembled from the cutting room floor of any given daytime soap	0
This is a visually stunning rumination on love, memory, history and the war between art and commerce	1
A fan film that for the uninitiated plays better on video with the sound turned down	0
At achieving the modest, crowd-pleasing goals it sets for itself	1

4 Experiments and Results

4.1 Dataset

The Stanford Emotion Treebank (SST-2) is a single-sentence classification task containing sentences from movie reviews and human annotations of their emotions [28]. The task is to classify the emotion of a given sentence. There are two emotion categories, which are the positive emotion category (1) and the negative emotion category (0). The emotion labels are only annotated on the sentence-level. Therefore, we consider SST-2 as a binary classification task, which classifies sentences into positive and negative emotions.

The sample size consists of a training set of 67, 350, a development set of 873, and a test set of 1, 821. It is a test set for performing a binary emotion classification task of positive and negative emotions. The evaluation criterion is accuracy. Examples with label (positive emotion, negative emotions) are shown in Table 2. Notice that since the sentences are derived from movie reviews and have human annotations of their emotions, some sentences are very long and others are very short, and the lengths are not uniform.

4.2 Evaluation Method

We choose accuracy, precision, recall, F1 value, macro avg, and weighted avg as evaluation criteria. Accuracy is defined as the percentage of results predicted correctly in relation to the total sample. Precision, which refers to the predicted outcome, refers to the probability that of all samples predicted to be true, that sample is actually true. Recall, which is specific to the original sample, is defined as the probability of being predicted as true in a sample that is actually true. F-Score, the summed average of precision and recall, which considers both precision and recall achieving the highest balance between the two. Macro avg, the average of all the label results. Weighted avg, The weighted average of all the label results.

4.3 Results and Discussion

Our final distillation results we obtained for the two distillation models are: Distil BERT-I retaining layers 1, 2, 4, 5, 7, and 9; Distil BERT-II retaining layers 1, 3, 6, 8, 10, and

Table 3. Sentence-DistilBERT's precision, recall, F1-score, macro-avg, and weighted avg.

	Precision	Recall	F1-score
Negative	0.9086	0.9477	0.9277
Positive	0.9518	0.9155	0.9333
Macro avg	0.9302	0.9316	0.9305
Weighted avg	0.9315	0.9306	0.9307

Table 4. Accuracy of ESDBERT with other models on the SST-2 dataset

Model	Accuracy
ESDBERT	92.8%
bmLSTM	91.8%
Charformer-Base	91.6%
DistilBERT	91.3%
BERT Base	91.2%
CNN-RNF-LSTM	90.0%

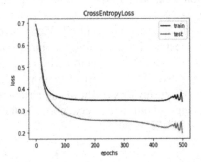

Fig. 2. ESDBERT's cross-entropy loss function.

11. The total model volume is almost the same as BERT, and the processing speed is about 50% faster relative to BERT.

As can be seen in Table 3, a relatively good balance between precision and recall can be achieved at F1 of 0.9333. Macro avg is the average of all labeled results of about 0.93, and the weighted avg is the weighted average of all labeled results of about 0.93.

The accuracy of the results evaluated was compared with the Dummy classifier. Dummy Classifier is a classifier that makes predictions using simple rules. Usually, this classifier is used as a simple baseline to compare with other (real) classifiers. The comparison results are as follows: The Dummy classifier score was 84.7%. Our accuracy is 92.8%. DistilBERT is 60% the size of BERT. Our model ESDBERT is 50% BERT size. Compared with BERT and DistilBERT's accuracy on SST-2, the results are shown in the Table 4. The accuracy of our model on the SST-2 dataset is 92.8%, which is higher than BERT and DistilBERT.

We evaluate the convergence of model learning by means of cross-entropy loss values. The cross-entropy value is used to describe the difference between the predicted and true values of the model. A lower cross-entropy value indicates better convergence. As shown in Fig. 2, the overall trend is downward convergence, which means that the model performs well.

5 Concludes

In this paper, we propose to apply Sentence-BERT to a text emotion classification task using transfer learning. Through transfer learning and continuous fine-tuning of the model, semantic sentence vectors based on sentence networks and their related algorithms are introduced into text emotion classification, better word vectors are obtained by setting two different DistilBERT models, which in turn improve the semantic richness of the sentence vectors, and finally the regression model is trained to achieve emotion classification. And the size of the model is further reduced by knowledge distillation. Our model achieves 92.8% accuracy on the SST-2 dataset, which is higher than models such as BERT and DistilBERT.

For future work, we will further optimize the model to improve the accuracy of emotion classification and explore more distillation strategies. We also want to create a suitable dataset for fine-grained emotion classification.

References

1. Fan, W., Bifet, A.: Mining big data: current status and forecast to the future. ACM SIGKDD Explorations Newsl. **14**(2), 1–5 (2013)
2. Devlin, J., Chang, M.W., Lee, K., Toutanova, K.: BERT: pre-training of deep bidi-rectional transformers for language understanding. arXiv preprint arXiv:1810.04805 (2018)
3. Wang, A., Singh, A., Michael, J., Hill, F., Levy, O., Bowman, S.R.: GLUE: a multi-task benchmark and analysis platform for natural language understanding. arXiv preprint arXiv: 1804.07461 (2018)
4. Williams, A., Nangia, N., Bowman, S.R.: A broad-coverage challenge corpus for sentence understanding through inference. arXiv preprint arXiv:1704.05426 (2017)
5. Rajpurkar, P., Zhang, J., Lopyrev, K., Liang, P.: Squad: 100,000+ questions for machine comprehension of text. arXiv preprint arXiv:1606.05250 (2016)
6. Johnson, J., Douze, M., Jégou, H.: Billion-scale similarity search with GPUs. IEEE Trans. Big Data **7**(3), 535–547 (2019)
7. Reimers, N., Gurevych, I.: Sentence-BERT: sentence embeddings using siamese BERT-networks. arXiv preprint arXiv:1908.10084 (2019)
8. Chopra, S., Hadsell, R., LeCun, Y.: Learning a similarity metric discriminatively, with application to face verification. In: 2005 IEEE Computer Society Conference on Computer Vision and Pattern Recognition (CVPR 2005), vol. 1, pp. 539–546. IEEE (2005)
9. Liang, L., Li, Y., Wen, M., Liu, Y.: KG4Py: a toolkit for generating Python knowledge graph and code semantic search. Connect. Sci. **34**(1), 1384–1400 (2022)
10. Liu, Y., et al.: Roberta: a robustly optimized BERT pretraining approach. arXiv preprint arXiv: 1907.11692 (2019)

11. Gou, J., Yu, B., Maybank, S.J., Tao, D.: Knowledge distillation: a survey. Int. J. Comput. Vis. **129**(6), 1789–1819 (2021)
12. May, C., Wang, A., Bordia, S., Bowman, S.R., Rudinger, R.: On measuring social biases in sentence encoders. arXiv preprint arXiv:1903.10561 (2019)
13. Zhang, T., Kishore, V., Wu, F., Weinberger, K.Q., Artzi, Y.: BERTScore: evaluating text generation with BERT. arXiv preprint arXiv:1904.09675 (2019)
14. Qiao, Y., Xiong, C., Liu, Z., Liu, Z.: Understanding the Behaviors of BERT in Ranking. arXiv preprint arXiv:1904.07531 (2019)
15. Sanh, V., Debut, L., Chaumond, J., Wolf, T.: DistilBERT, a distilled version of BERT: smaller, faster, cheaper and lighter. arXiv preprint arXiv:1910.01108 (2019)
16. Jiao, X., et al.: TinyBERT: Distilling BERT for Natural Language Understanding (2019)
17. Sun, Z., Yu, H., Song, X., Liu, R., Yang, Y., Zhou, D.: MobileBERT: a Compact Task-Agnostic BERT for Resource-Limited Devices (2020)
18. Karim, R.: Illustrated: Self-Attention (2019). Towards Data Science
19. Tetko, I.V., Kůrková, V., Karpov, P., Theis, F. (eds.): ICANN 2019. LNCS, vol. 11728. Springer, Cham (2019). https://doi.org/10.1007/978-3-030-30484-3
20. Meng, H., Lin, Z., Yang, F., Xu, Y., Cui, L.: Knowledge distillation in medical data mining: a survey. In: 5th International Conference on Crowd Science and Engineering, pp. 175–182 (2021)
21. Li, Y., Sun, Y., Zhu, N.: BERTtoCNN: similarity-preserving enhanced knowledge distillation for stance detection. PLoS ONE **16**(9), e0257130 (2021)
22. Chen, T., Xu, R., He, Y., Wang, X.: Improving sentiment analysis via sentence type classification using BiLSTM-CRF and CNN. Expert Syst. Appl. **72**, 221–230 (2017)
23. Jiao, X., et al.: TinyBERT: distilling BERT for natural language understanding. arXiv preprint arXiv:1909.10351 (2019)
24. Cohen, G., Afshar, S., Tapson, J., Van Schaik, A.: EMNIST: extending MNIST to handwritten letters. In: 2017 International Joint Conference on Neural Networks (IJCNN), pp. 2921–2926. IEEE (2017)
25. Liu, Z.H., Lu, B.L., Wei, H.L., Chen, L., Li, X.H., Wang, C.T.: A stacked auto-encoder based partial adversarial domain adaptation model for intelligent fault diagnosis of rotating machines. IEEE Trans. Ind. Inf. **17**(10), 6798–6809 (2020)
26. Dukhan, M., Ablavatski, A.: Two-pass SoftMax algorithm. In: 2020 IEEE International Parallel and Distributed Processing Symposium Workshops (IPDPSW), pp. 386–395. IEEE (2020)
27. Zhang, K., Lin, S., Sun, H., Ma, L., Xu, J.: Dynamic time warping based clustering for time series analysis. In: Wang, S., Zhang, Z., Xu, Y. (eds.) IoTCare 2021, vol. 415, pp. 376–385. Springer, Cham (2022). https://doi.org/10.1007/978-3-030-94182-6_29
28. Hernandez, S., Larsen, S., Trager, S., Kaper, L., Groot, P.: Metallicities of young massive clusters in NGC 5236 (M83). Mon. Not. R. Astron. Soc. **473**(1), 826–837 (2018)

Gait Recognition for Laboratory Safety Management Based on Human Body Pose Model

Jiangxin He, Xin Kang[✉], and Fuji Ren

Faculty of Engineering, Tokushima University, 2-1, Minamijyosanjima-Cho, Tokushima 7708506, Japan
c612035051@tokushima-u.ac.jp, {kang-xin, ren}@is.tokushima-u.ac.jp

Abstract. Most of the important data and equipment storage places, such as laboratories, mainly rely on manual management and various biometric systems to ensure their security. Currently, the commonly used biometric systems include facial recognition, fingerprint recognition, voice recognition and gait recognition. Gait is a unique way of moving for each person. Compared with other biometrics, gait is difficult to imitate or fake and can accomplish the supervision tasks more efficiently. This paper proposes a novel Human Body Pose (HBP) model for gait recognition in laboratory environments. Specifically, we first extract the image of each frame from the video and extract the 2D human body poses in the form of people's joints and bones with OpenPose. Then we use a 3D pose library to estimate a 3D human pose by matching with the 2D pose. Finally, we employ a Convolutional Neural Network to extract the human temporal-spatial features for gait recognition. We train and validate our method to compare with the state-of-the-art methods on the CASIA gait dataset B. Experimental results show that our method outperforms the state-of-the-art methods in the case of cross-view and clothing changes.

Keywords: Gait recognition · OpenPose · Human body pose · CNN

1 Introduction

Laboratories and other places are facing great challenges in terms of information and equipment storage security. Currently, the main security management methods in laboratories are broadly divided into two types, which are the manual management and the intelligent system management. The limitations and drawbacks of manual management are becoming more and more obvious in today's society, where technology is developing at a rapid pace. Intelligent systems usually refer to biometric identification systems, including fingerprint recognition, face recognition, gait recognition, etc. [1, 2]. Since biometric features such as fingerprints and faces have a certain possibility of being forged, they still pose a certain threat to the security of laboratories, so we propose the use of gait recognition systems to further strengthen the security management of laboratory.

Gait recognition aims to be a method for identity validation through the unique posture and manner of human walking [3]. Compared with other biometric identification

© The Author(s), under exclusive license to Springer Nature Singapore Pte Ltd. 2022
S. Yang and H. Lu (Eds.): ISAIR 2022, CCIS 1701, pp. 323–331, 2022.
https://doi.org/10.1007/978-981-19-7943-9_28

technologies such as face recognition and fingerprint recognition, gait recognition has its unique advantages and characteristics. Firstly, gait features are difficult to disguise. Each person has some differences in height, weight, bone length, bone weight, muscle strength, walking center of gravity, and physiological conditions that affect walking posture [4], so it is very difficult to imitate other people's gait. Secondly, gait recognition is a long-distance and non-invasive recognition method. In the recognition process, it does not require the recognized person to be close to or directly touch the recognition equipment, and the information collection is relatively convenient. Thirdly, gait recognition is less affected by the incidentals of the recognized person. For example, when people wear high-density sunglasses, masks and other items, face recognition and iris recognition systems will not work properly.

The common gait recognition methods available today include sensor-based gait recognition [5], appearance-based gait recognition [6], and model-based gait recognition [7]. Sensor devices for gait recognition usually contain both wearable and non-wearable sensors [8, 9], so sensor-based gait recognition methods usually require specialized sensor devices that are difficult to implement in a general laboratory environment. The most used feature for appearance-based gait recognition methods is gait energy image [10]. However, appearance-based gait recognition methods still face the challenges of environmental interference and image noise removal.

In this paper, we use a model-based gait recognition method that returns the features of gait recognition to the human body itself [11], which means that such methods are more sensitive when the human pose changes.

The rest of this paper is organized as follows. Section 2 briefly reviews the related work about the model-based gait recognition methods. Section 3 depicts our proposed HBP model for gait recognition in laboratory environments. In Sect. 4, we report the experimental results of gait recognition based on CASIA gait dataset B and compare our results with the state-of-the-art methods. Finally, Sect. 5 concludes this paper.

2 Related Work

The usual implementation process of the model-based method is: first modeling the human body by labeling the body information (bones, joints, etc.); then designing static or dynamic feature quantities (such as the angle between bones attached to the same joint, the length of the bones, or other features); finally achieving gait recognition by comparing the feature quantities with the relevant parameters. As early as 2009, W. K et al. [12] proposed that gait recognition becomes difficult in the case of perspective change. Based on the GEI technology, a view transformation model (VTM) based on spatial GEI was created. The Singular Value Decomposition (SVD) technique was used, which can convert the corridor gait perspective data and probe gait viewpoint data into the same view direction, thus overcoming the effect of viewpoint change on gait recognition.

R.T. et al. [7] used shadows projected from the lower body joints to the walking plane for gait recognition, calculated joint angle trajectories by estimating the offset of the lower body skeleton from the joints, and finally calculated the temporal dimension of the trajectories and normalized the experimental method.

The DensePose [13] uses a grid to mark the human body surface to form a grid-like modeling of the human pose. However, DensePose can only build a grid on the human body surface from the camera's filming angle. It cannot build the parts that are not captured by the camera, resulting in incomplete information about the human body and thus making the experimental data incomplete.

In our proposed HBP model, the human body was modeled by using joints and bones extracted by OpenPose [14]. This method estimates the 2D human pose from a single RGB image of the human body and annotates the bones and joints of the human body.

3   Human Body Pose (HBP) Model for Gait Recognition

In our method HBP, we use 3D pose information as a feature quantity for gait recognition. First, we need to capture RGB walking videos of human body and extract 2D skeleton and joint models of human body by RGB image sequences. Then we estimate the 3D model from the 2D model of the human body, construct the coordinate system in space, and extract the features needed in the method. The framework of the method is shown in the Fig. 1.

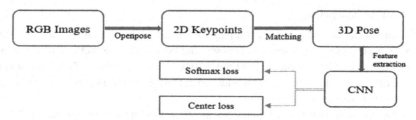

Fig. 1. The framework of HBP

3.1   Human Body Pose Estimation

In Fig. 2, a total of 25 human body joints are estimated and extracted by OpenPose, namely: Nose, Neck, RShoulder(R stands for Right, L stands for Left, and the subsequent R and L stand for the same meaning.), LShoulder and so on[1]. Because the size of the human body finally displayed on the image depends on the distance between the human body and the camera. In order to facilitate and more accurate information comparison, we subject the estimated human pose model to a simple normalization process. We define the distance between Neck and MidHip as the unit length, and since the currently extracted human body model is two-dimensional, take Neck as the origin. These works are beneficial to our follow-up work.

In order to solve the impact of the view change on the gait recognition, we need to convert a 2D human pose into a 3D human pose. The research in [15] shows that the method can estimate the 3D pose of the human body from each frame of images by matching 3D pose library.

---

[1] All of the joints in Fig. 2 are named "Nose, Neck, RShoulder, RElbow, RWrist, LShoulder,LElbow, LWrist, MidHip, RHip, RKnee, RAnkle, LHip, LKnee, LAnkle, REye, LEye, REar,LEar, LBigToe, LSmallToe, LHeel, RBigToe, RSmallToe and RHeel".

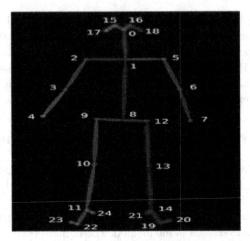

Fig. 2. The sample of the estimated 2D pose by OpenPose

3.2 Feature Extraction

According to the three-dimensional human pose to establish a spatial coordinate system, the X, Y and Z axes are defined as follows: the positive two directions of the X axis are the direction of human movement; the Y axis is perpendicular to the X axis and the positive direction is from the right shoulder to the left shoulder; the positive direction of the Z axis is vertically upward.

In the research, two feature quantities are used as comparison contents, F^{pose} and F^{motion}. F^{pose} represents a pose, which is represented by the collection of all human joint points, we have:

$$J_i = (x_i, y_i, z_i), \tag{1}$$

$$F^{pose} = [J_0, J_1, \ldots, J_N], \tag{2}$$

where $i \in \{0, 1, \ldots, N\}$ and $N = 24$, J is the coordinate of different joint points, and N represents the total of the joint points that be estimated. F^{motion} represents the change of the action, the change of posture between the adjacent two frames t and $t + 1$ can be expressed as:

$$F_t^{motion} = F_{t+1}^{pose} - F_t^{pose}, \tag{3}$$

Since both features are extracted frame by frame, so we can construct a feature matrix for the two defined features to fuse the two feature vectors, as:

$$F_t = F_t^{pose} + F_t^{motion}, \tag{4}$$

Because F_t^{motion} is the difference of F^{pose} between the frame t and $t + 1$, the total of F^{motion} will be one less than the total of F^{pose}. In order to make the number of two features consistent to make the matrix complete, we add a 0 vector for F^{motion} to the beginning to make the number of F^{pose} and F^{motion} be same. Then the two the constructed feature matrix can be complete. This feature matrix is used as a follow-up that the input of the CNN to extract the high-level temporal-spatial features.

3.3 Gait Recognition Network

Considering that the features used in the study are extracted on a per-frame basis and are continuous. Therefore, we adopt CNN as the network structure for feature extraction. In order to obtain high-level spatiotemporal features for gait recognition after processing through the CNN model, it is important to reduce intra-class differences and enlarge inter-class differences. Related studies in [16] show that a multi-loss strategy is employed to optimize the CNN network. Including softmax loss and center loss. The equation of the loss function is as follows:

$$L = L_{softmax} + L_{center},\qquad(5)$$

The softmax loss can classify the input features into different categories, which indicates that the softmax loss can expand the differences between different categories and thus achieve classification. The center loss can minimize the variation within each class to maintain the difference and separability of different class features. Since the dataset used in our comparative experiment is the CASIA gait dataset B, the amount of data is not very large, so we use a light-weight network structure with 7 convolutional layers (3×3) and 2 pooling layers (2×2).

4 Experiment

4.1 Dataset

In this study we use the CASIA gait dataset B to test the proposed method. It is a large-scale and multi-view gait dataset. Because the dataset is collected in an indoor environment and covers multiple views, it provides a better simulation of the laboratory environment. This dataset contains 124 subjects. Each subject contains three different walking states, including Normal Walking (NM), Walking with a Bag (BG) and Walking with a Coat (CL), and the dataset videos are from 11 different views.

4.2 Experimental Results

The experiment is conducted on the CASIA gait dataset B. We put the first 62 subjects into the training set and the rest into the testing set as a setup for comparison experiments with GEI + PCA [6], SPAE [17] and GaitGAN [18]. In the testing set, the gallery set consisted of the first 4 Normal Walking sequences and the probe set consisted of the remaining sequences as shown in Table 1.

In this study, experiments are conducted by using data from three views ($0°$, $90°$, $180°$) in the dataset because data from these perspectives are easier to simulate the laboratory environment. Table 2–4. list the experimental results of this method on the CASIA gait dataset B. In the experiment, the first 4 normal walking (NM01-04) sequences of a specific view are put into the gallery set, and the last 2 normal walking sequences (NM05-06), 2 walking sequences with bags (BG01-02), and 2 walking sequences with coats (CL01-02) are put into the probe sets of three sets of experiments respectively. For each set of experiments, there are 9 combinations. This means that there are 9 recognition rates in each table.

Table 1. Experimental setting on CASIA gait dataset B

	Training	Testing	
		Gallery set	Probe set
Num.	001–062	063–124	063–124
Sequence	NM01-06, BG01-02, CL01-02	NM01-04	NM05-06, BG01-02, CL01-02

Table 2. Recognition rates when the probe set is NM05-06 on CASIA gait dataset B

		Probe set view		
		0°	90°	180°
Gallery set view	0°	96.13	24.74	64.13
	90°	27.56	98.10	22.58
	180°	67.55	21.17	97.89

Table 3. Recognition rates when the probe set is BG01-02 on CASIA gait dataset B

		Probe set view		
		0°	90°	180°
Gallery set view	0°	75.23	16.33	35.68
	90°	20.98	71.16	15.56
	180°	43.84	16.17	62.49

Table 4. Recognition rates when the probe set is CL01-02 on CASIA gait dataset B

		Probe set view		
		0°	90°	180°
Gallery set view	0°	48.56	16.34	24.18
	90°	9.97	59.42	10.51
	180°	30.88	15.63	40.17

In the above table, we can see the recognition rates obtained by applying the method of this paper under three different conditions. In order to show more intuitively the effectiveness of the methods in this paper, in the following Fig. 3 and Fig. 4, we present in turn the results of the comparison between the methods used in this paper and the appearance-based gait recognition methods, namely GEI + PCA, SPAE and GaitGAN.

In the previous section, we introduced that the comparative experimental results are by comparable since the initial experimental settings are all the same. The Fig. 3 and 4 show the average recognition rates with the view variation and the same view.

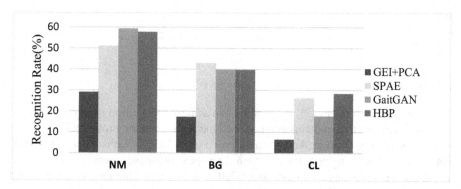

Fig. 3. The average recognition rates with the view variation

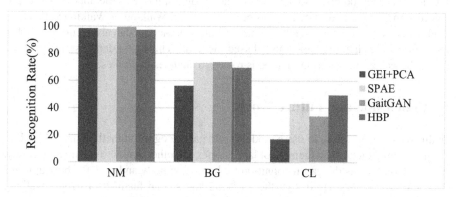

Fig. 4. The average recognition rates with the same view

The following Table 5 and Table 6 show the data for the above Fig. 3 and Fig. 4.

Table 5. The average recognition rates with the view variation

	GEI + PCA	SPAE	GaitGAN	HBP
NM	29.09	51.09	59.31	57.76
BG	17.30	42.92	39.78	39.72
CL	6.55	26.34	17.65	28.41

Table 6. The average recognition rates with the same view

	GEI + PCA	SPAE	GaitGAN	HBP
NM	98.45	98.12	99.46	97.37
BG	56.23	73.12	73.66	69.63
CL	16.93	43.28	33.87	49.38

4.3 Discussion

As we can see from the Fig. 3, our method can achieve recognition rate comparable to some of the more advanced appearance-based methods when the probe set is a Normal Walking or Walk with a Bag. And when the probe set is Walking with a Coat, our method can achieve a higher recognition rate than the appearance-based methods. This shows that the model-based approach can be applied to scenes with changing viewpoints and is robust to changes in clothing.

It also be seen from the Fig. 4, when the gallery set view is the same as the probe set view, our method can also achieve similar recognition rate as the appearance-based gait recognition methods when the probe set is Normal Walking or Walking with a bag. And when the probe set is "Walking with a Coat", our method can also achieve a higher recognition rate than the appearance-based methods. This again demonstrates that the model-based gait recognition method is robust to changes in clothes.

5　Conclusion and Future Work

In this paper, we propose to use a model-based gait recognition method named HBP to further strengthen the management of laboratories and other places to ensure their safety. This method returns the gait recognition to the human body and uses the human joints and bones as the basis to design the temporal and spatial features of people walking for recognition. In terms of datasets, this paper uses the CASIA gait dataset B for the experiment because the data of this dataset is taken from multiple perspectives and is indoors, which is similar to the laboratory environment, and the effect is more convincing. The experimental results show that the method can generally achieve a recognition rate similar to that of several relatively new appearance-based recognition methods, and the effect is better when the viewing angle changes and the clothes change. Future work starts from two points. 1. Whether it is possible to use more advanced human pose estimation methods to better and accurately extract human pose features to improve the recognition rate. 2. Collect more real-world datasets for testing to validate whether the method can work properly and efficiently.

References

1. Besbes, F., Trichili, H., Solaiman, B.: Multimodal biometric system based on fingerprint identification and iris recognition. In: 2008 3rd International Conference on Information and Communication Technologies: From Theory to Applications, pp. 1–5 (2008)
2. Deshpande, U.U., Malemath, V.S., Patil, S.M., et al.: Latent fingerprint identification system based on a local combination of minutiae feature points SN Comput. Sci. 2(3), 1–17 (2021). https://doi.org/10.1007/s42979-021-00615-7
3. Boyd, J.E., Little, J.J.: Biometric gait recognition. In: Tistarelli, M., Bigun, J., Grosso, E. (eds) Advanced Studies in Biometrics. Lecture Notes in Computer Science, vol 3161. Springer, Berlin, Heidelberg (2005)
4. Ball, A., Rye, D., Ramos, F., Velonaki, M.: Unsupervised clustering of people from 'skeleton' data. In: Proceedings of the Seventh Annual ACM/IEEE international conference on Human-Robot Interaction (HRI 2012). Association for Computing Machinery, vol. 225–226, New York (2012)
5. Marsico, M.D., Mecca, A.: A survey on gait recognition via wearable sensors. ACM Comput. Surv. 52(4), 39 (2020)
6. Han, J., Bhanu, B.: Individual recognition using gait energy image. IEEE Trans. Pattern Anal. Mach. Intell. 28(2), 316–322 (2006)
7. Tanawongsuwan, R., Bobick, A.: Gait recognition from time-normalized joint-angle trajectories in the walking plane. In: Proceedings of the 2001 IEEE Computer Society Conference on Computer Vision and Pattern Recognition. CVPR 2001, pp. II-II (2001)
8. Cha, Y., Kim, H., Kim, D.: Flexible piezoelectric sensor-based gait recognition. Sensors 18(2), 468 (2018)
9. Meng, Z., Fu, S., Yan, J., Liang, H., Zhou, A., Zhu, S., Ma, H., Liu, J., Yang, N.: Gait recognition for co-existing multiple people using millimeter wave sensing. Proc. AAAI Conf. Artif. Intell. 34(01), 849–856 (2020)
10. Lishani, A.O., Boubchir, L., Khalifa, E., et al.: Human gait recognition using GEI-based local multi-scale feature descriptors. Multimed. Tools Appl. 78, 5715–5730 (2019)
11. Borràs, R., Lapedriza, À., Igual, L.: Depth information in human gait analysis: an experimental study on gender recognition. In: Campilho, A., Kamel, M. (eds) Image Analysis and Recognition. ICIAR 2012. Lecture Notes in Computer Science, vol 7325. Springer, Berlin (2012)
12. Kusakunniran, W., Wu, Q., Li, H., Zhang, J.: Multiple views gait recognition using view transformation model based on optimized gait energy image. In: 2009 IEEE 12th International Conference on Computer Vision Workshops, ICCV Workshops, pp. 1058–1064 (2009)
13. Güler, R.A., Neverova, N., Kokkinos, I.: Densepose: dense human pose estimation in the wild. In: IEEE Conference on Computer Vision and Pattern Recognition (CVPR), pp. 7297–7306 (2018)
14. Cao, Z., Hidalgo, G., Simon, T., Wei, S.-E., Sheikh, Y.: OpenPose: realtime multi-person 2D pose estimation using Part Affiffiffinity Fields, 2018, pp. 1–14. arXiv:1812.08008.
15. Chen, C.-H., Ramanan, D.: 3D human pose estimation = 2D pose estimation + matching. In: IEEE Conference on Computer Vision and Pattern Recognition (CVPR), pp. 7035–7043 (2017)
16. Wen, Y., Zhang, K., Li, Z., Qiao, Y.: A discriminative feature learning approach for deep face recognition. In: European Conference on Computer Vision, pp. 499–515 (2016)
17. Yu, S., Chen, H., Wang, Q., Shen, L., Huang, Y.: Invariant feature extraction for gait recognition using only one uniform model. Neurocomputing 239, 81–93 (2017)
18. Yu, S., Chen, H., Reyes, E.B.G., Poh, N.: Gaitgan: invariant gait feature extraction using generative adversarial networks. In: Computer Vision and Pattern Recognition Workshops, pp. 532–539 (2017)

Use Active Learning to Construct Japanese Emoji Emotion Database

Xiudong Li, Xin Kang[✉], and Fuji Ren

Faculty of Engineering, Tokushima University, 2-1 Minamijyosanjima-cho,
Tokushima 770-8506, Japan
c612035052@tokushima-u.ac.jp, {kang-xin,
ren}@is.tokushima-u.ac.jp

Abstract. Emojis are now frequently used in online communication, which express rich meaningful information and emotional messages. However, communication will fail if the meaning of different Emojis is not well understood, especially for the speakers of different languages and those from different countries/regions. There are very few researches about the Emoji dataset currently, since the process of building an Emoji database is labor-intensive and time-consuming. To solve this problem, we propose an active learning-based framework for building Japanese text datasets containing Emoji. This approach aims to achieve fast and balanced labeling of data given a small and unevenly distributed source of Emoji data. The active learning algorithm selects unlabeled data with high information content for manual labeling and updates the model parameters with the manually labeled data, in which way a large Emoji database is iteratively constructed. The constructed Japanese Emoji database contains hundred types of Emojis, with at least hundred pieces of Our experiment suggests that the Emoji dataset can be efficiently constructed with balanced data and the result dataset can provide rich information for text emotion classification, by rendering an accuracy of over 82%.

Keywords: Emoji · Active learning · Database

1 Introduction

With the rise of social media, hieroglyphics, commonly referred to as "Emoji," have become one of the fastest growing forms of expression in the world. Emoji is an ideographic writing system born in Japan that provides a rich set of non-verbal cues to assist text communication. Unicode 11.0 specifies more than 2,500 emojis, ranging from facial expressions (such as 😃) to everyday objects (such as 🚚). Originally a visual aid for text communication, the non-verbal nature of Emoji has led some to believe that they are universal across cultures [1].

The rapid growth of Emoji began in 2011, when Apple iPhone added the Emoji keyboard to the iOS system, and Android mobile platform began to support Emoji in 2013. Emoji has penetrated into the modern network and network communication, and is now regarded as a natural and common form of expression [2]. In fact, Oxford

Dictionaries chose "⊕" as its word of the year for 2015. The global acceptance of Emoji indicates that its use is cross-cultural and normative. At the same time, there may be nuances in the use of Emoji in different cultures because of linguistic differences in how emojis express emotions, as well as differences in how they conceptualize topics.

Despite the ubiquity of emojis, there are still many questions regarding their use, especially regarding global differences in languages and countries/regions. In the studies related to Emoji, it can be found that according to the frequency of Emoji use, context and topic association, there will be understanding errors when using Emoji across cultures, which are very important [3]. Partly because they reveal how people communicate digitally on social platforms, but also because they offer a perspective from which to study different regions and cultures. Therefore, we want to study Emoji from the perspective of different languages.

In addition, in recent years, many studies have begun to detect the topic words in the text stream in the network to judge whether there is a negative emotion emergent topic, so as to deal with the related possible emergent situations [5, 6]. As of March 2019, there are 3,019 emojis in Unicode, nearly half of all text messages on Instagram contain emojis, and 5 billion of them are used daily on Facebook, demonstrating the influence of emojis in online communication. We believe it is very valuable to study the meaning of Emoji in more depth.

Previous Emoji research has focused more on optimizing the sentiment algorithm to improve the accuracy of the algorithm, and in the process of learning we believe that the current accuracy improvement has reached a bottleneck, Therefore, we decided to improve the accuracy of the final acquisition by improving the quality of the database. Based on this idea, we decided to study how to build a better database more quickly. The method we chose is to achieve this goal through active learning. In the past, a lot of Emoji-related research data was obtained through questionnaires, which was very inefficient. and some of the studies that collected data by themselves to build databases were not particularly well-developed because of the time required to build them, and there were various defects, such as the data were not evenly distributed and there were too few single data. By using active learning, the time required to build a database can be significantly reduced. And the distribution of data becomes more even as the amount of data increases, which greatly reduces the occurrence of a single piece of data and the amount of data is too small.

In this paper, we propose a database construction method based on active learning. Firstly, a large amount of data containing emoji is collected on the web, then it is preprocessed and the sentiment parameters are extracted by Bert. Then a small amount of data is manually labeled, and a large amount of labeled data is completed to build a database by the active learning method.

The rest of this paper is organized as follows. We review related work in Sect. 2. In Sect. 3, we describe the data collection and preprocessing, and introduce the active learning algorithm based on BERT for text sentiment classification. Section 4 describes the evaluation method of the experiments and analyzes the results of sentiment classification. Our conclusions and future work are given in Sect. 5.

2 Related Work

The use of Emoji is composed of the combination of language, social background and cultural customs [4], and is influenced by many factors such as cultural background, living environment and language. Environment and user groups. Cultural differences have a significant impact on the use of Emoji. Some specific uses of Emoji are closely related to cultural backgrounds. For example, users in Finland, India, and Pakistan use specific emojis based on their culture [7]. Chinese users are more likely than Spanish users to use emojis and other nonverbal cues to express negative emotions [3]. The study also found that people from Hong Kong and the United States used different emojis on user-generated restaurant re-view sites, which may reflect underlying cultural differences [8]. Due to cultural differences in Emoji use, an EmojiGrid was developed for cross-cultural research on food-related emotions, which reliably reflects established cultural characteristics [9]. This difference is evident not only between countries, but also within the same country [10]. The specific language environment can also affect the use of Emoji. Emoji show a high degree of context sensitivity in cross-language communication, which means that they are very dependent on their linguistic and textual environment [11]. For example, studies have shown that there is a strong similarity in Emoji use between the United Kingdom and the United States, as they both speak English, but the similarity is low when compared with other languages, such as Italian and Spanish [12]. Studies have also shown that Japanese teenagers have found innovative ways to use Emoji to manage their relationships and express their aesthetics in subculture-specific ways [13]. Through literature survey, we found that most of the previous research data were obtained in the form of questionnaire survey, so the amount of data obtained was not large. In particular, there may be a small amount of data for a given Emoji. Therefore, in this study, we attach great importance to these two points. We collect a large amount of data on the Internet to establish a database and use Active Learning model to achieve the balance between the data. Active Learning refers to the automatic selection of data request labels from a data set through automatic machine learning algorithms, which is also known as query learning or optimal experimental design in statistics [14, 15, 16]. By designing reasonable query function, Active Learning constantly picks out data from unlabeled data and adds them to the training set after labeling. Effective Active Learning data selection strategy can effectively reduce the cost of training, improve the recognition ability of the model, and achieve fast and balanced data tagging.

3 Constructing an Emotional Database Through Active Learning

3.1 Data Collection

For a long time, researchers have been using questionnaires or SNS social networks such as Twitter for data collection. The questionnaire method of data collection requires too much manpower and time to build a large and rich database. In contrast, data collection on Twitter is difficult due to the fact that Twitter users speak various languages, which makes the process of data collection more difficult. In this paper, we chose to collect data from the Japanese social network "Yay! "Yay!" is a social application where you can chat with people who have the same interests and share your moods with people who are interested in you. This SNS has a relatively even ratio of users, and by reducing the possibility of obtaining data from people of the same gender or from people of the same age, the data balance can be better ensured. Example Fig. 1 shows an example of the data.

Fig. 1. An example of data

The author of this data message shared his emotions at the time. It can be noticed that part of the text of this data shows happy emotions, but the attached 😭 Emoji contains sad emotions. We think it can be considered that through the combination of text and Emoji, the meaning of 😭 Emoji can be understood as moved to cry. Therefore, we believe that the emotion of the text part of a piece of data has a great influence on the emotion of Emoji, and We build a database based on the analysis of the emotions contained in the text. In order to attach importance to user privacy, During the data collection process, we only collect information related to text and Emoji. Information related to privacy, such as username and location, is not collected. Finally, the data information collected only includes text data.

We learned from the social network "Yay!" In the process of data collection, not all the data collected include Emoji. Therefore, we will complete the data set after several cycles of screening. In the process of screening, only the data information containing Emoji will be retained, and the data information without Emoji will be removed.

3.2 Text Sentiment Classification Based on BERT

After completing the dataset in order to analyze the sentiment of the text We chose to use BERT to extract features from the text, BERT: Bidirectional Encoder Representation from Transformers, BERT is a natural language processing model developed by Google that learns bidirectional representations of text. significantly improves the ability to understand unlabeled text in many different tasks in context. In order to select the BERT model for Japanese text, this study chose to use the "BERT Japanese Pretrained Model" published by the KurohashiKawara Research Laboratory of Kyoto University, which can achieve an accuracy of over 90.2. In the process of using BERT, we mainly use JUMAN + + tool to parse the morphological elements of text sentences considering the semantic rationality of word sequences, and then feed them into the BERT model, and then use pooling to calculate the representative vectors of the sentences, and apply the pooling strategy to obtain the corresponding text features.

3.3 Introduction to Active Learning Algorithm

Active learning continuously selects data from unlabeled data by designing a reasonable query function to add annotations to the training set. An effective active learning data selection strategy can effectively reduce the cost of training and improve the recognition ability of the model at the same time.

The steps of active learning are:

Each round begins by passing the current model.

step 1. Determine a Query Selection strategy.

step 2. Find the most informative sample.

step 3. Manually annotate data.

step 4. Add the newly annotated data to the training dataset.

step 5. Retrain the model based on the current data.

until the model's performance reaches a goal condition, or there are no conditions left to annotate data anyway

In the Active Learning framework, the most important thing is how to design a query strategy to judge the value of the sample, that is, whether it is worth to be labeled. However, the value of samples is not immutable. It is not only related to samples themselves, but also related to tasks and models. As a simple example, an 🙏 Emoji being used in a text expressing gratitude is often valuable to the training of a classification model because it is difficult to discriminate. However, an 😱 Emoji used in a text expressing fear becomes less important because it is not difficult for the model to discriminate it. Therefore, the design of query strategy is not simple and static, and needs to be set according to the specific environment, problem, and needs. In terms of algorithms, We choose Uncertainty Sampling to achieve the goal of perfect and balanced data.

Picking out the samples that the current model is least confident in, usually the closer the samples are to the edge of the hyperplane classification, the more likely they are to be uncertain.

$$x^* = \mathrm{argmax} f(x; P_\theta) \tag{1}$$

$$f(x; P_\theta) = f_{LC}(x; P_\theta) + f_{SM}(x; P_\theta) + f_{LE}(x; P_\theta), \tag{2}$$

$$f_{LC}(x; P_\theta) = 1 - P_\theta(\hat{y}|x), \tag{3}$$

$$f_{SM}(x; P_\theta) = P_\theta(\hat{y}_1|x) - P_\theta(\hat{y}_2|x), \tag{4}$$

$$f_{LE}(x; P_\theta) = \sum_i^k P_\theta(y_i|x), \tag{5}$$

P_θ represents the BERT model; x represents the text; y represents the sentiment; $\hat{y}$ represents the best sample; k represents the number of sentiment categories.

4 Experiment

Since the number of data in the database finally constructed in this paper is relatively large, We chose a more subjective judgment method in the judgment method. We randomly selected 600 pieces of data in the database, and firstly, 300 pieces of data were manually labeled with emotion to get a "data answer", and then the initial 20 pieces of data and the initial 60 pieces of data were labeled by the active learning model at a rate of 10% of the total data each time. The other 300 pieces of data are labeled, and then Accuracy is obtained from the data labeled by the active learning model and the manually labeled data.

In the evaluation index of the experiment in this study we choose to use dichotomous classification index.

To evaluate the method, we use T for True, F for False, P for Positive, N for Negative. first observe the predicted result (P or N), and then compare the predicted result with the actual result to give the judgment result (T or F). The number of samples that are actually True and classified as True, TP; the number of samples that are actually False but classified as True, FP; the number of samples that are actually False and classified as False, TN; the number of samples that are actually True but classified as False, FN.

The accuracy rate is the percentage of the total number of correctly predicted results.

$$Accuracy = \frac{TP + TN}{TP + TN + FP + FN} \tag{6}$$

Precision is the proportion of samples with positive and correct predictions to all samples with positive predictions.

$$Precision = \frac{TP}{TP + FP} \tag{7}$$

Recall is the proportion of samples with positive and correct predictions to all samples that are actually positive.

$$Recall = \frac{TP}{TP + FP}, \tag{8}$$

The F1-score is a metric that combines precision and recall.

$$F_1 - score = \frac{2*Precision*Recall}{Precision + Recall} \tag{9}$$

According to the accuracy obtained by each round of labeling of the active learning model, it can be seen that the accuracy of the labeling data of the active learning model has significantly increased. It can be seen from Table 1 that although the higher the initial training data, the higher the accuracies obtained, the accuracies basically reached the same level at the beginning of the sixth round, and the final accuracies reached 82%. It can be seen from Fig. 2 and Fig. 3 that the accuracies reached a stable stage when the cycle reached the seventh round. Through this experiment, it can be proved that the method of using active learning model can greatly reduce the manpower and time needed to build the Japanese Emoji Emotion Database. The final correct rate of this experiment can reach 0.82 while the accuracy, recall, and F1 score reach 0.91, 0.93, and 0.92, respectively.

Table 1. Accuracy per cycle.

Total	Test	Initial	1	2	3	4	5	6	7	8	9	10	All
600	300	20	0.33	0.43	0.49	0.56	0.61	0.75	0.8	0.8	0.81	0.82	0.82
600	300	60	0.46	0.54	0.59	0.63	0.69	0.76	0.79	0.8	0.81	0.82	0.82

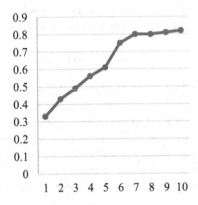

Fig. 2. Initial 20 per cycle Accuracy   **Fig. 3.** Initial 60 per cycle Accuracy

Here we discuss some data examples obtained during the experiment. Figure 4 shows the distribution of the sentiment categories for the 10 Emoji. Table 2 shows several emotion categories generated during the use of

🌀by Japanese language users. We found a significant correlation between Emoji and sentiment categories. For example, 😓the Emoji itself is closer to Sad in sentiment, and it is also obvious that Sad occupies a higher proportion of the sentiment categories, with 57 in Sad, 35 in Unease, and 8 in Anger out of 100 data.

Through subjective analysis, we found that Emoji can express a variety of emotion categories. For example, 😊this Emoji out of the 100 data collected, there are 30 in Happy, 6 in Love, 24 in Sad, 18 in Unease, and 22 in Surprise. Occupying 5 of the 6 emotion categories, with only anger not appearing. It can be seen that even though the original meaning of 😊is relatively clear, it has changed its original emotion because it is used by the user in various moods.

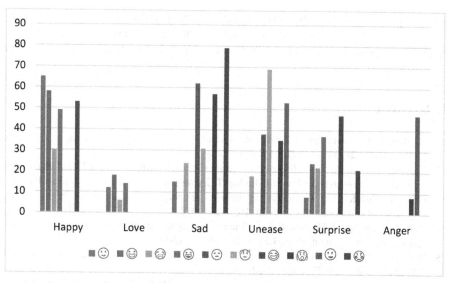

Fig. 4. Emotional category distribution of Emoji

Table 2. Several emotions that occur when using 😶

case study	translation	Emotional
今出かけて足をくじいた 😶	I sprained my leg just now 😶	Sad
うっかり学校の花瓶を割ってしまったらどうしよう 😶	Accidentally broke the school vase how to do 😶	Unease
ありがとう 😶	Thank you 😶	Happy
きょうプロポーズは成功した 😶	The proposal went off today 😶	Love
友人から念願のゲームをもらった 😶	My friend gave me the game I always wanted 😶	Surprise

5 Conclusions

The main purpose of our research is to create a Japanese Emoji Emotion Database for various future studies in order to address misunderstandings of Emoji arising from worldwide differences in language and country/region. We propose to use active learning algorithms to select unlabeled data with high information content for manual determination of the data labels. At the same time, we use the manually labeled data to update the model parameters, and so on repeatedly iterate through the cycle to complete the automated labeling of large data sets for the purpose of quickly building sentiment databases. This method can also be used to quickly build sentiment databases for other languages. We finally construct a Japanese Emoji database with 100 emojis (100 pieces of data for each) by subjective judgment method, The amount of work required to build the database is greatly reduced by using active learning methods. The data volume of a certain Emoji data was prevented from being extremely rare, and the purpose of data distribution averaging was achieved. As future work, this study intends to construct Emoji sentiment databases for other languages (such as Chinese, English, Russian, etc.) to enable data comparison.

References

1. Al Rashdi, F.: Functions of Emojis in WhatsApp interaction among Omanis. Discourse Context Media **26**, 117–126 (2018)
2. Njenga, K.: Social media information security threats: anthropomorphic Emoji analysis on social engineering, in Paper Presented at the IT Convergence and Security 2017 (Seoul) (2018)
3. Chik, A., Vasquez, C.: A comparative multimodal analysis of restaurant reviews from two geographical contexts. Vis. Commun. **16**, 3–26 (2017)
4. Derks, D., Fischer, A.H., Bos, A.E.R.: The role of emotion in computer-mediated communication: a review. Comput. Hum. Behav. **24**, 766–785 (2008)
5. Derks, D., Bos, A.E., Von Grumbkow, J.: Emoticons and online message interpretation. Soc. Sci. Comput. Rev. **26**, 379–388 (2008)
6. Gao, M., Zhang, Z., Yu, G., Arık, S.Ö., Davis, L.S., Pfister, T.: Consistency-based semi-supervised active learning: towards minimizing labeling cost. In: Vedaldi, A., Bischof, H., Brox, T., Frahm, J.-M. (eds.) ECCV 2020. LNCS, vol. 12355, pp. 510–526. Springer, Cham (2020). https://doi.org/10.1007/978-3-030-58607-2_30
7. Cheng, L.: Do I mean what I say and say what I mean? A cross cultural approach to the use of emoticons & Emojis in CMC messages. Fonseca J. Commun. (2017)
8. Kaneko, D., Toet, A., Ushiama, S., Brouwer, A.-M., Kallen, V., van Erp, J.B.F.: EmojiGrid: a 2D pictorial scale for cross-cultural emotion assessment of negatively and positively valenced food. Food Res. Int. **115**, 541–551 (2019)
9. Ljubešić, N., Fišer, D.: A global analysis of Emoji usage. In: Paper Presented at the Proceedings of the 10th Web as Corpus Workshop (2016)
10. Barbieri, F., Kruszewski, G., Ronzano, F., Saggion, H.: How cosmopolitan are Emojis?: exploring Emojis usage and meaning over different languages with distributional semantics In: Paper Presented at the 2016 ACM on Multimedia Conference (2016)
11. Sugiyama, S.: Kawaii meiru and Maroyaka neko: mobile Emoji for relationship maintenance and aesthetic expressions among Japanese teens. First Monday **20**, 1 (2015)
12. Barbieri, F., Ronzano, F., Saggion, H.: What does this Emoji mean? A vector space skip-gram model for Twitter Emojis. In: Paper presented at the International Conference on Language Resources and Evaluation, LERC (2016)
13. Tauch, C., Kanjo, E.: The roles of Emojis in mobile phone notifications. In: Paper Presented at the 2016 ACM International Joint Conference on Pervasive and Ubiquitous Computing: Adjunct (Heidelberg) (2016)
14. Settles, B.: Active learning literature survey (2009)
15. Gilyazev, R., Turdakov, D.Y.: Active learning and crowdsourcing: a survey of optimization methods for data labeling. Program. Comput. Softw. **44**(6), 476–491 (2018)
16. Schroder, C., Niekler, A.: A survey of active learning for text classification using deep neural networks, arXiv preprint arXiv:2008.07267 (2020)

Target-Driven Autonomous Robot Exploration in Mappless Indoor Environments Through Deep Reinforcement Learning

Wenxuan Shuai[1,2], Mengxing Huang[1,2(✉)], Di Wu[1,2,3(✉)], Gang Cao[3], and Zikai Feng[1,2]

[1] Information and Communication Engineering, Hainan University, Haikou 570228, HI, China
huangmx09@163.com, hainuwudi@163.com
[2] State Key Laboratory of Marine Resource Utilization in South China Sea, Haikou 570228, China
[3] Control Science and Engineering with the Department of Automation, Shanghai Jiao Tong University, Shanghai 200240, SH, China

Abstract. In this paper, we present a deep reinforcement learning (DRL)-based autonomous end-to-end system for wheeled robots in an unmapped environment. Potential Waypoints (PWPs) are obtained along the way towards the global target for possible better navigation directions. Based on the available data, we use a novel heuristics function to evaluate and select the optimal waypoint. Following the waypoints, the robot is guided towards the global goal. A local navigation system based on DRL is developed to generate the motion policy that guide the robot move between waypoints and towards global goal. The Proximal Policy Optimization algorithm and long short-term memory form the basic foundation of the DRL network. A special reward system is created to steer the robot away from dynamic impediments and to maintain a smooth trajectory. a long short-term memory architecture is used to alleviate the local optimum problem and help avoid obstacles out of the current range of sensors. Experiments demonstrate that the proposed method, which does not rely on a map or prior knowledge in complicated static as well as dynamic situations, has an advantage over similar exploration methods.

Keywords: Autonomous exploration · DRL · Global navigation · Local navigation

1 Introduction

Owing to the intensive study of Simultaneous localization and mapping (SLAM) [1, 2] and the continuous research into autonomous vehicles' capacity to execute the navigation and mapping tasks in past few decades [3], autonomous exploration has become a field that is receiving a lot of attention. However, unlike normal navigation mission or regular environment exploration which only aims to guide the vehicle reach the goal or map the surroundings. There are two issues with fully autonomous goal-driven exploration.

S. Yang and H. Lu (Eds.): ISAIR 2022, CCIS 1701, pp. 341–351, 2022.
https://doi.org/10.1007/978-981-19-7943-9_30

To have the best chance of achieving the overall objective, the exploration robot must first choose where to go. Navigating toward a predetermined global goal is necessary, as opposed to purely exploration-driven systems that place a high priority on navigating towards as-yet unknown areas of the world while recording a map. This needs to be taken into account while choosing intermediate places in the environment [4]. The system must directly identify potential navigation paths from the sensor data in the absence of prior knowledge or a clear picture of the overall objective. In [5, 6] the map boundaries, which show areas of open space in the landscape, can be used to determine Potential Waypoints (PWP) for exploration. Following the planning of a route, navigation is carried out in the direction of the chosen PWP. Second, a motion policy that is independent of map data must be acquired because map data is insufficient. Neural networks have been developed for reliable robot navigation as a result of the popularity and capabilities of deep reinforcement learning techniques. Robots can execute intentional movements that are produced by the neural network outputs. Robots' ability to adapt to varied environments is significantly improved by the use of neural networks.[7] demonstrated the viability of training Deep Reinforcement Learning (DRL) algorithms on actual robots and implementing them for demanding tasks. [8] demonstrated the feasibility of learning-based navigation in an unknown setting and combined RGB-D and lidar sensors to increase the resilience of the robot navigation in the continuous action space. Deep Deterministic Policy Gradient (DDPG) was employed by [9] as the local planner for the task of interior navigation, while the Continuous Action Fitted Value Iteration (CAFVI) algorithm was used as the planner for the task of aerial freight delivery. Through DRL, an agent control policy can be trained to accomplish the desired result in an uncharted environment [10]. However, due to its reactive character and lack of global knowledge, the local optimal problem is frequently encountered for large-scale navigation tasks [11].

In this research, we combine an efficient global planner with learning-based navigation to optimize the exploration system. We optimized the heuristic function of global planning and the network. The mission to explore and map out an uncharted environment in the direction of a predetermined overall objective can be more effectively accomplished by the optimized system. To prevent the robot from colliding with moving obstacles and to provide a smooth robot trajectory, a novel reward function is developed. The proposed completely autonomous exploration system is as depicted in Fig. 1. The primary contributions of this study might be listed as follows as compared to some previous studies:

- Developed a Potential Waypoint(PWP) detection global planner combined with neural network motion planner for robot exploration.
- Designed an information-based function for heuristics calculation taking the DRL training range constraints into account when evaluating PWP.
- Proposed a novel reward function to provide a smooth route for the robot and prevent collisions with obstacles.

The rest of this paper is structured as follows. Description of the proposed exploration system are presented in Sect. 2. The results of the experiments are presented and evaluated in Sect. 3. Sect. 4 serves as this paper's conclusion.

2 Autonomous Exploration

In order to accomplish autonomous navigation and exploration in an uncharted environment, we proposed the method of combining global navigation and DRL-based navigation. The exploration framework which consists of deep reinforcement learning-based local navigation and global navigation with optimal waypoint selection from PWP. The local planner is a Proximal Policy Optimization (PPO) [12] with Long Short-Term Memory structure network. The network is denoted as LPPO in the rest of the paper.

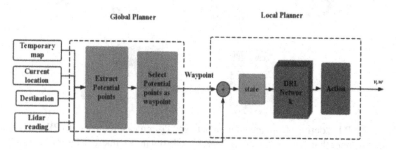

Fig. 1. Proposed system

2.1 Global Navigation

Selecting intermediate waypoints for local navigation from the available PWPs is necessary to direct the agent to investigate and navigate toward the global goal. Since there is no prior information about the areas to explore, it is impossible for the agent to get the optimal path. The agent must therefore investigate the uncharted territory while traveling to the target. It is necessary to collect and store in the robot's memory any PWP from its immediate surroundings as the map's initial information is not provided. For the purpose of acquiring new PWP, three strategies are implemented:

- If there is a value difference between two successive laser measurements that exceeds a certain threshold (usually set as the physical dimensions of the robot), indicating that the agent can cross the alleged chasm. Then a PWP is added in the range of these two sequential laser readings (it is typically set in the center area of the sequential readings in case of obstacles around).
- For readings outside of the laser sensors' maximum range, the results are delivered as a non-numerical type. The unstored non numerical reading could be considered as free undetected space in the environment. Obviously, the agent needs to explore the free undetected area. Thus, if a non-numerical value is returned by successive laser readings, a PWP is added to the environment. Due to the LSTM structure, the obstacles detected in previous instants could be avoided and no PWP would be added in that area even though it has not been explored
- If an intermediate target currently chosen is too far from the robot's position, a path planner is used to locate a path, and a new node is inserted along it.

Figure 2 shows illustrations of PWP extraction from the environment. Any PWPs that are discovered to be close to obstacles during the subsequent exploration phase will be removed from memory. The laser reading from an area that the agent has already visited won't add any PWP. And a new waypoint is chosen. A new point will be selected instead.

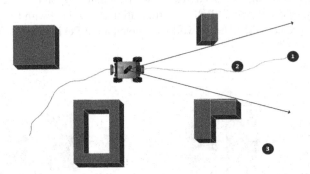

Fig. 2. (a) PWP 1 is derived from the interval between laser measurements. (b) PWP 2 is extracted from a path planner that planned a path to PWP 1. (c) From non-numerical laser readings, the blue PWP 3 is derived.

We proposed a Distance Limited Information (DLI) evaluation method to select waypoints. Each candidate PP's fitness is assessed using the DLI approach as follows:

$$h(c_i) = tan\left(e^{\rho_1 [\, d(p_t, c_i)]^2}\right)\rho_1 + e^{\frac{d(c_i, g)}{\rho_1}} \tag{1}$$

where e is the Euler number, ρ_1 are the two-step distance limits. The two-step distance restriction is set in accordance with the DRL training environment's area size. $d(p_t, c_i)$ Represents the Euclidean distance between agent's position p at t and candidate PWP. The second parameter $d(c_i, g)$ is the Euclidean distance between the potential point and the global target. Under the evaluation of DLI method, the PWP with the lowest score will be regarded as the optimal path point of local navigation.

2.2 The Dynamics Model of Wheeled Robot

The reduced-order model of wheeled robots can be described by the following differential equations.

$$\begin{bmatrix} x \\ y \\ \theta \end{bmatrix} = \begin{bmatrix} \cos\theta \\ \sin\theta \\ 0 \end{bmatrix} v + \begin{bmatrix} 0 \\ 0 \\ 1 \end{bmatrix} \omega \tag{2}$$

where (x, y) are the coordinates of the center of mass of m, θ is the angle between the axis of the robot and the horizontal axis, as shown in Fig. 3.

For the sake of simplicity, the robot's control inputs are considered to be its linear velocity v and rotational velocity ω. The control challenge entails designing (v, ω) in a way that allows the robot to be drawn to the goal point securely. Without a map, it is challenging to automatically generate a path that can be reached, and the problem is even more difficult in uncharted territory with unpredictable and dynamic obstacles. As a result, we take the DRL-based policy into account and continuously map the information that is available to the action space. Let

$$\begin{bmatrix} \omega \\ v \end{bmatrix} = F(p, yaw, S_n) \tag{3}$$

where yaw is the robot's current yaw angle, p is the relative location between the target point and the robot, and S_n is the state sequence over the last n moments. The challenge lies in training a network to obtain the implicit mapping F $(\cdot)$, which will enable the robot to travel automatically from its starting point to its goal position without colliding.

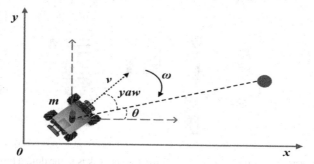

Fig. 3. The coordinate relation used for task-oriented navigation.

2.3 Local Navigation

The local navigation policy is trained separately in a simulated environment using DRL. The motion policy is trained using a neural network architecture based on PPO and LSTM. PPO is described in Eq. 5, θ is the policy parameter, $\hat{E}_t$ is the empirical expectation over time, $r_t(\theta)$ stands for the action probability ratio of the current policy $\pi_\theta(a \mid s)$ and the action probability ratio of the previous strategy $\pi_{\theta old}(a|s)$. $\hat{A}_t$ is the estimated advantage at time t and ε is a hyper-parameter which is an entropy factor set to 0.1 or 0.2 to encourage exploration and assist in setting the range of policy updates.

$$L^{CLIP}(\theta) = E_t\big[\min(r_t(\theta)A_t, \text{clip}(r_t(\theta), 1 - \varepsilon, 1 + \varepsilon)A_t)\big] \tag{4}$$

The robot's Local navigation process is shown in Fig. 4. The red box symbolizes the assessment network, and the blue box the policy network. Two processes make up the entire deep learning-based local navigation process: collecting samples and changing parameters. The following are the specific steps: The policy network for the robot at time i receives an input of s_i during the sample collection step, and then outputs the appropriate policy that is applied to sample the action. The state s_{i+1} at time $i + 1$ and the reward r_i are given to the robot when the environment changes, and s_i, a_i, r_i, and s_{i+1} are saved in the experience set. The robot uses the experience set's stored samples to update the policy parameters during the policy updating stage. We create the network architecture depicted in Fig. 5 in order to put the concerns previously raised into action. Laser data and other data are included in the input state (including speed of robot and positions of robot, waypoints and global goal). First, a feedforward deep neural network (DNN) with two fully connected layers known as the first hidden layer and the second hidden layer is employed to extract features from the input vector. LSTM receives the DNN output as an input. The "memory gate" and "forgetting gate" of the LSTM allow for the calculation of the weights of the states at different time instants in terms of learning.

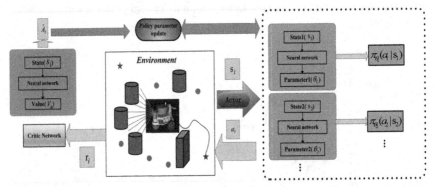

Fig. 4. The framework of Local Navigation. The actor network is in the dotted box, and the critic network is in the red box (Color figure online)

The robot's linear and rotational velocities, as determined by Gaussian sampling, are the policy network's output action. In this work, the range of angular velocity is [0, 1], and the range of linear speed is [0, 0.6]. The sigmoid function and tanh function, which correlate to variance and mean respectively, are activation functions of the output layer. Although the evaluation network's structure is similar to that of a policy network, its output layer is value estimation at current time.

The following is the proposed reward function:

$$r(s_t, a_t) = \begin{cases} r_g & \text{If } D_t < \eta_D \\ r_c & \text{If collision happen} \\ \rho_2(D_t - D_P) + \rho_3(v - |\omega|) & \text{otherwise} \end{cases} \quad (3)$$

There are three factors that determine the reward r for the state-action pair (s_t, a_t) at timestep t. If the current timestep's distance D_t from the target is less than the threshold η_D, which means the robot has reached the target position. A positive goal reward r_g is applied. Considering the actual size of robot, we set $\eta_D = 0.1$ m. Additionally, a collision is detected when the gap between the robot and an obstruction is less than 0.1 m. After that, a negative collision reward r_c is used. If neither of these circumstances holds true, an immediate reward is given based on the current distance D_t between the robot and the target point, the distance D_P between the robot and the target point at the previous time instant, the current linear velocity v, and the current angular velocity ω. It is evident that the reward function has taken route smoothness and collision avoidance into account. That is to say, to encourage the robot to reach the target point faster and to prevent excessive revolutions while travelling, ρ_2 and ρ_3 should be carefully chosen.

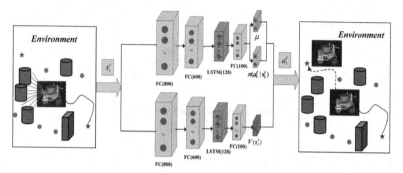

Fig. 5. The. Overview of the network architecture.

3 Simulation and Evaluation

To execute the end-to-end navigation strategy, the training of the neural network is needed. Allowing robots to freely explore a wide range in the actual world is unrealistic and expensive. As a result, to train the neural networks, we employed a simulation environment based on Gazebo.

We define a training as successful when the robot's most recent 100 training missions in the setting of a simulations have a success rate greater than 80%. Any episode that over 500 is considered to have failed the navigation during the training phase. To improve the network's generalization ability, it is also vital to train in different environments. The parameters are given as $v_{max}= 0.5$ m/s, $v_{min} = 0$, $\omega_{max}= 1$ rad/s, $\omega_{min}= 0$, $r_g = 80$, $r_c = -100$, $\rho_1= 5$, $\rho_2 = 100$ and $\rho_3 = 5$. In Table 1, other parameters are listed.

In a simulation environment based on the Gazebo, we trained and evaluated the network. Prior to doing qualitative and quantitative data analytics, we compared the three methods—DDPG, TD3, and LPPO—in the simulation environment. We compared the robot's propensity for navigation in various settings. Figure 6 and Table 2 display the navigational situation and the average distance travelled for each scenario and each approach. It can be clearly seen that in three scenarios the paths that LPPO selected are safest and most effective. Table 2 demonstrated that the average length of LPPO's route is the shortest.

In a simulated 10 × 10 m-sized landscape as depicted in Fig. 7 and Fig. 8, the entire exploration system was trained to test the system's ability to execute the complete exploration mission. Gaussian noise was added to the sensor and action values. To facilitate generalization and policy exploration. We compared the DDPG-based method without global navigation strategy, the TD3 algorithm combined with global navigation

Table 1. Selection parameters.

Parameters	Value
Actor learning rate	0.003
Critic learning rate	0.003
Discount factor	0.99
Generalization advantage estimation λ	0.95
Batch size	256
Clip parameter ε	0.2

Table 2. Average path length(m).

	Scenario I	Scenario II
DDPG	4.894	×
TD3	4.537	7.894
LPPO	4.282	7.047

Table 3. The first complete exploration test

	Av.$L(m)$	Av.$T(s)$	Goals
DDPG	×	×	×
TD3	33.702	132.47	3/5
LPPO	24.141	98.34	5/5

Table 4. The second complete exploration test

	Av.$L(m)$	Av.$T(s)$	Goals
DDPG	×	×	×
TD3	31.513	127.73	4/5
LPPO	23.328	90.13	5/5

strategy and our method: the LPPO combined with global navigation strategy to evaluate robot's capacity to navigate various challenging surroundings. Each method was tested five times in two different environments for experiments. The recorded data includes average path length (L) in meters, average travel time (T) in seconds and how many times has the robot successfully reached the goal. The result of simulation experiment is shown in Fig. 7, Fig. 8, Table 3 and Table 4. As the result demonstrated, all the experimental indexes of LPPO method combined with global planner were the best.

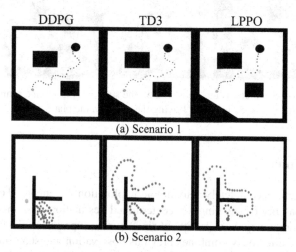

(a) Scenario 1

(b) Scenario 2

Fig. 6. In Scenario 1 a relatively simple environment. Three approaches can smoothly travel over major obstructions. When the goal point is surrounded by walls in Scenario 2, the DDPG method can't find a route to bypass the wall and reach the goal point. The TD3 method and LPPO method manage to reach the target point successfully. the LPPO choose a relatively safe and fast route.

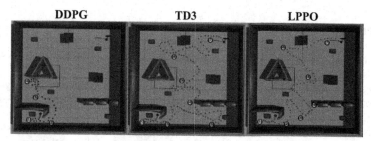

Fig. 7. The first explorations missions' routes. We can see that the DDPG method soon hit the obstacle and failed. Due to introduction of LSTM structure, the LPPO spent less time while returning in the phase of 1 to 2. In the phase of 3 to 4 and 6 to 7, the LPPO took a better route.

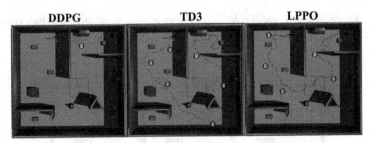

Fig. 8. The second explorations missions' route. The start point is set in a semi enclosed room. It can be seen that LPPO took less time leaving the room. In the phase of 2 to 3, a better route is selected by LPPO.

4 Conclusions

This paper presents a completely autonomous exploration system based on DRL to realize robot's capability of reaching a predetermined destination, documenting the environment, and completing the task without direct human supervision. The introduction of LSTM structure effectively combines previous observation and state information with the current state, which is advantageous for reliable and robust navigation. Moreover, the local optimum dilemma is alleviated by the introduction of the global navigation strategy and LSTM structure. Considering both safety and route optimization, the acquired experimental findings demonstrate that the suggested system operates relatively near to the optimal result that the path planner may obtain given a known environment.

References

1. Taketomi, T.: Visual slam algorithms: a survey from 2010 to 2016. Inf. Process. Soc. Jpn. Trans. Comput. Vis. Appl. **9**(1), 16 (2017)
2. Dong, K., Yong, K., Jin, L., Il, S.: A scene-based dependable indoor navigation system. In: 2016 IEEE/RSJ International Conference on Intelligent Robots and Systems, pp. 1530–1537. IEEE, Daejeon (2016)
3. Feras, D., Timothy, M., Ben, U., Peter, C.: Vision-only autonomous navigation using topometric maps. In: 2013 IEEE/RSJ International Conference on Intelligent Robots and Systems, pp. 1923–1929. IEEE, Tokyo (2013)
4. Reinis, C., Il, S., Jin, L.: Information-based heuristics for learned goal-driven exploration and mapping. In: 18th International Conference on Ubiquitous Robots, pp. 571–578. IEEE, Gangwon-do (2021)
5. Gao, W., Booker, M., Adiwahono, A., Yuan, M., Wang, J.: An improved frontier-based approach for autonomous exploration. In: 15th International Conference on Control, Automation, Robotics and Vision, pp. 292–297. IEEE, Marina Bay Sands (2018)
6. Reinis, C.: Goal-oriented obstacle avoidance with deep reinforcement learning in continuous action space. Electronics **9**(3), 411 (2020)
7. Gu, S., Holly, E., Lillicrap, T., Levine, S.: Deep reinforcement learning for robotic manipulation with asynchronous off-policy updates. In: 2017 IEEE International Conference on Robotics and Automation, pp. 3389–3396. IEEE, Marina Bay Sands (2017)
8. Surmann, H.: Deep reinforcement learning for real autonomous mobile robot navigation in indoor environments. arXiv preprint arXiv:2005.13857 (2020)

9. Faust, A., Oslund, K., Ramirez, O., et al.: PRM-Rl: Long-range robotic navigation tasks by combining reinforcement learning and sampling-based planning. In: 2018 IEEE International Conference on Robotics and Automation, pp. 5113–5120. IEEE, Brisbane (2018)

10. Sugiyama, M.: Statistical Reinforcement Learning: Modern Machine Learning Approaches, 1st edn. CRC Press, Tokyo (2015)

11. Aberdeen, D.: Policy-Gradient Algorithms for Partially Observable Markov Decision Processes. The Australian National University Press, Australia (2003)

12. Schulman, J., Wolski, F., Dhariwal, P., Radlford, A., Klimov, O.: Proximal policy optimization algorithms. arXiv preprint arXiv:1707.06347 (2017)

13. Huimin, L., Li, Y., Chen, M., et al.: Brain intelligence: go beyond artificial intelligence. Mob. Netw. Appl. **23**, 368–375 (2018)

14. Huimin, L., Li, Y., Shenglin, M., et al.: Motor anomaly detection for unmanned aerial vehicles using reinforcement learning. IEEE Internet Things J. **5**(4), 2315–2322 (2018)

Background Subtraction Based on Visual Saliency

Hongrui Zhang[1,2], Mengxing Huang[1,2(✉)], Di Wu[1,2,3(✉)], Zikai Feng[1,2],
and Ruihua Yu[1,2]

[1] School of Information and Communication Engineering, Hainan University, Haikou 570228,
China
huangmx09@163.com, hainuwudi@163.com
[2] State Key Laboratory of Marine Resource Utilization in South China Sea, Haikou 570228,
China
[3] Department of Automation, Shanghai Jiao Tong University, Shanghai 200240, China

Abstract. Visual salience plays a significant role in the process of real life to quickly extract necessary information from complex scenes. The state-of-the-art algorithms impose restrictions on various reality conditions, such as dynamic background and lighting, which will lead to misjudgment and false detection. To alleviate the problem that dynamic background is hard to be compensated, this paper proposes a background subtraction method based on visual saliency, which can fully release the advantages of human visual saliency. Experimental comparison is firstly conducted to confirm that the visual salient region is a potential moving target area. Then feature corner samples is extracted from this area, and sparse optical flow method is adopted to determine the moving target in the current frame. To further enhance the perception ability of moving target in dynamic background, an improved vibe method based on partially random background updating strategy is developed to realize accurate moving object extraction. In addition, the results of motion perception are purposefully used for background set updating. Experimental results indicate that the proposed model can effectively extract the moving target.

Keywords: Visual saliency · Vibe · Moving target prediction · Background subtraction

1 Introduction

Background subtraction is to extract moving objects in a video sequence at the pixel level. In a broad sense, A background subtraction is composed of a dynamic background dataset, a comparison formula for extracting foreground pixels, and an update method for the background dataset [1]. The background subtraction algorithm classifies each pixel of the video sequence into one of the following two categories: foreground for moving objects or background. Since the development of the Gaussian mixture model, background subtraction has made prominent progress, partly due to the availability of pixel-wise annotated datasets such as I2R and CDnet 2014. Modern algorithms such as

© The Author(s), under exclusive license to Springer Nature Singapore Pte Ltd. 2022
S. Yang and H. Lu (Eds.): ISAIR 2022, CCIS 1701, pp. 352–362, 2022.
https://doi.org/10.1007/978-981-19-7943-9_31

Vibe [2] and SuBSENCE [13] remain sensitive to a shaking scene or a shaking camera. More recently, deep learning based on algorithms emerged with the work of Lim [4], which opened the path for novel algorithms [5] is inseparable from the incremental HashRate. These background subtraction algorithms focus on detecting moving objects with a bottom-up method.

The development of visual saliency makes it possible for top-down methods to extract moving targets. Two main factors affect the saliency of human eyes. One is that the surrounding areas with distinct contrast or peculiar difference from the surrounding areas attract bottom-up attention. The other is determined by people's cognition factors, such as knowledge, expectations, and current goals, to form top-down attention [6]. The second factor of visual significance has the magical ability to filter complex backgrounds. A lot of intensive work exploits this selective vision mechanism, such as salient image segmentation [7], autonomous robot grasp [8], video compression [9], moving target tracking [10], advanced driver assistance [11], and many other aspects have achieved excellent results [16, 17].

In this paper, we focus on the excellent ability of the human eye gaze to filter out complex scenes and propose a background subtraction algorithm based on visual saliency. This algorithm demonstrates the relationship between eye fixation prediction areas and potential moving objects but also focuses on solving the problem of dynamic background establishment in background subtraction. The algorithm consists of two stages: moving object research and detection. In the stage of moving object research, the state-of-the-art visual saliency prediction algorithm is to perceive the eye gaze area. After that, according to the prediction results of visual saliency, the saliency regions of possible moving objects are extracted by the binarization method of an adaptive threshold. The feature corners are sparse samples in this region. Finally, the sparsity optical flow method is combined to determine whether the moving target exists in the current frame. In the stage of moving object extraction, we can distinguish possible moving frames from the video. Therefore, an improved vibe algorithm adopts the conservative background updating method. The improved vibe algorithm can effectively solve the ghost problem and background updating problem in the initial Vibe algorithm. Figure 1 shows the algorithm.

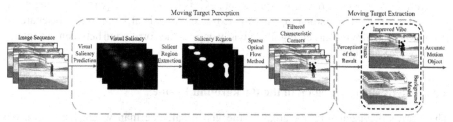

Fig. 1. Our proposed moving object detection algorithm based on visual saliency takes extensive advantage of human eye saliency to extract potential moving objects and reduces the influence of complex backgrounds on the extraction of foreground objects.

2 Relationship Between Visual Saliency and Potential Movement Targets

2.1 Potential Moving Target Attracting Visual Saliency

To discuss the relationship between potential moving targets and visual salience in the form of quantitative comparison, we designed a comparison experiment that involves six different application scenarios, all from CDnet2014 [12]. Considering that the visual salience map is a probability map that is unfit for direct comparison with the truth map (binary image) of moving object detection, we designed a visual salience region extraction algorithm (see Sect. 3 for details) to generate the salience region from the visual salience map. Precision and Pearson's linear correlation coefficient (CC) quantify and compare the correlation between the salient region map and the truth map of moving target detection. Table 1 shows the selected six scenes and the relationship between the saliency region map and the truth map of moving object detection.

Table 1. Quantitative index results between saliency region maps and truth maps.

Scene	Precision	CC
Badminton	0.6745	0.5003
Canoe	0.6967	0.5498
PETS2006	0.7945	0.5011
Snowfall	0.5937	0.6282
Fluid Highway	0.4520	0.5247
Turbulence3	0.7722	0.5618

As demonstrated in Table 1, in each scene, a visual saliency map is generated by leveraging the picture with moving objects through the Res-net structure. The average accuracy rate between the processed saliency region and the truth value is 66.39%, and the average Pearson's correlation coefficient (CC) is 54.43%. The quantitative index we selected exceeds 50%, indicating that the extracted visual saliency area is inseparable from the actual moving target. Figure 2 vividly depicts the correlation between the optical saliency area and the moving target.

2.2 Visual Saliency Region in the Background Frame

There are still visual salience areas in the visual salience map when there is only a pure background environment. For this reason, we quantitatively compared the dynamic background with the static on the changes over time. Five scene patterns select from the CDnet2014 data set, including three static scenes (pedestrians, snowfall, streetCornerAt-Night) and two dynamic Scenarios (canoe, fountain02). We quantitatively evaluated the similarity degree of the significant areas of human eye gaze between two consecutive frames by three quantitative indicators, Pearson's linear correlation coefficient (CC), structural similarity index (SSIM), and peak signal-to-noise ratio (PSNR), respectively. Table 2 reveals the results.

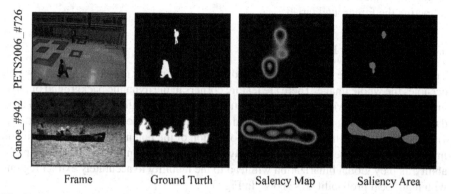

Frame   Ground Turth   Saliency Map   Saliency Area

Fig. 2. Two examples demonstrate that visual salience focus on moving objects. In PETS2006 and Canoe scenes, the moving target is similar to the extracted visual saliency region.

Table 2. Quantitative index results between two consecutive frames in five different scenarios.

Scene	CC	SSIM	PSNR
Canoe	0.7622	0.9359	25.6178
Fountain02	0.9363	0.9888	35.8613
Pedestrians	0.9667	0.9872	47.6578
Snowfall	0.9512	0.9749	41.5312
StreetCornerAtNight	0.9656	0.9884	38.2886

In the three groups of static scenes, CC, SSIM, and PSNR between consecutive frames are all kept at high levels, which indicates that in the static background, the saliency areas of the human eye gaze are almost independent of bad weather or night conditions. In the two groups of dynamic scenes (Canoe, Fountain02), the continuous inter-frame CC and PSNR in the Canoe scene are far lower than those in other scenes. However, the three evaluation indexes in the Fountain02 scene are slightly lower than those in static scenes. The reason is that the dynamic scene of the Canoe is an expansive water surface. The influence of illumination and other factors lead to leapfrog changes in the saliency area of the human eyes.

3   The Proposed Algorithm

A background subtraction method based on visual saliency solves the following moving target detection problem with a top-down mindset. The algorithm includes two main steps. The first is moving object perception, which adopts a sparse optical flow method based on visual saliency to extract the moving state of moving objects. The second step is moving target extraction utilizing an improved vibe algorithm. The locomotor target perception realizes the accurate updating of the background data set, thereby effectively extracting the foreground target.

3.1 Moving Target Perception

The traditional sparse optical flow method extracts the region of feature corners, which occupies the whole image. There are feature corners in the dynamic background of moving target detection, which leads to the motion feature corner information in the backdrop dataset of the moving target detection and contributes to subsequent misjudgment. The visual saliency map shows the motion information of the potential moving object in the image, and its essence is a probability gray scale map. Segmenting the gray-scale probability map by global binarization will lead to the inability to accurately extract regions with high local probability, as shown in Fig. 3.

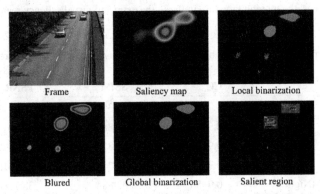

Fig. 3. One example is a salient region based on human eye saliency. The example picture shows that the local and global binarization collaborate to solve the problem that the traditional binarization method is inadaptable to extract regions with high local probability. (source: CDnet 2014 / baseline / highway / # 949)

To solve this problem, we adopted Bernsen's method. The method is that the $(2\omega + 1) \times (2\omega - 1)$ window centers on the pixel (i, j) to calculate the threshold $T(i, j)$ of each pixel. The gray value of the pixel point (i, j) is $f(i, j)$. The threshold formula display is (1).

$$T(i, j) = \frac{1}{2} \times (\max f(i + m, j + n) + \min f(i + m, j + n)) \tag{1}$$

In (1), $m \in [-\omega, +\omega]$, $n \in [-\omega, +\omega]$, the value of ω can be determined according to the input size of the image. We set ω is 15 in this paper. If the gray value exceeds the threshold value, the pixel assigns 1 and the target pixel; otherwise, it determines 0, and the background pixel to obtain a binary image $b(i, j)$, as shown in (2).

$$b(i, j) = sign(f(i, j) - T(i.j)) \tag{2}$$

The noise generated by Bernsen's method in Fig. 3. As a result, we have blurred the binary image results in Fig. 3. The fuzzification formula of point (x, y) is (3).

$$p(x, y) = \frac{1}{(2n + 1)^2} \sum_{j=y-n}^{y+n} \sum_{i=x-n}^{x+n} f(i, j) \qquad (3)$$

Otsu, a global binarization method, is adopted by us to accurately extract the human eye saliency region, as shown in Fig. 3.

The salient area of the eye saliency map will change with the change of the moving target, and it will be almost unchanged in the case of static background and partial dynamic background. In the case of full dynamic background, the salient area will have a long-distance inter-frame jump. The moving object perception takes advantage of this characteristic of the eye saliency region. In a video sequence, the video image of three consecutive frames is $f_{k-1}(x, y), f_k(x, y)$, and $f_{k+1}(x, y)$, and the corresponding saliency image is $e_{k-1}(x, y)$, $e_k(x, y)$, and $e_{k+1}(x, y)$. Shi-Tomas feature corner extraction the feature corner set extracted in the frame $f_{k-1}(x, y)$ is N_{k-1}, and the extraction effect is shown in Fig. 4.

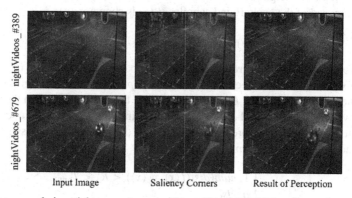

Fig. 4. The example is a night scene (source: CDnet 2014 / nightVideos / streetCornerAtNight / # 389 & 679) to illustrate the effectiveness and robustness of moving object perception. The red dots are feature corners extracted from visual saliency areas.

The sparse optical flow method formula solves the state vector V_1, V_2, S_1 and S_2 between successive frames. On this basis, the concept of optical flow length L is proposed, and its mathematical definition is (4).

$$L^2 = (x_k - x_{k-1})^2 + (y_k - y_{k-1})^2 \qquad (4)$$

In Eq. (4), (x_k, y_k) is the coordinate of the characteristic point at the time k, and (x_{k-1}, y_{k-1}) is the coordinate of the feature point at time $k - 1$. The optical flow length vector set of continuous frames is $V_L = (L_1^2, L_2^2, L_3^2, \cdots L_{n-1}^2, L_n^2)$. According to the state, vector sets V_1, V_2, S_1, and S_2, the corresponding optical flow length sets V_{L1}, V_{L2}, S_{L1}, and S_{L2} can be obtained straightway. The feature corners in the sparse optical flow method belong to potential moving targets, so the moving targets are detected by the optical flow length extracted from consecutive frames. The specific method is to set the static background threshold α and the dynamic background threshold β and b_k is the result of moving target perception for the k frame with the assistance of (5)

$$b_k = \begin{cases} 0, \arg(V_{L1} \cup V_{L2})\langle \alpha \text{ or } \arg\{(S_{L1} - V_{L1}) \cup (S_{L2} - V_{L2})\}\rangle \beta \\ 1, else \end{cases} \quad (5)$$

Through experimental verification, the background threshold value α sets to [0.5, 1.5] and β sets to [5, 10]. More examples are demonstrated in Fig. 4 to illustrate the background detection results.

3.2 Moving Object Extraction

In Sect. 3.1 of this paper, human eye saliency combined with the sparse optical flow method completes the formidable project of moving target perception, so in the initialization process of the background model, the perceived background frame is directly selected as the initial frame to establish the background model. N pixel values are randomly sampled from neighborhood $N_B(x)$ of the pixel point x as the background model $B(x)$ is composed of the background samples. $B(x)$ is shown in (6).

$$B(x) = \{v_1(x), v_2(x), \cdots, v_k(x), \cdots, v_n(x)\} \quad (6)$$

$v_k(x)$ represents the $k'th$ background sample in the background model $B(x)$.

The pixel value of the detected pixel point x is $p(x)$, and each background sample $v_k(x)$ in the background model $B(x)$ is calculated. If the result is less than the matching threshold value R and the number is less than the minimum matching number T_{min}, the pixel point x determines the foreground; otherwise, the pixel point x is assigned as the background. The formula is depicted at (7).

$$S(x) = \begin{cases} 1, num(dist(I(x), v_k(x)) < R) < T_{min} \\ 0, else \end{cases} \quad (7)$$

$S(x) = 1$ represents the foreground of the binarized image, and $S(x) = 0$ represents the background. The above formula (7) depicts that the decision-making stage mainly involves two parameters independently the matching threshold R and the minimum matching number T_{min}. The matching threshold R classifies each pixel, and the minimum matching number T_{min} is a fixed global parameter. Generally, the matching threshold R is 20 and the minimum matching number is 2.

After the pixel matching course, it is a conservative updating strategy based on moving target perception. When the current frame f_k is perceived as a moving target frame $b_k = 1$, all pixels are not updated to the background dataset. The b_k is the result of moving target perception for the k frame. When the current frame f_k is perceived as the background frame $b_k = 0$, the background dataset is partially updated according to the number of foreground pixels detected in the background frame. The specific implementation is to set the background to be updated M_T and foreground detection threshold δ. It assumes that when $b_k = 0$ occurs, the number of foreground pixel points detected from f_k is C. If the number of foreground pixels C is less than the foreground detection threshold δ, the background frame is randomly replaced by one frame in the background model B. Otherwise, the background frame will be added to the background to be updated set M_T. The frame in the M_T will be deleted, if it stays in the M_T for 1 s. The background frame in the set M_T to be updated will be updated to the background model B with the probability $p = 1/\varphi(t)$ to replace any background sample V_x. The expression of $\varphi(t)$ is as follows (8), where t is the number of background frames in the M_T set, and *fps* is the frame rate.

$$\varphi(t) = 0.5fps \times sign(t - 0.5fps) \tag{8}$$

4 Experimental Results

In this section, we report our experimental results and compare the proposed algorithm with previous technologies, i.e., Vibe [2], GMM [14], SuBSENSE [13]. The benchmark data set for video monitoring is CDnet2014. To quantitatively evaluate the performances of the algorithms, we have computed the F-measure and adopted mean statistics for each evaluation index [15].

4.1 Comparison on Background

In most scenes, all moving object detection algorithms can output the background accurately when there is only the background. However, the compared algorithms will produce adverse reactions in the dynamic backdrop or shaking cameras.

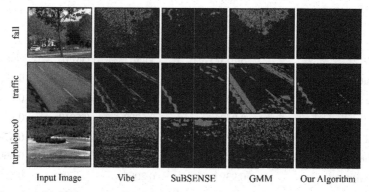

Fig. 5. Results of background comparison. The selected pictures (from top to bottom) are fall-1100 (dynamicBackground), traffic-1132 (cameraJitter), and turbulence0–1608 (turbulence).

We selected three dynamic categories on the CDnet2014 dataset for comparison. The apparent difference between them and the static background is that there is a dynamic background or a shaking camera. These dynamic factors greatly increase the difficulty of background modeling of the GMM algorithm, thus leading to a large number of misjudgments. The Vibe algorithm can reduce misjudgment due to its independent update mechanism of a single pixel, but the effect is still unsatisfactory. The SuBSENCE algorithm considers the relevant information of the domain space, thus reducing the area range of misjudgment to a certain extent and achieving good results. But in Fig. 5, it can be seen more intuitively that our algorithm is better than SuBSENCE. Our algorithm borrows the high-level human eye saliency mechanism and can mask and ignore the ambient regions autonomously. Our algorithm can't deal with the shaking camera perfectly. But compared with other algorithms, we also have improvements.

4.2 Performance on CDnet2014

The average values of various indicators are shown in Table 3. Our algorithm has reached the most prominent position under "Bad Weather" and "Turbulence" scenarios. Integrating the ability of human eye saliency to filter complex backgrounds into moving target detection improves the accuracy of the background dataset and enhances the robustness. Our algorithm also performs well in "Baseline", "Camera Jitter", "Dynamic Background", and "Shadow" scenes. SuBSENCE method integrates color intensity and LBSP texture features into Vibe to improve accuracy. In "Low Frame Rate", "Intermittent Object Movement", and "Night Videos" scenes, our algorithm results are not satisfactory. The sparse optical flow method is obligatory to meet three preconditions for moving target perception. However, in "Low Frame Rate" and "Intermittent Object Movement" scenes, these conditions cannot be affordable, resulting in the unsatisfactory effect of our algorithm. In "Night Videos" scenes, because of the bottom-up saliency of car lights, it is easy to lead to deviation in the extraction of eye saliency regions, which reduces the accuracy.

Table 3. Comparison of the foreground detection results in terms of the f-measure on cdnet2014 dataset.

Category	SuBSENCE	Vibe	GMM	Ours
Bad Weather	0.8945	0.7077	0.6758	0.8967
Baseline	0.9450	0.8193	0.5424	0.7747
Camera Jitter	0.8406	0.6088	0.5212	0.7576
Dynamic Background	0.9711	0.5531	0.5095	0.8717
Intermittent Object Motion	0.8947	0.5423	0.4504	0.6609
Low Framerate	0.9393	0.2066	0.1705	0.4552
Night Video	0.5035	0.3187	0.2627	0.2706
Shadow	0.9788	0.8050	0.7552	0.8819
Turbulence	0.7998	0.6900	0.4987	0.8643

5 Conclusion

This paper proposes a Background Subtraction algorithm based on visual saliency. This algorithm realizes the combination of human eye saliency and moving object detection. Meanwhile, it proves that human eye saliency tends to focus on potential moving targets and analyzes the changes in human eye visual saliency under different backgrounds. Human visual saliency has the advanced ability to solve complex scenes. It overcomes the severe challenges brought by dynamic backgrounds and achieves gratifying results. The experimental results show that the Background Subtraction Based on Visual Saliency is capable of multiple scene tasks and has better detection ability in simple background conditions.

Acknowledgements. This work was founded by the National Key Research and Development Program of China (2018YFB1404400), the Scientific Research Fund Project of Hainan University (KYQD(ZR)-21007), the Natural Science Foundation of Hainan Province (621QN212), the Hainan Provincial Natural Science Foundation of China (622RC618).

References

1. Li, L., Wang, Z., Hu, Q., et al.: Adaptive nonconvex sparsity based background subtraction for intelligent video surveillance. IEEE Trans. Industr. Inf. **17**(6), 4168–4178 (2020)
2. Barnich, O., Van Droogenbroeck, M.: ViBe: A universal background subtraction algorithm for video sequences. IEEE Trans. Image Process. **20**(6), 1709–1724 (2010)
3. Jiang, S., Lu, X.: WeSamBE: a weight-sample-based method for background subtraction. IEEE Trans. Circuits Syst. Video Technol. **28**(9), 2105–2115 (2017)
4. Lim, L.A., Keles, H.Y.: Foreground segmentation using convolutional neural networks for multiscale feature encoding. Pattern Recogn. Lett. **112**, 256–262 (2018)
5. Bouwmans, T., Javed, S., Sultana, M., et al.: Deep neural network concepts for background subtraction: a systematic review and comparative evaluation. Neural Netw. **117**, 8–66 (2019)
6. Borji, A., Sihite, D.N., Itti, L.: What stands out in a scene? A study of human explicit saliency judgment. Vis. Res. **91**, 62–77 (2013)
7. Wang W., et al.: Salient object detection driven by fixation prediction. In: Proceedings of the IEEE conference on computer vision and pattern recognition, pp. 1711–1720, IEEE, Salt City (2018)
8. Kim H., Ohmura Y., Kuniyoshi Y.: Memory-based gaze prediction in deep imitation learning for robot manipulation. arXiv preprint arXiv:2202.04877 (2022)
9. Feng Y., et al.: Gaze-driven video streaming with saliency-based dual-stream switching. In: 2012 Visual Communications and Image Processing, pp. 1–6, IEEE, San Diego (2012)
10. Zhang D., Yang T.: Visual object tracking algorithm based on biological visual information features and few-shot learning. Computational Intelligence and Neuroscience, 2022 (2022)
11. Schwehr J., Willert V.: Driver's gaze prediction in dynamic automotive scenes. In: 2017 IEEE 20th International Conference on Intelligent Transportation Systems (ITSC), pp. 1–8. IEEE, Yokohama (2017)
12. Wang Y., Jodoin P. M., Porikli F., et al.: CDnet 2014: an expanded change detection benchmark dataset. In: Proceedings of the IEEE conference on computer vision and pattern recognition workshops, pp.387–394. IEEE, Columbus (2014)
13. St-Charles, P.L., Bilodeau, G.A., Bergevin, R.: SuBSENSE: a universal change detection method with local adaptive sensitivity. IEEE Trans. Image Process. **24**(1), 359–373 (2014)

14. Stauffer, C., Grimson, W.E.L.: Adaptive background mixture models for real-time tracking. In: Proceedings of the 1999 IEEE Computer Society Conference on Computer Vision and Pattern Recognition, pp. 246–252. Fort Collins, IEEE (1999)
15. Xu, Y., Ji, H., Zhang, W.: Coarse-to-fine sample-based background subtraction for moving object detection. Optik **207**, 164195 (2020)
16. Wu, E.Q., Xiong, P., Tang, Z.R., et al.: Detecting dynamic behavior of brain fatigue through 3-D-CNN-LSTM. IEEE Trans. Syst. Man Cybernet.: Syst. **52**(1), 90–100 (2021)
17. Wu, E.Q., Cao, Z., Sun, P.Z.H., et al.: Inferring cognitive state of pilot's brain under different maneuvers during flight. IEEE Trans. Intell. Transp. Syst. **23**, 1–11 (2022)
18. Lu, H., Qin, M., Zhang, F., et al. RSCNN: A CNN-based method to enhance low-light remote-sensing images
19. Huimin, L., Li, Y., Shenglin, M., et al.: Motor anomaly detection for unmanned aerial vehicles using reinforcement learning. IEEE Internet Things J. **5**(4), 2315–2322 (2018)
20. Huimin, L., Li, Y., Chen, M., et al.: Brain Intelligence: go beyond artificial intelligence. Mobile Netw. Appl. **23**, 368–375 (2018)
21. Huimin, L., Zhang, M., Xu, X.: Deep fuzzy hashing network for efficient image retrieval. IEEE Trans. Fuzzy Syst. (2020). https://doi.org/10.1109/TFUZZ.2020.2984991

Image Rectification of Industrial Equipment Nameplate Based on Progressive Probabilistic Hough Transform

Han Li, Hong Bao[✉], and Yan Ma

Beijing Key Laboratory of Information Service Engineering, Beijing Union University,
Beijing 100101, China
baohong@buu.edu.cn

Abstract. In this paper, we put forward an industrial nameplate picture correction method based on Progressive Probabilistic Hough Transform. Our method can effectively correct the image tilt caused by the wrong shooting direction. Even the oblique images taken from a long distance have certain effects. We also introduce the Mining Equipment Nameplate Dataset. The frame of the industrial nameplate is quadrilateral. The two sides of the nameplate border in the photo will cross each other after being extended. This result is caused by the tilt of the shooting angle. Our method firstly grays the picture. Then binarizes the image and Gaussian smoothing filter. We use the Progressive Probabilistic Hough Transform to locate the two longest line segments in the picture. The four endpoints of the two line segments are the four endpoints of the quadrilateral. Finally, the correct picture is obtained by perspective transformation. Our method makes the nameplate text more visible, and the detection method is fast and effective. The pictures obtained by experiments are clearer and easier to observe. In the second half of the article, we list some experimental results. Our method can well handle the requirements in actual production.

Keywords: Progressive probabilistic hough transform · OCR · Image processing · Perspective transformation · Hough transform · Industrial nameplate detection

1 Introduction

The record of equipment information in industrial maintenance is the critical link to industrial system maintenance. The equipment information record can help the laboratory to know the running status of the equipment in the later stage. After the equipment enters the testing organization, it is necessary to establish files for long-term records until it's scrapped. Equipment nameplate is a like human ID card, which is used to obtain critical information and essential parameters. This information can provide critical information support for operation and maintenance personnel. In the face of aging, corrosion, rust, other failures, and scrap treatment, it is indispensable to obtain equipment information safely, quickly, and effectively in the process of industrial process.

© The Author(s), under exclusive license to Springer Nature Singapore Pte Ltd. 2022
S. Yang and H. Lu (Eds.): ISAIR 2022, CCIS 1701, pp. 363–372, 2022.
https://doi.org/10.1007/978-981-19-7943-9_32

Target detection technology can be trained and detected according to fixed datasets, so as to obtain image positioning or critical feature information of the object. Equipment nameplates often show inclined photographs, and there are many outside areas in nameplates. This paper is dedicated to solving the influence of irrelevant regions. We put forward a professional Mining Equipment Nameplate Dataset (MEND), and a machine learning method based on Progressive Probabilistic Hough Transform to detect the specific position of the nameplate. Then the outside areas in the image are removed by perspective transformation. Finally, we use DBNet [1] to select 20 different nameplate images on MEND dataset for comparative experiments. This method has a fast positioning speed and shows a good detection effect.

2 Related Works

Image processing technology is a significant research content in machine vision. Combined with many pictures and prior knowledge analysis, is know that there are many straight lines in equipment nameplate photos. The four most extended lines form the frame of the industrial nameplate. Most nameplate photos are taken at an oblique angle. The affected photo borders have different lengths on both sides. In order to facilitate text detection and improve detection accuracy, it is necessary to carry out the perspective transformation on the image. The four corners of the industrial nameplate can be located by the machine learning. For example, Lai [2] et al. invented a method for detecting the bold text lines in the picture of equipment nameplate, RTLD, which can locate and detect the text examples of equipment in the field. RTLD can directly detect the corner points of nameplate equipment. The natural scene recognizer (ORSTR) designed by Chen [3] et al. uses a correction module based on neural network to process curved and multi-directional texts. Li [4] et al. put forward an application of nameplate detection and recognition based on machine vision, which uses seed algorithm to eliminate unnecessary interference factors. Paying attention to the shape similarity between square billboards and industrial nameplates, Panhwar [5] et al. added the shape detection of signboards to enhance the efficiency of text detection.

The standard Hough Transform algorithm and the improved Hough Transform algorithm are applied to many machine vision applications. For example, Zhao [6] et al. integrated Hough Transform into the deep learning framework that transformed the detection of semantic lines into the problem of the midpoint in parameter space. Kundu [7] et al. integrated Hough Transform into the process of physical sign extraction. Lapinskij [8] et al. proposed a cumulus vision detection method based on Hough Transform and Canny edge detection. Chen [9] proposed an improved Hough Transform algorithm to realize lane detection, Guo [10] proposed gesture recognition based on an improved Hough Transform algorithm, and Zhang [11] proposed a straight line extraction algorithm based on an improved random Hough Transform.

The Machine learning method based on Hough Transform is widely used to detect sensitive shapes. Because it has a fast detection speed for planar graphics. Hough Transform has been used in various applications since its discovery. The innovation of this paper is to detect and locate the corner coordinates of two line segments based on Progressive Probabilistic Hough Transform. Our method has a faster detection speed and higher detection accuracy. It can preprocess the image perfectly and add it to the end-to-end text detection program.

3 Methodology

3.1 Feature Transformation Based on Hough Transform

Hough Transformation. Hough Transformation is a method used to recognize the shape of an image. The basic principle of Hough Transformation is to use the duality of points and lines. Establish a Cartesian coordinate system according to image space. Every straight line in the image can transform into a point in the parameter space. For the convenience of understanding, here we call the parameter space Hough space and vice versa. The straight line formula is as follow:

$$y = k * x + b \tag{1}$$

In the Cartesian coordinate system, the k parameter represents slope, and the b parameter represents intercept. All straight lines passing through a point (x_0, y_0) in the image space satisfy $y_0 = k * x_0 + b$.

A straight line of Hough space K and B is obtained by the point (x_0, y_0). The expression is $b = -k * x_0 + y_0$. In the same way, a straight line in the Cartesian coordinate system can be obtained by passing through the (k_0, b_0) point in Hough space. The representative expression is as follow:

$$b_0 = k_0 * x + y \tag{2}$$

Therefore, every line in the image space has (x_n, y_n) corresponding to k_0 and b_0 in Hough space, so the problem of line detection in the image space can be transformed into the problem of points in Hough space by Hough Transform. Broadly speaking, every graph can be detected by obtaining the graph formula. Such as detecting curves of arbitrary shape features.

Progressive Probabilistic Hough Transform. Progressive Probabilistic Hough Transform can detect the shape more finely and the length of the line segment in the image space.

Progressive Probabilistic Hough Transform adds the definition of superposition based on Hough Transform. The principle of Progressive Probabilistic Hough Transform is not difficult to understand. Firstly, a feature point in the image space is randomly extracted and marked as a point on a particular straight line; Then extract a feature point and check whether the point is on the straight line; Then Hough Transform is carried out to determine whether to accumulate the weights of the points, to select the largest point in the parameter space. Then get the endpoint of the other end of the line segment along the straight line existing at this point.

In this way, the feature of line segment length in image processing can be transformed into the weight of points in parameter space. As long as the length of the calculated line segment is greater than a certain threshold, it can be considered a good line segment output.

3.2   Corner Detection Based on Double Line Segment Interception

After explaining the principles of Hough Transform and Progressive Probabilistic Hough Transform, the latter is applied to the actual scene. Hough Transform is often used to detect straight lines in images, while Progressive Probabilistic Hough Transform can detect both ends of line segments. As long as I select the two largest points in.

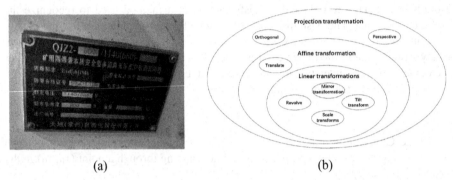

(a)   (b)

Fig. 1. (a)The two longest sides of the nameplate image are detected.(b) The Relationship among Perspective Transformation, Affine Transformation, and Linear Trans-formation.

Hough space, they respectively represent the two most extended line segments in the image space in Cartesian coordinate system. Corner detection is to select the vertex coordinates of the two line segments, and four corner points of the nameplate can be obtained according to the two ends of the line segments (see Fig. 1(a)).

According to the images, two endpoints of two straight lines are obtained, and there are four endpoints in total. According to the coordinate position comparison of the four corners, the correct coordinates are obtained, which correspond to the upper left corner, upper right corner, lower left corner, and lower right corner of the nameplate in the picture.

3.3   Nameplate Correction Based on Perspective Transformation

In this part, the coordinates of four corners obtained by Progressive Probabilistic Hough Transform are projected. The principle is to project a graphic on a plane to a specified plane through a projection matrix. When it comes to projection transformation, we have to mention its two subsets: affine transformation and linear transformation. This paper shows their containment relationship (see Fig. 1(b)).

The linear transformation has nothing to do with the matrix. The linear transformation includes image rotation, tilt transform, scaling, and their combination and superposition. The origin of image coordinates after linear transformation remains unchanged. After transformation, a straight line is still a straight line, and parallel straight lines are still parallel after transformation.

Affine transformation is also called affine projection. The affine transformation includes linear transformation. In geometry, a vector space is transformed linearly and then translated into another vector space. Affine transformation equals linear transformation plus translation. We explain the concrete principle by a formula.

Suppose there are two vector spaces, k and j:

$$K = (x, y)J = (x', y')$$

(3)

The vector space is changed from K to J, which will be transformed by the following formula:

$$J = K \times w + b$$

(4)

The formula will be split to get:

$$x' = w_{00} \times x + w_{01} \times y + b_0$$

(5)

$$y' = w_{10} \times x + w_{11} \times y + b_0$$

(6)

Convert to matrix multiplication:

$$\begin{bmatrix} x' \\ y' \end{bmatrix} = \begin{bmatrix} w_{00} & w_{01} & b_0 \\ w_{10} & w_{11} & b_1 \end{bmatrix} \begin{bmatrix} x \\ y \\ 1 \end{bmatrix} = M \begin{bmatrix} x \\ y \\ 1 \end{bmatrix}$$

(7)

Affine transformation also needs a matrix M to realize translation, scaling, rotation, and flip transformation. The transformation between two vector spaces is realized by parameter matrix M. Affine transformation achieves the transformation of two vector spaces.

Perspective transformation is also called projection transformation. In this paper, the irregular quadrilateral in the 2D image is transformed into a standard rectangle by projection transformation. Using the four corners obtained by Progressive Probabilistic Hough Transform, the position coordinates of the four corners of the industrial nameplate are intercepted. The irregular quadrilateral formed by four corners is projected on the specified plane by a projection matrix. The principle of perspective transformation is introduced in three steps.

1. General formula of perspective transformation:

$$\begin{bmatrix} u' & v' & \omega' \end{bmatrix} = \begin{bmatrix} u & v & \omega \end{bmatrix} \begin{bmatrix} a_{11} & a_{12} & a_{13} \\ a_{21} & a_{22} & a_{23} \\ a_{31} & a_{32} & a_{33} \end{bmatrix}$$

(8)

Parameters u and v are from the original picture, defining $\omega = 1$, $a_{33} = 1$, and the picture coordinates (x, y) obtained by perspective transformation. In which x and y satisfy:

$$x = \frac{x'}{\omega'} y = \frac{y'}{\omega'}$$

(9)

2. Because the perspective transformation matrix has eight parameters, it needs four coordinates to correspond to eight equations to be solved. Linear transformation and affine transformation are two special forms of perspective transformation. The expressions of transformed x_n and y_m satisfy:

$$x_n = \frac{x'}{\omega'} = \frac{a_{11} \times u + a_{21} \times v + a_{31} \times 1}{a_{13} \times u + a_{23} \times v + 1 \times 1} \tag{10}$$

$$y_m = \frac{y'}{\omega'} = \frac{a_{12} \times u + a_{22} \times v + a_{32} \times 1}{a_{13} \times u + a_{23} \times v + 1 \times 1} \tag{11}$$

3. By solving the equations, eight parameters needed for perspective transformation are obtained.

A new planar image is obtained by multiplying a two-dimensional image by a projection transformation matrix. Using the condition that the perspective center, image point, and target point are collinear, according to the perspective rotation law, the shadow-bearing surface is rotated by a certain angle around the perspective axis. Destroy the original projection light beam and keep the projection geometry unchanged to obtain the target matrixv (Fig. 2).

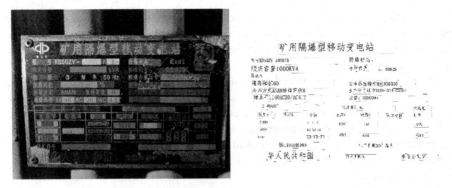

Fig. 2. Text of nameplate and label

4   Experiment

4.1   Mining Equipment Nameplate Dataset

We have established a dataset: MEND, which is suitable for text detection and character recognition of industrial nameplates. The pictures collected in this experiment are all from this dataset. All pictures of this dataset are from the industrial equipment nameplate photos of some mining enterprises collected in China. The dataset contains more than 700 nameplate pictures of industrial equipment under different conditions, which are divided into 586 training set photos and 137 test set photos.

The centralized data photos are inconsistent. Such too strong and poor lighting conditions, partial occlusion, distorted shape, pollution, rotation, and irregular shape photos. This makes our dataset more challenging than other datasets.

This dataset identifies the text instances on all images and records the text content (see Fig. 3). Therefore, this dataset can be used as a text detection model experiment and character recognition experiment for industrial equipment nameplates. It is a powerful help to end-to-end text detection and recognition. We will use this dataset to carry out follow-up work in the future.

4.2 Comparative Experiment

Ordinary equipment nameplate photographs are inclined, and there are a lot of outside areas around the nameplate pattern. This will seriously degrade the performance of text detection. The text detection model only needs to detect text instances. Text examples have a good effect only in the case of document-level scanning. Therefore, it is necessary to discharge the colorful areas of the text examples on the deformed nameplate. This will definitely improve the accuracy of the detector.

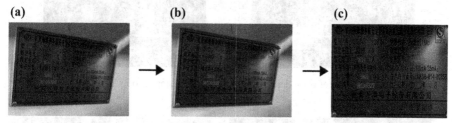

Fig. 3. (a) Original image; (b) The two most extended line segments of the industrial nameplate are intercepted by using the progressive probabilistic hough transform; (c) The final result after perspective transformation.

In order to transform the irregular quadrilateral nameplate in the photograph into a regular rectangle, this experiment consists of six steps. This paper shows the simplified process (see Fig. 3).

The nameplate required by this method has obvious characteristics and is easy to extract. The image was first miniaturized to reduce the experimental time. Use the Pillow.shape function to reduce the image by ten times. For the detect the edge of the image and convert the reduced resolution thumbnail into a grayscale image to obtain the peripheral contour of the grayscale image (see Fig. 4 (a)).

Then binarize the image. To improve the efficiency of the Progressive Probabilistic Hough Transform in detecting long straight lines, we used Gaussian smoothing. The small line segments are connected into a long straight line (see Fig. 5).

The Progressive Probabilistic Hough Transform method mentioned in this paper is used to detect the double line segments of the Gaussian smoothed image. We get the corner coordinates of the thumbnail in the Cartesian coordinate system through two line segments. Enlarging the value of corner coordinates by ten times is the target corner position of the initial image (see Fig. 4(b)).

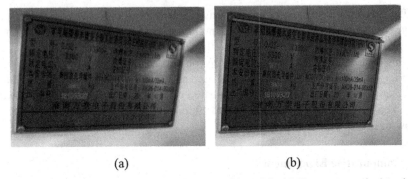

(a)   (b)

Fig. 4. (a)Gray diagram of the nameplate. (b)The position of double line segments in the original image.

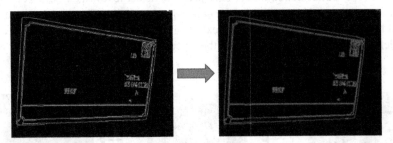

Fig. 5. After edge detection, apply the Gaussian smoothing filter.

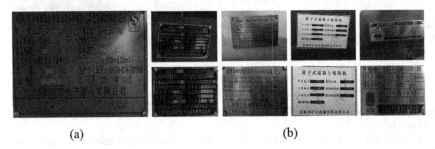

(a)   (b)

Fig. 6. (a)After correction, the pictures were tested by DBNet. (b)The pictures after corrected.

After locating the corner coordinates of the nameplate, use the perspective transformation matrix to transform the area into a standard rectangle (see Fig. 6(a)).

To verify the effectiveness of the two-line detection and perspective transformation methods, we use the differential binarization model to make a comparative test on the nameplate images. Figure 7 is the result after text detection.

We list the experimental results of double line segment recognition and correction for ordinary pictures (see Fig. 6(b)). DB model uses the lightweight backbone ResNet-18. It can simplify the binarization process in the segmented network, so it has higher accuracy and more accurate recognition performance. The following is the result of double-line segment recognition and correction for ordinary pictures.

5 Conclusions

Aiming at the problem that the picture of industrial equipment nameplate has an irregular shape, which leads to the decline of the accuracy of text detection and recognition, we put forward a correction module.

The principle of this module is based on Progressive Probabilistic Hough Transform. The module includes two tasks: double long line segment detection based on Progressive Probabilistic Hough Transform and perspective transformation of the image.

This module is helpful in transforming irregular nameplates into rectangles close to the standard. Our method is huseful for text detection and character recognition. This method is time-consuming and simple. It has accuracy and faster speed, not inferior to the deep learning method, and strong practicability. This method has the accuracy and speed not belong to the deep learning model. It has strong practicability in industrial life. We will consider adding it to end-to-end text detection in the future.

References

1. Liao, M., Wan, Z., Yao, C., et al.: Real-time scene text detection with differentiable binarization. In: Proceedings of the AAAI Conference on Artificial Intelligence, vol. 34, no. 07, pp. 11474–11481 (2020)
2. Lai, J., Guo, L., Qiao, Y., et al.: Robust text line detection in equipment nameplate images. In: 2019 IEEE International Conference on Robotics and Biomimetics (ROBIO), pp. 889–894. IEEE (2019)
3. Chen, X., Zhang, Z., Qiao, Y., et al.: Orientation robust scene text recognition in natural scene. In:2019 IEEE International Conference on Robotics and Biomimetics (ROBIO), pp. 901–906. IEEE (2019)
4. Li, J., Zhang, W., Han, R.: Application of machine vision in defects inspection and character recognition of nameplate surface. In: 2014 13th International Symposium on Distributed Computing and Applications to Business, Engineering and Science, pp. 295–298. IEEE (2014)
5. Panhwar, M.A., Memon, K.A., Abro, A., et al.: Signboard detection and text recognition using artificial neural networks. In: 2019 IEEE 9th International Conference on Electronics Information and Emergency Communication (ICEIEC), pp. 16–19. IEEE (2019)
6. Zhao, K., Han, Q., Zhang, C.-B., Xu, J., Cheng, M.M.: Deep hough transform for semantic line detection. IEEE Trans. Pattern Anal. Mach. Intell. **44**(9), 4793–4806 (2022). https://doi.org/10.1109/TPAMI.2021.3077129
7. Kundu, S., Malakar, S., Geem, Z.W., et al.: Hough transform-based angular features for learning-free handwritten keyword spotting. Sensors **21**(14), 4648 (2021)
8. Lapušinskij, A., Suzdalev, I., Goranin, N., et al.: The application of Hough transform and Canny edge detector methods for the visual detection of cumuliform clouds. Sensors **21**(17), 5821 (2021)
9. Yang, C., Shi, J., Liu, C.: Lane recognition algorithm based on improved hough transform. Autom. Pract. Technol. (2021)
10. Chuangshi, G., Zhaohui, M.: Gesture recognition based on progressive hough transform algorithm. Comput. Syst. Appl. **27**(4), 243–248 (2018)

11. Xuan, Z., Yan, Y.: Straight-line extraction algorithm based on improved randomized Hough transform. Inf. Technol. **41**(12), 6–9 (2017)
12. He, K., Zhang, X., Ren, S., et al.: Deep residual learning for image recognition. In: Proceedings of the IEEE Conference on Computer Vision and Pattern Recognition, pp. 770–778 (2016)
13. Huimin, L., Li, Y., Chen, M., et al.: Brain Intelligence: go beyond artificial intelligence. Mob. Netw. Appl. **23**, 368–375 (2018)
14. Lu, H., Zhang, M., Xu, X., Li, Y., Shen, H.T.: Deep fuzzy hashing network for efficient image retrieval. IEEE Trans. Fuzzy Syst. **29**(1), 166–176 (2020). https://doi.org/10.1109/TFUZZ.2020.2984991
15. Hu, L., Qin, M., Zhang, F., Du, Z., Liu, R.: RSCNN: a CNN-based method to enhance low-light remote-sensing images. Rem. Sens. **13**(1), 62 (2020)

Author Index

Printed in the United States
by Baker & Taylor Publisher Services